grokking
Simplicity

taming complex software with functional thinking

Eric Normand

Foreword by Guy Steele and Jessica Kerr

MANNING

SHELTER ISLAND

For online information and ordering of this and other Manning books, please visit
www.manning.com. The publisher offers discounts on this book when ordered in quantity. For more
information, please contact

  Special Sales Department
  Manning Publications Co.
  20 Baldwin Road, PO Box 761
  Shelter Island, NY 11964
  Email: orders@manning.com

Manning Publications Co.	Development editor: Jenny Stout
20 Baldwin Road	Technical development editor: Alain Couniot
Shelter Island, NY 11964	Review editor: Ivan Martinović
	Production editor: Lori Weidert
	Copy editor: Michele Mitchell
	Proofreader: Melody Dolab
	Technical proofreader: Jean-François Morin
	Typesetter: Jennifer Houle
	Cover designer: Leslie Haimes

ISBN: 9781617296208

Printed and bound by CPI Group (UK) Ltd, Croydon, CR0 4YY

Get the eBook FREE!

(PDF, ePub, Kindle, and liveBook all included)

We believe that once you buy a book from us, you should be able to read it in any format we have available. To get electronic versions of this book at no additional cost to you, purchase and then register this book at the Manning website.

Go to https://www.manning.com/freebook and follow the instructions to complete your pBook registration.

That's it!
Thanks from Manning!

contents

14 Functional tools for nested data   355

15 Isolating timelines   391

18 Reactive and onion architectures   509

19 The functional journey ahead   541

foreword

Guy Steele

I've been writing programs for over 52 years now. I still find it exciting, because there are always new problems to tackle and new things to learn. My programming style has changed quite a bit over the decades, as I learn new algorithms, new programming languages, and new techniques for organizing my code.

When I first learned to program, in the 1960s, a well-accepted methodology was to draw a flowchart for the program before writing actual code. Every computation was represented by a rectangular box, every decision by a diamond, and every input/output operation by some other shape. The boxes were connected by arrows representing the flow of control from one box to another. Then writing the program was just a matter of writing code for the contents of each box in some order, and whenever an arrow pointed anywhere but the next box you were about to code, you would write a `goto` statement to indicate the necessary transfer of control. The problem was that flowcharts were two-dimensional but code was one-dimensional, so even if the structure of a flowchart looked nice and neat on paper, it could be hard to understand when written out as code. If you drew arrows on your code from each `goto` statement to its destination, the result often resembled a mound of spaghetti, and in those days we indeed talked about the difficulties of understanding and maintaining "spaghetti code."

The first big influence on my programming style was the "structured programming" movement of the early 1970s. Looking back, I see *two* big ideas that came out of that community-wide discussion. Both of them are techniques for **organizing control flow**. The idea, which became famous, was that most control flow could be expressed in terms of a few simple patterns: sequential execution, multiway decisions such as `if-then else` and `switch` statements, and repetitive execution such as `while` loops and `for` loops. This was sometimes oversimplified into the slogan "No `goto` statements!"—but the important thing was the patterns, and if you used the patterns consistently you found that you rarely needed to use an actual `goto` statement. The second idea, less famous but no less important, was that sequential statements could be grouped into blocks that should be properly nested, and that a non-local transfer of control may jump to the end of a block or out of a block (think of `break` and `continue`) but should not jump into a block from outside.

When I first learned the ideas of structured programming, I did not have access to a structured programming language. But I found myself writing my Fortran code a little more carefully, organizing it according to the principles of structured programming. I even found myself writing low-level assembly language code as if I were a compiler translating from a structured programming language into machine instructions. I found that this discipline made my programs easier to write and to maintain. Yes, I was still writing `goto` statements or branch instructions, but almost always according to one of the standard patterns, and that made it much easier to see what was going on.

In the bad old days when I wrote Fortran code, all the variables needed in a program were declared right up front, all together in one place, followed by the executable code. (The COBOL language rigidly formalized this specific organization; variables were declared in the "data division" of a program, which began with the actual words "DATA DIVISION." This was then followed by the code, which always began with the actual words "PROCEDURE DIVISION.") Every variable could be referred to from any point in the code. That made it hard to figure out, for any specific variable, exactly how it might be accessed and modified.

The second big influence that changed my programming style was "object-oriented programming," which for me encompasses a combination and culmination of early ideas about objects, classes, "information hiding," and "abstract data types." Again, looking back I see *two* big ideas that came out of this grand synthesis, and both have to do with **organizing access to data**. The first idea is that variables should be "encapsulated" or "contained" in some way, to make it easier to see that only certain parts of the code can read or write them. This can be as simple as declaring local variables within a block rather than at the top of the program, or as elaborate as declaring variables within a class (or module) so that only methods of that class (or procedures within the module) can access them. Classes or modules can be used to guarantee that sets of variables obey certain consistency properties, because methods or procedures can be coded to ensure that if one variable is updated, then related variables are also appropriately updated. The second idea is inheritance, meaning that one can define a more complicated object by extending simpler ones, adding new variables and methods, and perhaps overriding existing methods. This second idea is made possible because of the first one.

At the time that I learned about objects and abstract data types, I was writing a lot of Lisp code, and while Lisp itself is not a purely object-oriented language, it is pretty easy to use Lisp to implement data structures and to access those data structures only through approved methods (implemented as Lisp functions). If I paid attention to organizing my data, I got many of the benefits of object-oriented programming, even though I was coding in a language that did not enforce that discipline.

The third big influence on my programming style was "functional programming," which is sometimes oversimplified into the slogan "No side effects!" But this is not realistic. Understood properly, functional programming provides techniques for **organizing side effects** so that they don't occur just *anywhere*—**and that is the subject of this book**.

Once again, there are actually two big ideas that work together. The first big idea is to distinguish *computations*, which have no effect on the outside world and produce the same result even when executed multiple times, from *actions*, which may produce different results each time they are executed and may have some *side effect* on the outside world, such as displaying text on a screen, or launching a rocket. A program is easier to understand if organized into standard patterns that make it easier to figure out which parts might have side effects and which parts are "merely computations." The standard patterns may be divided into two sub-categories: those typically used in single-threaded programs (sequential execution) and those typically used in multi-threaded programs (parallel execution).

The second big idea is a set of techniques for processing collections of data—arrays, lists, databases—"all at once" rather than item by item. These techniques are most effective when the items can be processed independently, free of side effects and their influence, so once again the second idea works better thanks to the first idea.

In 1995 I helped to write the first full specification for the Java programming language; the next year I helped to write the first standard for JavaScript (the ECMAScript standard). Both these languages were clearly object-oriented; indeed, in Java there is no such thing as a global variable—every variable must be declared within some class or method. And both those languages have no `goto` statement; the language designers concluded that the structured programming movement had succeeded, and `goto` was no longer needed. Nowadays millions of programmers get along just fine without `goto` statements and global variables.

But what about functional programming? There are some purely functional languages such as Haskell that are widely used. You can use Haskell to display text on a screen, or to launch a rocket, but the use of side effects within Haskell is subject to a very strict discipline. One consequence is that you can't just drop a print statement anywhere you want in the middle of a Haskell program to see what's going on.

On the other hand, Java, JavaScript, C++, Python, and so many others are not *purely* functional languages, but have adopted ideas from functional programming that make them much easier to use. And this is the punchline: once you understand the key principles for organizing side effects, these simple ideas can be used in *any* programming language. This book, *Grokking Simplicity*, shows you how to do that. It may seem long, but it's an easy read, filled with practical examples and sidebars that explain the technical terms. I was drawn in, really enjoyed it, and learned a couple of new ideas that I am eager to apply in my own code. I hope you enjoy it, too!

Jessica Kerr
Jessitron, LLC

When I first learned programming, I loved it for its predictability. Each of my programs was simple: it was small, it ran on one machine, and it was easy for one person (me) to use. Loving software development is something different. Software is not small. It is not written by one person. It runs on many machines, in many processes. It accommodates different people, including people who don't care how the software works.

Useful software doesn't get to be simple.

What's a programmer to do?

For sixty years, the techniques of functional programming have grown in the minds of computer scientists. Researchers like to make positive statements about what can never happen.

This last decade or two, developers have been adopting these techniques in business software. This is good timing, because it corresponds with the dominance of web applications: every app is a distributed system, downloaded to unknown computers, clicked on by unknown people. Functional programming is well suited. Whole categories of hard-to-find bugs can never happen.

But functional programming does not transfer peacefully from academia to business software. We are not using Haskell. We aren't starting from scratch. We depend on runtimes and libraries outside our control. Our software interacts with many other systems; it is not enough to output an answer. It is a long way from FP-land to legacy business software.

Eric has undertaken this journey for us. He delved into functional programming, found its most helpful essences, and brought them to us where we are.

Gone are the strict typing, the "pure" languages, the category theory. Here instead we notice the code that interacts with the world, choose to leave data unchanged, and break code apart for better clarity. Instead of high-minded abstractions, here are degrees and levels of abstraction. Instead of eschewing state, here are ways to safely keep state.

Eric offers new ways to perceive our existing code. New diagrams, new smells, new heuristics. Yes, this came out of a journey into functional programming—yet, when he makes his ways of thinking explicit so that we can use them too, he creates something new. Something that will help all of us with our creations.

My simple programs were not useful to the world. Our useful software will never be simple. But we can make more of our code simpler than it was. And we can manage those crucial bits that interact with the world. Eric unwinds these contradictions for us.

This book will make you better at programming—and more, at software development.

preface

I was first introduced to functional programming (FP) in the form of Common Lisp back in 2000 when I took an Artificial Intelligence class at my university. At first, Lisp appeared spare and foreign compared to the object-oriented languages I was used to. But by the end of the semester, I had built many assignments in Lisp, and it started to feel comfortable. I had gotten a taste of FP, even if I had only just begun to understand it.

Over the years, my use of functional programming deepened. I wrote my own Lisp. I read books on Lisp. I started doing my assignments from other classes in it. And from there, I was introduced to Haskell and eventually Clojure in 2008. In Clojure I found my muse. It was built on the 50-year tradition of Lisp, but on a modern and practical platform. And the community was churning through ideas about computation, the nature of data, and the practical engineering of large software systems. It was a hotbed of philosophy, computer science, and engineering. And I ate it up. I blogged about Clojure and eventually built a company to teach Clojure.

Meanwhile, awareness of Haskell was also on the rise. I worked in Haskell professionally for a few years. Haskell had a lot in common with Clojure, but there were also a lot of differences. How could we define *functional programming* to include both Clojure and Haskell? That question led to the seed of this book.

That first seed was the idea of actions, calculations, and data as the primary distinction of the functional programming paradigm. If you ask any functional programmer, they will agree this distinction is essential to the practice of FP, though few would agree it is the defining aspect of the paradigm. That looked like cognitive dissonance. People tend to teach the way they were taught. I saw an opportunity in that cognitive dissonance to help people learn FP in a new way.

I worked on many drafts of the book. One was very theoretical. One was showing off the impressive features of FP. One was extremely didactic. One was entirely narrative. But eventually, with a lot of coaching from my editor, I arrived at the current incarnation which treats functional programming as a set of skills. Basically, it was picking skills that are common in FP circles, but are rare outside of them. Once I decided on that approach, planning the book was just a matter of finding those skills, organizing them, and prioritizing them. The writing proceeded very quickly after that.

Of course, the book can't cover every skill. Functional programming is at least sixty years old. There are a lot of techniques that deserve to be taught well that I just didn't have room for. I'm sure people would object to some of my omissions, but I'm confident that the skills I did include are important parts of the professional functional programmer's repertoire. Further, they open the doors to more skills. I hope that other authors take the skills in this book as a starting point for discussion and further teaching.

My main goal with *Grokking Simplicity* was to at least start the process of legitimizing functional programming as a practical option for professional programmers. When a programmer wants to learn object-oriented programming, they can find many books on the subject written just for them, the beginning professional. Those books name patterns and principles and practices that the learner can build their skills upon. Functional programming does not have the same pedagogical literature. What books exist are mainly academic, and those that try to appeal to industry, in my opinion, fail to capture the most foundational concepts. But the knowledge and experience are out there in the minds of thousands of functional programmers. I hope this book inspires FP literature to bloom out of the hard-won skills of functional programmers everywhere.

acknowledgments

I would like to first of all thank Rich Hickey and the entire Clojure community for being a fountain of philosophical, scientific, and engineering ideas related to programming. You've been a huge inspiration to me. I'm sure you'll recognize many of the ideas in this book as stemming directly from the Clojure mindset.

I must thank my family, especially Virginia Medinilla, Olivia Normand, and Isabella Normand, for supporting me during the writing with encouragement, patience, and love. Thanks also to Liz Williams who advised me throughout.

Thank you to Guy Steele and Jessi Kerr for your attention to the book. It is a generous act to see a thing for what it is, and I believe you saw the purpose of the book. And thanks, of course, for sharing your personal experiences in the foreword.

Finally, I want to thank the folks at Manning. Bert Bates, thanks for the countless hours of meandering discussion that, somehow, led to the book being finished. Thanks for the continuous coaching on how to be a better teacher. And thanks for the patience and support while I figured out what the book needed to be. Also, sorry if it's hard to look at non-FP in the same way. Thanks to Jenny Stout for keeping the whole project straight. Thanks to Jennifer Houle for the beautiful design of the book. And thanks to everyone else at Manning who was involved. I know this was a hard book in many ways.

To all the reviewers: Michael Aydinbas, James J. Byleckie, Javier Collado, Theo Despoudis, Fernando García, Clive Harber, Fred Heath, Colin Joyce, Oliver Korten, Joel Luukka, Filip Mechant, Bryan Miller, Orlando Méndez, Naga Pavan Kumar T., Rob Pacheco, Dan Posey, Anshuman Purohit, Conor Redmond, Edward Ribeiro, David Rinck, Armin Seidling, Kaj Ström, Kent Spillner, Serge Simon, Richard Tuttle, Yvan Phelizot, and Greg Wright, your suggestions helped make this a better book.

about this book

Who should read this book

Grokking Simplicity was designed for programmers with 2–5 years of experience. I expect you to know at least one programming language. It will help if you have built a system sizeable enough to feel the pain we've all felt when systems scale. The code examples are written in a style of JavaScript that emphasizes readability. If you can read C, C#, C++, or Java, you should have little trouble

How this book is organized: a roadmap

This book is organized into two parts and nineteen chapters. Each part introduces a fundamental skill and then explores the other skills that fundamental skill opens up. Each part ends with a capstone about design and architecture in a functional programming context. Part 1, which starts in chapter 3, introduces the distinction between actions, calculations, and data. Part 2, which starts in chapter 10, introduces the idea of first-class values. There is a high-level tour of the possibilities that these skills open up in chapter 2.

- Chapter 1 introduces the book and the main idea of functional programming.

- Chapter 2 gives a high-level tour of what is possible using the skills in this book.

Part 1: Actions, calculations, and data

- Chapter 3 begins the first part by introducing the practical skills for distinguishing between actions, calculations, and data.

- Chapter 4 teaches us how to refactor code into calculations.

- Chapter 5 shows how we can improve actions if they cannot be refactored to calculations.

- Chapter 6 teaches an important immutability discipline called *copy-on-write*.

- Chapter 7 teaches a complimentary immutability discipline called *defensive copying*.

- Chapter 8 introduces a way of organizing our code according to layers of meaning.

- Chapter 9 helps us analyze the layers according to maintenance, testing, and reuse.

Part 2: First-class abstractions

- Chapter 10 starts the second part by introducing the idea of first-class values.

- Chapter 11 teaches you how to give any function superpowers.

- Chapter 12 shows us how we can create and use tools that iterate over arrays.

- Chapter 13 helps us build complex calculations out of the tools from chapter 12.

- Chapter 14 introduces functional tools for dealing with nested data while touching on recursion.

- Chapter 15 introduces the notion of timeline diagrams as a way to analyze the execution of your code.

- Chapter 16 shows how to safely share resources between timelines without introducing bugs.

- Chapter 17 shows how you can manipulate the ordering and repetition of actions to avoid bugs.

- Chapter 18 caps off part 2 with a discussion of two architectural patterns for building services in functional programming.

- Chapter 19 finishes the book with a retrospective and guidance for further learning.

You should read the book from the beginning and in order. Each chapter builds on the last. Be sure to do the exercises. *Noodle on it* exercises don't have an answer. They are there to help you formulate your own opinions on subjective matters. *It's your turn* exercises have answers. They are intended to give you practice and to reinforce the skills you learn through realistic scenarios. Feel free to pause at any time in the book. No one has mastered FP by reading books alone. If you've learned something important, put the book down and let it sink in. The book will be there when you're ready.

About the code

There is code throughout the book. The code is written in JavaScript using a style that emphasizes clarity instead of current best practices. I use JavaScript not to advocate that you do functional programming in JavaScript. JavaScript, in fact, is not great at FP. However, because it doesn't have a lot of FP features, this makes it a great language for teaching FP. We have to build a lot of functional constructs ourselves. By doing that, we understand them deeply. We also appreciate when they are provided by a language such as Haskell or Clojure.

The parts of the text that are code are clear. References to variables and other pieces of syntax that appear inline in the text use a `fixed-width font like this` to separate them from normal text. There are also code listings that use the same font. Sometimes code is highlighted to indicate that something has changed from previous steps. And the top-level variables and function names are **bold** to help them stand out. I also use underlining to draw attention to relevant parts of the code.

Source code for the examples in this book is available for download from the publisher's website at https://www.manning.com/books/grokking-simplicity.

liveBook discussion forum

Purchase of *Grokking Simplicity* includes free access to a private web forum run by Manning Publications where you can make comments about the book, ask technical questions, and receive help from the author and from other users. To access the forum, go to https://livebook.manning.com/#!/book/grokking-simplicity/discussion. You can also learn more about Manning's forums and the rules of conduct at https://livebook.manning.com/#!/discussion.

Manning's commitment to our readers is to provide a venue where a meaningful dialogue between individual readers and between readers and the author can take place. It is not a commitment to any specific amount of participation on the part of the author, whose contribution to the forum remains voluntary (and unpaid). We suggest you try asking the author some challenging questions lest his interest stray! The forum and the archives of previous discussions will be accessible from the publisher's website as long as the book is in print.

Other online resources

There are too many online and offline resources related to functional programming to list them all. And none are canonical enough to merit special mention. I would like to encourage you, though, to seek out local functional programming groups. We learn better when learning is social.

If you would like additional material related specifically to this book, I maintain links to resources and other materials at https://grokkingsimplicity.com.

about the author

ERIC NORMAND is an experienced functional programmer, trainer, speaker, and writer on all things functional programming. He hails from New Orleans. He started programming in Lisp in 2000. He creates Clojure training material at PurelyFunctional.tv. He also consults with companies to use functional programming to better serve business objectives. You can find him speaking internationally at programming conferences. His writing, speaking, training, and consulting can be found at LispCast.com

Welcome to Grokking Simplicity | 1

In this chapter

- Learn the definition of functional thinking.

- Understand how this book is different from other books on functional programming.

- Discover the primary distinction that functional programmers make when they look at code.

- Decide whether this book is for you.

In this chapter, we will define functional thinking and how its major distinction helps working programmers build better software. We will also get an overview of the journey ahead through two major insights that functional programmers experience.

What is functional programming?

Programmers ask me all the time what functional programming (FP) is and what it's good for. What FP is good for is difficult to explain because it is a general-purpose paradigm. It's good for everything. We'll see where it really shines in just a few pages.

The typical definition of functional programming makes it seem completely impractical.

Defining functional programming is difficult, too. Functional programming is a huge field. It's used in both the software industry and in academia. However, most of what has been written about it is from academia.

Grokking Simplicity takes a different approach from the typical book about functional programming. It is decidedly about the industrial uses of functional programming. Everything in this book needs to be practical for working software engineers.

You may come across definitions from other sources, and it's important to understand how they relate to what we're doing in this book. Here is a typical definition paraphrased from Wikipedia:

functional programming (FP), *noun*.
1. a programming paradigm characterized by the use of <u>mathematical functions</u> and the avoidance of <u>side effects</u>
2. a programming style that uses only <u>pure functions</u> without <u>side effects</u>

we need to define the underlined terms

Let's pick apart the underlined terms.

Side effects are anything a function does other than returning a value, like sending an email or modifying global state. These can be problematic because the side effects happen every time your function is called. If you need the return value and not the side effects, you'll cause things to happen unintentionally. It is very common for functional programmers to avoid unnecessary side effects.

these are why we run software in the first place!

Pure functions are functions that depend only on their arguments and don't have any side effects. Given the same arguments, they will always produce the same return value. We can consider these *mathematical functions* to distinguish them from the language feature called /functions/. Functional programmers emphasize the use of pure functions because they are easier to understand and control.

The definition implies that functional programmers completely avoid side effects and *only* use pure functions. But this is not true. Working functional programmers will use side effects and impure functions.

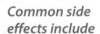

Common side effects include

- Sending an email
- Reading a file
- Blinking a light
- Making a web request
- Applying the brakes in a car

The problems with the definition for practical use

The definition might work well for academia, but it has a number of problems for the working software engineer. Let's look at the definition again:

functional programming (FP), *noun*.
1. a programming paradigm characterized by the use of mathematical functions and the avoidance of side effects

2. a programming style that uses only pure functions without side effects

There are three main problems with this definition for our purposes.

Problem 1: FP needs side effects

The definition says FP avoids side effects, but side effects are the very reason we run our software. What good is email software that doesn't send emails? The definition implies that we completely avoid them, when in reality, we use side effects when we have to.

Problem 2: FP is good at side effects

Functional programmers know side effects are necessary yet problematic, so we have a lot of tools for working with them. The definition implies that we *only* use pure functions. On the contrary, we use impure functions a lot. We have a ton of functional techniques that make them easier to use.

Problem 3: FP is practical

The definition makes FP seem like it's mostly mathematical and impractical for real-world software. There are many important software systems written using functional programming.

The definition is especially confusing to people who are introduced to FP through the definition. Let's see an example of a well-intentioned manager who reads the definition on Wikipedia.

 **Vocab time**

Side effects are any behavior of a function besides the return value.

Pure functions depend only on their arguments and don't have any side effects.

The definition of FP confuses managers

Imagine a scenario where Jenna, the eager programmer, wants to use FP for an email-sending service. She knows FP will help architect the system to improve dependability. Her manager doesn't know what FP is, so he has to look up the definition on Wikipedia.

The manager looks up "functional programming" on Wikipedia:

. . . the avoidance of side effects . . .

He Googles "side effect." **Common side effects include**

- *sending an email*
- *. . .*

Later that day . . .

We treat functional programming as a set of skills and concepts

We're not going to use the typical definition in this book. FP is many things to many people, and it is a huge field of study and practice.

I've talked with many working functional programmers about what they find most useful from FP. *Grokking Simplicity* is a distillation of the skills, thought processes, and perspectives of working functional programmers. Only the most practical and powerful ideas made it into this book.

In *Grokking Simplicity*, you won't find the latest research or the most esoteric ideas. We're only going to learn the skills and concepts you can apply today. While doing this research I've found that the most important concepts from FP apply even in object-oriented and procedural code, and across all programming languages. The real beauty of FP is that it deals with beneficial, universal coding practices.

Let's take a crack at the skill any functional programmer would say is important: the distinction between actions, calculations, and data.

GroKKing Simplicity is a distillation of the best practices of working functional programmers.

Distinguishing actions, calculations, and data

When functional programmers look at code, they immediately begin to classify code into three categories:

1. Actions

2. Calculations

3. Data

Here are some snippets of code from an existing codebase. You need to be more careful with the snippets with stars.

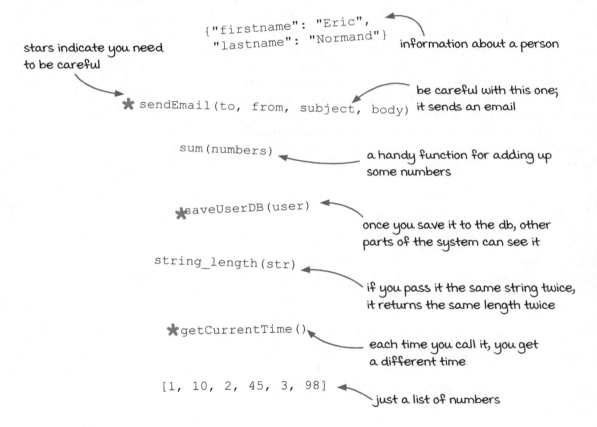

```
{"firstname": "Eric",
 "lastname": "Normand"}
```
information about a person

stars indicate you need to be careful

★ sendEmail(to, from, subject, body)   be careful with this one; it sends an email

sum(numbers)   a handy function for adding up some numbers

★saveUserDB(user)   once you save it to the db, other parts of the system can see it

string_length(str)   if you pass it the same string twice, it returns the same length twice

★getCurrentTime()   each time you call it, you get a different time

[1, 10, 2, 45, 3, 98]   just a list of numbers

The starred functions need caution because they depend on when they are run or how many times they are run. For instance, you don't want to send an important email twice, nor do you want to send it zero times.

The starred snippets are *actions*. Let's separate those from the rest.

Functional programmers distinguish code that matters when you call it

Let's draw a line and move all of the functions that depend on when you call them to one side of the line:

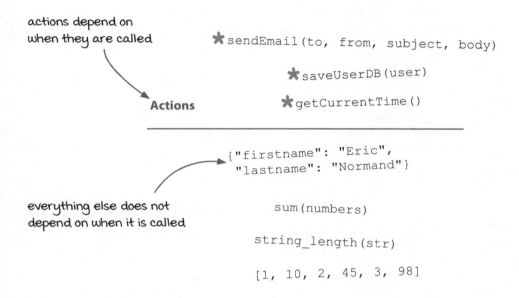

actions depend on
when they are called

Actions

everything else does not
depend on when it is called

```
* sendEmail(to, from, subject, body)

    * saveUserDB(user)

* getCurrentTime()
```

```
{"firstname": "Eric",
 "lastname": "Normand"}
```

```
sum(numbers)
```

```
string_length(str)
```

```
[1, 10, 2, 45, 3, 98]
```

This is a very important distinction. Actions (everything above the line) depend on when they are called or how many times they are called. We have to be extra careful with them.

However, the stuff below the line is much easier to work with. It does not matter when you call a sum. It will give you the correct answer any time. And it doesn't matter how many times you call it. It won't have an effect on the rest of the program or the world outside the software.

But there is another distinction we can make: Some of the code is executable and some is inert. Let's draw another line on the next page.

Functional programmers distinguish inert data from code that does work

We can draw another line between *calculations* and *data*. Neither calculations nor data depend on when or how many times they are used. The difference is that calculations can be executed, while data cannot. Data is inert and transparent. Calculations are opaque, meaning that you don't really know what a calculation will do until you run it.

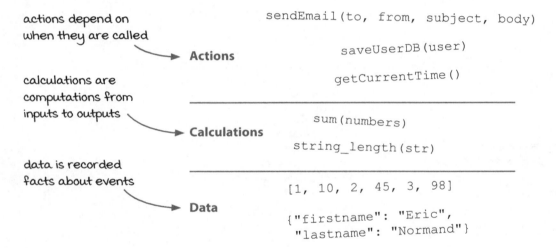

actions depend on when they are called

Actions

```
sendEmail(to, from, subject, body)

saveUserDB(user)

getCurrentTime()
```

calculations are computations from inputs to outputs

Calculations

```
sum(numbers)

string_length(str)
```

data is recorded facts about events

Data

```
[1, 10, 2, 45, 3, 98]

{"firstname": "Eric",
 "lastname": "Normand"}
```

The distinction between actions, calculations, and data is fundamental to FP. Any functional programmer would agree that this is an important skill. Most other concepts and skills in FP are built on top of it.

It's important to emphasize that functional programmers are not averse to using code in any of the three categories because they are all important. However, they do recognize the tradeoffs and try to use the best tool for the job. In general, they prefer data to calculations and calculations to actions. Data is the easiest to work with.

It's worth emphasizing this again: **Functional programmers see these categories when they look at any code**. It's the primary perspective difference of FP. There are a number of skills and concepts that revolve around this distinction. We will focus on these skills throughout the rest of Part 1.

Let's see what this distinction can tell us about a simple task management service.

Functional programmers prefer data to calculations and prefer calculations to actions.

Functional programmers see actions, calculations, and data

Distinguishing actions, calculations, and data is fundamental to FP. You couldn't really do FP without it. This may be obvious, but just so we are all on the same page, let's go through a simple scenario that illustrates the three categories.

Let's imagine a cloud service for project management. As the clients mark their tasks as completed, the central server sends email notifications.

Where are the actions, calculations, and data? In other words, how does a functional programmer see what's going on?

the server sends an email based on that decision. sending the email is an **action**

Step 1: The user marks a task as completed.

This triggers a UI event, which is an *action*, since it depends on how many times it happens.

the central cloud server receives messages from many clients and decides what to do. the decision is made with **calculations**

Step 2: The client sends a message to the server.

Sending the message is an *action*, but the message itself is *data* (inert bytes that must be interpreted).

Step 3: The server receives the message.

Receiving a message is an *action*, since it depends on how many times it happens.

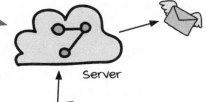

Server

Step 4: The server makes a change to its database.

Changing the internal state is an *action*.

Step 5: The server makes a decision of who to notify.

Making a decision is a *calculation*. Given the same inputs, your server would make the same decision.

the message itself is **data**, but sending the message is an **action**

Client

Step 6: The server sends an email notification.

Sending an email is an *action*, since sending the same email twice is different from sending it once.

we distinguish between deciding (**calculation**) and carrying out the decision (**action**)

If this doesn't make sense to you now, don't worry, because we're going to spend the whole first part of this book understanding how to make this distinction, why we make it, and how to improve our code because of it. As we've talked about before, the distinction between actions, calculations, and data is the first big idea in this book.

The three categories of code in FP

Let's go over the characteristics of the three categories:

FP has tools for using each category

1. Actions

Anything that depends on when it is run, or how many times it is run, or both, is an *action*. If I send an urgent email today, it's much different from sending it next week. And of course, sending the same email 10 times is different from sending it 0 times or 1 time.

Actions

- Tools for safely changing state over time
- Ways to guarantee ordering
- Tools to ensure actions happen exactly once

2. Calculations

Calculations are computations from input to output. They always give the same output when you give them the same input. You can call them anytime, anywhere, and it won't affect anything outside of them. That makes them really easy to test and safe to use without worrying about how many times or when they are called.

Calculations

- Static analysis to aid correctness
- Mathematical tools that work well for software
- Testing strategies

3. Data

Data is recorded facts about events. We distinguish data because it is not as complex as executable code. It has well-understood properties. Data is interesting because it is meaningful without being run. It can be interpreted in multiple ways. Take a restaurant receipt as an example: It can be used by the restaurant manager to determine which food items are popular. And it can be used by the customer to track their dining-out budget.

Data

- Ways to organize data for efficient access
- Disciplines to keep records long term
- Principles for capturing what is important using data

This distinction is the beginning of functional thinking, and it's the starting point for what you'll learn in this book.

How does distinguishing actions, calculations, and data help us?

FP works great for distributed systems, and most software written today is distributed

FP is a buzzword these days. It's important to know if it's just a trend that will one day die down, or if there is something essential about it.

FP is not a trend. It is one of the oldest programming paradigms, which has roots in even older mathematics. The reason it is gaining popularity only now is that, due to the internet and a proliferation of devices such as phones, laptops, and cloud servers, we need a new way of looking at software that takes into account multiple pieces of software communicating over networks.

Once computers talk over networks, things get chaotic. Messages arrive out of order, are duplicated, or never arrive at all. Making sense of what happened when, basically *modeling change over time*, is very important but also difficult. The more we can do to eliminate a dependency on when or how many times a thing runs, the easier it will be to avoid serious bugs.

Data and calculations do not depend on how many times they are run or accessed. By moving more of our code into data and calculations, we sweep that code clean of the problems inherent in distributed systems.

The problems still remain in actions, but we've identified and isolated them. Further, FP has a set of tools for working with actions to make them safer, even in the uncertainty of distributed systems. And because we've moved code out of actions and into calculations, we can give more attention to the actions that need it most.

> *Three rules of distributed systems*
>
> 1. Messages arrive out of order.
> 2. Each message may arrive 0, 1, or more times.
> 3. If you don't hear back, you have no idea what happened.

once you go distributed, things get really complicated

Why is this book different from other FP books?

This book is *practical* for software engineering

A lot of the discussion around FP is academic. It's researchers exploring the theory. Theory is great until you have to put it into practice.

Many FP books focus on the academic side. They teach recursion and continuation-passing style. This book is different. *Grokking Simplicity* distills the pragmatic experience of many professional functional programmers. They appreciate the theoretical ideas but have learned to stick to what works.

This book uses real-world scenarios

You won't find any definitions of Fibonacci or merge sort in this book. Instead, the scenarios in this book mimic situations you might actually encounter at your job. We apply functional thinking to existing code, to new code, and to architecture.

This book focuses on software design

It's easy to take a small problem and find an elegant solution. There's no need for architecture when you're writing FizzBuzz. It's only when things get big that design principles are needed.

Many FP books never need to design because the programs are so small. In the real world, we do need to architect our systems to be maintainable in the long term. This book teaches functional design principles for every level of scale, from the line of code to the entire application.

This book conveys the richness of FP

Functional programmers have been accumulating principles and techniques since the 1950s. A lot has changed in computing, but much has stood the test of time. This book goes deep to show how functional thinking is more relevant now than ever.

This book is language agnostic

Many books teach the features of a particular functional language. This often means that people using a different language cannot benefit.

This book uses JavaScript for code examples, which is not great for *doing* FP. However, JavaScript has turned out to be great for *teaching* FP precisely because it isn't perfect. The limitations of the language will cause us to stop and think.

And even though it uses JavaScript for the examples, this is not a book about FP in JavaScript. Focus on the thinking, not on the language.

The code examples have been written for clarity, not to suggest any particular JavaScript style. If you can read C, Java, C#, or C++, you will be able to follow.

What is functional thinking?

Functional thinking is the set of skills and ideas that functional programmers use to solve problems with software. That's a big set of skills. This book aims to guide you through two powerful ideas that are very important in functional programming: (1) distinguishing actions, calculations, and data and (2) using first-class abstractions. These are not the only ideas in FP, but they will give you a solid and practical foundation on which to build. And they will take you from beginner to professional functional programmer.

Each idea brings with it associated skills. They also correspond with the two parts of this book. Each part teaches practical, line-by-line and function-by-function skills and caps off with a chapter or two on design for a higher-level picture of what's going on.

Let's go over the two big ideas and what skills you'll learn in each part.

Part 1: Distinguishing actions, calculations, and data

As we've seen, functional programmers separate all code into one of three categories: actions, calculations, or data. They may not use these same terms, but that's what we'll call them in this book. These categories correspond to how difficult the code is to understand, test, and reuse. We've already begun to discover this important distinction in this chapter. Throughout this first part of the book, we'll learn to identify the category of any piece of code, refactor actions into calculations, and make actions easier to work with. The design chapters look at how identifying layers in our code can help make it maintainable, testable, and reusable.

Part 2: Using first-class abstractions

Programmers of all kinds will find common procedures and name them to be reused later. Functional programmers do the same but can often reuse more procedures by passing in procedures to the procedures. The idea may sound crazy, but it's extremely practical. We'll learn how to do it and how to avoid overdoing it. We'll cap it off with two common designs called reactive architecture and onion architecture.

It will be quite a journey. But let's not get ahead of ourselves. We're still in part 1! Before we begin our journey, let's lay out some ground rules for what we'll learn.

Ground rules for ideas and skills in this book

FP is a big topic. We won't be able to learn "the whole thing." We will have to pick and choose what to learn. These ground rules will help us choose practical knowledge for the working programmer.

1. The skills can't be based on language features

There are a lot of functional programming languages out there that have features made to support FP. For instance, many functional languages have very powerful type systems. If you are using one of those languages, that's great! But even if you're not, functional thinking can help you. We'll only focus on skills that are language-feature agnostic. That means that even though type systems are cool, we will only mention them here or there.

2. The skills must have immediate practical benefit

FP is used in both industry and academia. In academia, they sometimes focus on theoretically important ideas. That's great, but we want to keep it practical. This book will only teach skills that can benefit you here and now. In fact, the ideas we will learn are beneficial even if they don't show up in your code. For example, just being able to identify actions can help you better understand certain bugs.

3. The skills must apply regardless of your current code situation

Some of us are starting brand new projects, with no code yet written. Some of us are working on existing codebases with hundreds of thousands of lines of code. And some of us are somewhere in between. The ideas and skills in this book should help us, regardless of our situation. We're not talking about a functional rewrite here. We need to make pragmatic choices and work with the code we've got.

 **Brain break**

There's more to go, but let's take a break for questions

Q: I use an object-oriented (OO) language. Will this book be useful?

A: Yes, the book should be useful. The principles in the book are universally applicable. Some of them are similar to OO design principles you might be familiar with. And some of them are different, stemming from a different fundamental perspective.

Functional thinking is valuable, regardless of what language you use.

Q: Every time I've looked into FP, it has been so academic and math-based. Is this book more of the same?

A: No! Academicians like FP because calculations are abstract and easy to analyze in papers. Unfortunately, researchers dominate the FP conversation.

However, there are many people working productively using FP. Though we keep an eye on the academic literature, functional programmers are mostly coding away at their day jobs like most professional programmers. We share knowledge with each other about how to solve everyday problems. You will find some of that knowledge in this book.

Q: Why JavaScript?

A: That's a really good question. JavaScript is widely known and available. If you're programming on the web, you know at least a little bit. The syntax is pretty familiar to most programmers. And, believe it or not, JavaScript does have everything you need for FP, including functions and some basic data structures.

That said, it's far from perfect for FP. However, those imperfections let us bring up the principles of FP. Learning to implement a principle in a language that doesn't do this by default is a useful skill, especially since most languages don't have this by default.

Q: Why is the existing FP definition not enough? Why use the term "functional thinking"?

A: That's also a great question. The standard definition is a useful extreme position to take to find new avenues of academic research. It is essentially asking "What can we accomplish if we don't allow side effects?" It turns out that you can do quite a lot, and a lot of it is interesting for industrial software engineering.

However, the standard definition makes some implicit assumptions that are hard to uncover. This book teaches those assumptions first. "Functional thinking" and "functional programming" are mostly synonymous. The new term simply implies a fresh approach.

Conclusion

Functional programming is a large, rich field of techniques and principles. However, it all starts with the distinction between actions, calculations, and data. This book teaches the practical side of FP. It can apply in any language and to any problem. There are thousands of functional programmers out there, and I hope this book will convince you to count yourself among us.

Summary

- The book is organized into two parts that correspond to two big ideas and related skills: distinguishing actions, calculations, and data and using higher-order abstractions.

- The typical functional programming definition has served academic researchers, but until now, there hasn't been a satisfactory one for software engineering. This explains why FP can feel abstract and impractical.

- Functional thinking is the skills and concepts of FP. It's the main topic of this book.

- Functional programmers distinguish three categories of code: actions, calculations, and data.

- Actions depend on time, so they are the hardest to get right. We separate them so we can devote more focus to them.

- Calculations do not depend on time. We want to write more code in this category because they are so easy to get right.

- Data is inert and require interpretation. Data is easy to understand, store, and transmit.

- This book uses JavaScript for examples, since it has familiar syntax. We will learn a few JavaScript concepts when we need them.

Up next . . .

Now that we have taken a good first step into functional thinking, you might wonder what programming with functional thinking actually looks like. In the next chapter, we'll see examples of solving problems using the big ideas that form the structure of this book.

In this chapter

- See examples of functional thinking applied to real problems.

- Understand why stratified design can help organize your software.

- Learn how actions can be visualized in timelines.

- See how timelines help you discover and resolve problems having
  to do with timing.

This chapter will give a broad overview of the two big ideas we will address
in this book. Your main goal should be to get a taste of thinking with FP.
Don't worry about understanding everything right away. Remember that
each of these ideas will be addressed in several chapters later on. This will
be a whirlwind tour of functional thinking in action.

Welcome to Toni's Pizza

Welcome to Toni's Pizza. The year is 2118. It turns out people still like pizza in the future. But all of the pizza is made by robots. And the robots are programmed in JavaScript. Go figure.

Toni has applied a lot of functional thinking to the code that runs her restaurants. We're going to take a brief tour through some of her systems, including the kitchen and her inventory, and see how she has applied the two levels of functional thinking.

Just so you don't have to flip back, here are the two levels again. Here's how Toni uses them.

Part 1: Distinguishing actions, calculations, and data

Toni is sure to distinguish the code that uses ingredients and other resources (action) from code that doesn't (calculations). In this chapter, we'll dip into some examples of each category; then we'll see how she organizes the code into layers using the principles of *stratified design*.

Part 2: Using first-class abstractions

Toni's kitchen is a distributed system because multiple robots work together to cook the pizzas. We'll peek in as Toni uses *timeline diagrams* to understand how her system operates (sometimes unsuccessfully). We also see how Toni uses *first-class functions* (functions that take functions as arguments) to coordinate her robots so she can successfully scale up the baking.

Toni   Robot

Part 1: Distinguishing actions, calculations, and data

Toni's pizza business has grown a lot and has faced scaling problems. However, she has kept on top of those challenges with dili-
gent use of functional thinking. The primary way she has applied
functional thinking is the most fundamental: distinguishing
actions, calculations and data. Every functional programmer
needs to make this distinction that tells us which parts of our code
are easy (calculations and data) and which need more attention.

If you looked at Toni's code, you'd see the three main categories
of code:

*examples of
categories*

1. Actions

The actions are anything that depend on when they are called or
how many times they are called. The actions use ingredients or
other resources, like the oven or delivery van, so Toni has to be
really careful with how they are used.

Example actions

- Roll out dough
- Deliver pizza
- Order ingredients

2. Calculations

The calculations represent decisions or planning. They don't
affect the world when they run. Toni likes them because she can
use them any time and any place without worrying about them
messing up her kitchen.

Example calculations

- Double a recipe
- Determine a shopping list

3. Data

Toni represents as much as she can with immutable data. That
includes the accounting, inventory, and the recipes for her pizzas.
Data is very flexible since it can be stored, transfered over the
network, and used in multiple ways.

Example data

- Customer orders
- Receipts
- Recipes

These examples are all parts of Toni's pizza business. But the distinction applies at all levels, from the lowest JavaScript expression
to the largest function. We'll learn how these three categories
interact when they call each other in chapter 3.

Making the distinction between these three categories is vital to
FP, though functional programmers might not use these same
words to describe them. **By the end of Part 1, you will feel very
comfortable identifying actions and calculations, and moving
code between them.** Let's take a look at how Toni uses stratified
design in her codebase.

Organizing code by "rate of change"

A first glimpse of stratified design

Over time, Toni's software has had to change and grow with her business. Using functional thinking, she has learned to organize her code to minimize the cost of making changes.

Imagine we draw out a spectrum. On the bottom, we put the stuff that changes the least frequently. On the top, we put the stuff that changes the most frequently.

What parts of Toni's software would go on the bottom, and what would go on the top? Certainly the JavaScript language changes the most slowly. In the bottom layer are all of the built-in language constructs like arrays and objects. In the middle, there is all of the stuff about making pizza. Then on the top go all of the specifics about her business, like what's on the menu this week.

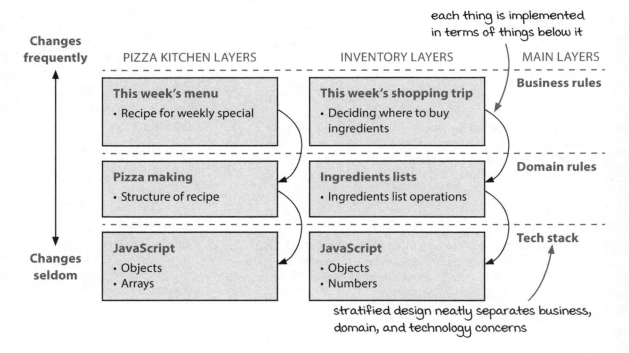

Each layer is built on layers beneath it. That means that each piece of code is built on a more stable foundation. By building our software in this way, we ensure we will make code changes as easy as possible. Stuff at the top is easy to change because very little other code relies on it. Things at the bottom, of course, might change, but are much less likely to.

Functional programmers call this architectural pattern *stratified design* because it creates layers. In generic terms, we think of three main layers: business rules, domain rules, and tech stack.

We will go deeper into stratified design in chapters 8 and 9. It's a great way to organize code to improve testing, reuse, and maintenance.

Part 2: First-class abstractions

As applied to a robotic kitchen

Toni's kitchen just has one robot right now, and she's starting to get scaling problems. She can't bake fast enough to satisify her customers. Following is a *timeline diagram* of the actions one robot takes to make a pizza.

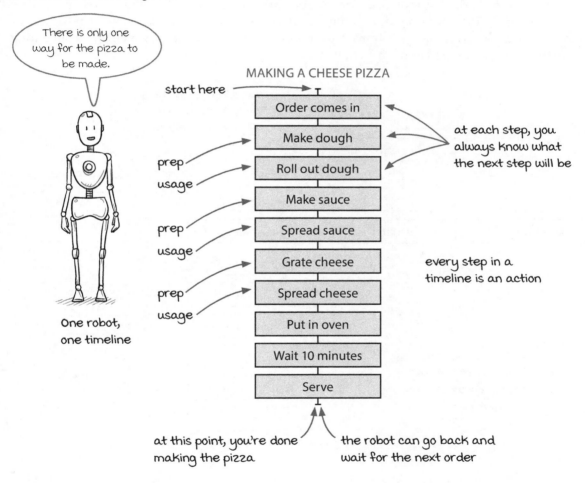

We use the timeline diagram to understand how actions will execute over time. Remember, actions depend on when they are run, so it is important to make sure they run in the right order. We will see Toni manipulate the diagram to make her kitchen more efficient. We'll learn everything she does, including how to draw these diagrams, and more, starting in chapter 15. For now, let's just sit back and watch her work. We don't need to understand it all right away.

Timelines visualize distributed systems

Toni's one robot makes good pizza, but it's not fast enough. It is purely sequential. She is sure that there is a way to get three robots working together on one pizza. She can divide the work into three parts that can happen in parallel: making the dough, making the sauce, and grating the cheese.

However, once she has more than one robot working, she has a distributed system. Actions can run out of order. Toni can draw a timeline diagram to help her understand what the robots will do when they run their programs. Each robot gets its own timeline, which looks something like this. We will learn to draw these in part 2.

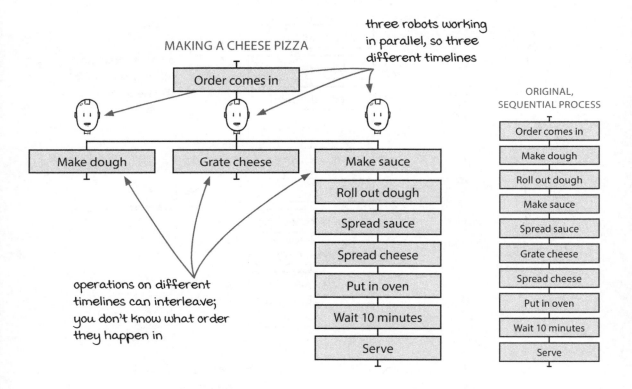

The timeline diagram will help Toni understand problems in her program, but she has failed to account for different orderings of actions. When she ran the three-robot kitchen at the restaurant that night, it was a disaster. Many pizzas came out wrong. There are many ways these timelines can run that will make bad pizzas.

Multiple timelines can execute in different orderings

In the timeline diagram, there is no coordination between different timelines by default. There is nothing in the diagram saying to wait for another timeline to finish, so no waiting occurs. The actions in different timelines can also occur out of order. For instance, the dough can be finished after the sauce. In that case, the sauce robot will start rolling out the dough before the dough is ready.

DOUGH TAKES LONGER

Order comes in

Grate cheese · Make sauce

Roll out dough

Spread sauce

Spread cheese

Put in oven

Wait 10 minutes

Serve

Make dough

dough not ready until after the other robot tried to roll it out

Or the cheese could be finished last. The sauce robot will start spreading the cheese before it's ready.

CHEESE TAKES LONGER

Order comes in

Make dough · Make sauce

Roll out dough

cheese not ready until after the other robot tried to spread it

Spread sauce

Spread cheese

Grate cheese

Put in oven

Wait 10 minutes

Serve

In fact, there are six ways the preparations could be interleaved, and the sauce is finished last in only two of them. Only when the sauce is finished last will you get a good pizza.

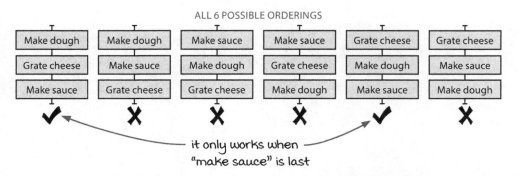

ALL 6 POSSIBLE ORDERINGS

Make dough	Make dough	Make sauce	Make sauce	Grate cheese	Grate cheese
Grate cheese	Make sauce	Make dough	Grate cheese	Make dough	Make sauce
Make sauce	Grate cheese	Grate cheese	Make dough	Make sauce	Make dough
✔	✘	✘	✘	✔	✘

it only works when "make sauce" is last

The hard fact of distributed systems is that uncoordinated timelines run in weird orders. Toni needs to coordinate the robots to guarantee that they don't start assembling the pizza before the three ingredients are ready.

Hard-won lessons about distributed systems

Toni does a postmortem

Toni learns the hard way that moving from a sequential program to a distributed system is not easy. She will need to focus on the actions (things that depend on time) to make sure they happen in the right order.

Here's what I learned last night.

1. Timelines are uncoordinated by default.

The dough might not be ready yet, but the other timelines just keep going. She needs to get the timelines to coordinate.

2. You cannot rely on the duration of actions.

Just because the sauce usually takes the longest doesn't mean it always does. The timelines need to be independent of order.

3. Bad timing, however rare, can happen in production.

It worked fine in her tests, but once the dinner rush came in, the rare event became common. The timelines need to get a good result every time.

4. The timeline diagram reveals problems in the system.

She should have seen from the diagram that the cheese might not be ready in time. Use the timeline diagram to understand the system.

There must be a way for the three robots to work together.

We await your instructions.

Cutting the timeline: Making the robots wait for each other

Toni is going to give us a first look at a technique we will learn in chapter 17 called *cutting a timeline*. It's a way to coordinate multiple timelines working in parallel, implemented as a *higher-order operation*. Each of the timelines will do work independently, then wait for each other to finish when they are done. That way, it doesn't matter which one finishes first. Let's watch her do it.

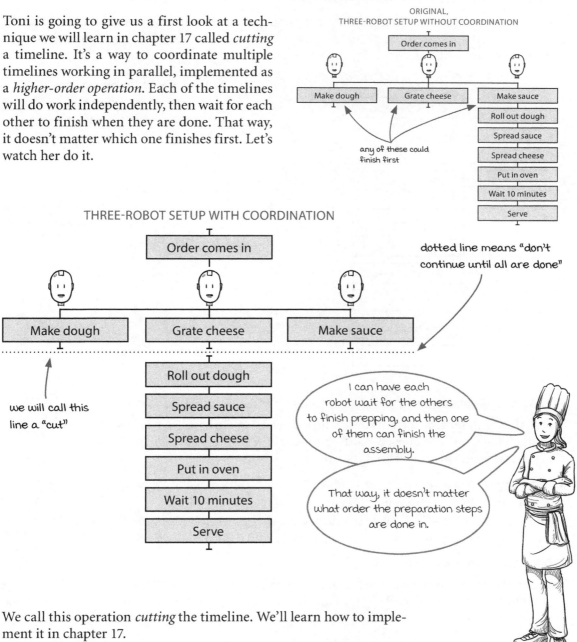

We call this operation *cutting* the timeline. We'll learn how to implement it in chapter 17.

Toni tries it that night at the restaurant and it is a total success.

Positive lessons learned about timelines

Retrospective on coordinating robots

The three-robot system worked great at the restaurant. Pizzas came out in record time, and they were all perfectly prepared. Toni's application of the cutting technique ensured that the actions happened in the right order.

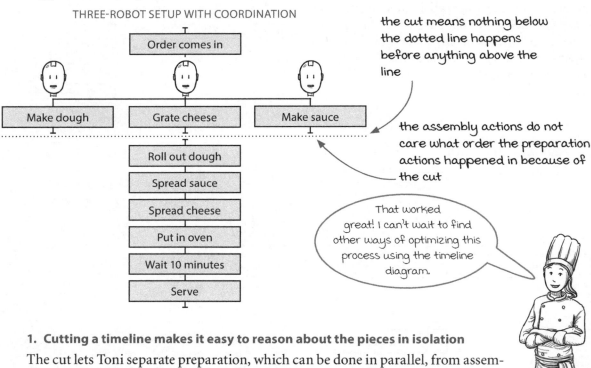

THREE-ROBOT SETUP WITH COORDINATION

the cut means nothing below the dotted line happens before anything above the line

the assembly actions do not care what order the preparation actions happened in because of the cut

That worked great! I can't wait to find other ways of optimizing this process using the timeline diagram.

1. Cutting a timeline makes it easy to reason about the pieces in isolation

The cut lets Toni separate preparation, which can be done in parallel, from assembly, which happens in sequence. Cutting timelines lets you reason about shorter timelines without worrying about the order.

2. Working with timeline diagrams helps you understand how the system works through time

Now that Toni understands timeline diagrams, she trusts how things will run. Timelines are a useful tool for visualizing parallel and distributed systems.

3. Timeline diagrams are flexible

Toni figured out what she wanted to happen and drew the timeline. Then all she had to do was figure out a simple way to code it up. Timeline diagrams give you a way to model coordination between timelines.

We will learn about cutting and other higher-order operations in part 2. But for now, that marks the end of our tour!

Conclusion

In this chapter, we got a high-level view of some of the functional ideas we'll see later in the book.

We watched as Toni got a lot of mileage from applying functional thinking to her pizza restaurant software. She organized her actions and calculations according to stratified design to minimize the cost of maintenance. We will learn to do this in chapters 3 through 9. Toni was also able to scale the kitchen to multiple robots and avoid some nasty timing bugs. We will learn to draw and manipulate timeline diagrams in chapters 15 through 17.

Unfortunately, we won't revisit Toni. But we will see very similar scenarios so we can learn the exact same processes she used.

Summary

- Actions, calculations, and data are the first and most important distinction functional programmers make. We need to learn to see them in all code we read. We'll start to apply this distinction in chapter 3.

- Functional programmers apply stratified design to make their code easier to maintain. The layers help organize code by rate of change. We see the exact process of stratified design in chapters 8 and 9.

- Timeline diagrams can help you visualize how actions will run over time. They can help you see where actions will interfere with each other. We'll learn the process of drawing timeline diagrams in chapter 15.

- We learned to cut timelines to coordinate their actions. Coordinating them helps us guarantee that they perform their actions in the proper order. We'll see exactly how to cut timelines in chapter 17 in a very similar scenario to the pizza kitchen.

Up next . . .

We just got an example of how functional thinking can be applied to a practical scenario. After that high-level overview, let's get down to the nitty-gritty of functional thinking: distinguishing between actions, calculations, and data.

Part 1

· ·

Actions, calculations, and data

We will learn many skills on our journey into the world of functional programming. But first we must equip ourselves with a fundamental skill. That skill is the ability to distinguish three categories of code: actions, calculations, and data. Once we learn that distinction, a vast landscape of powerful ideas is available to us. We will learn to refactor actions to become calculations, making our code easier to test and read. We will improve the design of actions to be more reusable. We will make data immutable so that we can rely on it for keeping records. And we will learn a way to organize and understand our code as layers of meaning. But first, we must learn to see actions, calculations, and data.

· ·

In this chapter

- Learn the differences between actions, calculations, and data.

- Distinguish between actions, calculations, and data when thinking about a problem, coding, and reading existing code.

- Track actions as they spread throughout your code.

- Be able to spot actions in existing code.

We've already seen the categories of actions, calculations, and data at a glance. In this chapter, we're going to learn how to identify these three categories in real life and in code. As we've talked about before, it's the first step in doing functional programming. By identifying these categories, you'll see how calculations are often overlooked and how infectious actions can be.

Actions, calculations, and data

Functional programmers distinguish between actions, calculations, and data (ACD).

Actions	Calculations	Data
Depend on how many times or when it is run	Computations from input to output	Facts about events
Also called *functions with side-effects, side-effecting functions, impure functions*	**Also called** *pure functions, mathematical functions*	
Examples: Send an email, read from a database	**Examples**: Find the maximum number, check if an email address is valid	**Examples**: The email address a user gave us, the dollar amount read from a bank's API

We apply this distinction throughout the development process. For instance, you might find functional programmers using these concepts in the following situations:

1. Thinking about a problem

Even before we begin coding, functional programmers try to break it down into actions, calculations and data. This will help us clarify the parts that need special attention (actions), what data we will need to capture, and what decisions we will need to make (calculations).

2. Coding a solution

While we're coding, functional programmers will reflect the three categories in their code. For instance, data will be separated from calculations, which are separated from actions. Further, we will always ask whether an action couldn't be rewritten as a calculation, or whether a calculation couldn't be data.

3. Reading code

When we read code, we are always conscious of what goes in what category, especially actions. We know that actions are tricky because they depend on time, so we always look for hidden actions. In general, functional programmers will look for ways to refactor the code to better separate actions, calculations, and data.

In this chapter, we're going to look at all three categories. We will also look at how we can apply them in the three situations listed. Let's get to it!

 **Vocab time**

Calculations are *referentially transparent* because a call to a calculation can be replaced by its result. For instance, + is a calculation. 2 + 3 always results in 5, so you could replace the code 2 + 3 with 5 and have an equivalent program. That means you can call 2 + 3 zero, one, or more times and get the same result.

Actions, calculations, and data apply to any situation

Let's check out a situation that we encounter frequenty in our lives: going grocery shopping.

If a nonfunctional programmer were to sketch out the process of shopping, it might look roughly like the following. On the left, we'll categorize each of the steps into actions, calculations, and data (ACD).

Actions **depend on how many times or when they are run.**

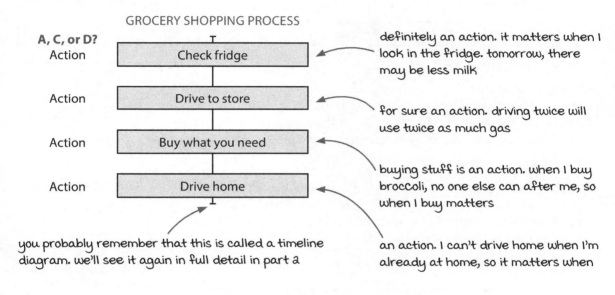

GROCERY SHOPPING PROCESS

A, C, or D?

Action — Check fridge — definitely an action. it matters when I look in the fridge. tomorrow, there may be less milk

Action — Drive to store — for sure an action. driving twice will use twice as much gas

Action — Buy what you need — buying stuff is an action. when I buy broccoli, no one else can after me, so when I buy matters

Action — Drive home — an action. I can't drive home when I'm already at home, so it matters when

you probably remember that this is called a timeline diagram. we'll see it again in full detail in part 2

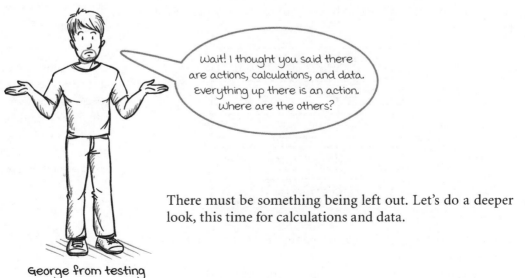

Wait! I thought you said there are actions, calculations, and data. Everything up there is an action. Where are the others?

There must be something being left out. Let's do a deeper look, this time for calculations and data.

George from testing

We can't accept that everything is an action. Though we might rarely find only actions in extremely simple situations, this one isn't so simple. We've got a good outline of the shopping process. Let's go through each step and see if we can find what we're missing.

Check fridge

Checking the fridge is an **action** because *when* we check matters. The information about what food we have is **data**. We will call it a *current inventory*.

Data | Current inventory |

Drive to store

Driving to the store is a complex activity. It's definitely an **action**. However, there are some pieces of **data** in there; for instance, the location of the store and directions to get there. Because we're not building a self-driving car, we'll leave this step alone.

Buy what you need

Buying stuff is definitely an **action**, but you could break this down further. How do you know what you need? This depends on how you shop, but a simple way to do it is to make a list of everything you want but don't already have.

desired inventory – current inventory = shopping list

In fact, this is using a piece of **data** we generated in the first step: the *current inventory*. We can break "buying what you need" into a few pieces:

Data | Current inventory |
Data | Desired inventory |
Calculation | Inventory "minus" |
Data | Shopping list |
Action | Buy from list |

GROCERY SHOPPING PROCESS

Check fridge
Drive to store
Buy what you need
Drive home
Store the food

inventory "minus" is a calculation because for the same inputs it gives the same outputs

calculations are often decisions, such as this one, which decides what to buy. separating actions from calculations is like separating deciding what to buy from buying it.

Drive home

We could break down driving home further, but that is beyond the scope of this exercise.

Let's rebuild our process with all of this new stuff in it.

Let's draw out a more complete diagram of the process. We will separate out the actions, calculations, and data into separate columns for clarity. We can also draw arrows to represent data being outputted by and inputted to actions and calculations.

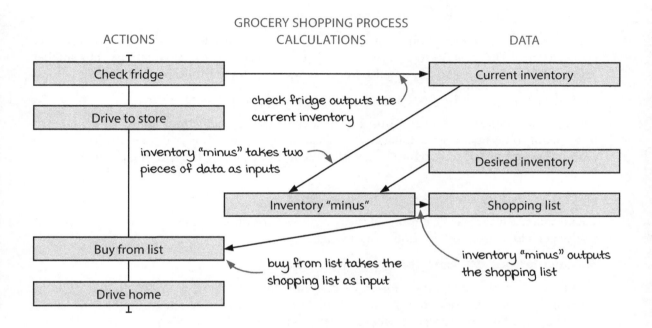

We could definitely go deeper and start pulling these things even further apart into actions, calculations, and data. The more you pull things apart, the richer your model will be.

For instance, we could pull "check fridge" apart even further and make actions to check the fridge and freezer separately. Each action would generate a separate piece of data, which we would have to combine. Or, "buy from list" could be composed out of "add to cart" and "check out" actions.

Of course, we could make it as complex as we wanted to. What's important for functional programmers is to be aware that actions can be complex miasmas of actions, calculations, and data. Don't be satisfied until you've broken them apart.

Lessons from our shopping process

1. We can apply the ACD perspective to any situation

It may be difficult to see at first, but the more you do it, the better you'll get at it.

2. Actions can hide actions, calculations, and data

What seems like a simple action might actually be made of multiple pieces from any of the categories. Part of functional programming is digging deeper to pull apart actions into smaller actions, calculations, and data, and also knowing when to stop pulling apart.

3. Calculations can be composed of smaller calculations and data

We didn't see a great example of this, but data can hide in calculations as well. This is often benign, but sometimes it is advantageous to break things apart. Usually it takes the form of one calculation getting broken up into two, with data output from the first passing to the second as input.

4. Data can only be composed of more data

Luckily, data is just data. That is one of the reasons we seek out data so eagerly. If you've got data, you've got a lot of guarantees about how it will behave.

5. Calculations often happen "in our heads"

One reason we take calculations for granted, even if they are there, is that they often take the form of thought processes. For instance, we might figure out what to buy throughout the shopping trip. There was never a point where we sat down and made a list of what we wanted to buy. It all happened in our heads.

However, once we realize this, it makes it easier to spot calculations. We can ask ourselves, "Do we need to make any decisions? Is there anything we can plan ahead?" Decisions and planning make good candidates for calculations.

This shopping scenario was a good application of the ACD perspective to a problem before we've coded it. But what does it look like when we apply ACD to code we are writing? We are going to go further with a real coding problem. But first, a word about data.

Deep dive: Data

What is data?

Data is facts about events. It is a record of something that happened. Functional programmers tap into the rich tradition of record-keeping that started thousands of years ago.

How do we implement data?

Data is implemented in JavaScript using the built-in data types. These include numbers, strings, arrays, and objects, among others. Other languages have more sophisticated ways of implementing data. For instance, Haskell lets you define new data types that encode the important structure of your domain.

How does data encode meaning?

Data encodes meaning in structure. The structure of your data should mirror the structure of the problem domain you are implementing. For instance, if the order of a list of names is important, you should choose a data structure that maintains order.

Immutability

Functional programmers use two main disciplines for implementing immutable data:

1. **Copy-on-write.** Make a copy of data before you modify it.

2. **Defensive copying.** Make a copy of data you want to keep.

We will learn about these disciplines in chapters 6 and 7.

Examples

- A list of foods to buy
- Your first name
- My phone number
- A receipt for a meal

What are the advantages of data?

Data is useful mostly because of what it can't do. Unlike actions and calculations, it cannot be run. It is inert. That is what lets it be so well understood.

1. **Serializable.** Actions and calculations have trouble being serialized to be run on another machine without a lot of trouble. Data, however, has no problem being transmitted over a wire or stored to disk and read back later. Well-preserved data can last for thousands of years. Will your data last that long? I can't say. But it sure will last longer than code for a function.

2. **Compare for equality.** You can easily compare two pieces of data to see if they are equal. This is impossible for calculations and actions.

3. **Open for interpretation.** Data can be interpreted in multiple ways. Server access logs can be mined to debug problems. But they can also be used to know where your traffic is coming from. Both use the same data, with different interpretations.

Disadvantages

Interpretation is a double-edged sword. Although it's an advantage that data can be interpreted in different ways, it is a disadvantage that data must be interpreted to be useful. A calculation can run and be useful, even if we don't understand it. But data needs a machine to interpret it. Data has no meaning without interpretation. It's just bytes.

Much of the skill of functional programming is about how to represent data so that it can be interpreted now and reinterpreted in the future.

 # Brain break

There's more to go, but let's take a break for questions

Q: Is all data facts about events? What about facts about a person or another entity?

A: That's a really good question. Even information about a person enters the system at a certain time. For example, we might store the first and last name of a user in the database. That's definitely data. But where did it come from? If we trace it back, we might find that it was received as part of a "create user" web request. The receipt of that web request is an event. The web request was processed and interpreted, and some parts of it were stored in the database. So yes, you can *interpret* the name as a fact about a person, but it originates as a specific *event*, the web request.

data, *mass noun*.

1. facts about events

2. factual information used as a basis for reasoning, discussion, or calculation

3. information obtained from an input device that must be processed to be meaningful

The "facts about events" definition is straight out of the dictionary. Of course, there are various definitions from different dictionaries. But this definition is the perfect one for functional programming because it highlights two points. First, it emphasizes the necessity of interpretation. Most data goes through many levels of interpretation in its lifetime, from bytes, to characters, to JSON, to user information.

MULTIPLE LEVELS OF INTERPRETATION OF A WEB REQUEST

Second, it highlights that software engineers build information systems. Our systems receive and process information (some of which has errors), make decisions from it (such as what to store and who to email), then take action based on those decisions (actually sending the emails).

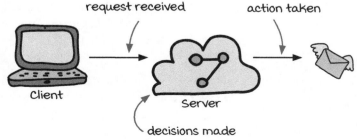

Applying functional thinking to new code

A new marketing tactic at CouponDog

CouponDog has a huge list of people interested in coupons. They send out a weekly email newsletter full of coupons. People love it!

In order to grow the list, the chief marketing officer (CMO) has a plan. If someone recommends CouponDog to 10 of their friends, they get better coupons.

The company has a big database table of email addresses. Along with that, they have counted how many times each person has recommended CouponDog to their friends.

They also have a database of coupons. These are ranked as "bad," "good," and "best." The "best" coupons are reserved for people who recommend a lot. Everyone else gets "good" coupons. They never send out "bad" coupons.

the number of times they have recommended the newsletter to friends

EMAIL DATABASE TABLE

email	rec_count
john@coldmail.com	2
sam@pmail.co	16
linda1989@oal.com	1
jan1940@ahoy.com	0
mrbig@pmail.co	25
lol@lol.lol	0

COUPON DATABASE TABLE

coupon	rank
MAYDISCOUNT	good
10PERCENT	bad
PROMOTION45	best
IHEARTYOU	bad
GETADEAL	best
ILIKEDISCOUNTS	good

CLOUD EMAIL SERVICE

these two get "best" coupons because rec_count >= 10

> **Referral plan**
>
> Refer 10 friends and get better coupons.

Your job is to implement the software to send out the right coupons to the right people. Can you have it by Friday?

cmo

 ## It's your turn

Don't worry about getting the wrong answer. It's just about exploring the ideas.

The new marketing plan looks simple, but is it? In order to work, what does our code need to know, decide, and do? Write down as many things as you can think of. They don't need to be detailed. And we don't need to put them in order yet. There are a few examples to get you started. Remember: there's no right or wrong answer. We'll categorize them on the next page.

EMAIL DATABASE TABLE

email	rec_count
john@coldmail.com	2
sam@pmail.co	16
linda1989@oal.com	1
jan1940@ahoy.com	0
mrbig@pmail.co	25
lol@lol.lol	0

COUPON DATABASE TABLE

coupon	rank
MAYDISCOUNT	good
10PERCENT	bad
PROMOTION45	best
IHEARTYOU	bad
GETADEAL	best
ILIKEDISCOUNTS	good

CLOUD EMAIL SERVICE

> *Referral plan*
>
> Refer 10 friends and get better coupons.

some examples to get you started

send an email

read subscribers from the database

rank of each coupon

write your ideas here

✏️ It's your turn

Here are the things the CouponDog team came up with. Now we need to categorize them. Write an A, C, or D next to each one to categorize them into the three main categories: actions, calculations, and data.

- Send an email A ← example
- Read subscribers from the database
- The ranking of each coupon
- Reading the coupons from the database
- The subject of the email
- An email address
- A recommendation count
- Deciding which email someone gets
- A subscriber record
- A coupon record
- A list of coupon records
- A list of subscriber records
- The body of the email

depends on when or how many times it is called \

> **Three Primary Categories**
>
> A   Action ←
> C   Calculation
> D   Data

computation from inputs to outputs

✏️ Answer

- A   Send an email
- A   Read subscribers from the database
- D   The ranking of each coupon
- A   Reading coupons from the database
- D   The subject of the email
- D   An email address
- D   A recommendation count
- C   Deciding which email someone gets
- D   A subscriber record
- D   A coupon record
- D   A list of coupon records
- D   A list of subscriber records
- D   The body of the email

If you want, go back and categorize the parts you came up with on the previous page.

Drawing the coupon email process

We're going to go through one way we could diagram this process, although there are definitely different ways to implement this same plan. What you should pay attention to is the action/calculation/data (ACD) distinction that we make along the way.

email	rec_count
john@coldmail.com	2
sam@pmail.co	16
linda1989@oal.com	1
jan1940@ahoy.com	0
mrbig@pmail.co	25
lol@lol.lol	0

code	rank
MAYDISCOUNT	good
10PERCENT	bad
PROMOTION45	best
IHEARTYOU	bad
GETADEAL	best
ILIKEDISCOUNTS	good

1. Let's start with fetching subscribers from the database

We are going to need to fetch subscribers from the database, which is an **action**. Since if we fetch them today, we'll get back different subscribers than we would from fetching them tomorrow, it depends on when it is run. When we fetch the subscribers from the database, we get a list of customer records out. Those records are **data**.

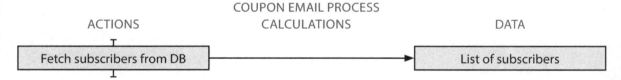

2. Fetching the coupons from the database

Fetching coupons is a similar **action**. The database of coupons is constantly changing, so when we run it matters. But once we have fetched the coupons, we have a record of what was in the database at that point in time. As **data**, it is a fact of the DB query event.

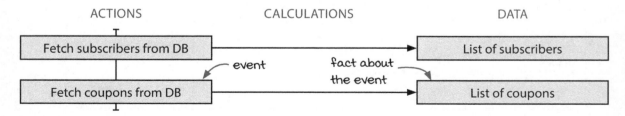

So far, this is pretty straightforward. Now that we have our two main pieces of data from the database, we can start making some decisions. This data will be used in the next step to decide who gets what emails.

3. Generating the emails to send

It may be different from what you're used to, but functional programmers often generate the data they will need separately from using the data. It's just like making a shopping list before you go shopping instead of figuring out what to buy as you walk through the store.

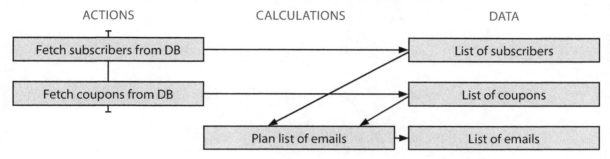

The result of generating the list of emails is some data that we can use in the next step. The list of emails is a plan for what emails to send.

4. Sending the emails

Once we have a plan for what emails to send, we can execute the plan. It's as simple as looping through the big list of emails and sending each one off. At this point, all of the decisions have been made.

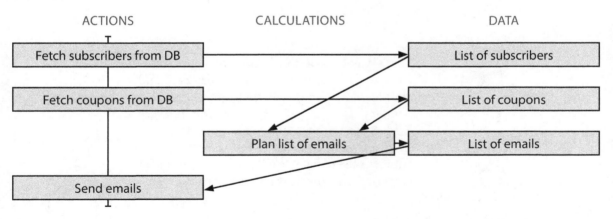

At this point, we're done with the major outline of the process, but how do we plan a list of all of the emails to be sent?

Zooming into generating emails

Planning out all of the emails you're going to send before you send them may feel foreign, but it's quite common to do so in functional programming. Let's zoom into this calculation and see how it is made of smaller calculations. Here it is as we've already seen it.

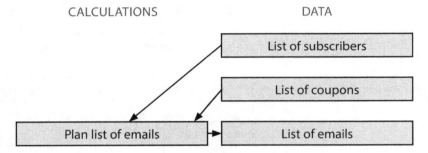

CALCULATIONS   DATA

The calculation takes two lists: one of subscribers and one of coupons. It returns a list of emails.

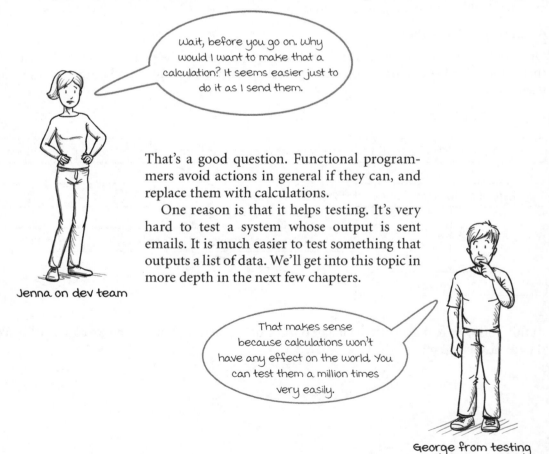

Wait, before you go on. Why would I want to make that a calculation? It seems easier just to do it as I send them.

That's a good question. Functional programmers avoid actions in general if they can, and replace them with calculations.

One reason is that it helps testing. It's very hard to test a system whose output is sent emails. It is much easier to test something that outputs a list of data. We'll get into this topic in more depth in the next few chapters.

Jenna on dev team

That makes sense because calculations won't have any effect on the world. You can test them a million times very easily.

George from testing

So, where was I? Ah, yes. Let's take this calculation and see how we might implement it with smaller calculations.

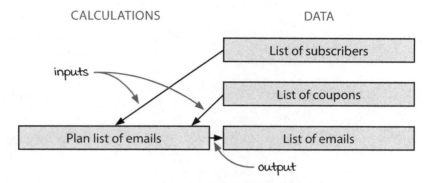

First, we could calculate lists of "good" coupons and "best" coupons.

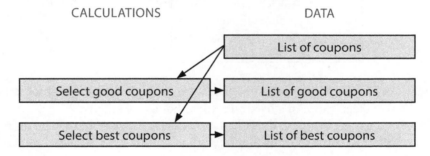

Then, we could make a calculation that decides whether a subscriber gets the good or best ones.

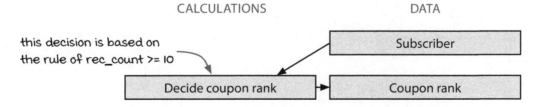

Now we can put them together to make a calculation that plans a single email given a single subscriber.

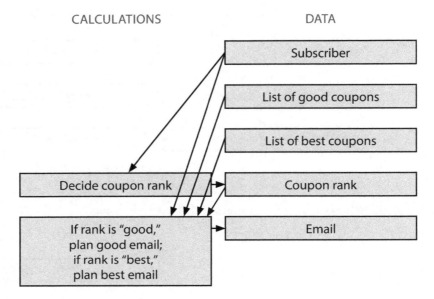

To plan the list of emails, we just have to loop through the list of subscribers and plan one email each. We can keep those in a list and return that list of emails.

We can keep breaking up the calculations as far as we need to. The more you break them up, the easier they become to implement. At some point, they are easy enough that the implementation becomes obvious. Let's implement one right now.

Implementing the coupon email process

Let's start implementing the three boxes—one calculation and two pieces of data—that we see in this section of the diagram.

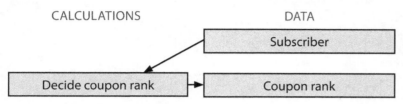

The subscriber's data from the database

We know that the subscriber data comes from a table like we see on the right. In JavaScript, one way to represent this data is as a plain JavaScript object. It would look like this:

```
var subscriber = {
  email: "sam@pmail.com",
  rec_count: 16
};
```

each row becomes an object like this

In functional programming, we represent data with simple data types like this. This is straightforward and will serve our purposes.

The coupon rank is a string

We previously decided that the coupon rank would be a string. It could be any type, really, but making it a string is convenient. It corresponds to the values in the rank column of the coupon table.

```
var rank1 = "best";
var rank2 = "good";
```

ranks are strings

Deciding a coupon rank is a function

In JavaScript, we typically represent calculations as functions. The inputs to the calculation are the arguments, and the output is the return value. The computation is the code in the function body.

```
function subCouponRank(subscriber) {
  if(subscriber.rec_count >= 10)
    return "best";
  else
    return "good";
}
```

input

computation

output

We have encoded the decision of which rank a subscriber should get into a neat, testable, and reusable package—a function.

EMAIL DATABASE TABLE

email	rec_count
john@coldmail.com	2
sam@pmail.co	16
linda1989@oal.com	1
jan1940@ahoy.com	0
mrbig@pmail.co	25
lol@lol.lol	0

COUPON DATABASE TABLE

code	rank
MAYDISCOUNT	good
10PERCENT	bad
PROMOTION45	best
IHEARTYOU	bad
GETADEAL	best
ILIKEDISCOUNTS	good

> **Remember:**
> A calculation is a computation from inputs to outputs. It does not depend on when or how many times it is called. Given the same inputs, it will give the same outputs.

Let's implement one more section of the diagram, which is how to select only coupons of a given rank out of a big list of coupons.

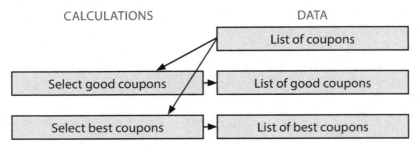

The coupon's data from the database

Just like we did for a subscriber, we can represent a coupon with a JavaScript object:

```
var coupon = {
  code: "10PERCENT",
  rank: "bad"
};
```

each row becomes an object like this

COUPON DATABASE TABLE

code	rank
MAYDISCOUNT	good
10PERCENT	bad
PROMOTION45	best
IHEARTYOU	bad
GETADEAL	best
ILIKEDISCOUNTS	good

The table will be a JavaScript array of similar objects.

The calculation to select coupons by rank is a function

Like before, we will use a function to implement our calculation. The inputs will be a list of mixed-rank coupons and a rank. The output will be a list of coupons all with that same rank.

```
function selectCouponsByRank(coupons, rank) {
  var ret = [];
  for(var c = 0; c < coupons.length; c++) {
    var coupon = coupons[c];
    if(coupon.rank === rank)
      ret.push(coupon.code);
  }
  return ret;
}
```

inputs

initialize an empty array

loop through all coupons

if it's of the rank we want, add the coupon string to the array

return the array

output

Let's verify that `selectCouponsByRank()` is indeed a calculation. Does it give you a different answer if you pass it through the same arguments? No. The same coupons and rank will result in the same output list each time. Does it matter how many times you run it? No. You can run this as many times as you want without any effect on the outside. It is a calculation.

We have one more major section of the diagram to implement, which is the one that plans an individual email.

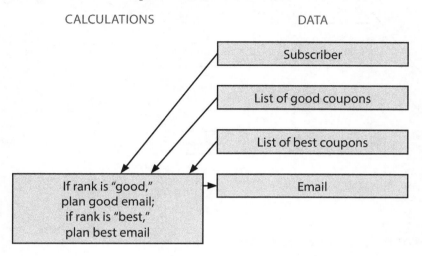

An email is just data

We will represent the email before it is sent as data. It's composed of a *from* address, a *to* address, a *subject*, and a *body*. We can implement it using a JavaScript object.

```
var message = {
  from: "newsletter@coupondog.co",
  to: "sam@pmail.com",
  subject: "Your weekly coupons inside",
  body: "Here are your coupons ..."
};
```

this object contains everything you need to send an email. no decisions need to be made

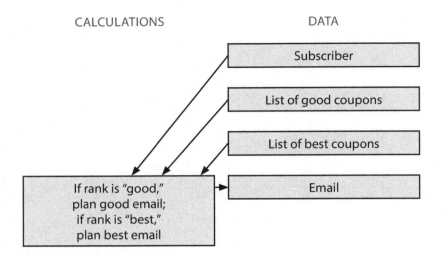

The calculation to plan one email for a subscriber

Like before, we will use a function to implement our calculation. We will need to input the subscriber to send the email to, but, perhaps less obviously, we will want to know the coupons to send them as well. At this point, we have not decided which coupons they will get, so we will pass in two different lists: the good coupons and the best coupons. The output will be a single email, represented as data.

```
function emailForSubscriber(subscriber, goods, bests) {        ← inputs
  var rank = subCouponRank(subscriber);
  if(rank === "best")        ← decide the rank
    return {        ← create and return an email
      from: "newsletter@coupondog.co",
      to: subscriber.email,
      subject: "Your best weekly coupons inside",
      body: "Here are the best coupons: " + bests.join(", ")
    };
  else // rank === "good"        ← create and return an email
    return {
     from: "newsletter@coupondog.co",
     to: subscriber.email,
     subject: "Your good weekly coupons inside",
     body: "Here are the good coupons: " + goods.join(", ")
    };
}
```

Notice that this is just a calculation. All it does is decide what the email should look like, which it returns as data. It does not have any other effect outside of itself.

We have most of the pieces we need, so now let's see how we can put them together to send this email campaign.

Planning all emails

We have a calculation to plan a single email from a single subscriber. Now we need a calculation to plan a list of emails from a list of subscribers. We can use a loop, as we have before.

```javascript
function emailsForSubscribers(subscribers, goods, bests) {
  var emails = [];
  for(var s = 0; s < subscribers.length; s++) {
    var subscriber = subscribers[s];
    var email = emailForSubscriber(subscriber, goods, bests);
    emails.push(email);
  }
  return emails;
}
```

we will see a better way to loop, called map(), in part 2

generating all emails is just a loop around generating one email

Sending the emails is an action

We need to implement this action in JavaScript. Typically, actions are implemented as functions, just as calculations are. That makes it hard to see at a glance what is a calculation and what is an action. Actions frequently need inputs (arguments) and outputs (return values), so we will use a function to implement it. We will just be careful to remember that it is an action.

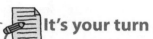**It's your turn**

Is this function an action, a calculation, or data?

Answer: A calculation. It doesn't depend on when it is run.

```javascript
function sendIssue() {
  var coupons     = fetchCouponsFromDB();
  var goodCoupons = selectCouponsByRank(coupons, "good");
  var bestCoupons = selectCouponsByRank(coupons, "best");
  var subscribers = fetchSubscribersFromDB();
  var emails = emailsForSubscribers(subscribers, goodCoupons, bestCoupons);
  for(var e = 0; e < emails.length; e++) {
    var email = emails[e];
    emailSystem.send(email);
  }
}
```

the action that ties it all together

Now we have our entire feature coded. We started with the most constrained category, the data, then we added in calculations to derive more data from those, and finally we put it all together with actions, the least constrained. We coded data, then calculations, then actions. We see this pattern frequently in functional programming.

Now that we've written some code, we will see what functional thinking looks like when applied to reading existing code. But first, a word about calculations.

Common order of implementation

1. Data
2. Calculations
3. Actions

 **Brain break**

There's more to go, but let's take a break for questions

Q: Why would you generate all of the emails before you send them? Isn't that inefficient? What if you have millions of customers?

A: Good question. This system might not work well when there are lots and lots of customers because we could run out of memory. But it also might work just fine! The fact is that we don't know. It would be unwise to optimize this prematurely.

However, we know we want to grow our number of subscribers, so we should at least consider making this scalable. If we do have too much data to fit in memory at the same time, we can still use almost all of this code. `emailsForSubscribers()` takes an array of subscribers. There is nothing in this code that requires that to be all subscribers. It can be a small array of subscribers, say, the first 20. Certainly we can hold 20 emails in memory at once.

Then we could loop through and do all subscribers in groups of 20. We would only need to modify `fetchSubscribersFromDB()` to make it return those groups of subscribers instead of all of them. Here is the modified `sendIssue()`:

```
function sendIssue() {
  var coupons     = fetchCouponsFromDB();
  var goodCoupons = selectCouponsByRank(coupons, "good");
  var bestCoupons = selectCouponsByRank(coupons, "best");
  var page = 0;                                          ⟵ start at page 0
  var subscribers = fetchSubscribersFromDB(page);        ⟵
  while(subscribers.length > 0) {    ⟵                    loop until we fetch
    var emails = emailsForSubscribers(subscribers,       empty page
                              goodCoupons, bestCoupons);

    for(var e = 0; e < emails.length; e++) {
      var email = emails[e];
      emailSystem.send(email);
    }
    page++;                          ⟵
    subscribers = fetchSubscribersFromDB(page);   ⟵      go to next page
  }
}
```

Notice that the calculations did not change. We optimized our system inside of the action. In a well-written system, the calculations define timeless, often abstract ideas like "the emails for this list of zero or more subscribers." Reading those in from the database into memory is an action. The action can just read in a smaller number.

Deep dive: Calculations

What are calculations?

Calculations are computations from inputs to outputs. No matter when they are run, or how many times they are run, they will give the same output for the same inputs.

How do we implement calculations?

We typically represent calculations as functions. That's what we do in JavaScript. In languages without functions, we would have to use something else, like a class with a method.

How do calculations encode meaning?

Calculations encode meaning as computation. A calculation represents some computation from inputs to outputs. When or how you use it depends on whether that calculation is appropriate for the situation.

Why prefer calculations to actions?

Calculations have benefits compared to actions:

1. They're much easier to test. You can run them as many times as you want or wherever you want (local machine, build server, testing machine) in order to test them.

2. They're easier to analyze by a machine. A lot of academic research has gone into what's called "static analysis." It's essentially automated checks that your code makes sense. We won't get into that in this book.

3. They're very composable. Calculations can be put together into bigger calculations in very flexible ways. They can also be used in what are called "higher-order" calculations. We'll get to those in chapter 14.

. . . .

Much of functional programming is doing with calculations what is typically done with actions outside of FP.

Examples of calculations

- Addition and multiplication
- String concatenation
- Planning a shopping trip

What worries do calculations avoid?

Functional programmers prefer using calculations instead of actions when possible because calculations are so much easier to understand. You can read the code and know what it is going to do. There's a whole list of things you *don't* have to worry about:

1. What else is running at the same time

2. What has run in the past and what will run in the future

3. How many times you have already run it

Disadvantage

Calculations do have their downside, which they share with actions. You can't really know what calculations or actions are going to do without running them.

Of course, you, the programmer, can read the code and sometimes see what it will do. But as far as your running software is concerned, a function is a black box. You give it some inputs and an output comes out. You can't really do much else with a function except run it.

If you can't live with this disadvantage and you need something understandable, you must use data instead of calculations or actions.

What are they typically called?

Outside of this book, calculations are typically called *pure functions* or *mathematical functions*. We call them *calculations* in *Grokking Simplicity* to avoid ambiguities with specific language features such as JavaScript functions.

Applying functional thinking to existing code

Functional programmers will also apply functional thinking when they are reading existing code. They will always be on the lookout for actions, calculations, and data.

Let's look at some of Jenna's code for sending affiliates their commissions. `sendPayout()` is an action that transfers money to a bank account.

> This is pretty functional, right? It's only got one action. . . . Right?

```
function figurePayout(affiliate) {
  var owed = affiliate.sales * affiliate.commission;
  if(owed > 100) // don't send payouts less than $100
    sendPayout(affiliate.bank_code, owed);
}
```

we highlight the "one action" Jenna is talking about

```
function affiliatePayout(affiliates) {
  for(var a = 0; a < affiliates.length; a++)
    figurePayout(affiliates[a]);
}
```

```
function main(affiliates) {
  affiliatePayout(affiliates);
}
```

Jenna on dev team

Jenna is not correct. This code is not very functional. And there is more than just one action here. Let's take a closer look at it. It will reveal how difficult actions can be to work with. And we'll finally hint at the techniques we will see later on.

So, let's get started.

We'll start by highlighting the one line we know is an action. Then, step-by-step, we will see the dependence on time spread over the code. Watch!

```
function figurePayout(affiliate) {
  var owed = affiliate.sales * affiliate.commission;
  if(owed > 100) // don't send payouts less than $100
    sendPayout(affiliate.bank_code, owed);
}

function affiliatePayout(affiliates) {
  for(var a = 0; a < affiliates.length; a++)
    figurePayout(affiliates[a]);
}

function main(affiliates) {
  affiliatePayout(affiliates);
}
```

we highlight the action

1. We start with the original line that we know is an action. We know it's an action because transferring money to an account does depend on when it is done or how many times it is done. We highlight it.

```
function figurePayout(affiliate) {
  var owed = affiliate.sales * affiliate.commission;
  if(owed > 100) // don't send payouts less than $100
    sendPayout(affiliate.bank_code, owed);
}

function affiliatePayout(affiliates) {
  for(var a = 0; a < affiliates.length; a++)
    figurePayout(affiliates[a]);
}

function main(affiliates) {
  affiliatePayout(affiliates);
}
```

the whole function is an action because it calls an action

we highlight the line where we call figurePayout(), a known action

2. An action, by definition, depends on when it is run or how many times it is run. But that means that the function figurePayout() that is calling sendPayout() also depends on when it is run. So it, too, is an action. We highlight the whole function and the place where it is called.

```
function figurePayout(affiliate) {
  var owed = affiliate.sales * affiliate.commission;
  if(owed > 100) // don't send payouts less than $100
    sendPayout(affiliate.bank_code, owed);
}

function affiliatePayout(affiliates) {
  for(var a = 0; a < affiliates.length; a++)
    figurePayout(affiliates[a]);
}

function main(affiliates) {
  affiliatePayout(affiliates);
}
```

highlight the whole function since it calls an action

called here

3. By the same logic, we now have to highlight the entire function definition of affiliatePayout() and any place where it is called.

```
function figurePayout(affiliate) {
  var owed = affiliate.sales * affiliate.commission;
  if(owed > 100) // don't send payouts less than $100
    sendPayout(affiliate.bank_code, owed);
}

function affiliatePayout(affiliates) {
  for(var a = 0; a < affiliates.length; a++)
    figurePayout(affiliates[a]);
}

function main(affiliates) {
  affiliatePayout(affiliates);
}
```

it's all actions

4. Of course, the inevitable actionhood of main() also follows from the same logic. The entire program is an action because of one tiny call to an action deep in the code.

Actions spread through code

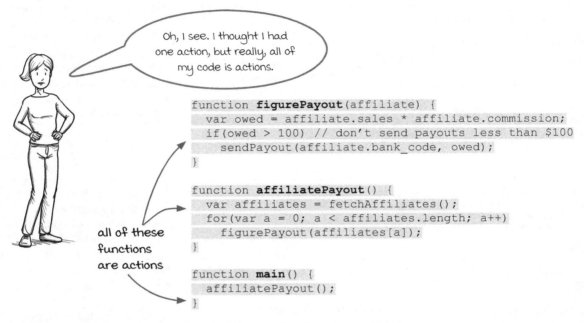

Oh, I see. I thought I had one action, but really, all of my code is actions.

```
function figurePayout(affiliate) {
  var owed = affiliate.sales * affiliate.commission;
  if(owed > 100) // don't send payouts less than $100
    sendPayout(affiliate.bank_code, owed);
}

function affiliatePayout() {
  var affiliates = fetchAffiliates();
  for(var a = 0; a < affiliates.length; a++)
    figurePayout(affiliates[a]);
}

function main() {
  affiliatePayout();
}
```

all of these functions are actions

We didn't mean to pick on Jenna's code. This was just an example of typical code that hasn't been written with functional thinking in mind.

What this example demonstrates is one of the properties of actions that make them so darn difficult to work with. Actions spread. If you call an action in a function, that function becomes an action. If you call that function in another function, it becomes an action. One little action somewhere and it spreads all over.

It's one of the reasons functional programmers tend to avoid actions if possible. You have to be careful where you use them, because as soon as you do, they start to spread.

So how do you use actions if they're so dangerous?

George from testing

That's a good question. Functional programmers do use actions, but they tend to use them very carefully. The care they put into using them makes up a large part of functional thinking. We'll address a lot of it in the next few chapters of the book.

Actions can take many forms

Functional programmers differentiate between actions, calculations, and data, but most languages do not. Languages like JavaScript make it very easy to accidentally call actions. It makes our jobs harder, I'm sorry to say, but functional programmers do learn to manage. The trick is to recognize them for what they are.

Let's look at some of the actions you can find in JavaScript. You probably used these just the other day. Actions can show up in all sorts of places.

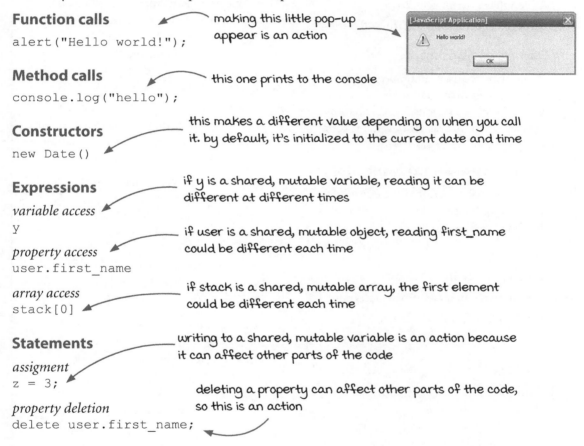

Function calls

making this little pop-up appear is an action

```
alert("Hello world!");
```

Method calls

this one prints to the console

```
console.log("hello");
```

Constructors

this makes a different value depending on when you call it. by default, it's initialized to the current date and time

```
new Date()
```

Expressions

variable access

```
y
```

if y is a shared, mutable variable, reading it can be different at different times

property access
```
user.first_name
```

if user is a shared, mutable object, reading first_name could be different each time

array access
```
stack[0]
```

if stack is a shared, mutable array, the first element could be different each time

Statements

assigment
```
z = 3;
```

writing to a shared, mutable variable is an action because it can affect other parts of the code

property deletion
```
delete user.first_name;
```

deleting a property can affect other parts of the code, so this is an action

All of these bits of code are actions. They each will cause different results depending on when or how many times they are run. And wherever they are used, they spread.

Luckily, we don't have to make a laundry list of all the actions we should be on the lookout for. We simply ask ourselves, "Does it depend on when or how many times it runs?"

Deep dive: Actions

What are actions?

Actions are anything that have an effect on the world or are affected by the world. As a rule of thumb, actions depend on when or how many times they are run.

• When they are run—*Ordering*

• How many times they are run—*Repetition*

How are actions implemented?

In JavaScript, we use functions to implement actions. It is unfortunate that we use the same construct for both actions and calculations. That can get confusing. However, it is something you can learn to work with.

How do actions encode meaning?

The meaning of an action is the effect it has on the world. We should make sure the effect it has is the one we want.

Examples

• Sending an email

• Withdrawing money from an account

• Modifying a global variable

• Sending an ajax request

What are they typically called?

Outside of this book, actions are typically called *impure functions, side-effecting functions,* or *functions with side effects.* We call them actions in *Grokking Simplicity* to avoid ambiguities with specific language features such as JavaScript functions.

Actions are super important in functional programming. We'll be spending the next few chapters learning to work with their limitations.

Actions pose a tough bargain

A. They are a pain to deal with.

B. They are the reason we run our software in the first place.

That's one nasty bargain, if you ask me. But it's what we have to live with, regardless of the paradigm we work in. Functional programmers accept the bargain, and they have a bag of tricks for how to best deal with actions. We can take a look at a few of the tricks:

1. Use fewer actions if possible. We can never get all the way down to zero actions, but if an action isn't required, use a calculation instead. We look at that in chapter 15.

2. Keep your actions small. Remove everything that isn't necessary from the action. For instance, you can extract a planning stage, implemented as a calculation, from the execution stage, where the necessary action is carried out. We explore this technique in the next chapter.

3. Restrict your actions to interactions with the outside. Your actions are all of those things that are affected by the world outside or can affect the world outside. Inside, ideally, is just calculations and data. We'll see this more when we talk about the onion architecture in chapter 18.

4. Limit how dependent on time an action is. Functional programmers have techniques for making actions a little less difficult to work with. These techniques include making actions less dependent on when they happen and how many times they are run.

Conclusion

In this chapter, we saw how the three categories of actions, calculations, and data are applied at three different times. We saw how calculations can be thought of as planning or deciding. In that case, data is the plan or decision. Then you can execute the plan with an action.

Summary

- Functional programmers distinguish three categories: actions, calculations, and data. Learning this distinction is your first task as a functional programmer.

- Actions are things that depend on when or how many times they are run. Usually, these are things that affect the world or are affected by the world.

- Calculations are computations from inputs to outputs. They don't affect anything outside of themselves, and hence it doesn't matter when or how many times they are run.

- Data is facts about events. We record the facts immutably since the facts don't change.

- Functional programmers prefer data over calculations, and they prefer calculations over actions.

- Calculations are easier to test than actions since calculations always return the same answer for a given input.

Up next . . .

We've learned how to see the three categories in our code. However, that is not enough. Functional programmers will want to transform code from actions to calculations in order to gain the benefts of calculations. We'll see how in the next chapter.

In this chapter

- Observe how information enters and leaves a function.

- Discover functional techniques to make code more testable and reusable.

- Learn how to extract calculations from actions.

In this chapter, we're going to do a lot of refactoring. We're going to look at an existing piece of software, add some features, and then refactor calculations out of the actions. This improves the reuse and testability of the code.

Welcome to MegaMart.com!

Where your shopping cart is always full

MegaMart is an online store. One of its key features, and how it stays competitive, is that the shopping cart always shows you the total cost of its contents—even while you're shopping.

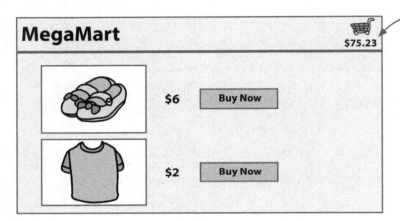

shopping cart shows
up-to-date total

MegaMart reveals its secret code to you

No NDA required

global variables for
the cart and total

```
var shopping_cart = [];
var shopping_cart_total = 0;

function add_item_to_cart(name, price) {
  shopping_cart.push({
    name: name,
    price: price
  });
  calc_cart_total();
}

function calc_cart_total() {
  shopping_cart_total = 0;
  for(var i = 0; i < shopping_cart.length; i++) {
    var item = shopping_cart[i];
    shopping_cart_total += item.price;
  }
  set_cart_total_dom();
}
```

add a record to
cart array to add
items to cart

update total because
cart just changed

sum all the item prices

update DOM to
reflect new total

The final line updates the *document object model* (*DOM*), which is how web programmers modify a web page in the browser.

Vocab time

The *document object model* (*DOM*) is the in-memory representation of an HTML page in a browser.

Calculating free shipping

Your new assignment

MegaMart wants to offer free shipping if the order total is at least $20. We need to put an icon next to the buy button if adding that item to the cart will bump the cart over $20.

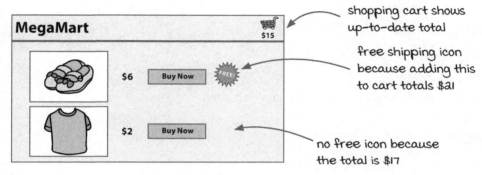

shopping cart shows
up-to-date total

free shipping icon
because adding this
to cart totals $21

no free icon because
the total is $17

The imperative way to do it

Sometimes the imperative way is the most straightforward

We could just write a function that adds little icons to all of the buttons. We'll refactor it to be more functional in a few pages.

get all buy buttons on
the page, then loop
through them

```
function update_shipping_icons() {
  var buy_buttons = get_buy_buttons_dom();
  for(var i = 0; i < buy_buttons.length; i++) {
    var button = buy_buttons[i];
    var item = button.item;
    if(item.price + shopping_cart_total >= 20)
      button.show_free_shipping_icon();
    else
      button.hide_free_shipping_icon();
  }
}
```

figure out if they get
free shipping

show or hide the icon
appropriately

Then we call this new function at the end of `calc_cart_total()`, so every time the total changes, we update all of the icons.

```
function calc_cart_total() {
  shopping_cart_total = 0;
  for(var i = 0; i < shopping_cart.length; i++) {
    var item = shopping_cart[i];
    shopping_cart_total += item.price;
  }
  set_cart_total_dom();
  update_shipping_icons();
}
```

the same function
from before

we add a line to
update the icons

> **MegaMart dev team motto**
>
> It works; ship it!

Calculating tax

Your next assignment

We now need to calculate the amount of tax and update it every time the cart total changes. Again, this will be easy to add to the existing implementation, but this isn't the functional programming way.

write a new function

```
function update_tax_dom() {
  set_tax_dom(shopping_cart_total * 0.10);
}
```

multiply the total by 10%

update the dom

Then, like before, we call it after we calculate the new cart total in `calc_cart_total()`.

```
function calc_cart_total() {
  shopping_cart_total = 0;
  for(var i = 0; i < shopping_cart.length; i++) {
    var item = shopping_cart[i];
    shopping_cart_total += item.price;
  }
  set_cart_total_dom();
  update_shipping_icons();
  update_tax_dom();
}
```

add a line to update the tax on the page

It works; ship it!

Jenna on dev team

We need to make it more testable

The code contains business rules that are not easy to test

Every time the code changes, George has to write a test to do the following:

1. Set up a browser

2. Load a page

3. Click buttons to add items to the cart

4. Wait for the DOM to update ◄—— it should be easier than this!

5. Scrape the value out of the DOM

6. Parse the string into a number

7. Compare it to the expected value

> Can we make it easier to test? I haven't seen my kids in six days!

George from testing

George from testing's code notes

```
function update_tax_dom() {
  set_tax_dom(shopping_cart_total * 0.10);
}
```

the business rule George needs to test (total * 0.10)

only way to get answer is scraping DOM

need to set up global variable before testing

George from testing's suggestions

In order to test it easily, complete these steps:

- Separate the business rules from the DOM updates.

- Get rid of those global variables!

these suggestions map really well to functional programming. we'll see how in a few pages

> **MegaMart testing team motto**
>
> 100% coverage or you don't go home.

We need to make it more reusable

The accounting and shipping departments want to use our code

Accounting and shipping want to reuse our code, but they can't for a few reasons:

Accounting and shipping want to use your code but they can't. Can we give them what they need?

- The code reads the shopping cart from a global variable, but they need to process orders from the database, not the variable

- The code writes directly to the DOM, but they need to print tax receipts and shipping labels

Jenna on dev team's code notes

Jenna on dev team

```
function update_shipping_icons() {
  var buy_buttons = get_buy_buttons_dom();
  for(var i = 0; i < buy_buttons.length; i++) {
    var button = buy_buttons[i];
    var item = button.item;
    if(item.price + shopping_cart_total >= 20)
      button.show_free_shipping_icon();
    else
      button.hide_free_shipping_icon();
  }
}
```

the business rule they want to reuse (>=20)

this function can only be run after shopping_cart _total is set

there's no way to get the answer out since there's no return value

these will only work if the DOM has been set up

Jenna on dev team's suggestions

Do these things to make it reusable:

- Don't depend on global variables.

- Don't assume the answer goes in the DOM.

- Return the answer from the function.

Jenna's suggestions also map well to functional programming. we'll see how in a few pages

Distinguishing actions, calculations, and data

The first thing we should look at is what category each function belongs in. This will give us some idea of our code and how we can improve it. We can mark each function with either an A, C, or D, depending on its category.

```
var shopping_cart = []; A            these globals are
var shopping_cart_total = 0; A       mutable: actions

function add_item_to_cart(name, price) { A
  shopping_cart.push({
    name: name,                      modifies a global
    price: price                     variable: action
  });
  calc_cart_total();                 reads from the DOM: action
}

function update_shipping_icons() { A
  var buy_buttons = get_buy_buttons_dom();
  for(var i = 0; i < buy_buttons.length; i++) {
    var button = buy_buttons[i];
    var item = button.item;
    if(item.price + shopping_cart_total >= 20)
      button.show_free_shipping_icon();
    else
      button.hide_free_shipping_icon();
  }                                  modifies the DOM: action
}

function update_tax_dom() { A
  set_tax_dom(shopping_cart_total * 0.10);
}                                    modifies the DOM: action

function calc_cart_total() { A
  shopping_cart_total = 0;
  for(var i = 0; i < shopping_cart.length; i++) {
    var item = shopping_cart[i];
    shopping_cart_total += item.price;   modifies a global var: action
  }
  set_cart_total_dom();
  update_shipping_icons();
  update_tax_dom();
}
```

Key

A Action
C Calculation
D Data

Remember:

Actions spread. We only have to identify one action inside a function for the whole function to be an action.

All of the code is actions. There are no calculations or data. Let's see how functional programming can give Jenna and George what they are asking for.

Functions have inputs and outputs

Every function has inputs and outputs. The *inputs* are information from the outside that a function uses in its computation. The *outputs* are information or actions that leave the function. We call a function for its outputs. The inputs are what the function needs in order to give us the outputs we want.

Here is a function with inputs and outputs annotated:

```
var total = 0;

function add_to_total(amount) {
  console.log("Old total: " + total);
  total += amount;
  return total;
}
```

the arguments are inputs

reading a global is an input

printing to the console is an output

modifying a global is an output

the return value is an output

It's all about tracking information in and information and effects out.

Inputs and outputs can be implicit or explicit

The *explicit inputs* are the arguments. The *explicit output* is the return value. Any other way information enters or leaves the function is implicit.

```
var total = 0;

function add_to_total(amount) {
  console.log("Old total: " + total);
  total += amount;
  return total;
}
```

arguments are explicit inputs

reading a global is an implicit input

printing is an implicit output

modifying a global is an implicit output

the return value is an explicit output

Implicit inputs and outputs make a function an action

If we eliminate all implicit inputs and outputs from an action, it becomes a calculation. The trick is to replace the implicit inputs with arguments, and to replace the implicit outputs with return values.

 **Vocab time**

Functional programmers call these implicit inputs and outputs *side effects*. They are not the main effect of the function (which is to calculate a return value).

Explicit inputs
- Arguments

Implicit inputs
- Any other input

Explicit outputs
- Return value

Implicit outputs
- Any other output

Testing and reuse relate to inputs and outputs

Remember George and Jenna? They were concerned about testability and reusability. They gave us some suggestions for making our code better:

George from testing

- Separate business rules from DOM updates

- Get rid of global variables

Jenna on dev team

- Don't depend on global variables

- Don't assume the answer goes in the DOM

- Return the answer from the function

These suggestions are all about removing implicit inputs and outputs. Let's take a closer look.

George 1: Separate business rules from DOM updates

DOM updates are outputs since they are information leaving the function. And because they aren't part of the return value, they are implicit. We still need the DOM update somewhere so the user can see the information, but George is asking us to extract the business rule separate from the implicit output of DOM updates.

George 2: Get rid of global variables

Reading from globals is implicit inputs and writing to globals is implicit outputs. He is asking us to eliminate these implicit inputs and outputs. We can replace them with arguments and a return value.

Jenna 1: Don't depend on global variables

This request is the same as George's second. She is asking us to eliminate implicit inputs and outputs.

Jenna 2: Don't assume the answer goes in the DOM

Our function writes directly to the DOM. As we have already said, it is an implicit output. We can replace the implicit output with a return value.

Jenna 3: Return the answer from the function

Jenna is asking us directly to use an explicit output instead of an implicit one.

George's and Jenna's suggestions for improving testability and reusability map to our functional concepts of implicit and explicit inputs and outputs. Let's see how we can apply these to extract calculations.

Extracting a calculation from an action

Let's follow the process of extracting a calculation from an action. First, we'll isolate the calculation code, then convert its inputs and outputs to arguments and return values.

Inside of the original function, we see that there is a block of code that does the work of calculating the total. We will extract this code to its own function before modifying it.

Original

```
function calc_cart_total() {
  shopping_cart_total = 0;
  for(var i = 0; i < shopping_cart.length; i++) {
    var item = shopping_cart[i];
    shopping_cart_total += item.price;
  }

  set_cart_total_dom();
  update_shipping_icons();
  update_tax_dom();
}
```

let's extract this into a function

Extracted

```
function calc_cart_total() {



  calc_total();
  set_cart_total_dom();
  update_shipping_icons();
  update_tax_dom();
}

function calc_total() {
  shopping_cart_total = 0;
  for(var i = 0; i < shopping_cart.length; i++) {
    var item = shopping_cart[i];
    shopping_cart_total += item.price;
  }
}
```

we call the new function in its place

We create and name a new function and paste in the code as its body. Where the code originally was, we call our new function. At the moment, the new function is an action. We will continue to work on the new function to turn it into a calculation.

The refactoring we just did might be called an *extract subroutine*. As an operation, it leaves the code working just as it was.

 **Noodle on it**

The operation we did in step 2 leaves the code working as it was before. Operations that do that are called *refactorings*. We want to cultivate a sense of code that changes without breaking. Why is it beneficial to change code but keep it working?

We need to convert our new function into a calculation. To do that, it's important to identify the inputs and outputs.

This function has two outputs and one input. The outputs are both writes to the same global variable, `shopping_cart_total`. The input is a read from the global variable `shopping_cart`.

These outputs and inputs need to be converted from implicit to explicit.

> Assigning a global variable is an *output* because data is leaving the function.
>
> Reading a global variable is an *input* because data is entering the function.

```
                              output
function calc_total() {
  shopping_cart_total = 0;           input
  for(var i = 0; i < shopping_cart.length; i++) {
    var item = shopping_cart[i];
    shopping_cart_total += item.price;
  }
}                       output
```

The two outputs were writes to the same global variable. We can replace these both with a single return value. Instead of writing to the global variable, we will write to a local variable, which we return. Then we write to the global variable in the original function using the return value.

use the return value to set the global variable

Current

```
function calc_cart_total() {
  calc_total();
  set_cart_total_dom();
  update_shipping_icons();
  update_tax_dom();
}
```

move the assignment outside to the caller

```
function calc_total() {
  shopping_cart_total = 0;
  for(var i = 0; i < shopping_cart.length; i++) {
    var item = shopping_cart[i];
    shopping_cart_total += item.price;
  }
}
```

operate on the local variable

Eliminated outputs

```
function calc_cart_total() {
  shopping_cart_total = calc_total();
  set_cart_total_dom();
  update_shipping_icons();
  update_tax_dom();
}
```

convert it to a local variable

```
function calc_total() {
  var total = 0;
  for(var i = 0; i < shopping_cart.length; i++) {
    var item = shopping_cart[i];
    total += item.price;
  }
  return total;
}
```

return the local

 Noodle on it

We've just done a significant change. Will the code work at this point?

We have gotten rid of the two implicit outputs. Up next is the implicit input.

We've already eliminated the implicit outputs. The last thing to do is convert the implicit input to an argument. We add the argument `cart` and use it in the function.

We then have to add that argument where it is called.

we pass shopping_cart as an argument

Current

```
function calc_cart_total() {
  shopping_cart_total = calc_total();
  set_cart_total_dom();
  update_shipping_icons();
  update_tax_dom();
}

function calc_total() {
  var total = 0;
  for(var i = 0; i < shopping_cart.length; i++) {
    var item = shopping_cart[i];
    total += item.price;
  }
  return total;
}
```

we read from it in two places

Eliminated inputs

```
function calc_cart_total() {
  shopping_cart_total = calc_total(shopping_cart);
  set_cart_total_dom();
  update_shipping_icons();
  update_tax_dom();
}

function calc_total(cart) {
  var total = 0;
  for(var i = 0; i < cart.length; i++) {
    var item = cart[i];
    total += item.price;
  }
  return total;
}
```

add an argument and use it instead of global

At this point, `calc_total()` is a calculation. The only inputs and outputs are arguments and return values.

And we've successfully extracted a calculation.

All of George and Jenna's concerns are covered

George from testing

✔ Separate business rules from the DOM updates

✔ Get rid of global variables

Jenna on dev team

✔ Don't depend on global variables

✔ Don't assume the answer goes in the DOM

✔ Return the answer from the function

how to calculate the cart total is definitely a business rule

calc_total() no longer relies on global variables

yes, it no longer reads from global variables

it doesn't update the DOM

now it has a return value

Extracting another calculation from an action

Now let's follow the same process again, this time for
`add_item_to_cart()`. We'll follow the same steps, choosing a
suitable section, extracting it, then converting inputs and
outputs.

Let's choose the section of code that modifies the shopping cart.
That will make a good calculation. Let's extract it into a new
function.

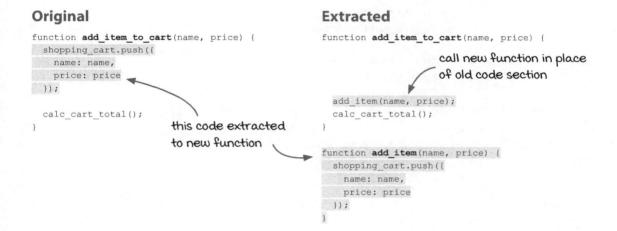

Original

```
function add_item_to_cart(name, price) {
  shopping_cart.push({
    name: name,
    price: price
  });

  calc_cart_total();
}
```

this code extracted
to new function

Extracted

```
function add_item_to_cart(name, price) {




  add_item(name, price);
  calc_cart_total();
}

function add_item(name, price) {
  shopping_cart.push({
    name: name,
    price: price
  });
}
```

call new function in place
of old code section

We make a new function called `add_item()` to put the section of
code into. It will need `name` and `price` arguments. Then we
replace the old code with a call to the new one.

Like we said before, this could be a refactoring called *extract
subroutine*. The extracted function is an action, because it modifies the global `shopping_cart` array. Let's turn it into a
calculation.

 **Noodle on it**

We just extracted a function. Did that change the behavior of
the system?

We just extracted a piece of code from add_item_to_cart() to a new function add_item(). Now we're going to convert that new function into a calculation. We need to identify its implicit inputs and outputs.

add_item() reads from a global variable, which is an input. And it modifies the array in that value by calling push(), which is an output.

```
function add_item(name, price) {
  shopping_cart.push({
    name: name,
    price: price
  });
}
```

we modify the array with .push()

we read the global shopping_cart variable

> **Remember:**
>
> Reading a global variable is an *input* because data is entering the function.
>
> Modifying a global array is an *output* because data is leaving the function.

Now that we have identified the implicit input and output, let's convert them to arguments and return values. Let's start with the input.

We were originally referring directly to the global variable shopping_cart. Instead, we add an argument to add_item(). The function will refer to that variable instead of the global variable.

pass global in as argument

Current

```
function add_item_to_cart(name, price) {
  add_item(name, price);
  calc_cart_total();
}

function add_item(name, price) {
  shopping_cart.push({
    name: name,
    price: price
  });
}
```

refer to argument instead of global

Eliminated input

```
function add_item_to_cart(name, price) {
  add_item(shopping_cart, name, price);
  calc_cart_total();
}

function add_item(cart, name, price) {
  cart.push({
    name: name,
    price: price
  });
}
```

add argument

We then have to pass the global variable in as an argument. We've turned the implicit input into an explicit input as an argument.

But we are still modifying the global array by calling .push(), which is an implicit output. Let's tackle that on the next page.

We had one implicit input and one implicit output. We've already converted the input to an argument. There's just the output left, which we will tackle now.

The output we identified was modifying the array stored in `shopping_cart`. We don't want to modify it. Instead, we want to return a modified copy. Let's see what that looks like.

Vocab time

Copying a mutable value before you modify it is a way to implement immutability. It's called *copy-on-write*. We'll get into the details in chapter 6.

assign return value to
global in original function

Current

```
function add_item_to_cart(name, price) {

  add_item(shopping_cart, name, price);
  calc_cart_total();
}

function add_item(cart, name, price) {

  cart.push({
    name: name,
    price: price
  });

}
```

make a copy and assign
it to local variable

Eliminated output

```
function add_item_to_cart(name, price) {
  shopping_cart =
    add_item(shopping_cart, name, price);
  calc_cart_total();
}

function add_item(cart, name, price) {
  var new_cart = cart.slice();
  new_cart.push({
    name: name,
    price: price
  });
  return new_cart;
}
```

modify copy

return copy

We create a copy, modify it, then return the copy. In the original function, we assign the return value to the global variable. We've converted the implicit output into a return value.

That marks the end of the extraction. `add_item()` no longer has any implicit inputs or outputs. That makes it a calculation.

 Deep dive

In JavaScript, there is no direct way to copy an array. In this book, we will use the `.slice()` method, like this:

```
array.slice()
```

We will get into the details in chapter 6.

 **Noodle on it**

We avoided modifying the cart by making a copy. Would this still be a calculation if we modified the array passed as an argument? Why or why not?

It's your turn

Here is the code we've written. We extracted `add_item()` to make it more testable and reusable. Does `add_item()` satisfy all of George and Jenna's concerns?

```
function add_item_to_cart(name, price) {
  shopping_cart = add_item(shopping_cart, name, price);
  calc_cart_total();
}

function add_item(cart, name, price) {
  var new_cart = cart.slice();
  new_cart.push({
    name: name,
    price: price
  });
  return new_cart;
}
```

Check if all of George and Jenna's concerns are covered

George from testing

☐ Separate business rules from the DOM updates

☐ Get rid of global variables

Jenna on dev team

☐ Don't depend on global variables

☐ Don't assume the answer goes in the DOM

☐ Return the answer from the function

 Answer

Yes! All of the concerns have been addressed.

🧠 Brain break

There's more to go, but let's take a break for questions

Q: It looks like the amount of code is increasing. Is that normal? Isn't less code better?

A: In general, less code is better. But our total lines of code are increasing.

We're making new functions, which take at least two lines of code each: one line for the function signature and one for the closing curly brace. However, breaking things into functions will pay off over time.

We're already starting to see the payoff. Our code is becoming more reusable and testable. Two other departments can use these functions. And our tests will be shorter.

Finally, we're not done yet! Just wait :)

Q: Are reusability and testability the only concerns that functional programming helps with?

A: Absolutely not! FP does help with those, but there's a lot more out there. We'll get to concurrency, architecture, and data modeling by the end of the book. Also, FP is a big field, and this book cannot cover all of it.

Q: I see that you're making certain calculations useful on their own, outside of the use case that it was developed for. Is that important?

A: Yes, for sure. One thing that we like to do in functional programming is to pull things apart, which makes more, smaller things. Smaller things are easier to reuse, test, and understand.

Q: In the calculations we extracted, we are still modifying a variable. I heard that in functional programming, everything is immutable. What gives?

A: That's a great question. Immutability states that a thing shouldn't be modified after it is created. However, during its creation, it needs to be initialized, and that requires modifying it. For instance, you might need to initialize the values in an array. After that, you don't modify it. But right at the beginning, you are adding items.

The places where we modify local variables or local values are all newly created values that need to be initialized. They are local, so nothing outside the function can see them. When the initialization is done, we return them. We expect to maintain the discipline not to modify them. We'll go deep into immutability in chapter 6.

Step-by-step: Extracting a calculation

Extracting a calculation from an action is a repeatable process. Here are the steps.

1. Select and extract the calculation code

Select a suitable chunk of code for extraction. Refactor that chunk into a new function. You may have to add arguments where appropriate. Make sure to call the new function where the chunk was in the old function.

2. Identify the implicit inputs and outputs of the function

Identify the inputs and outputs of the new function. The inputs are anything that can affect the result between calls to the function. And the outputs are anything that can be affected by calling that function.

Example inputs include arguments, reads from variables outside the function, queries of a database, and so on.

Example outputs include return value, modifying a global variable, modifying a shared object, sending a web request, and so on.

3. Convert inputs to arguments and outputs to return values

One at a time, convert inputs to arguments and outputs to return values. If you add return values, you may need to assign that value to a local variable in the original function.

It's important to note here that we want our arguments and return values to be immutable values—that is, they don't change. If we return a value and some piece of our function later changes it, that's a kind of implicit output. Similarly, if something changes the argument values after our function has received them, that is a kind of implicit input. We'll learn way more about immutable data in chapter 6, including why we use it and how to enforce it. For now, let's just assume we don't change them.

📝 It's your turn

The accounting department wants to use our tax calculation, but it's tied to a DOM update. Extract the tax calculation from update_tax_dom(). Use the space that follows. An answer is on the next page.

```
function update_tax_dom() {
  set_tax_dom(shopping_cart_total * 0.10);
}
```

accounting wants
this computation

> ### Extracting a calculation
>
> 1. Select and extract the code.
> 2. Identify implicit inputs and outputs.
> 3. Convert inputs to arguments and outputs to return values.

if you need a reminder,
here are the steps

use this space to
write your code

 **Answer**

Our task was to extract the tax calculation from update_tax_dom(). Let's first extract the code into a new function called calc_tax().

Original

```
function update_tax_dom() {
  set_tax_dom(shopping_cart_total * 0.10);
}
```

Extracted

```
function update_tax_dom() {
  set_tax_dom(calc_tax());
}

function calc_tax() {
  return shopping_cart_total * 0.10;
}
```

there's just one implicit input and no implicit outputs

We extract the small mathematical expression that is the argument to set_tax_dom() into calc_tax(). That function has just one implicit input and no implicit outputs. Its only output is the explicit return value.

Let's replace the implicit input with an explicit argument.

Extracted

```
function update_tax_dom() {
  set_tax_dom(calc_tax());
}

function calc_tax() {
  return shopping_cart_total * 0.10;
}
```

Done

```
function update_tax_dom() {
  set_tax_dom(calc_tax(shopping_cart_total));
}

function calc_tax(amount) {
  return amount * 0.10;
}
```

nice, clean tax calculation that the accountants can use

Now we're done. We've extracted a function and replaced all of its implicit inputs and outputs with explicit ones. It's now a calculation, and it's quite reusable. This one represents a business rule.

It's your turn

Check if all of George and Jenna's concerns are covered in the `calc_tax()` business rule we just extracted.

```
function update_tax_dom() {
  set_tax_dom(calc_tax(shopping_cart_total));
}

function calc_tax(amount) {
  return amount * 0.10;
}
```

George from testing

☐ Separate business rules from the DOM updates.

☐ Get rid of global variables.

Jenna on dev team

☐ Don't depend on global variables.

☐ Don't assume the answer goes in the DOM.

☐ Return the answer from the function.

 ## Answer

Yes! All of the concerns have been addressed.

📝 It's your turn

The shipping department wants to use the code to determine which shipments are free.
Extract a calculation for `update_shipping_icons()`. Use the space that follows. An
answer is on the next page.

```
function update_shipping_icons() {
  var buy_buttons = get_buy_buttons_dom();
  for(var i = 0; i < buy_buttons.length; i++) {
    var button = buy_buttons[i];
    var item = button.item;
    if(item.price + shopping_cart_total >= 20)
      button.show_free_shipping_icon();
    else
      button.hide_free_shipping_icon();
  }
}
```

shipping department
wants to use this rule

Extracting a calculation

1. Select and extract the code.
2. Identify implicit inputs and outputs.
3. Convert inputs to arguments and outputs to return values.

if you need a reminder,
here are the steps

use this space to
write your code

 **Answer**

Our task was to extract the logic that determines if free shipping is offered. Let's start by extracting that code; then we'll turn it into a calculation.

Original

```
function update_shipping_icons() {
  var buy_buttons = get_buy_buttons_dom();
  for(var i = 0; i < buy_buttons.length; i++) {
    var button = buy_buttons[i];
    var item = button.item;
    if(item.price + shopping_cart_total >= 20)
      button.show_free_shipping_icon();
    else
      button.hide_free_shipping_icon();
  }
}
```

Extracted

```
function update_shipping_icons() {
  var buy_buttons = get_buy_buttons_dom();
  for(var i = 0; i < buy_buttons.length; i++) {
    var button = buy_buttons[i];
    var item = button.item;
    if(gets_free_shipping(item.price))
      button.show_free_shipping_icon();
    else
      button.hide_free_shipping_icon();
  }
}

function gets_free_shipping(item_price) {
  return item_price + shopping_cart_total >= 20;
}
```

just one implicit input, a read from a global variable

Now that we have extracted `gets_free_shipping()`, we can turn it into a calculation by eliminating the implicit input.

Extracted

```
function update_shipping_icons() {
  var buy_buttons = get_buy_buttons_dom();
  for(var i = 0; i < buy_buttons.length; i++) {
    var button = buy_buttons[i];
    var item = button.item;
    if(gets_free_shipping(
                   item.price))
      button.show_free_shipping_icon();
    else
      button.hide_free_shipping_icon();
  }
}

function gets_free_shipping(item_price) {
  return item_price + shopping_cart_total >= 20;
}
```

Done

```
function update_shipping_icons() {
  var buy_buttons = get_buy_buttons_dom();
  for(var i = 0; i < buy_buttons.length; i++) {
    var button = buy_buttons[i];
    var item = button.item;
    if(gets_free_shipping(shopping_cart_total,
                   item.price))
      button.show_free_shipping_icon();
    else
      button.hide_free_shipping_icon();
  }
}

function gets_free_shipping(total, item_price) {
  return item_price + total >= 20;
}
```

It's your turn

Check if all of George and Jenna's concerns are covered in the `get_free_shipping()` business rule we just extracted.

```
function update_shipping_icons() {
  var buy_buttons = get_buy_buttons_dom();
  for(var i = 0; i < buy_buttons.length; i++) {
    var button = buy_buttons[i];
    var item = button.item;
    if(gets_free_shipping(shopping_cart_total, item.price))
      button.show_free_shipping_icon();
    else
      button.hide_free_shipping_icon();
  }
}

function gets_free_shipping(total, item_price) {
  return item_price + total >= 20;
}
```

George from testing

- [ ] Separate business rules from the DOM updates.

- [ ] Get rid of global variables.

Jenna on dev team

- [ ] Don't depend on global variables.

- [ ] Don't assume the answer goes in the DOM.

- [ ] Return the answer from the function.

 **Answer**

Yes! All of the concerns have been addressed.

Let's see all of our code in one place

Here is our new code. Let's tag these functions with A, C, or D to
get a sense of how much code is in each category.

```
var shopping_cart = [];  A
var shopping_cart_total = 0;  A
```
← global vars: actions

```
function add_item_to_cart(name, price) {  A
  shopping_cart = add_item(shopping_cart, name, price);
  calc_cart_total();
}
```
← reading a global
var: action

```
function calc_cart_total() {  A
  shopping_cart_total = calc_total(shopping_cart);
  set_cart_total_dom();
  update_shipping_icons();
  update_tax_dom();
}
```
← reading a global
var: action

```
function update_shipping_icons() {  A
  var buttons = get_buy_buttons_dom();
  for(var i = 0; i < buttons.length; i++) {
    var button = buttons[i];
    var item = button.item;
    if(gets_free_shipping(shopping_cart_total, item.price))
      button.show_free_shipping_icon();
    else
      button.hide_free_shipping_icon();
  }
}
```
← reading a global var: action

Remember:

We only have to
find one action in a
function for the
whole function to be
an action

```
function update_tax_dom() {  A
  set_tax_dom(calc_tax(shopping_cart_total));
}
```
← reading a global var: action

```
function add_item(cart, name, price) {  C
  var new_cart = cart.slice();
  new_cart.push({
    name: name,
    price: price
  });
  return new_cart;
}
```
← remember, this is a common
way to copy an array

← no implicit inputs or outputs

```
function calc_total(cart) {  C
  var total = 0;
  for(var i = 0; i < cart.length; i++) {
    var item = cart[i];
    total += item.price;
  }
  return total;
}
```
← no implicit inputs or outputs

```
function gets_free_shipping(total, item_price) {  C
  return item_price + total >= 20;
}
```
← no implicit inputs or outputs

```
function calc_tax(amount) {  C
  return amount * 0.10;
}
```
← no implicit inputs or outputs

Conclusion

After the changes we made, everybody is happy. George from testing got home to see his kids this weekend. They grow so fast! And Jenna reports that the accounting and shipping departments like the new code. They put it to use right away with no problems.

And don't forget the CEO. He's happy because the stock of MegaMart just went up, all thanks to your new free shipping icons. Don't expect any bonus, though.

However, Kim from the dev team has some ideas about how to improve the design of our code.

Summary

- Functions that are actions will have implicit inputs and outputs.

- Calculations have no implicit inputs or outputs by definition.

- Shared variables (such as globals) are common implicit inputs and outputs.

- Implicit inputs can often be replaced by arguments.

- Implicit outputs can often be replaced by return values.

- As we apply functional principles, we'll find the ratio of code in actions to code in calculations shifting toward calculations.

Up next . . .

We've seen how we can extract calculations from our actions to improve the quality of our code. However, sometimes we can't extract any more calculations. We will always have actions. Can we improve those actions that we can't get rid of? Yes. And that's the topic of the next chapter.

Improving the design of actions | 5

In this chapter

- Discover how eliminating implicit inputs and outputs can enhance reusability.

- Learn to improve the design of our code by pulling things apart.

In the last chapter, we learned how eliminating all implicit inputs and outputs can convert an action into a calculation. However, you can't eliminate all of them. You need some actions. In this chapter, we see how even eliminating some of the inputs and outputs can improve the design of actions.

Aligning design with business requirements

Choosing a better level of abstraction that matches usage

The refactoring from actions to calculations that we did was fairly mechanical. It doesn't always lead to the best possible design. That takes a more human touch. Let's look at that now. In fact, Kim has an idea for how to improve it.

The function `gets_free_shipping()` is not quite right. The idea was to know if an order with the current cart and a new item would result in free shipping. But this doesn't ask about the order, it asks about a total plus an item's price. It takes the wrong arguments.

We want to know if an order results in free shipping, not if a total plus an item price does.

Kim on dev team

these arguments are not the ones we want

```
function gets_free_shipping(total, item_price) {
  return item_price + total >= 20;
}
```

We also have a subtle duplication. We're adding an item price to a total in two places. Duplication isn't always bad, but it is a code smell. *Code smell* means an indicator of a potential problem.

we are duplicating the calculation of the total of the cart (item + total)

```
function calc_total(cart) {
  var total = 0;
  for(var i = 0; i < cart.length; i++) {
    var item = cart[i];
    total += item.price;
  }
  return total;
}
```

Vocab time

A *code smell* is a characteristic of a piece of code that might be a symptom of deeper problems.

We want to change

```
gets_free_shipping(total, item_price)
```

to

```
gets_free_shipping(cart)
```

this function signature answers the question "does this cart get free shipping?"

And we need to get rid of the duplication by reusing the `calc_total()` function.

Aligning the function with business requirements

This isn't refactoring, really, since we're changing the behavior

First, let's review our goal: `gets_free_shipping()` should take
a cart and return whether the total of that cart is greater than or
equal to 20.

get the total using our
handy calculation

Original

```
function gets_free_shipping(total,
                             item_price) {
  return item_price + total >= 20;
}
```

With new signature

```
function gets_free_shipping(cart) {

  return calc_total(cart) >= 20;
}
```

Our function now operates on the cart data structure instead of on
a total and a price. This makes sense because as an e-commerce
company, shopping carts are a primary entity type.

   Because the signature changed, we need to modify the functions that were using the old one.

Original

```
function update_shipping_icons() {
  var buttons = get_buy_buttons_dom();
  for(var i = 0; i < buttons.length; i++) {
    var button = buttons[i];
    var item = button.item;



    if(gets_free_shipping(
       shopping_cart_total,
       item.price))
      button.show_free_shipping_icon();
    else
      button.hide_free_shipping_icon();
  }
}
```

create a new cart that
contains the item

With new signature

```
function update_shipping_icons() {
  var buttons = get_buy_buttons_dom();
  for(var i = 0; i < buttons.length; i++) {
    var button = buttons[i];
    var item = button.item;
    var new_cart = add_item(shopping_cart,
                             item.name,
                             item.price);
    if(gets_free_shipping(
       new_cart))

      button.show_free_shipping_icon();
    else
      button.hide_free_shipping_icon();
  }
}
```

call the improved
function

Now our function does what we need. It tells us if a shopping cart
gets free shipping.

 **Noodle on it**

What are your first impressions of this code transformation? We're using a calculation that creates a modified copy of the cart, but it's not modifying the existing
cart. This is the most functional code we have written. What words would you use
to describe it?

 **Brain break**

There's more to go, but let's take a break for questions

Q: The lines of code keep going up! How is this better?

A: Lines of code is a decent metric for how hard a codebase is to write and maintain. But it's not perfect. Another way to measure maintenance difficulty is by how big each function is. Small functions are easier to understand and get right. Notice that our calculations are pretty small. They're also cohesive and reusable. Plus, we're not done yet :)

Q: Every time we run `add_item()`, we're making a copy of the cart array. Won't that get expensive?

A: Yes and no. It is definitely more expensive than modifying a single array. However, modern runtimes and garbage collectors handle this very well. In fact, we make copies of things all the time without thinking about it. JavaScript has immutable strings. Every time you concatenate two strings, you are making a new string. All of the characters have to be copied over.

Besides, the benefits outweigh the cost. Being able to make modified copies without changing the original is very useful, as we'll see throughout this book. And if that part of the code does get too slow, we can optimize it later. Let's not optimize prematurely. We'll go deeper into copying in chapters 6 and 7.

Principle: Minimize implicit inputs and outputs

Implicit inputs are all of the inputs that aren't arguments. And implicit outputs are all of the outputs that aren't the return value. We've been writing functions with no implicit inputs and outputs. We call those calculations.

However, calculations aren't the only thing that this principle applies to. Even actions would do well to eliminate implicit inputs and outputs. Even if you can't eliminate all implicit inputs and outputs, the more you can eliminate, the better.

A function with implicit inputs and outputs is like a component hardwired to other components. It's not modular. It can't be used in another place. And its behavior depends on the behavior of the parts it's connected to. By converting implicit inputs and outputs to explicit ones, we are making the component modular. Instead of solder, it's got a connector that's easy to detach.

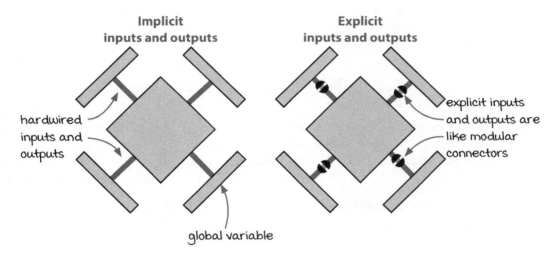

Implicit inputs limit when you can call a function. Remember how we could only calculate the tax when the `shopping_cart_total` variable was set? What about if something else was using that variable? You'd have to make sure no other code was running while you calculated the tax.

Implicit outputs limit when you can call the function as well. You can only call the function if you want that output to happen. What if you don't want to output to the DOM at that time? What if you need the result, but put somewhere else?

Because you're limited by when you can run it, functions with implicit inputs and outputs are harder to test. You have to set up all the inputs, run the test, then check the outputs. The more inputs and outputs, the harder it is to test.

Calculations are easiest to test because they have no implicit inputs and outputs. But any that you can eliminate will improve the testability and reusability of your actions, even if you don't cross into calculation land.

Reducing implicit inputs and outputs

If it truly is a principle, it should apply universally. Let's apply the principle of minimal implicit inputs and outputs to `update_shipping_icons()`. We can convert the implicit input to an explicit input, in the form of an argument.

add the argument and read it instead of global

Original

we are reading a global variable here

```
function update_shipping_icons() {
  var buttons = get_buy_buttons_dom();
  for(var i = 0; i < buttons.length; i++) {
    var button = buttons[i];
    var item = button.item;
    var new_cart = add_item(shopping_cart,
                            item.name,
                            item.price);
    if(gets_free_shipping(new_cart))
      button.show_free_shipping_icon();
    else
      button.hide_free_shipping_icon();
  }
}
```

With explicit argument

```
function update_shipping_icons(cart) {
  var buttons = get_buy_buttons_dom();
  for(var i = 0; i < buttons.length; i++) {
    var button = buttons[i];
    var item = button.item;
    var new_cart = add_item(cart,
                            item.name,
                            item.price);
    if(gets_free_shipping(new_cart))
      button.show_free_shipping_icon();
    else
      button.hide_free_shipping_icon();
  }
}
```

We've changed the signature of this function, so we need to update the caller. Here is the function that calls `update_shipping_icons()`:

Original

here's where we're calling it in the original code

```
function calc_cart_total() {
  shopping_cart_total =
    calc_total(shopping_cart);
  set_cart_total_dom();
  update_shipping_icons();
  update_tax_dom();
}
```

Passing argument

we pass it as an argument

```
function calc_cart_total() {
  shopping_cart_total =
    calc_total(shopping_cart);
  set_cart_total_dom();
  update_shipping_icons(shopping_cart);
  update_tax_dom();
}
```

 ## Noodle on it

We just applied a principle to this function and eliminated an implicit input. It was an action before, and it still is an action. After applying the principle, is the function better? Can it be reused in more circumstances? Can it be tested more easily?

It's your turn

Here is the code for all of the actions we have so far. How many global variable reads can you convert into arguments? After you identify them, convert them into arguments. The answer is on the next page.

```
function add_item_to_cart(name, price) {
  shopping_cart = add_item(shopping_cart,
                           name, price);
  calc_cart_total();
}

function calc_cart_total() {
  shopping_cart_total = calc_total(shopping_cart);
  set_cart_total_dom();
  update_shipping_icons(shopping_cart);
  update_tax_dom();
}

function set_cart_total_dom() {
 ...
 shopping_cart_total
 ...
}
```

we haven't seen the code for this function, but the frontend team says we can add the argument

```
function update_shipping_icons(cart) {
  var buy_buttons = get_buy_buttons_dom();
  for(var i = 0; i < buy_buttons.length; i++) {
    var button = buy_buttons[i];
    var item = button.item;
    var new_cart = add_item(cart, item.name, item.price);
    if(gets_free_shipping(new_cart))
      button.show_free_shipping_icon();
    else
      button.hide_free_shipping_icon();
  }
}

function update_tax_dom() {
  set_tax_dom(calc_tax(shopping_cart_total));
}
```

 **Answer**

We can convert many global variable reads to arguments:

the only places we read
shopping_cart global

Original   **Eliminating reads to globals**

```
function add_item_to_cart(name, price) {
  shopping_cart = add_item(shopping_cart,
                           name, price);
  calc_cart_total();
}
```

```
function add_item_to_cart(name, price) {
  shopping_cart = add_item(shopping_cart,
                           name, price);
  calc_cart_total(shopping_cart);
}
```

```
function calc_cart_total() {
  shopping_cart_total =
    calc_total(shopping_cart);
  set_cart_total_dom();
  update_shipping_icons(shopping_cart);
  update_tax_dom();
}
```

```
function calc_cart_total(cart) {
  var total =
    calc_total(cart);
  set_cart_total_dom(total);
  update_shipping_icons(cart);
  update_tax_dom(total);
  shopping_cart_total = total;
}
```

we write to shopping_cart_total,
but we don't read it anywhere

```
function set_cart_total_dom() {
  ...
  shopping_cart_total
  ...
}
```

```
function set_cart_total_dom(total) {
  ...
  total
  ...
}
```

```
function update_shipping_icons(cart) {
  var buttons = get_buy_buttons_dom();
  for(var i = 0; i < buttons.length; i++) {
    var button = buttons[i];
    var item = button.item;
    var new_cart = add_item(cart,
                            item.name,
                            item.price);
    if(gets_free_shipping(new_cart))
      button.show_free_shipping_icon();
    else
      button.hide_free_shipping_icon();
  }
}
```

```
function update_shipping_icons(cart) {
  var buttons = get_buy_buttons_dom();
  for(var i = 0; i < buttons.length; i++) {
    var button = buttons[i];
    var item = button.item;
    var new_cart = add_item(cart,
                            item.name,
                            item.price);
    if(gets_free_shipping(new_cart))
      button.show_free_shipping_icon();
    else
      button.hide_free_shipping_icon();
  }
}
```

```
function update_tax_dom() {
  set_tax_dom(calc_tax(shopping_cart_total));
}
```

```
function update_tax_dom(total) {
  set_tax_dom(calc_tax(total));
}
```

Giving the code a once-over

Let's go through and check for any other things we can clean up.
We're looking not only for functional principles to apply, but also
for other things like duplication and unnecessary functions.

Here are all of the actions:

```
function add_item_to_cart(name, price) {
  shopping_cart = add_item(shopping_cart, name, price);
  calc_cart_total(shopping_cart);
}
```

this function is what will be
called when we click a "buy
now" button

```
function calc_cart_total(cart) {
  var total = calc_total(cart);
  set_cart_total_dom(total);
  update_shipping_icons(cart);
  update_tax_dom(total);
  shopping_cart_total = total;
}
```

this function seems a little
superfluous. why not just do
this in add_item_to_cart()?

we write to this global but nothing reads
from it anywhere. we can get rid of it

```
function set_cart_total_dom(total) {
  ...
}
```

```
function update_shipping_icons(cart) {
  var buy_buttons = get_buy_buttons_dom();
  for(var i = 0; i < buy_buttons.length; i++) {
    var button = buy_buttons[i];
    var item = button.item;
    var new_cart = add_item(cart, item.name, item.price);
    if(gets_free_shipping(new_cart))
      button.show_free_shipping_icon();
    else
      button.hide_free_shipping_icon();
  }
}
```

the rest seems fine for now

```
function update_tax_dom(total) {
  set_tax_dom(calc_tax(total));
}
```

We've identified two promising cleanups: First, shopping
_cart_total, the global variable, is not being read anywhere.
Second, calc_cart_total() is a superfluous function. Let's do
the cleanup on the next page.

We identified two things on the last page: `shopping _cart_total` was not being used, and the function `calc _cart_total()` was superfluous. Let's inline its code into `add_item_to_cart()`, where it was called.

Original

```
function add_item_to_cart(name, price) {
  shopping_cart = add_item(shopping_cart,
                           name, price);
  calc_cart_total(shopping_cart);



}

function calc_cart_total(cart) {
  var total = calc_total(cart);
  set_cart_total_dom(total);
  update_shipping_icons(cart);
  update_tax_dom(total);
  shopping_cart_total = total;
}
```

Improved

```
function add_item_to_cart(name, price) {
  shopping_cart = add_item(shopping_cart,
                           name, price);

  var total = calc_total(shopping_cart);
  set_cart_total_dom(total);
  update_shipping_icons(shopping_cart);
  update_tax_dom(total);
}
```

get rid of calc_cart_total() and global var shopping_cart_total and move everything into add_item_to_cart()

The rest of the code is not shown because there were no more changes to make. Now that our actions have improved, let's go through our actions and group them by layers of meaning.

Noodle on it

It seems that we have finally significantly decreased the number of lines in actions. Did it have to take so long? Could we have taken a more direct route?

Categorizing our calculations

By grouping our calculations, we learn something about layers of meaning

I'd like to explore the calculations a bit more. Let's put a C (for cart) on each function that knows the structure of the shopping cart. That is, it knows it's an array with items in it. Let's put an I (for item) on each function that knows the structure of an item. And we'll put a B (for business) by the functions about business rules.

> **Key**
>
> **C** Cart operation
> **I** Item operation
> **B** Business rule

```
                            C   I
function add_item(cart, name, price) {
  var new_cart = cart.slice();
  new_cart.push({
    name: name,
    price: price
  });
  return new_cart;
}
```

remember, .slice() is how you copy an array in JavaScript

```
                        C   I   B
function calc_total(cart) {
  var total = 0;
  for(var i = 0; i < cart.length; i++) {
    var item = cart[i];
    total += item.price;
  }
  return total;
}
```

this definitely knows the cart structure, but it could be considered a business rule, too, since it defines how megamart determines the total

```
                              B
function gets_free_shipping(cart) {
  return calc_total(cart) >= 20;
}
```

```
                      B
function calc_tax(amount) {
  return amount * 0.10;
}
```

Over time, we'll see these groupings become more distinct. Keep an eye out for them. They will become layers of meaning in our code. I wanted to bring this up now, because we're right here in the code. We'll definitely get deeper into it in chapters 8 and 9. For right now, just enjoy. These layers happen when you start pulling things apart. And, speaking of pulling things apart, let's look at a principle that is all about that.

💡 Principle: Design is about pulling things apart

Functions give us a very natural way to separate concerns. Functions separate what value is provided as an argument from how the value is used. Very often, we are tempted to put things together. Bigger, more complex things feel more substantial. But things that are pulled apart can always be composed back together. The hard part is figuring out useful ways to pull them apart.

Easier to reuse

Smaller, simpler functions are easier to reuse. They do less. They make fewer assumptions.

Easier to maintain

Smaller functions are easier to understand and maintain. They have less code. They are often obviously right (or wrong).

Easier to test

Smaller functions are easier to test. They do one thing, so you just test that one thing.

Even if there is no identifiable problem in a function, if you see something you can pull out, it's worth at least trying to extract it. It might lead to a better design.

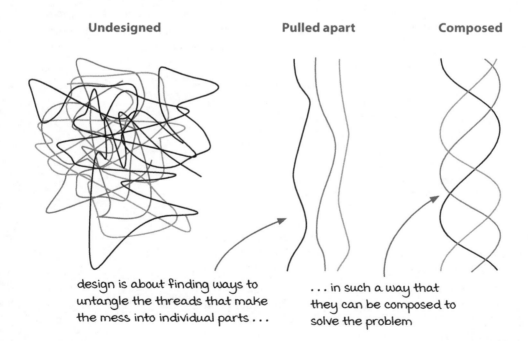

Undesigned   **Pulled apart**   **Composed**

design is about finding ways to untangle the threads that make the mess into individual parts . . .

. . . in such a way that they can be composed to solve the problem

Improving the design by pulling `add_item()` apart

Here is our trusty `add_item()`. It doesn't do very much. It adds an item to a cart. Or does it? Let's take a closer look. It turns out this function does four distinct things:

```
function add_item(cart, name, price) {
  var new_cart = cart.slice();                    1. make a copy of an array
  new_cart.push({                                 2. build an item object
    name: name,
    price: price                                  3. add the item to the copy
  });
  return new_cart;                                4. return the copy
}
```

This function knows both the structure of the cart and the structure of the item. We can pull out the item into its own function.

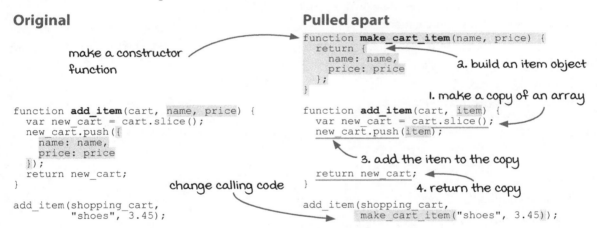

Original

make a constructor function

```
function add_item(cart, name, price) {
  var new_cart = cart.slice();
  new_cart.push({
    name: name,
    price: price
  });
  return new_cart;
}
add_item(shopping_cart,
         "shoes", 3.45);
```

change calling code

Pulled apart

```
function make_cart_item(name, price) {
  return {
    name: name,
    price: price                    2. build an item object
  };
}
                                    1. make a copy of an array
function add_item(cart, item) {
  var new_cart = cart.slice();
  new_cart.push(item);
                                    3. add the item to the copy
  return new_cart;
}                                   4. return the copy
add_item(shopping_cart,
         make_cart_item("shoes", 3.45));
```

By pulling this function out, we have made a function that knows about the structure of items, but not about the structure of carts, and a function that knows about the structure of carts, but not about the structure of items. That means that the cart and item structures can evolve independently. For instance, if you need to switch from the cart being implemented as an array to it being implemented as a hash map, you could do this with few changes.

As for #1, #3, and #4, we actually want them to be together. Making a copy before modifying a value is a strategy for implementing immutability called *copy-on-write*, so we will keep them together. We'll learn all about that in chapter 6.

This function is not specific to carts and items. Let's change the names of the function and arguments on the next page.

Extracting a copy-on-write pattern

We just separated a nice little function. When we look at the code, we see it's just adding an item to an array using a copy-on-write discipline. It's a generic operation. But the name is not very generic. It's very specific to shopping carts.

names are specific

```
function add_item(cart, item) {
  var new_cart = cart.slice();
  new_cart.push(item);
  return new_cart;
}
```

implementation is general

Imagine if we changed the names of the function and two arguments to something more generic:

generic names that work for any array and element

Original (specific)

```
function add_item(cart, item) {
  var new_cart = cart.slice();
  new_cart.push(item);
  return new_cart;
}
```

General

```
function add_element_last(array, elem) {
  var new_array = array.slice();
  new_array.push(elem);
  return new_array;
}
```

Then we could define add_item() very simply:

```
function add_item(cart, item) {
  return add_element_last(cart, item);
}
```

We've extracted a very reusable utility function that can work on any array and element, not just carts and items. The cart probably won't be the last array we'll want to add items to. We will want to use immutable arrays at some point, too. We'll go much deeper into immutability in chapters 6 and 7.

Using `add_item()`

`add_item()` used to take three arguments, cart, name, and price:

```
function add_item(cart, name, price) {
  var new_cart = cart.slice();
  new_cart.push({
    name: name,
    price: price
  });
  return new_cart;
}
```

Now it only takes two, the cart and the item:

```
function add_item(cart, item) {
  return add_element_last(cart, item);
}
```

We extracted a separate function for constructing the item:

```
function make_cart_item(name, price) {
  return {
    name: name,
    price: price
  };
}
```

That means we need to modify the functions that call `add_item()` so that they pass in the correct number of arguments:

Original

```
function add_item_to_cart(name, price) {

  shopping_cart = add_item(shopping_cart,
                           name, price);
  var total = calc_total(shopping_cart);
  set_cart_total_dom(total);
  update_shipping_icons(shopping_cart);
  update_tax_dom(total);

}
```

Using new version

```
function add_item_to_cart(name, price) {
  var item = make_cart_item(name, price);
  shopping_cart = add_item(shopping_cart,
                           item);
  var total = calc_total(shopping_cart);
  set_cart_total_dom(total);
  update_shipping_icons(shopping_cart);
  update_tax_dom(total);
}
```

We construct the item first, then pass it to `add_item()`. And that's that. Let's get a new, broad look at our calculations.

Categorizing our calculations

Now that we've modified the code, let's look at the calculations once more. Let's put a C (for cart) on each function that knows the structure of the shopping cart. That is, it knows it's an array with items in it. Let's put an I (for item) on each function that knows the structure of an item. We'll put a B (for business) by the functions about business rules. And now we'll add an A (for array) for array utility functions.

> **Key**
>
> **C** Cart operation
> **I** Item operation
> **B** Business rule
> **A** Array utility

```
function add_element_last(array, elem) {
  var new_array = array.slice();
  new_array.push(elem);
  return new_array;              A
}

function add_item(cart, item) {
  return add_element_last(cart, item);   C
}

function make_cart_item(name, price) {
  return {
    name: name,                    I
    price: price
  };
}

function calc_total(cart) {
  var total = 0;
  for(var i = 0; i < cart.length; i++) {   C  I  B
    var item = cart[i];
    total += item.price;
  }
  return total;
}

function gets_free_shipping(cart) {
  return calc_total(cart) >= 20;
}                                   B

function calc_tax(amount) {
  return amount * 0.10;        B
}
```

we separated these three things. these used to be one function

this function is interesting! it ties together three concepts

these three functions haven't changed

🧠 Brain break

There's more to go, but let's take a break for questions

Q: **Why are we categorizing the functions into utility, cart, and business rule again?**

A: Good question. This is just a preview of some of the design skills we'll get to later. Eventually, we will want to organize these groupings into distinct and separate layers. But it's good to see the same things a few times to help it sink in.

Q: **So what is the difference between a business rule and a cart operation? Isn't this an e-commerce store? Isn't the whole business about shopping carts?**

A: Imagine it like this: Most e-commerce stores have shopping carts. We can imagine these shopping cart operations existing at any number of stores. They are generic for e-commerce stores. However, the business rules are particular to the operations of this business, MegaMart. If we went to another store, we would expect a shopping cart, but we wouldn't expect to see the same free shipping rule.

Q: **Can a function be both a business rule and a cart operation?**

A: Great question! Well, at this point, yes. But it is a code smell we might want to address when we start talking about layers. If business rules have to know that the cart is an array, that might be a problem. Business rules change faster than lower-level constructs like shopping carts. If we were going to keep going with the design, we'd want to pull those out in some way. For now, we'll leave it as it is.

It's your turn

`update_shipping_icons()` is our largest function—it is probably doing the most. Following, you'll see a list of things it's doing, grouped into categories:

```
function update_shipping_icons(cart) {
  var buy_buttons = get_buy_buttons_dom();
  for(var i = 0; i < buy_buttons.length; i++) {
    var button = buy_buttons[i];
    var item = button.item;
    var new_cart = add_item(cart, item);
    if(gets_free_shipping(new_cart))
      button.show_free_shipping_icon();
    else
      button.hide_free_shipping_icon();
  }
}
```

Things this function does

1. Getting all buttons

2. Looping through buttons

3. Getting the button's items

4. Creating a new cart with that item

5. Checking whether the cart requires free shipping

6. Showing or hiding the icons

buy button operations

cart and item operations

DOM operation

Your task is to pull those things apart into functions that deal only with one category. Give it a shot. There are many ways to do it correctly.

use this space to write your code

Answer

There are many ways to pull this function apart. Here is one way that tries to keep clear what is doing what. You could have pulled it apart in an entirely different way, and that's okay.

buy button operation

```
function update_shipping_icons(cart) {
  var buy_buttons = get_buy_buttons_dom();
  for(var i = 0; i < buy_buttons.length; i++) {
    var button = buy_buttons[i];
    var item = button.item;
    var hasFreeShipping =
      gets_free_shipping_with_item(cart, item);
    set_free_shipping_icon(button, hasFreeShipping);
  }
}
```

1. getting all buttons

2. looping through buttons

3. getting the button's item

cart and item operation

```
function gets_free_shipping_with_item(cart, item) {
  var new_cart = add_item(cart, item);
  return gets_free_shipping(new_cart);
}
```

4. creating a new cart with that item

5. checking whether the cart requires shipping

DOM operation

```
function set_free_shipping_icon(button, isShown) {
  if(isShown)
    button.show_free_shipping_icon();
  else
    button.hide_free_shipping_icon();
}
```

6. showing or hiding the icons

There is certainly more that could be done. This arrangement has the advantage of separating button operations from item and cart operations. This was a useful exercise. However, the code was okay as it was, so let's just leave it going forward.

Smaller functions and more calculations

Here is our new code. Let's tag these functions with A, C, or D to
get a sense of how much code is in which category:

```
                A
var shopping_cart = [];          ◄──── global var: action
                     A
function add_item_to_cart(name, price) {
  var item = make_cart_item(name, price);
  shopping_cart = add_item(shopping_cart, item);
  var total = calc_total(shopping_cart);  ◄── reading global
  set_cart_total_dom(total);                  var: action
  update_shipping_icons(shopping_cart);
  update_tax_dom(total);
}
                        A
function update_shipping_icons(cart) {
  var buttons = get_buy_buttons_dom();
  for(var i = 0; i < buttons.length; i++) {  modifying the
    var button = buttons[i];                 DOM: action
    var item = button.item;
    var new_cart = add_item(cart, item);
    if(gets_free_shipping(new_cart))
      button.show_free_shipping_icon();  ◄──
    else
      button.hide_free_shipping_icon();
  }
}
                    A             modifying the
function update_tax_dom(total) {  DOM: action
  set_tax_dom(calc_tax(total));
}
                    C
function add_element_last(array, elem) {
  var new_array = array.slice();
  new_array.push(elem);  ◄──── no implicit inputs or outputs
  return new_array;
}
               C
function add_item(cart, item) {      no implicit inputs or outputs
  return add_element_last(cart, item); ◄──
}
                  C
function make_cart_item(name, price) {
  return {
    name: name,  ◄────── no implicit inputs or outputs
    price: price
  };
}
              C
function calc_total(cart) {
  var total = 0;
  for(var i = 0; i < cart.length; i++) {
    var item = cart[i];               no implicit inputs or outputs
    total += item.price;  ◄──
  }
  return total;
}
                 C
function gets_free_shipping(cart) {   no implicit inputs or outputs
  return calc_total(cart) >= 20;  ◄──
}
              C
function calc_tax(amount) {      no implicit inputs or outputs
  return amount * 0.10;  ◄──
}
```

> **Key**
>
> **A** Action
> **C** Calculation
> **D** Data

> *Remember:*
>
> We only have to
> find one action in a
> function for the
> whole function to be
> an action.

Conclusion

Kim's design guidance seems to have helped the organization of our code. We see that our actions now don't need to know the structure of our data. And we are starting to see a number of useful and reusable interface functions emerge.

And it's a good thing we've done this now, because although MegaMart does not know it yet, there are more bugs lurking in the shopping cart. What are they? We'll get to that! But first, we need to take a closer look at immutability.

Summary

- In general, we want to eliminate implicit inputs and outputs by replacing them with arguments and return values.

- Design is about pulling things apart. They can always be put back together.

- As we pull things apart, and as functions have single responsibilities, we will find that they are easy to organize around concepts.

Up next . . .

We will come back to design soon in chapter 8. In the next two chapters, we will take a close look at immutability. How do we implement it in new code while still being able to interact with existing code?

Staying immutable in a mutable language | 6

In this chapter

- Apply a copy-on-write discipline to ensure that data is not changed.
- Develop copy-on-write operations for arrays and objects.
- Make copy-on-write work well for deeply nested data.

We've been talking about immutability, and we've even implemented it in some places. In this chapter, we're going to dive deep. We'll learn to make immutable versions of all of the common JavaScript array and object operations we're used to using.

Can immutability be applied everywhere?

We've already implemented some shopping cart operations using a copy-on-write discipline. Remember: That means we made a copy, modified the copy, then returned the copy. But there are a number of shopping cart operations we haven't done yet. Here is a list of the operations we need or might need for the shopping cart and for shopping cart items:

Vocab time

We say data is *nested* when there are data structures within data structures, like an array full of objects. The objects are *nested* in the array. Think of *nesting* as in Russian nesting dolls—dolls within dolls within dolls.

We say data is *deeply nested* when the nesting goes on for a while. It's a relative term, but an example might be objects within objects within arrays within objects within objects . . . The nesting can go on a long time.

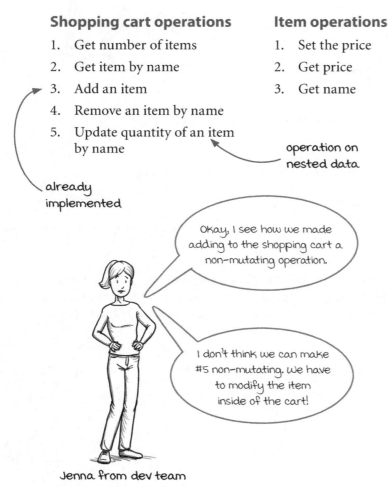

Shopping cart operations

1. Get number of items
2. Get item by name
3. Add an item
4. Remove an item by name
5. Update quantity of an item by name

Item operations

1. Set the price
2. Get price
3. Get name

operation on nested data

already implemented

Okay, I see how we made adding to the shopping cart a non-mutating operation.

I don't think we can make #5 non-mutating. We have to modify the item inside of the cart!

Jenna from dev team

Jenna is skeptical that all of these operations can be done immutably. The fifth operation is harder, because it is modifying an item inside of a shopping cart. We call that *nested data*. How can we implement immutability on nested data? Well, let's find out.

Categorizing operations into reads, writes, or both

We can categorize an operation as either a read or a write

Let's look at each of our operations in a new way. Some of our operations are *reads*. We are getting some information out of the data without modifying it. These are easy cases because nothing is being modified. Those don't need any other work. Reads that get information from their arguments are calculations.

The rest of our operations are *writes*. They modify the data in some way. These will require a discipline, because we don't want to modify any of the values that may be in use somewhere else.

> **Reads**
> • Get information out of data
> • Do not modify the data
>
> **Writes**
> • Modify the data

Shopping cart operations

1. Get number of items. }
2. Get item by name. } reads
3. Add an item.
4. Remove an item by name. }
5. Update quantity by name. } writes

Three of our shopping cart operations are writes. We will want to implement these using an immutable discipline. As we've seen before, the discipline we'll use is called *copy-on-write*. It's the same discipline used in languages like Haskell and Clojure. The difference is those languages implement the discipline for you.

Because we're in JavaScript, mutable data is the default, so we the programmers have to apply the discipline ourselves explicitly in the code.

What about an operation that reads and writes?

Sometimes we may want to modify the data (a write) *and* get some information out of it (read) at the same time. If you're curious about that, we will get to that in just a few pages. The short answer is "Yes, you can do that." You'll see the long answer on page 122.

Item operations

1. Set the price. } write
2. Get the price. }
3. Get the name. } reads

 **Language safari**

Immutable data is a common feature in functional programming languages, though not all of them have it by default. Here are some functional languages that are immutable by default:
• Haskell
• Clojure
• Elm
• Purescript
• Erlang
• Elixir

Others have immutable data in addition to mutable data by default. And some trust the programmer to apply the discipline where they choose.

The three steps of the copy-on-write discipline

The copy-on-write discipline is just three steps in your code. If you implement these steps, you are doing copy-on-write. And if you replace every part of your code that modifies the global shopping cart with a copy-on-write, the shopping cart will never change. It will be immutable.

There are three steps of the copy-on-write discipline to be performed whenever you want to modify something that is immutable:

1. Make a copy.

2. Modify the copy (as much as you want!).

3. Return the copy.

> ### Reads
> - Get information out of data
> - Do not modify the data
>
> ### Writes
> - Modify the data

Let's look at the function `add_element_last()` from the last chapter, which implements copy-on-write:

```
function add_element_last(array, elem) {
    var new_array = array.slice();
    new_array.push(elem);
    return new_array;
}
```

we want to modify array

1. make a copy

2. modify the copy

3. return the copy

Why does this work? How does this avoid modifying the array?

1. We make a copy of the array, but never modify the original.

2. The copy is within the local scope of the function. That means no other code has access to it while we modify it.

3. After we're done modifying it, we let it leave the scope (we return it). Nothing will modify it after that.

So here's a question. Is `add_element_last()` a read or a write?

It doesn't modify the data, and now it returns information, so it must be a read! We've essentially converted a write into a read. We'll talk more about that soon.

Copy-on-write converts writes into reads.

Converting a write to a read with copy-on-write

Let's look at another operation that modifies the cart. This one removes an item from the cart based on the name.

```
function remove_item_by_name(cart, name) {
  var idx = null;
  for(var i = 0; i < cart.length; i++) {
    if(cart[i].name === name)
      idx = i;
  }
  if(idx !== null)
    cart.splice(idx, 1);
}
```

cart.splice() modifies the cart array

Is an array the best data structure to represent a shopping cart? Probably not. But this is the system as MegaMart implemented it. For now, at least, we have to work with what we found.

What does `cart.splice()` do?

`.splice()` is a method on arrays that lets you remove items from an array.

remove one item

```
cart.splice(idx, 1)
```

at index idx

`.splice()` can do other things with different combinations of arguments, but we don't use those things here.

This function modifies the cart (via `cart.splice()`). If we pass in the global `shopping_cart` to `remove_item _by_name()`, it will modify the global shopping cart.

However, we don't want to modify the shopping cart anymore. We want to treat our shopping cart as immutable. Let's apply a copy-on-write discipline to the `remove_item_by_name()` function.

We have a function that modifies the shopping cart, and we want it to use a copy-on-write discipline. First, we'll make a copy of the cart.

make a copy of the cart and save it to a local var

Current

```
function remove_item_by_name(cart, name) {

  var idx = null;
  for(var i = 0; i < cart.length; i++) {
    if(cart[i].name === name)
      idx = i;
  }
  if(idx !== null)
    cart.splice(idx, 1);
}
```

With copy of argument

```
function remove_item_by_name(cart, name) {
  var new_cart = cart.slice();
  var idx = null;
  for(var i = 0; i < cart.length; i++) {
    if(cart[i].name === name)
      idx = i;
  }
  if(idx !== null)
    cart.splice(idx, 1);
}
```

We're making a copy, but we're not doing anything with it. On the next page, we will change all code that modifies the cart argument to modify the copy of the cart.

We just made a copy; now we need to use it. Let's replace all usages of the original cart with our new copy.

> **Rules of copy-on-write**
>
> ✔ 1. Make a copy.
>   2. Modify the copy.
>   3. Return the copy.

Current

```
function remove_item_by_name(cart, name) {
  var new_cart = cart.slice();
  var idx = null;
  for(var i = 0; i < cart.length; i++) {
    if(cart[i].name === name)
      idx = i;
  }
  if(idx !== null)
    cart.splice(idx, 1);
}
```

Modifying copy

```
function remove_item_by_name(cart, name) {
  var new_cart = cart.slice();
  var idx = null;
  for(var i = 0; i < new_cart.length; i++) {
    if(new_cart[i].name === name)
      idx = i;
  }
  if(idx !== null)
    new_cart.splice(idx, 1);
}
```

Now we aren't modifying the original at all. But the copy is stuck inside the function. Next, let's let it out by returning it.

> **Rules of copy-on-write**
>
> ✔ 1. Make a copy.
> ✔ 2. Modify the copy.
>   3. Return the copy.

On the last page, we had gotten rid of all the modifications to the cart array. Instead, we modified a copy. Now we can do the last step of the copy-on-write and return the copy.

At this point, we have a fully working copy-on-write implementation of the function. The only thing left to do now is to change the code where we used it.

Wherever we use this function, we need to make a small change. For example, the delete from cart button calls this function, which used to modify the global cart. Since it no longer modifies the cart, we have to reassign. Here's an example.

> *Rules of copy-on-write*
> ✔ 1. Make a copy.
> ✔ 2. Modify the copy.
>   3. Return the copy.

Current

```
function remove_item_by_name(cart, name) {
  var new_cart = cart.slice();
  var idx = null;
  for(var i = 0; i < new_cart.length; i++) {
    if(new_cart[i].name === name)
      idx = i;
  }
  if(idx !== null)
    new_cart.splice(idx, 1);

}
```

Returning the copy

```
function remove_item_by_name(cart, name) {
  var new_cart = cart.slice();
  var idx = null;
  for(var i = 0; i < new_cart.length; i++) {
    if(new_cart[i].name === name)
      idx = i;
  }
  if(idx !== null)
    new_cart.splice(idx, 1);
  return new_cart;
}
```

return the copy

And now we have a fully working copy-on-write version of the function. The only thing left to do now is to change how we use it. Let's do that next.

> *Rules of copy-on-write*
> ✔ 1. Make a copy.
> ✔ 2. Modify the copy.
> ✔ 3. Return the copy.

On the last page, we had gotten rid of all the modifications to the cart array. Instead, we modified a copy. Now we can do the last step of the copy-on-write and return the copy.

this function used to modify the global

now we have to modify the global in the caller

Current

```
function delete_handler(name) {

  remove_item_by_name(shopping_cart, name);
  var total = calc_total(shopping_cart);
  set_cart_total_dom(total);
  update_shipping_icons(shopping_cart);
  update_tax_dom(total);

}
```

With copy-on-write

```
function delete_handler(name) {
  shopping_cart =
    remove_item_by_name(shopping_cart, name);
  var total = calc_total(shopping_cart);
  set_cart_total_dom(total);
  update_shipping_icons(shopping_cart);
  update_tax_dom(total);

}
```

We will need to go to each call site for remove_item_by_name() and assign its return value to the global shopping_cart. We won't do that here. It's pretty boring.

Complete diff from mutating to copy-on-write

We've made a few changes over a few pages. Let's see it all in one place:

Original mutating version

```
  var idx = null;
  for(var i = 0; i < cart.length; i++) {
    if(cart[i].name === name)
      idx = i;
  }
  if(idx !== null)
    cart.splice(idx, 1);

}

function delete_handler(name) {

  remove_item_by_name(shopping_cart, name);
  var total = calc_total(shopping_cart);
  set_cart_total_dom(total);
  update_shipping_icons(shopping_cart);
  update_tax_dom(total);
}
```

Copy-on-write version

```
function remove_item_by_name(cart, name) {
  var new_cart = cart.slice();
  var idx = null;
  for(var i = 0; i < new_cart.length; i++) {
    if(new_cart[i].name === name)
      idx = i;
  }
  if(idx !== null)
    new_cart.splice(idx, 1);
  return new_cart;
}

function delete_handler(name) {
  shopping_cart =
    remove_item_by_name(shopping_cart, name);
  var total = calc_total(shopping_cart);
  set_cart_total_dom(total);
  update_shipping_icons(shopping_cart);
  update_tax_dom(total);
}
```

These copy-on-write operations are generalizable

We are going to do very similar copy-on-write operations all over.
We can generalize the ones we've written so that they are more
reusable, just like we did with add_element_last().

Let's start with array's .splice() method. We use .splice()
in remove_item_by_name().

Original

```
function removeItems(array, idx, count) {

  array.splice(idx, count);

}
```

Copy-on-write

```
function removeItems(array, idx, count) {
  var copy = array.slice();
  copy.splice(idx, count);
  return copy;
}
```

Now we can use it in remove_item_by_name().

Previous copy-on-write

```
function remove_item_by_name(cart, name) {
  var new_cart = cart.slice();
  var idx = null;
  for(var i = 0; i < new_cart.length; i++) {
    if(new_cart[i].name === name)
      idx = i;
  }
  if(idx !== null)
    new_cart.removeItems(idx, 1);
  return new_cart;
}
```

removeItems()
copies the
array so we
don't have to

Copy-on-write using splice()

```
function remove_item_by_name(cart, name) {

  var idx = null;
  for(var i = 0; i < cart.length; i++) {
    if(cart[i].name === name)
      idx = i;
  }
  if(idx !== null)
    return removeItems(cart, idx, 1);
  return cart;
}
```

bonus! we don't have to
make a copy of the array
if we don't modify it

Because we will likely use these operations a lot, implementing
them in a reusable way can save a lot of effort. We won't need to
copy the boilerplate of copying the array or object all over.

JavaScript arrays at a glance

One of the basic collection types in JavaScript is the *array*. Arrays in JavaScript represent ordered collections of values. They are heterogeneous, meaning they can have values of different types in them at the same time. You can access elements by index. JavaScript's arrays are different from what are called *arrays* in other languages. You can extend and shrink them—unlike arrays in Java or C.

Lookup by index `[idx]`

This gets the element at `idx`. Indexes start at 0.

```
> var array = [1, 2, 3, 4];
> array[2]
3
```

Set an element `[] =`

The assignment operator will mutate an array.

```
> var array = [1, 2, 3, 4];
> array[2] = "abc"
"abc"
> array
[1, 2, "abc", 4]
```

Length `.length`

This contains the number of elements in the array. It's not a method, so don't use parentheses.

```
> var array = [1, 2, 3, 4];
> array.length
4
```

Add to the end `.push(el)`

This mutates the array by adding `el` to the end and returns the new length of the array.

```
> var array = [1, 2, 3, 4];
> array.push(10);
5
> array
[1, 2, 3, 4, 10]
```

Remove from the end `.pop()`

This mutates the array by dropping the last element and returns the value that was dropped.

```
> var array = [1, 2, 3, 4];
> array.pop();
4
> array
[1, 2, 3]
```

Add to the front `.unshift(el)`

This mutates the array by adding `el` to the array at the beginning and returns the new length.

```
> var array = [1, 2, 3, 4];
> array.unshift(10);
5
> array
[10, 1, 2, 3, 4]
```

Remove from the front `.shift()`

This mutates the array by dropping the first element (index 0) and returns the value that was dropped.

```
> var array = [1, 2, 3, 4];
> array.shift()
1
> array
[2, 3, 4]
```

Copy an array `.slice()`

This creates and returns a shallow copy of the array.

```
> var array = [1, 2, 3, 4];
> array.slice()
[1, 2, 3, 4]
```

Remove items `.splice(idx, num)`

This mutates the array by removing `num` items starting at `idx` and returns the removed items.

```
> var array = [1, 2, 3, 4, 5, 6];
> array.splice(2, 3); // remove 3 elements
[3, 4, 5]
> array
[1, 2, 6]
```

It's your turn

Here's an operation for adding a contact to a mailing list. It adds email addresses to the end of a list stored in a global variable. It's being called by the form submission handler.

```
var mailing_list = [];

function add_contact(email) {
  mailing_list.push(email);
}

function submit_form_handler(event) {
  var form = event.target;
  var email = form.elements["email"].value;
  add_contact(email);
}
```

Your task is to convert this into a copy-on-write form. Here are some clues:

1. add_contact() shouldn't access the global variable. It should take a mailing_list as an argument, make a copy, modify the copy, then return the copy.

2. Wherever you call add_contact(), you need to assign its return value to the mailing_list global variable.

Modify the code provided to make it follow a copy-on-write discipline. The answer is on the next page.

write your answer here

 **Answer**

We had two things we needed to do:

1. `add_contact()` shouldn't access the global variable. It should take a `mailing_list` as an argument, make a copy, modify the copy, then return the copy.

2. Wherever you call `add_contact()`, you need to assign its return value to the `mailing_list` global variable.

Here is how we could modify the code:

Original

```
var mailing_list = [];

function add_contact(email) {


  mailing_list.push(email);

}

function submit_form_handler(event) {
  var form = event.target;
  var email =
    form.elements["email"].value;

  add_contact(email);
}
```

Copy-on-write

```
var mailing_list = [];

function add_contact(mailing_list,
                     email) {
  var list_copy = mailing_list.slice();
  list_copy.push(email);
  return list_copy;
}

function submit_form_handler(event) {
  var form = event.target;
  var email =
    form.elements["email"].value;
  mailing_list =
    add_contact(mailing_list, email);
}
```

What to do if an operation is a read and a write

Sometimes a function plays two roles at the same time: It modifies a value and it returns a value. The `.shift()` method is a good example. Let's see an example:

```
var a = [1, 2, 3, 4];
var b = a.shift();
console.log(b); // prints 1
console.log(a); // prints [2, 3, 4]
```

returns a value

var a was modified

`.shift()` returns the first element of the array at the same time as it modifies the array. It's both a read and a write.

How can you convert this to a copy-on-write?

In copy-on-write, we are essentially converting a write to a read, which means we need to return a value. But `.shift()` is already a read, so it already has a return value. How can we make this work? There are two approaches.

1. Split the function into read and write.

2. Return two values from the function.

We will see both. When you have the choice, you should prefer the first approach. It more cleanly separates the responsibilities. As we saw in chapter 5, design is about pulling things apart.

We'll see the first approach first.

Two approaches
1. Split function.
2. Return two values.

Splitting a function that does a read and write

There are two steps to this technique. The first is to split the read from the write. The second is to convert the write to a copy-on-write operation. That is done in the same way as any write operation.

Splitting the operation into read and write

The read of the `.shift()` method is simply its return value. The return value of `.shift()` is the first element of the array. So we just write a calculation that returns the first element of the array. It's a read, so it shouldn't modify anything. Because it doesn't have any hidden inputs or outputs, it's a calculation.

```
function first_element(array) {
  return array[0];
}
```

just a function that returns the first element (or undefined if the list is empty). it's a calculation

We don't need to convert `first_element()`, because as a read, it won't modify the array.

The write of the `.shift()` method doesn't need to be written, but we should wrap up the behavior of `.shift()` in its own function. We'll discard the return value of `.shift()` just to emphasize that we won't use the result.

```
function drop_first(array) {
  array.shift();
}
```

perform the shift but drop the return value

Convert the write into a copy-on-write

We have successfully separated the read from the write. But the write (`drop_first()`) mutates its argument. We should convert it to copy-on-write.

Mutating

```
function drop_first(array) {

  array.shift();

}
```

Copy-on-write

```
function drop_first(array) {
  var array_copy = array.slice();
  array_copy.shift();
  return array_copy;
}
```

textbook copy-on-write here

Splitting the read from the write is the preferred approach because it gives us all of the pieces we need. We can use them separately or together. Before, we were forced to use them together. Now we have the choice.

Returning two values from one function

This second approach, like the first approach, also has two steps. The first step is to wrap up the `.shift()` method in a function we can modify. That function is going to be both a read and a write. The second step is to convert it to be just a read.

Wrap up the operation

The first one is to wrap up the `.shift()` method in a function we control and can modify. But in this case, we don't want to discard the return value.

```
function shift(array) {
  return array.shift();
}
```

Convert the read and write to a read

In this case, we need to convert the `shift()` function we've written to make a copy, modify the copy, and return both the first element and the modified copy. Let's see how we can do that.

Mutating

```
function shift(array) {


  return array.shift();




}
```

Copy-on-write

```
function shift(array) {
  var array_copy = array.slice();
  var first = array_copy.shift();
  return {
    first : first,
    array : array_copy
  };
}
```

we use an object to return two separate values

Another option

Another option is to use the approach we took on the previous page and combine the two return values into an object:

```
function shift(array) {
  return {
    first : first_element(array),
    array : drop_first(array)
  };
}
```

Because both of those functions are calculations, we don't need to worry about the combination; it will also be a calculation.

It's your turn

We just wrote copy-on-write versions of the `.shift()` method on arrays. Arrays also have a `.pop()` method, which removes the last item in the array and returns it. Like `.shift()`, `.pop()` is both a read and a write.

Your task is to convert this read and write to a read in the two different versions. Here is an example of how `.pop()` works:

```
var a = [1, 2, 3, 4];
var b = a.pop();
console.log(b); // prints 4
console.log(a); // prints [1, 2, 3]
```

Convert `.pop()` into copy-on-write versions.

1. Split the read and write into two functions

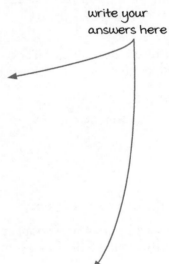

write your
answers here

2. Return two values from one function

 **Answer**

Our task was to rewrite `.pop()` to use a copy-on-write discipline. We will implement it in two separate ways.

1. Split the read and write into two operations

The first thing we'll need to do is create two wrapper functions to implement the read and write portions separately.

```
function last_element(array) {
  return array[array.length - 1];
}
```
← this is a read

```
function drop_last(array) {
  array.pop();
}
```
← this is a write

The read is done. We won't need to modify it anymore. But the write will need to be converted into a copy-on-write operation.

Original

```
function drop_last(array) {

  array.pop();

}
```

Copy-on-write

```
function drop_last(array) {
  var array_copy = array.slice();
  array_copy.pop();
  return array_copy;
}
```

2. Return two values

We start by creating a wrapper function for the operation. It doesn't add any new functionality, but it will give us something to modify.

```
function pop(array) {
  return array.pop();
}
```

Then we modify it to follow a copy-on-write discipline.

Original

```
function pop(array) {

  return array.pop();



}
```

Copy-on-write

```
function pop(array) {
  var array_copy = array.slice();
  var first = array_copy.pop();
  return {
    first : first,
    array : array_copy
  };
}
```

🧠 Brain break

There's more to go, but let's take a break for questions

Q: How is the copy-on-write `add_element_to_cart()` **a read?**

A: The function `add_element_to_cart()` that implements the copy-on-write discipline is a read because it doesn't modify the cart. You can look at it like it's asking a question. The question might be "What would this cart look like if it also had this element?"

This last question is a hypothetical question. A lot of important thinking and planning is done with answers to hypothetical questions. Remember, calculations are often used for planning. We'll see more examples in the pages to come.

Q: The shopping cart uses an array, and we have to search through the array to find the element with the given name. Is array the best data structure for this? Wouldn't an associative data structure like an object be better?

A: Yes, it may be better to use an object. We often find that, in existing code, data structure decisions have already been made and we can't easily change them. That's the case here. We'll have to continue with the shopping cart as an array.

Q: It seems like a lot of work to implement immutability. Is it worth it? Can it be easier?

A: JavaScript doesn't have much of a standard library. It can feel like we're always writing routines that should be part of the language. On top of that, JavaScript does not help us much with copy-on-write. In many languages, you would have to write your own routines for copy-on-write. It's worth taking the time to ask if it's worth the work.

First, you don't have to write new functions. You can do it inline. However, it's often more work. There's a lot of repeated code, and each time you write it, you have to be focused enough to get it right. It's much better to write the operations once and reuse them.

Fortunately, there are not that many operations that you'll need. Writing these operations may feel tedious at first, but soon you won't be writing new ones from scratch. You'll be reusing the existing ones and composing them to make newer, more powerful ones.

Because it can be a lot of work up front, I suggest only writing the functions when you need them.

It's your turn

Write a copy-on-write version of `.push()`, the array method. Remember, `.push()` adds one element to the end of an array.

```
function push(array, elem) {
```
← write your implementation here

```
}
```

Answer

```
function push(array, elem) {
  var copy = array.slice();
  copy.push(elem);
  return copy;
}
```

It's your turn

Refactor add_contact() to use the new push() function from the last exercise. Here is the existing code:

```
function add_contact(mailing_list, email) {
  var list_copy = mailing_list.slice();
  list_copy.push(email);
  return list_copy;
}


function add_contact(mailing_list, email) {




}
```

write your implementation here

Answer

```
function add_contact(mailing_list,
                     email) {
  var list_copy = mailing_list.slice();
  list_copy.push(email);
  return list_copy;
}
```

```
function add_contact(mailing_list,
                     email) {

  return push(mailing_list, email);

}
```

✎ It's your turn

Write a function `arraySet()` that is a copy-on-write version of the array assignment operator.

Example:

make a copy-on-write
version of this operation

write your
implementation here

```
a[15] = 2;

function arraySet(array, idx, value) {



}
```

✎ Answer

```
function arraySet(array, idx, value) {
  var copy = array.slice();
  copy[idx] = value;
  return copy;
}
```

Reads to immutable data structures are calculations

I think I get what these reads and writes have to do with actions, calculations, and data.

Reads to mutable data are actions. But reads to immutable data are calculations.

Writes modify data, so if we get rid of all of the writes, the data is effectively immutable.

Kim from dev team

Reads to mutable data are actions

If we read from a mutable value, we could get a different answer each time we read it, so reading mutable data is an action.

Writes make a given piece of data mutable

Writes modify data, so they are what make the data mutable.

If there are no writes to a piece of data, it is immutable

If we get rid of all of the writes by converting them to reads, the data won't ever change after it is created. That means it's immutable.

Reads to immutable data structures are calculations

Once we do make the data immutable, all of those reads become calculations.

Converting writes to reads makes more code calculations

The more data structures we treat as immutable, the more code we have in calculations and the less we have in actions.

Applications have state that changes over time

We now have the tools to go through all of our code and convert everything to use immutable data everywhere. We convert all of the writes to reads. But there is a big problem that we haven't faced: If everything is immutable, how can your application keep track of changes over time? How can the user add an item to their cart if nothing ever changes?

Kim makes a good point. We've implemented immutability everywhere, but we need one place that is still mutable so we can keep track of changes over time. We do have that place. It's the `shopping_cart` global variable.

By definition, we need mutable data. How will the application work if the cart can't change?

We are assigning new values to the `shopping_cart` global variable. It always points to the current value of the cart. In fact, we could say we are *swapping* in new values of the shopping cart.

Kim from dev team

swapping
1. read
2. modify
3. write

```
shopping_cart = add_item(shopping_cart, shoes);
```

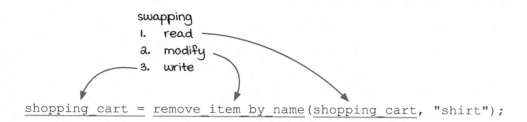

swapping
1. read
2. modify
3. write

```
shopping_cart = remove_item_by_name(shopping_cart, "shirt");
```

The `shopping_cart` global variable is always going to point to the current value, and whenever we need to modify it, we'll use this swapping pattern. This is a very common and powerful pattern in functional programming. Swapping makes it really easy to implement an undo command. We will revisit swapping and make it more robust in part 2.

Immutable data structures are fast enough

Let's be very clear: In general, immutable data structures use more memory and are slower to operate on than their mutable equivalents.

Every time we change something, we make a copy? That can't be efficient!

That said, there are many high-performance systems written using immutable data, including high-frequency trading systems, where performance is vitally important. That's pretty good empirical proof that immutable data structures are fast enough for common applications. However, here are some more arguments.

George from testing

We can always optimize later

Every application has performance bottlenecks that are hard to predict while you're developing. Common wisdom dictates that we avoid optimizing before we're sure the part we're optimizing will make a difference.

Functional programmers prefer immutable data by default. Only if they find that something is too slow will they optimize for performance with mutable data.

Garbage collectors are really fast

Most languages (but certainly not all) have had years of research and hard work, making the garbage collector very fast. Some garbage collectors have been optimized so much that freeing memory is only one or two machine instructions. We can lean on all of that hard work. However, do try it for youself in your language.

We're not copying as much as you might think at first

If you look at the copy-on-write code that we've written so far, none of it is copying that much. For instance, if we have 100 items in our shopping cart, we're only copying an array of 100 references. We aren't copying all of the items themselves. When you just copy the top level of a data structure, it's called a *shallow copy*. When you do a shallow copy, the two copies share a lot of references to the same objects in memory. This is known as *structural sharing*.

Functional programming languages have fast implementations

We are writing our own immutable data routines on top of JavaScript's built-in data structures, using very straightforward code. This is fine for our application. However, languages that support functional programming often have immutable data structures built-in. These data structures are much more efficient than what we are doing. For instance, Clojure's built in data structures are very efficient and were even the source of inspiration for other languages' implementations.

How are they more efficient? They share a lot more structure between copies, which means less memory is used and less pressure is put on the garbage collector. They're still based on copy-on-write.

Copy-on-write operations on objects

So far, we've only made copy-on-write operations for JavaScript arrays. We need a way to set the price on a shopping cart item, which is represented with an object. The steps are the same:

1. Make a copy.

2. Modify the copy.

3. Return the copy.

We can make a copy of an array with the `.slice()` method. But there's no equivalent way to make a copy of an object in JavaScript. What JavaScript does have, however, is a way of copying all keys and values from one object to another. If we copy all of the keys and values into an empty object, we've effectively made a copy. This method is called `Object.assign()`. Here's how you use it to make a copy:

```
var object = {a: 1, b: 2};
var object_copy = Object.assign({}, object);
```

 how you copy an
object in JavaScript

We'll use this method for copying objects. Here's how we can use it to implement `set_price()`, which sets the price of an item object:

Original

```
function setPrice(item, new_price) {

  item.price = new_price;

}
```

Copy-on-write

```
function setPrice(item, new_price) {
  var item_copy = Object.assign({}, item);
  item_copy.price = new_price;
  return item_copy;
}
```

The basic idea is just the same as for arrays. You can apply this to any data structure at all. Just follow the three steps.

Vocab time

Shallow copies only duplicate the top-level data structure of nested data. For instance, if you have an array of objects, a shallow copy will only duplicate the array. The objects inside will be shared with both the original and the copy of the array. We will compare shallow and deep copies later on.

When two pieces of nested data share some of their references, it is called *structural sharing*. When it's all immutable, structural sharing is very safe. Structural sharing uses less memory and is faster than copying everything.

JavaScript objects at a glance

JavaScript's Objects are very much like hash maps or associative arrays that you find in other languages. Objects in JavaScript are collections of key/value pairs, where the keys are unique. The keys are always strings, but the values can be any type. Here are the operations we will use in our examples:

Look up by key `[key]`

This looks up the value corresponding to `key`. If the key doesn't exist, you'll get `undefined`.

```
> var object = {a: 1, b: 2};
> object["a"]
1
```

Look up by key `.key`

You can also use a dot notation to access the values. This is convenient if `key` fits into JavaScript's tokenization syntax rules.

```
> var object = {a: 1, b: 2};
> object.a
1
```

Set value for key `.key` or `[key]` `=`

You can assign a value to a key using either syntax, which mutates the object. It sets the value for key. If key exists, it replaces the value. If the key doesn't exist, it adds to it.

```
> var object = {a: 1, b: 2};
> object["a"] = 7;
7
> object
{a: 7, b: 2}
> object.c = 10;
10
> object
{a: 7, b: 2, c: 10}
```

Remove a key/value pair `delete`

This method mutates the object by removing a key/value pair given the key. You can use either look-up syntax.

```
> var object = {a: 1, b: 2};
> delete object["a"];
true
> object
{b: 2}
```

Copy an object `Object.assign(a, b)`

This one is complicated. `Object.assign()` copies all key/values pairs from object b to object a (mutating it). We can use it to make a copy of b by copying all key/value pairs to an empty object.

```
> var object = {x: 1, y: 2};
> Object.assign({}, object);
{x: 1, y: 2}
```

List the keys `Object.keys()`

If we want to iterate through the key/value pairs in an object, we can do it indirectly by asking the object for all of its keys using the function `Object.keys()`. That returns an array of the keys in an object, which we can then loop through.

```
> var object = {a: 1, b: 2};
> Object.keys(object)
["a", "b"]
```

It's your turn

Write a function `objectSet()` that is a copy-on-write version of the object assignment operator.

Example:

```
o["price"] = 37;
```

make a copy-on-write
version of this

```
function objectSet(object, key, value) {
```

write your
implementation here

```
}
```

Answer

```
function objectSet(object, key, value) {
  var copy = Object.assign({}, object);
  copy[key] = value;
  return copy;
}
```

It's your turn

Refactor `setPrice()` to use `objectSet()`, which we just wrote in the last exercise.
  Existing code:

```
function setPrice(item, new_price) {
  var item_copy = Object.assign({}, item);
  item_copy.price = new_price;
  return item_copy;
}
```

Write a function `setQuantity()`, using `objectSet()`, that sets the quantity of an item. Make sure it implements the copy-on-write discipline.

```
function setQuantity(item, new_quantity) {
```

write your
implementation here

```
}
```

Answer

```
function setQuantity(item, new_quantity) {
  return objectSet(item, "quantity", new_quantity);
}
```

📝 It's your turn

Write a function setQuantity(), using objectSet(), that sets the quantity of an item. Make sure it implements the copy-on-write discipline.

```
function setQuantity(item, new_quantity) {



}
```

write your implementation here ←

📝 Answer

```
function setQuantity(item, new_quantity) {
  return objectSet(item, "quantity", new_quantity);
}
```

It's your turn

Write a copy-on-write version of the delete operator, which removes a key from an object.
  Example:

```
> var a = {x : 1};
> delete a["x"];          make a copy-on-write
> a                        version of this
{}
                                   write your
                                   implementation here
function objectDelete(object, key) {




}
```

Answer

```
function objectDelete(object, key) {
  var copy = Object.assign({}, object);
  delete copy[key];
  return copy;
}
```

Converting nested writes to reads

We still have one write left to convert to a read on our shopping cart. The operation that updates the price of an item given its name is still a write. However, that operation is interesting because it is modifying a nested data structure. It is modifying the item object inside of the shopping cart array.

It's usually easier to convert the write for the deeper operation first. We implemented `setPrice()` in the exercise on page 137. We can use `setPrice()`, which operates on items, inside of `setPriceByName()`, which operates on carts.

typical copy-on-write pattern of copying and modifying the copy

Original

```
function setPriceByName(cart, name, price) {

  for(var i = 0; i < cart.length; i++) {
    if(cart[i].name === name)
      cart[i].price =
        price;
  }

}
```

Copy-on-write

```
function setPriceByName(cart, name, price) {
  var cartCopy = cart.slice();
  for(var i = 0; i < cartCopy.length; i++) {
    if(cartCopy[i].name === name)
      cartCopy[i] =
        setPrice(cartCopy[i], price);
  }
  return cartCopy;
}
```

we call a copy-on-write operation to modify the nested item

Nested writes follow the same pattern as non-nested writes. We make a copy, modify the copy, then return the copy. The only difference with nested operations is that we do another copy-on-write operation to modify the nested one.

If we modified the item directly, like we were doing in the original code, then our data would not be immutable. The references in the cart array may not change, but the values they refer to do change. That's unnacceptable. The entire nested data structure has to remain unchanged for it to be immutable.

This is a very important concept. Everything in the nested data structure, from the top to the bottom, must be immutable. When we update a nested piece of data, we need to copy the inner value and all of the values on the way up to the top. It's so important that we'll spend a couple of pages really understanding what is getting copied.

What gets copied?

Let's say we have three items in a shopping cart: a t-shirt, shoes, and socks. Let's take an inventory of our arrays and objects so far. We have one Array (the shopping cart) and three objects (a t-shirt, shoes, and socks in cart).

We want to set the price of the t-shirt to $13. To do that, we use the nested operation `setPriceByName()`, like so:

```
shopping_cart = setPriceByName(shopping_cart, "t-shirt", 13);
```

Let's step through the code and count what gets copied:

```
function setPriceByName(cart, name, price) {
  var cartCopy = cart.slice();                        ⟵ copy array
  for(var i = 0; i < cartCopy.length; i++) {
    if(cartCopy[i].name === name)
      cartCopy[i] = setPrice(cartCopy[i], price);     we call setPrice() only once,
  }                                                   when the loop finds the
  return cartCopy;                                    t-shirt
}

function setPrice(item, new_price) {
  var item_copy = Object.assign({}, item);            copy object
  item_copy.price = new_price;
  return item_copy;
}
```

We started with one array and three objects. What got copied? Well, only one array (the shopping cart) and one object (the t-shirt). Two objects were not copied. What's going on?

We are making shallow copies of nested data, which results in structural sharing. That's a lot of vocabulary words in one sentence. Let's visualize it on the next page.

 **Vocab time**

Let's do a quick vocabulary review of some words we've already seen:
Nested data: Data structures inside data structures; we can talk about the *inner* data structure and the *top-level* data structure
Shallow copy: Copying only the top-level data structure in nested data
Structural sharing: Two nested data structures referencing the same inner data structure

Visualizing shallow copies and structural sharing

We started out with a shopping cart (one array) with three items (three objects). That's four pieces of data total. We want to set the price of the t-shirt to $13.

We then made a shallow copy of the shopping cart. At first, the copy pointed to the same objects in memory.

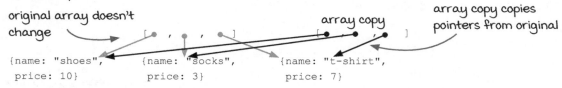

The loop eventually found the t-shirt and called `setPrice()` on it. That function created a shallow copy of the t-shirt Object and changed the price to 13.

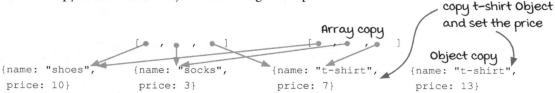

`setPrice()` returned that copy, and `setPriceByName()` assigned it in the array in place of the original t-shirt.

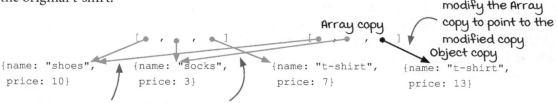

Although we had four pieces of data at the start (one array and three objects), only two of them (one array and one object) had to be copied. The other objects weren't modified so we didn't copy them. The original array and the copy are both pointing to everything that hasn't changed. That's the structural sharing that we've talked about before. As long as we don't modify those shared copies, it is totally safe. Making copies allows us to keep the original and the copy without worrying that it will change.

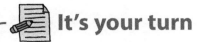 **It's your turn**

Let's imagine we have a `shopping_cart` that has four items:

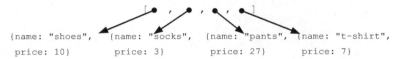

```
                    shopping_cart
                  [ •  ,  •  ,  •  ,  •  ]

{name: "shoes",   {name: "socks",   {name: "pants",   {name: "t-shirt",
 price: 10}        price: 3}         price: 27}        price: 7}
```

When we run this line of code

```
setPriceByName(shopping_cart, "socks", 2);
```

what has to be copied? Circle all of the pieces of data that are copied.

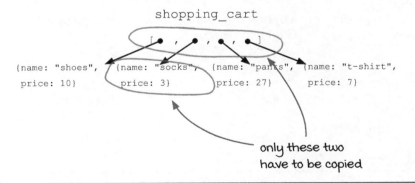 **Answer**

We only have to copy the item that changes and everything on the path up from it. In this case, the "socks" item changes, so it is copied, and the array containing it must change to contain the new copy, so it needs to be copied, too.

```
                    shopping_cart
                  [ •  ,  •  ,  •  ,  •  ]

{name: "shoes",   {name: "socks",   {name: "pants",   {name: "t-shirt",
 price: 10}        price: 3}         price: 27}        price: 7}
```

only these two
have to be copied

It's your turn

Write a copy-on-write version of this nested operation:

```
function setQuantityByName(cart, name, quantity) {
  for(var i = 0; i < cart.length; i++) {
    if(cart[i].name === name)
      cart[i].quantity = quantity;
  }
}


function setQuantityByName(cart, name, quantity) {




}
```

write your implementation here

Answer

```
function setQuantityByName(cart, name, quantity) {
  var cartCopy = cart.slice();
  for(var i = 0; i < cartCopy.length; i++) {
    if(cartCopy[i].name === name)
     cartCopy[i] =
        objectSet(cartCopy[i], 'quantity', quantity);
  }
  return cartCopy;
}
```

Conclusion

In this chapter we learned the ins and outs of the copy-on-write discipline. Although it's the same discipline you find in languages like Clojure and Haskell, in JavaScript you have to do all the work yourself. That's why it's convenient to wrap it up with some utility functions that handle everything for you. If you stick with those wrapper functions, you'll be fine. Sticking with it is why it's called a discipline.

Summary

- In functional programming, we want to use immutable data. It is impossible to write calculations on mutable data.

- Copy-on-write is a discipline for ensuring our data is immutable. It means we make a copy and modify it instead of modifying the original.

- Copy-on-write requires making a shallow copy before modifying the copy, then returning it. It is useful for implementing immutability within code that you control.

- We can implement copy-on-write versions of the basic array and object operations to reduce the amount of boilerplate we have to write.

Up next . . .

The copy-on-write discipline is nice. However, not all of our code will use the wrappers we wrote. Most of us have lots of existing code written without the copy-on-write discipline. We need a way of exchanging data with that code without it changing our data. In the next chapter, we will learn another discipline called *defensive copying*.

In this chapter

- Make defensive copies to protect your code from legacy code and other code you don't trust.

- Compare deep copies to shallow copies.

- Choose when to use defensive copies versus copy-on-write.

We've learned how to maintain immutability in our own code using copy-on-write. But we often have to interact with code that doesn't use the copy-on-write discipline. There are libraries and existing code that we know treat data as mutable. How can you pass your immutable data to it? In this chapter, we learn a practice for maintaining immutability when interacting with code that might change your data.

Immutability with legacy code

It's time again for MegaMart's monthly Black Friday sale (yes, they do one every month). The marketing department wants to promote old inventory to clear it out of the warehouse. The code they have to do that is old and has been added to over time. It works and is crucial for keeping the business profitable.

Hey! Could you make sure we run the Black Friday sale when they add an item to the cart? Black Friday is this Friday this month.

Chief marketing officer

Oh, I forgot! That code doesn't use copy-on-write. I wonder how we can safely exchange data with it.

> **Vocab time**
>
> In this book, we'll use the term *legacy code* to mean existing code (perhaps written with older practices) that we can't replace at the moment. We have to work with it as is.

All of the code we've been managing for the shopping cart has treated the cart as immutable using a copy-on-write discipline. However, the Black Friday promotion code does not. It mutates the shopping cart quite a lot. It was written years ago, it works reliably, and there's just no time to go back and rewrite it all. We need a way to safely interface with this existing code.

To trigger the Black Friday promotion, we'll need to add this line of code to add_item_to_cart().

Jenna from dev team

```
function add_item_to_cart(name, price) {
  var item = make_cart_item(name, price);
  shopping_cart = add_item(shopping_cart, item);
  var total = calc_total(shopping_cart);
  set_cart_total_dom(total);
  update_shipping_icons(shopping_cart);
  update_tax_dom(total);
  black_friday_promotion(shopping_cart);
}
```

we need to add this line of code, but it will mutate the shopping cart

Calling this function will violate copy-on-write, and we can't modify black_friday_promotion(). Luckily, there is another discipline that will let us call the function safely without violating copy-on-write. The discipline is called *defensive copying*. We use it to exchange data with code that mutates data.

Our copy-on-write code has to interact with untrusted code

The marketing team's Black Friday sale code is untrusted. We don't trust it because it doesn't implement the copy-on-write immutability discipline that our code follows.

Our code forms a *safe zone* where we trust all of the functions to maintain immutability. We can mentally relax while we're using code inside that circle.

The Black Friday code is outside of that safe zone, but our code still needs to run it. And in order to run it, we need to exchange data with it through its inputs and outputs.

Just to be extra clear: Any data that leaves the safe zone is potentially mutable. It could be modified by the untrusted code. Likewise, any data that enters the safe zone from untrusted code is potentially mutable. The untrusted code could keep references to it and modify it after sending it over. The challenge is to exchange data without breaking our immutability.

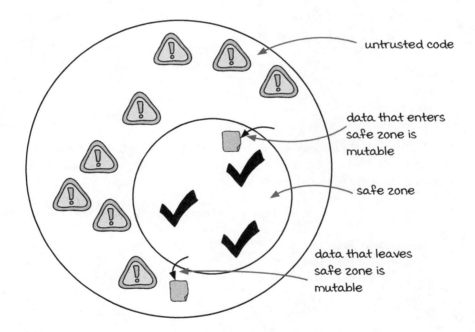

We've seen the copy-on-write pattern, but it won't quite help us here. In the copy-on-write pattern, we copy before modifying it. We know exactly what modifications will happen. We can reason about what needs to be copied. On the other hand, in this case, the Black Friday routine is so big and hairy that we don't know exactly what will happen. We need a discipline with more protective power that will completely shield our data from modification. That discipline is called *defensive copying*. Let's see how it works.

Defensive copying defends the immutable original

The solution to the problem of exchanging data with untrusted code is to make copies—two, in fact. Here's how it works.

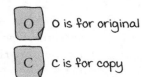

As data enters the safe zone from the untrusted code, we can't trust that the data is immutable. We immediately make a deep copy and throw away the mutable original. Since only trusted code has a reference to that copy, it's immutable. That protects you as data enters.

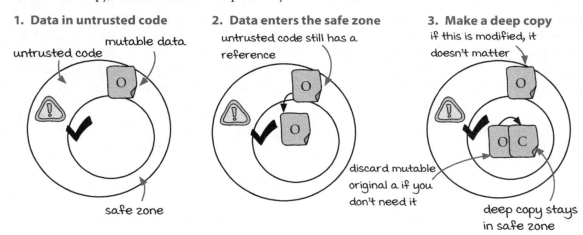

You still need protection when data leaves. As we've said before, any data that leaves the safe zone should be considered mutable because the untrusted code can modify it. The solution is to make a deep copy and send the copy to the untrusted code. That protects you as data leaves.

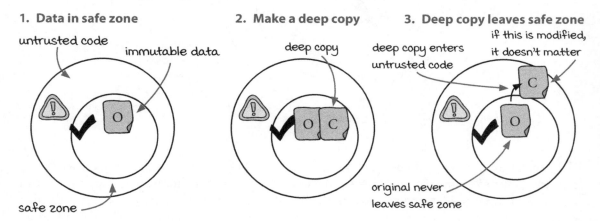

That's defensive copying in a nutshell. You make copies as data enters; you make copies as data leaves. The goal is to keep your immutable originals inside the safe zone and to not let any mutable data inside the safe zone. Let's apply this discipline to Black Friday.

Implementing defensive copies

We need to call a function that mutates its argument, but we don't want to break our hard-won immutable discipline. We can use *defensive copies* to protect data and maintain immutability. It's called defensive because you are defending your original from modifications.

`black_friday_promotion()` modifies its argument, the shopping cart. We can deep copy the shopping cart and pass the copy to the function. That way, it won't modify the original.

Original

```
function add_item_to_cart(name, price) {
  var item = make_cart_item(name, price);
  shopping_cart = add_item(shopping_cart,
                           item);
  var total = calc_total(shopping_cart);
  set_cart_total_dom(total);
  update_shipping_icons(shopping_cart);
  update_tax_dom(total);

  black_friday_promotion(shopping_cart);
}
```

Copy before sharing data

```
function add_item_to_cart(name, price) {
  var item = make_cart_item(name, price);
  shopping_cart = add_item(shopping_cart,
                           item);
  var total = calc_total(shopping_cart);
  set_cart_total_dom(total);
  update_shipping_icons(shopping_cart);
  update_tax_dom(total);
  var cart_copy = deepCopy(shopping_cart);
  black_friday_promotion(cart_copy);
}
```
copy data as it leaves

That's great, except we need the output from `black_friday_promotion()`. Its output is the modifications it does to the shopping cart. Luckily, it has modified `cart_copy`. But can we use `cart_copy` safely? Is it immutable? What if `black_friday_promotion()` keeps a reference to that shopping cart and modifies it later? These are the kinds of bugs you find weeks, months, or years later. The solution is to make another defensive copy as the data enters our code.

Copy before sharing data

```
function add_item_to_cart(name, price) {
  var item = make_cart_item(name, price);
  shopping_cart = add_item(shopping_cart,
                           item);
  var total = calc_total(shopping_cart);
  set_cart_total_dom(total);
  update_shipping_icons(shopping_cart);
  update_tax_dom(total);
  var cart_copy = deepCopy(shopping_cart);
  black_friday_promotion(cart_copy);

}
```

Copy before and after sharing data

```
function add_item_to_cart(name, price) {
  var item = make_cart_item(name, price);
  shopping_cart = add_item(shopping_cart,
                           item);
  var total = calc_total(shopping_cart);
  set_cart_total_dom(total);
  update_shipping_icons(shopping_cart);
  update_tax_dom(total);
  var cart_copy = deepCopy(shopping_cart);
  black_friday_promotion(cart_copy);
  shopping_cart = deepCopy(cart_copy);
}
```
copy data as it enters

And that's the defensive copy pattern. As we've seen, you protect yourself by making copies. You copy data as it leaves your system, and you copy it as it comes back in.

The copies we make need to be *deep copies*. We'll see how to implement that in just a moment.

The rules of defensive copying

Defensive copying is a discipline that maintains immutability when you have to exchange data with code that does not maintain immutability. We'll call that code you don't trust. Here are the two rules:

Rule 1: Copy as data leaves your code

If you have immutable data that will leave your code and enter code that you don't trust, follow these steps to protect your original:

1. Make a deep copy of the immutable data.

2. Pass the copy to the untrusted code.

Rule 2: Copy as data enters your code

If you are receiving data from untrusted code, that data might not be immutable. Follow these steps:

1. Immediately make a deep copy of the mutable data passed to your code.

2. Use the copy in your code.

 **Vocab time**

Deep copies duplicate all levels of nested data structures, from the top all the way to the bottom.

If you follow these two rules, you can interact with any code you don't trust without breaking your immutable discipline.

Note that these rules could be applied in any order. Sometimes you send data out, and then data comes back. That's what happens when your code calls a function from an untrusted library.

On the other hand, sometimes you receive data before you send data out. That happens when untrusted code calls a function in your code, like if your code is part of a shared library. Just keep in mind that the two rules can be applied in either order.

We are going to implement defensive copying a few more times. But before we move on to another implementation, let's keep working on the code we just saw for the Black Friday promotion. We can improve it by wrapping it up.

Also note that sometimes there is no input or output to copy.

Wrapping untrusted code

We have successfully implemented defensive copying, but the code is a bit unclear with all of the copying going on. Plus, we're going to have to call `black_friday_promotion()` many times in the future. We don't want to risk getting the defensive copying wrong. Let's wrap up the function in a new function that includes the defensive copying inside it.

We're going to need to call this function next month, too. Let's wrap it up so we can call it safely when we need it.

Kim from dev team

Original

```
function add_item_to_cart(name, price) {
  var item = make_cart_item(name, price);
  shopping_cart = add_item(shopping_cart,
                           item);
  var total = calc_total(shopping_cart);
  set_cart_total_dom(total);
  update_shipping_icons(shopping_cart);
  update_tax_dom(total);
  var cart_copy = deepCopy(shopping_cart);
  black_friday_promotion(cart_copy);
  shopping_cart =
    deepCopy(cart_copy);
}
```

extract this code into a new function

Extracted safe version

```
function add_item_to_cart(name, price) {
  var item = make_cart_item(name, price);
  shopping_cart = add_item(shopping_cart,
                           item);
  var total = calc_total(shopping_cart);
  set_cart_total_dom(total);
  update_shipping_icons(shopping_cart);
  update_tax_dom(total);


  shopping_cart =
    black_friday_promotion_safe(shopping_cart);
}

function black_friday_promotion_safe(cart) {
  var cart_copy = deepCopy(cart);
  black_friday_promotion(cart_copy);
  return deepCopy(cart_copy);
}
```

Now we can call `black_friday_promotion_safe()` without worry. It protects our data from modification. And now it's much more convenient and clear to see what's going on.

Let's look at another example.

It's your turn

MegaMart uses a third-party library for calculating payroll. You pass the function payrollCalc() through an array of employee records and it returns an array of payroll checks. The code is definitely untrusted. It will probably modify the employee array, and who knows what it does with the payroll checks.

Your job is to wrap it up in a function that makes it safe using defensive copies. Here's the signature of payrollCalc():

```
function payrollCalc(employees) {          ← make a defensive copy
  ...                                           version of this
  return payrollChecks;
}
```

Write the wrapper called payrollCalcSafe().

write your implementation here

```
function payrollCalcSafe(employees) {




}
```

Answer

```
function payrollCalcSafe(employees) {
  var copy = deepCopy(employees);
  var payrollChecks = payrollCalc(copy);
  return deepCopy(payrollChecks);
}
```

📝 It's your turn

MegaMart has another legacy system that serves up data about users of the software. You subscribe to updates to users as they change their settings.

But here's the thing: All the parts of the code that subscribe get the same exact user data. All of the references are to the same objects in memory. Obviously, the user data is coming from untrusted code. Your task is to protect the safe zone with defensive copying. Note that there is no data going back out to the unsafe zone—there's only mutable user data coming in.

You call it like this:

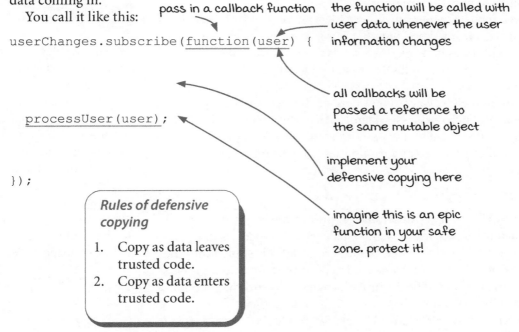

pass in a callback function

the function will be called with user data whenever the user information changes

```
userChanges.subscribe(function(user) {



    processUser(user);



});
```

all callbacks will be passed a reference to the same mutable object

implement your defensive copying here

imagine this is an epic function in your safe zone. protect it!

Rules of defensive copying

1. Copy as data leaves trusted code.
2. Copy as data enters trusted code.

📝 Answer

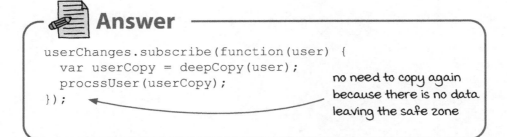

```
userChanges.subscribe(function(user) {
    var userCopy = deepCopy(user);
    procssUser(userCopy);
});
```

no need to copy again because there is no data leaving the safe zone

Defensive copying you may be familiar with

Defensive copying is a common pattern that you might find outside of the traditional places. You may have to squint to see it, though.

Defensive copying in web application programming interfaces (API)

Most web-based APIs are doing implicit defensive copying. Here's a scenario of how that might look.

A web request comes into your API as JSON. The JSON is a *deep copy* of data from the client that is serialized over the internet. Your service does its work, then sends the response back as a serialized *deep copy*, also in JSON. It's copying data on the way in and on the way back.

It's doing defensive copying. One of the benefits of a service-oriented or microservices system is that the services are doing defensive copying when they talk to each other. Services with different coding practices and disciplines can communicate without problems.

Defensive copying in Erlang and Elixir

Erlang and Elixir (two functional programming languages) implement defensive copying as well. Whenever two processes in Erlang send messages to each other, the message (data) is copied into the mailbox of the receiver. Data is copied on the way into a process and on the way out. The defensive copying is key to the high reliability of Erlang systems.

For more information on Erlang and Elixir, see https://www.erlang.org and https://elixir-lang.org.

We can tap into the same benefits that microservices and Erlang use in our own modules.

 **Vocab time**

When modules implement defensive copying when talking to each other, this is often called a *shared nothing architecture* because the modules don't share references to any data. You don't want your copy-on-write code to share references with untrusted code.

 **Brain break**

There's more to go, but let's take a break for questions

Q: Wait! Is it really okay to have two copies of the user data at the same time? Which is the real one that represents the user?

A: That's a great question, and it's one of the conceptual changes that people go through when learning functional programming. Many people are used to having a user object that represents a user of their software, and it's confusing to have two copies of the same object. Which one represents the user?

In functional programming, we don't represent the user. We record and process data about the user. Remember the definition of data: facts about events. We record facts, like the name of the user, about events, like them submitting a form. We can copy those facts as many times as we want.

Q: Copy-on-write and defensive copying seem very similar. Are they really different? Do we need both?

A: Copy-on-write and defensive copying are both used to enforce immutability, so it seems like we should only need one. The fact is that you could get away with only doing defensive copying, even inside the safe zone. That would enforce immutability just fine.

However, defensive copying makes deep copies. Deep copies are much more expensive than shallow copies because they copy the entire nested data structure from top to bottom. We don't need to make so many copies when we trust the code we're passing data to. So in order to save the processing and memory of all of those copies, we use copy-on-write when we can, which is everywhere inside the safe zone. The two disciplines work together.

It's important to compare the two approaches so that we can have a better understanding of when to use each. Let's do that now.

Copy-on-write and defensive copying compared

Copy-on-write

When to use it
Use copy-on-write when you need to modify data you control.

Where to use it
You should use copy-on-write everywhere inside the safe zone. In fact, the copy-on-write defines your immutability safe zone.

Type of copy
Shallow copy—relatively cheap

The rules

1. Make a shallow copy of the thing to modify.

2. Modify the copy.

3. Return the copy.

Defensive copying

When to use it
Use defensive copying when exchanging data with untrusted code.

Where to use it
Use defensive copying at the borders of your safe zone for data that has to cross in or out.

Type of copy
Deep copy—relatively expensive

The rules

1. Make a deep copy of data as it enters the safe zone.

2. Make a deep copy of data as it leaves the safe zone.

Deep copies are more expensive than shallow copies

The difference between a deep copy and a shallow copy is that a deep copy shares no structure with the original. Every nested object and array is copied. In a shallow copy, we can share a lot of the structure—anything that doesn't change can be shared.

Shallow copy

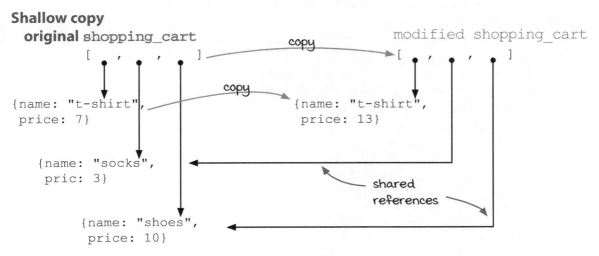

In a deep copy, we make copies of everything. We use a deep copy because we don't trust that any of it will be treated as immutable by the untrusted code.

Deep copy

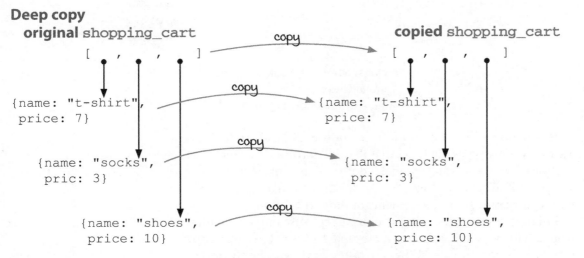

Deep copies are obviously more expensive. That's why we don't do them everywhere. We only do them where we can't guarantee that copy-on-write will be followed.

Implementing deep copy in JavaScript is difficult

Deep copy is a simple idea that should have a simple implementation. However, in JavaScript it is quite hard to get right because there isn't a good standard library. Implementing a robust one is beyond the scope of this book.

I recommend using the implementation from the Lodash library. Specifically, the function `.cloneDeep()` does a deep copy of nested data structures. The library is trusted by thousands if not millions of JavaScript developers.

see
`lodash.com`

see
`lodash.com/docs/#cloneDeep`

However, just for completeness, here is a simple implementation that may satisfy your curiosity. It should work for all JSON-legal types and functions.

```
function deepCopy(thing) {
  if(Array.isArray(thing)) {
    var copy = [];
    for(var i = 0; i < thing.length; i++)
      copy.push(deepCopy(thing[i]));
    return copy;
  } else if (thing === null) {
    return null;
  } else if(typeof thing === "object") {
    var copy = {};
    var keys = Object.keys(thing);
    for(var i = 0; i < keys.length; i++) {
      var key = keys[i];
      copy[key] = deepCopy(thing[key]);
    }
    return copy;
  } else {
    return thing;
  }
}
```

recursively make copies of all of the elements

strings, numbers, booleans, and functions are immutable so they don't need to be copied

This function will not hold up to the quirks of JavaScript. There are many more types out there that this will fail on. However, as an outline of what needs to be done, it does a decent job. It shows that arrays and objects need to be copied, but also that the function will recurse into all of the elements of those collections.

I highly recommend using a robust deep copy implementation from a widely used JavaScript library like Lodash. This deep copy function is just for teaching purposes and will not work in production.

It's your turn

The following statements are about the two types of copying we have seen, shallow and deep. Some statements are true for deep copying and some are true for shallow copies. And some are true for both! Write DC by the ones that apply to deep copying and SC for those that apply to shallow copying.

1. It copies every level of a nested structure.

2. It is much more efficient than the other because two copies can share structure.

3. It copies only the parts that change.

4. Because copies don't share structure, it is good for protecting the original from untrusted code.

5. It is useful for implementing a *shared nothing architecture*.

> **Key**
>
> **DC** deep copying
> **SC** shallow copying

Answer

1. DC; 2. SC; 3. SC; 4. DC; 5. DC.

A dialogue between copy-on-write and defensive copying

The topic: Which discipline is more important?

Copy-on-write:
Obviously, I'm more important. I help people keep their data immutable.

Defensive copying:

That doesn't make you more important. I help keep data immutable, too.

Well, my shallow copies are way more efficient than your deep copies.

Well, you only have to worry about that because you need to make a copy EVERY SINGLE TIME data is modified. I only need to make copies when data enters or leaves the safe zone.

Exactly my point! There wouldn't even be a safe zone without me.

Well, I suppose you're right about that. But your safe zone wouldn't be any use at all if it couldn't pass data to the outside. That's where all the existing code and libraries are.

Well, I really think they should be using me in those legacy codebases and libraries, too. They could learn a lot from a discipline like me. Convert their writes to reads, and the reads naturally become calculations.

Listen, that is never going to happen. Just accept it. There's too much code out there. There aren't enough programmers in the whole world to ever rewrite it all.

You're right! *(sobbing)* I should face facts. I'm worthless without you!

Oh, now I'm getting all emotional, too. *(tears running down face)* I can't live without you, either!

(hugs)   *(hugs)*

Oh, brother! Moving on . . .

It's your turn

The following statements are about immutability disciplines. Some are true for defensive copying and some are true for copy-on-write. And some are true for both! Write DC by the ones that apply to defensive copying and CW for those that apply to copy-on-write.

1. It makes deep copies.

2. It is cheaper than the other.

3. It is an important way to maintain immutability.

4. It copies data before modifying the copy.

5. It is used inside the safe zone to maintain immutability.

6. You use it when you want to exchange data with untrusted code.

7. It is a complete immutability solution. It can be used without the other.

8. It uses shallow copies.

9. It copies data before sending it to untrusted code.

10. It copies data it receives from untrusted code.

> *Key*
>
> **DC** defensive copying
> **CW** copy-on-write

Answer

1. DC; 2. CW; 3. DC and CW, 4. CW; 5. CW; 6. DC; 7. DC;
8. CW; 9. DC; 10. DC.

It's your turn

Your team has just started using a copy-on-write discipline to create a safe zone. Every time your team writes new code, they make sure to keep it immutable. A new task requires you to write code that interacts with existing code that does not keep the immutability discipline. Which of the following courses of action would ensure you maintain immutability? Check all the statements that apply. Justify your responses.

1. Use defensive copying when exchanging data with the existing code.

2. Use a copy-on-write discipline when exchanging data with the existing code.

3. Read the source code of the existing code to see if it modifies the data. If it doesn't, we don't need to use any special discipline.

4. Rewrite the preexisting code to use copy-on-write and call the rewritten code without defensive copying.

5. The code belongs to your team, so it's already part of the safe zone.

Answer

1. Yes. Defensive copying will protect your safe zone at the cost of memory and work to make the copies.

2. No. Copy-on-write only works when you are calling other functions that implement copy-on-write. If you're not sure, your existing code probably does not implement it.

3. Maybe. If you analyze the source code, you might discover that it doesn't modify the data you pass it. However, also be on the lookout for other things it might do, like pass the data to a third part of the code.

4. Yes. If you can afford it, a rewrite using copy-on-write would solve the problem.

5. No. Just because you own it does not mean it enforces the immutability discipline of your team.

Conclusion

In this chapter we learned a more powerful yet more expensive discipline for maintaining immutability called *defensive copying*. It's more powerful because it can implement immutability all by itself. It's more expensive because it needs to copy more data. However, when you use defensive copying in tandem with copy-on-write, you can get all of the benefits of both—power when you need it, but shallow copies for efficiency.

Summary

- Defensive copying is a discipline for implementing immutability. It makes copies as data leaves or enters your code.

- Defensive copying makes deep copies, so it is more expensive than copy-on-write.

- Unlike copy-on-write, defensive copying can protect your data from code that does not implement an immutability discipline.

- We often prefer copy-on-write because it does not require as many copies and we use defensive copying only when we need to interact with untrusted code.

- Deep copies copy an entire nested structure from top to bottom. Shallow copies only copy the bare minimum.

Up next . . .

In the next chapter, we will pull together everything we've learned so far and discover a way to organize our code to improve the design of our system.

Stratified design: Part 1 | 8

In this chapter

- Learn a working definition of software design.

- Understand stratified design and how it can help your team.

- Learn how to extract functions to make code cleaner.

- Discover why building software in layers helps you think better.

We've come to the last chapters in part 1, and it's time to look at the big picture. We're going to apply a design practice called stratified design. In stratified design, we write functions in terms of functions defined in lower layers. What are layers? And what are they for? Those questions will be answered in this chapter and the next. And with the concepts we learn, we'll be set up to succeed in part 2.

What is software design?

The programmers at MegaMart realize how important the shopping cart is to their software. But they don't think it's implemented very well.

Jenna from dev team

Jenna's frustration is an important signal that something is wrong. A good design should feel good. It should help your software development efforts all along the development cycle—from ideation, to coding, to testing, to maintenance.

In fact, that sounds like a good working definition of *software design* as we will treat it in this book.

software design, *noun.*
> using one's aesthetic sense to guide programming choices to improve the ease of coding, testing, and maintaining software

We don't want to get into a heated debate over what software design is. And you don't have to agree with that definition. But it is helpful to know the definition we will use in this book.

In this chapter, we're going to hone our aesthetic senses using the practice of *stratified design*. Let's get to it.

What is stratified design?

Stratified design is a technique for building software in layers. Each layer defines new functions in terms of the functions in the layers below it. By training our sense of design, we can find arrangements of layers that make our software flexible to change, readable, easy to test, and much more reusable. Here's what we mean by *layers*:

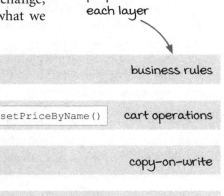

purpose of each layer

`gets_free_shipping()` `cartTax()`	business rules
`remove_item_by_name()` `calc_total()` `add_item()` `setPriceByName()`	cart operations
`removeItems()` `add_element_last()`	copy-on-write
`.slice()`	array built-ins

Let's be clear: Identifying these layers is hard. You need to know what to look for and what to do with what you find. There are too many factors involved to come up with an absolute formula for "the best design." However, we can develop a sense of good design, and we can follow that sense where it leads.

How do you develop a sense of good design? That's a hard thing to explain, but here's how we'll approach it in this chapter: We'll learn to read our code, looking for the signals that tell us where our design could be better. And we'll improve our design so we see what that is like, too. With some hard work and a little luck, we'll finish the chapter with the beginnings of a good design sense that you can continue to hone for years to come.

 **Vocab time**

Stratified design is a design technique that builds software in layers. It is a practice with long historical roots, with many contributions from many people. However, special mention goes to Harold Abelson and Gerald Sussman for documenting their insights into the practice.

Developing our design sense

The curse of expertise

Experts are notoriously bad at explaining what they do, though they can clearly do it very well. They have a highly trained model, but no way to describe that model to others. That's the curse of expertise. Even if you are good at something, you can't explain what you do. It's a black box.

One reason experts can't explain their black box is that the skill is so complex. The black box takes a huge variety of inputs and gives a huge variety of outputs.

The inputs to a stratified design sense

We can think of the inputs to stratified design as clues. We read our code, looking for clues, and use those to guide our actions. Here are some sources of clues we can use:

don't worry if you don't understand these yet. we'll get to them in this chapter and the next

Function bodies
- Length
- Complexity
- Levels of detail
- Functions called
- Language features used

Layer structure
- Arrow length
- Cohesion
- Level of detail

Function signatures
- Function name
- Argument names
- Argument values
- Return value

The outputs from a stratified design sense

Once we've taken in all of those inputs, we combine them somehow in our heads. Remember, even experts can't explain exactly what they do. But somehow people can learn to combine those inputs into complex decisions and actions in the code. Those decisions and actions might take many forms:

Organization
- Decide where a new function goes.
- Move functions around.

Implementation
- Change an implementation.
- Extract a function.
- Change a data structure.

Changes
- Choose where new code is written.
- Decide what level of detail is appropriate.

We are going to look at our code from many different angles and apply the patterns of stratified design to it. With any luck, your brain will do what it does best (finding patterns) and begin to see the patterns the way an expert does.

Patterns of stratified design

We're going to look at stratified design from many angles. But the primary way we'll organize this chapter and the next is by four patterns. We'll address pattern 1 in this chapter and the rest in the next chapter.

Pattern 1: Straightforward implementation

The layer structure of stratified design should help us build straightforward implementations. When we read a function with a straightforward implementation, the problem the function signature presents should be solved at the right level of detail in the body. Too much detail is a code smell.

Pattern 2: Abstraction barrier

Some layers in the graph provide an interface that lets us hide an important implementation detail. These layers help us write code at a higher level and free our limited mental capacity to think at a higher level.

Pattern 3: Minimal interface

As our system evolves, we want the interfaces to important business concepts to converge to a small, powerful set of operations. Every other operation should be defined in terms of those, either directly or indirectly.

Pattern 4: Comfortable layers

The patterns and practices of stratified design should serve our needs as programmers, who are in turn serving the business. We should invest time in the layers that will help us deliver software faster and with higher quality. We don't want to add layers for sport. The code and its layers of abstraction should feel comfortable to work in.

These patterns are abstract, so let's make them concrete. The scenarios, diagrams, explanations, and exercises should help make them part of your stratified design sense. Let's get started with pattern 1.

Pattern 1: Straightforward implementations

In this section, we're going to see how we can make our implementations clear to read. The layer structure of our design should help even our most powerful functions say what they do without undue complexity.

Let's rewind back to what Jenna was saying a few pages ago.

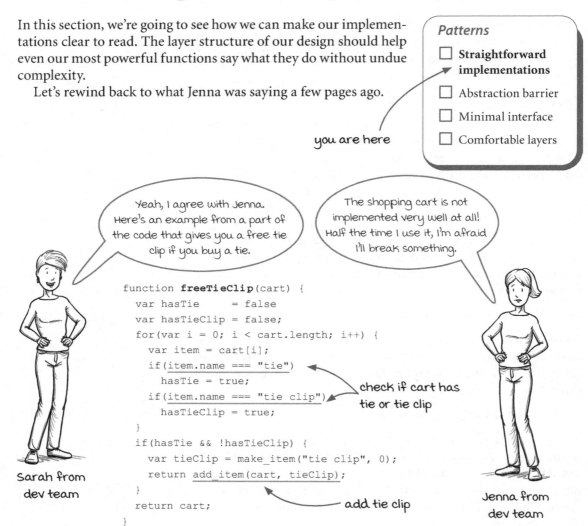

Patterns

☐ **Straightforward implementations**

☐ Abstraction barrier

☐ Minimal interface

☐ Comfortable layers

you are here

> Yeah, I agree with Jenna. Here's an example from a part of the code that gives you a free tie clip if you buy a tie.

> The shopping cart is not implemented very well at all! Half the time I use it, I'm afraid I'll break something.

```
function freeTieClip(cart) {
    var hasTie     = false
    var hasTieClip = false;
    for(var i = 0; i < cart.length; i++) {
        var item = cart[i];
        if(item.name === "tie")
            hasTie = true;
        if(item.name === "tie clip")
            hasTieClip = true;
    }
    if(hasTie && !hasTieClip) {
        var tieClip = make_item("tie clip", 0);
        return add_item(cart, tieClip);
    }
    return cart;
}
```

check if cart has tie or tie clip

add tie clip

Sarah from dev team

Jenna from dev team

The code is easy enough to follow, but there are many functions that loop through the shopping cart, check the items, and make some decision. These functions are designed ad hoc. The programmer isn't following any design principle. They are solving the problem at hand (adding a tie clip) with their knowledge of the shopping cart (it's an array). It's tiresome to write new code like this and difficult to maintain.

This code isn't following pattern 1: straightforward implementations. The code is full of details that aren't relevant at this level of thinking. Why should marketing campaigns have to know that the shopping cart is an array? Should a sale be liable to fail if there's an off-by-one error looping through the cart?

Desired shopping cart operations

The team decides to do a design sprint to get the shopping cart in shape. With their knowledge of the code, they start by coming up with a list of operations they would like to have. This is one way to get a feel for what your code should look like. These operations would then be used in place of the ad hoc code they write habitually.

On the left is a list of operations they want to have, with checkmarks indicating the ones they already have. On the right is the code for the ones they already have.

Patterns

☐ **Straightforward implementations**

☐ Abstraction barrier

☐ Minimal interface

☐ Comfortable layers

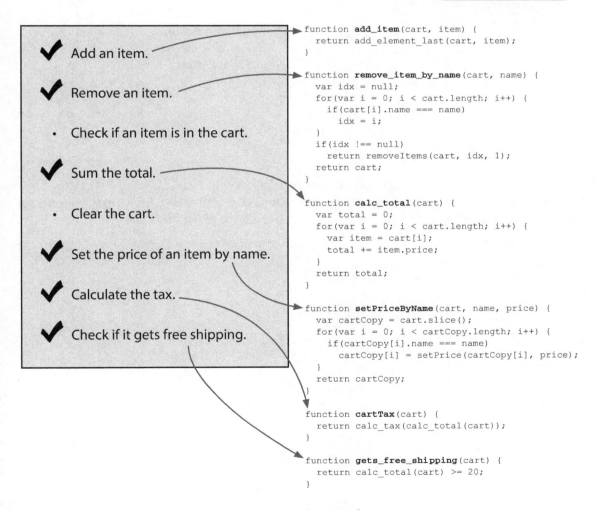

```
function add_item(cart, item) {
  return add_element_last(cart, item);
}

function remove_item_by_name(cart, name) {
  var idx = null;
  for(var i = 0; i < cart.length; i++) {
    if(cart[i].name === name)
      idx = i;
  }
  if(idx !== null)
    return removeItems(cart, idx, 1);
  return cart;
}

function calc_total(cart) {
  var total = 0;
  for(var i = 0; i < cart.length; i++) {
    var item = cart[i];
    total += item.price;
  }
  return total;
}

function setPriceByName(cart, name, price) {
  var cartCopy = cart.slice();
  for(var i = 0; i < cartCopy.length; i++) {
    if(cartCopy[i].name === name)
      cartCopy[i] = setPrice(cartCopy[i], price);
  }
  return cartCopy;
}

function cartTax(cart) {
  return calc_tax(calc_total(cart));
}

function gets_free_shipping(cart) {
  return calc_total(cart) >= 20;
}
```

- ✔ Add an item.
- ✔ Remove an item.
- • Check if an item is in the cart.
- ✔ Sum the total.
- • Clear the cart.
- ✔ Set the price of an item by name.
- ✔ Calculate the tax.
- ✔ Check if it gets free shipping.

There are two operations that we have not implemented yet. We will get to them soon.

Checking if an item is in the cart can help us

Listing all of the desired operations has given Kim a new perspective, and she sees a way to make freeTieClip() more straightforward.

> Wait! One of our missing functions, checking if an item is in the cart, can help us make freeTieClip() clearer.

```
function freeTieClip(cart) {
  var hasTie     = false
  var hasTieClip = false;
  for(var i = 0; i < cart.length; i++) {
    var item = cart[i];
    if(item.name === "tie")
      hasTie = true;
    if(item.name === "tie clip")
      hasTieClip = true;
  }
  if(hasTie && !hasTieClip) {
    var tieClip = make_item("tie clip", 0);
    return add_item(cart, tieClip);
  }
  return cart;
}
```

this for loop is just checking if two items are in the cart

Kim from dev team

If we had a function to check if an item was in the cart, we could use it instead of that low-level for loop. Low-level code is always a good candidate for extraction. The trick is that this for loop is checking for two different items. We'll have to call the same function twice.

```
function freeTieClip(cart) {
  var hasTie     = false;
  var hasTieClip = false;
  for(var i = 0; i < cart.length; i++) {
    var item = cart[i];
    if(item.name === "tie")
      hasTie = true;
    if(item.name === "tie clip")
      hasTieClip = true;
  }
  if(hasTie && !hasTieClip) {
    var tieClip = make_item("tie clip", 0);
    return add_item(cart, tieClip);
  }
  return cart;
}
```

extract for loop into function

```
function freeTieClip(cart) {
  var hasTie     = isInCart(cart, "tie");
  var hasTieClip = isInCart(cart, "tie clip");
  if(hasTie && !hasTieClip) {
    var tieClip = make_item("tie clip", 0);
    return add_item(cart, tieClip);
  }
  return cart;
}

function isInCart(cart, name) {
  for(var i = 0; i < cart.length; i++) {
    if(cart[i].name === name)
      return true;
  }
  return false;
}
```

The new implementation is shorter, which often helps make it clear. However, the implementation is also clearer to read because everything is happening at a similar level of detail.

Visualizing our function calls with a call graph

Let's look at the original implementation of the function `freeTieClip()` from another powerful perspective. We can read what functions it calls or language feature it uses and draw them, creating a *call graph*. Here we want to highlight the for loop and array index, so we'll include them.

Code

```
function freeTieClip(cart) {
  var hasTie     = false
  var hasTieClip = false;
  for(var i = 0; i < cart.length; i++) {
    var item = cart[i];
    if(item.name === "tie")
      hasTie = true;
    if(item.name === "tie clip")
      hasTieClip = true;
  }
  if(hasTie && !hasTieClip) {
    var tieClip = make_item("tie clip", 0);
    return add_item(cart, tieClip);
  }
  return cart;
}
```

Diagram

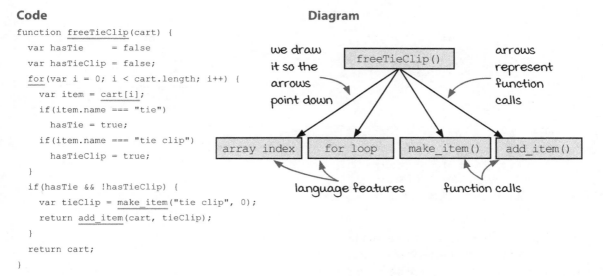

Do the boxes on the bottom layer all represent the same level of abstraction? No. It is very difficult to imagine functions we write (`make_item()` and `add_item()`) being on the same level as built-in language features (for loop and array index). Array index and for loop should be on a lower level. Let's express that in our diagram:

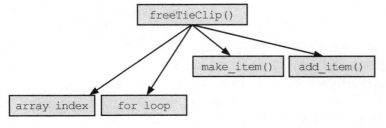

Now the diagram is showing us the same thing we sensed before when reading the code: `freeTieClip()` is implemented using parts that span different levels of abstraction. We can see that because the arrows are pointing to different layers. The difference in layers makes the implementation less obvious and hard to read.

How does our improved implementation look as a call graph?

Patterns

- ☐ **Straightforward implementations**
- ☐ Abstraction barrier
- ☐ Minimal interface
- ☐ Comfortable layers

Straightforward implementations call functions from similar layers of abstraction

We just saw that the call graph of freeTieClip() revealed that it was not a straightforward implementation since it called functions on vastly different layers of abstraction. It echoed the same sense we got when looking at the code.

Code   **Diagram**

```
function freeTieClip(cart) {
  var hasTie     = false;
  var hasTieClip = false;
  for(var i = 0; i < cart.length; i++) {
    var item = cart[i];
    if(item.name === "tie")
      hasTie = true;
    if(item.name === "tie clip")
      hasTieClip = true;
  }
  if(hasTie && !hasTieClip) {
    var tieClip = make_item("tie clip", 0);
    return add_item(cart, tieClip);
  }
  return cart;
}
```

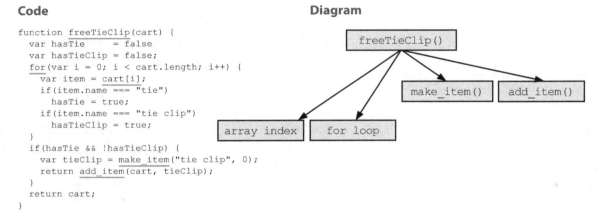

Now let's see what the new implementation looks like. We believe the code is more straightforward. We should expect the functions it calls to be at closer layers of abstraction.

we call it twice, but it only needs to be in the diagram once

Code   **Diagram**

```
function freeTieClip(cart) {
  var hasTie     = isInCart(cart, "tie");
  var hasTieClip = isInCart(cart, "tie clip");
  if(hasTie && !hasTieClip) {
    var tieClip = make_item("tie clip", 0);
    return add_item(cart, tieClip);
  }
  return cart;
}
```

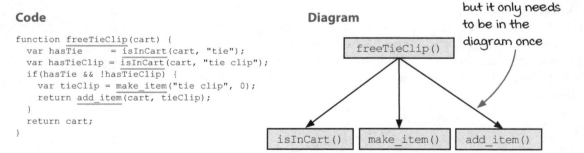

Indeed, we see that the functions that freeTieClip() calls are at a very similar layer of abstraction, if not the very same layer. If that's not clear yet, don't worry. We will see many more perspectives that will make it clear. For now, simply ask yourself this: What do you have to know about the shopping cart to be able to call those functions? Do you have to know that it's an array?

We don't. We can ignore that it's an array when using all three of those functions. Being able to ignore the same detail is one clue that they are at a similar layer of abstraction. And since they are at a similar layer, the implementation is straightforward.

Brain break

There's more to go, but let's take a break for questions

Q: Do I really need to look at the call graph? I could see the problems right in the code.

A: Good question. In this case, the code was obviously not straightforward. The call graph just confirmed it. From that perspective, we didn't really need the graph.

However, right now, we only have two layers in the graphs. As we add more functions, the diagram will have more layers, and the global view it gives you of your code will be very useful for seeing how your layers are structured as a system. That information is hard to get when looking at the small amount of code you can see at one time. The layer structure is an invaluable signal to feed your design sense.

Q: Do you really draw all of these diagrams?

A: That's a really good question. Most of the time we don't draw them. We imagine them. Once you get good at using them, you may be able to "draw" them in your mind.

However, a shared diagram, for example on a whiteboard, is a great communication tool. Design discussions run the risk of getting too abstract. A drawing can give you something concrete to refer to in order to avoid that problem.

Q: Are these layers real? Are they objective things that everyone agrees on?

A: Goodness! That's a tough philosophical question.

Stratified design is a practice—a particular perspective—that many people have learned to use. Think of it as goggles that give you a higher resolution view of the structure of your code. Use those goggles to find ways to improve the reusability, testability, and maintainability of your code. If they don't help at the moment, take them off. And if someone sees something different, trade goggles.

Q: I see more layers than you show even in these simple diagrams. Am I doing it wrong?

A: You are not doing it wrong. You may be focusing on a level of detail that is important for your purposes but unimportant to what is being taught. Please do explore as fine-grained or high-level as you want. Zoom in and out freely. Use those goggles!

Adding `remove_item_by_name()` to the graph

The graph we've drawn for `freeTieClip()` gave us a great perspective. We can extend that perspective to all of the operations we have for dealing with the shopping cart one at a time. Let's add the function `remove_item_by_name()` to the graph. We should underline all functions it calls and language features we want to highlight.

Code

```
function remove_item_by_name(cart, name) {
  var idx = null;
  for(var i = 0; i < cart.length; i++) {
    if(cart[i].name === name)
      idx = i;
  }
  if(idx !== null)
    return removeItems(cart, idx, 1);
  return cart;
}
```

Diagram

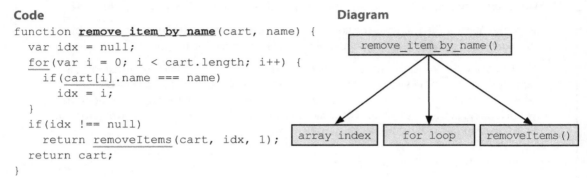

We want to extend the graph we already have with the boxes and arrows of this new diagram. Following is the graph we drew for `freeTieClip()`. Where should we draw `remove_item_by_name()`? We have five choices, which are all drawn as well:

Diagram

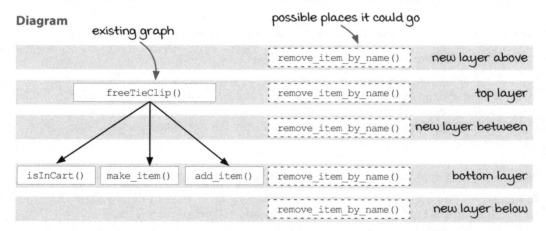

 **It's your turn**

The diagram shows five different layers where we could place `remove_item_by_name()`. Some create new layers; some add it to existing layers. Where should we add it? What information should we use to make that decision? We'll work through it on the next pages.

 **Answer**

There are many inputs that can help us place `remove_item_by_name()` on the appropriate layer. We can use the process of elimination:

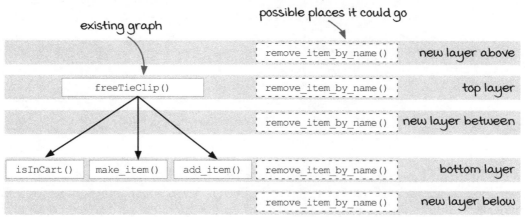

Does `remove_item_by_name()` go in the top layer? What is already in the top layer? Looking at the name of the function `freeTieClip()`, we see that it's a function about a marketing campaign. `remove_item_by_name()` is definitely not about marketing. It is a more general-purpose operation. It can be used for marketing campaigns, user interface (UI) operations, or any number of other purposes. And we can imagine marketing campaign functions at that top level calling `remove_item_by_name()`. Therefore, `remove_item_by_name()` must come below that layer to maintain downward arrows. We can eliminate the top two choices.

We can use function names as clues to which layer a function belongs in.

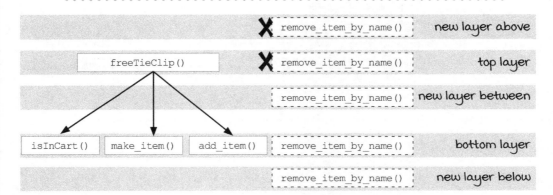

 **Answer**

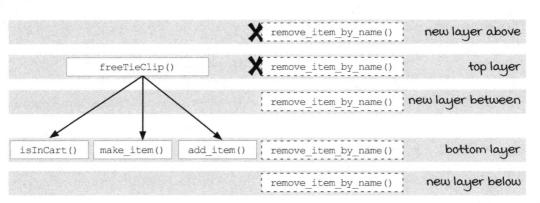

We've eliminated the top two choices because marketing campaigns (top layer) might call `remove_item_by_name()`. What about the bottom layer? The names in that layer all indicate operations on shopping carts and items. And `remove_item_by_name()` is also about shopping carts. That's our best candidate layer so far.

Can we eliminate the two other new layers to be certain? We can eliminate the new layer below. None of the functions in the bottom layer need to call `remove_item_by_name()`. That lets us eliminate the new layer below.

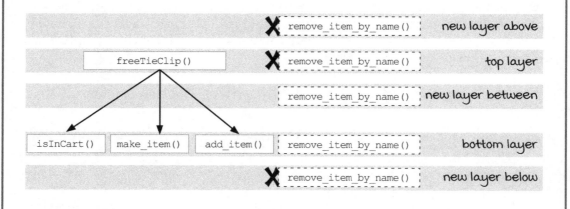

Answer

Because `remove_item_by_name()` is a general operation on shopping carts, like two other operations in the bottom layer, the bottom layer is our best choice. But there's still one new layer we haven't eliminated. Can we eliminate the new layer between?

Not 100%. But **we can look at what functions and language features the functions in the bottom layer call**. If there is a good overlap, it's a good sign that they belong on the same level.

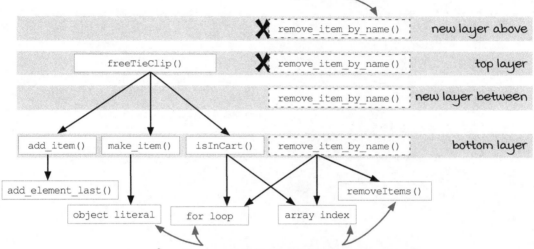

```
function isInCart(cart, name) {
  for(var i = 0; i < cart.length; i++) {
    if(cart[i].name === name)
      return true;
  }
  return false;
}


function make_item(name, price) {
  return {
    name: name,
    price: price
  };
}
```

```
function add_item(cart, item) {
  return add_element_last(cart, item);
}


function remove_item_by_name(cart, name) {
  var idx = null;
  for(var i = 0; i < cart.length; i++) {
    if(cart[i].name === name)
      idx = i;
  }
  if(idx !== null)
    return removeItems(cart, idx, 1);
  return cart;
}
```

`isInCart()` and `remove_item_by_name()` **both point to the same two boxes, which is good evidence that they belong on the same level**. We'll see later how to strengthen the case. For now, we've chosen the bottom layer as the best place to put it, right alongside `isInCart()`, `make_item()`, and `add_item()`.

It's your turn

Below you will see all of the shopping cart operations we have implemented. Some have already been added to the graph. Those are highlighted. The current diagram is at the bottom. Many functions have not been added.

Your task is to add the rest of the functions to the graph and arrange the functions (you can move existing ones, if you need to) into appropriate layers. The answer will be on the next page.

```
function freeTieClip(cart) {
  var hasTie     = isInCart(cart, "tie");
  var hasTieClip = isInCart(cart, "tie clip");
  if(hasTie && !hasTieClip) {
    var tieClip = make_item("tie clip", 0);
    return add_item(cart, tieClip);
  }
  return cart;
}

function add_item(cart, item) {
  return add_element_last(cart, item);
}

function isInCart(cart, name) {
  for(var i = 0; i < cart.length; i++) {
    if(cart[i].name === name)
      return true;
  }
  return false;
}

function remove_item_by_name(cart, name) {
  var idx = null;
  for(var i = 0; i < cart.length; i++) {
    if(cart[i].name === name)
      idx = i;
  }
  if(idx !== null)
    return removeItems(cart, idx, 1);
  return cart;
}
```

```
function calc_total(cart) {
  var total = 0;
  for(var i = 0; i < cart.length; i++) {
    var item = cart[i];
    total += item.price;
  }
  return total;
}

function gets_free_shipping(cart) {
  return calc_total(cart) >= 20;
}

function setPriceByName(cart, name, price) {
  var cartCopy = cart.slice();
  for(var i = 0; i < cartCopy.length; i++) {
    if(cartCopy[i].name === name)
      cartCopy[i] =
        setPrice(cartCopy[i], price);
  }
  return cartCopy;
}

function cartTax(cart) {
  return calc_tax(calc_total(cart));
}
```

Answer

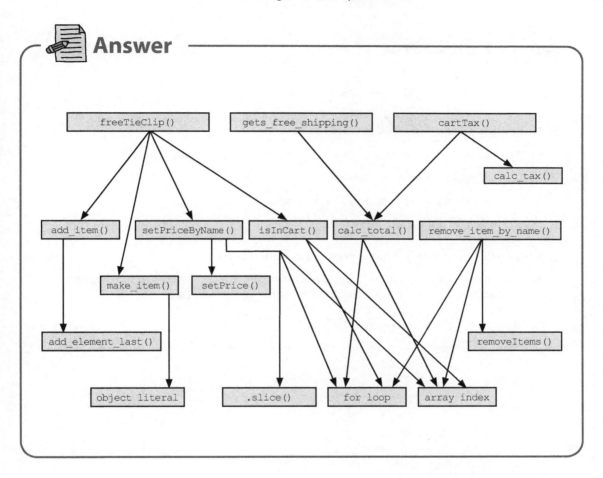

 **Brain break**

There's more to go, but let's take a break for questions

Q: My graph is similar, but different. Did I do it wrong?

   A: Well, probably not. If you got the following things right, your graph is fine:

   1.   All functions are on the graph.

   2.   Each function points to all functions it calls.

   3.   All arrows point down (not sideways or up).

Q: But why did you organize them into those specific layers?

   A: That's a really good question. Those layers in the diagram were chosen to correspond to layers of abstraction. Let's explain each of those layers on the next page.

All functions in a layer should serve the same pupose

This diagram has six layers. Each of those layers was an explicit choice. Nothing in this diagram is arbitrary. Although the process for deciding which layer something is in can be complex, it is good evidence that you've found good layers when you can give each layer a succinct purpose. All functions in that layer should serve that purpose. Let's do that now on this graph.

purpose for each layer

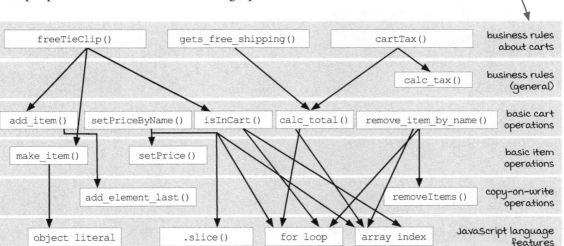

Each of these layers is a different level of abstraction. That is, when you are working on functions in one layer, there are some common details that you don't have to care about. For instance, when you're working on the "business rules about carts" layer, you don't have to worry about the detail that carts are implemented as arrays.

The diagram we have is a combination of facts (what functions call what) and some intuitive deductions (how they should be arranged into layers). It's a good, high-level representation of our code.

But remember, we want stratified design to help us write straightforward implementations. That's our first pattern. How can this diagram help us find those implementations? On the next few pages, we're going to look at different levels of details—different zoom levels—to focus on just the information we want at any given time.

Patterns

☐ **Straightforward implementations**

☐ Abstraction barrier

☐ Minimal interface

☐ Comfortable layers

Three different zoom levels

In our diagram, we can see the problems. But there is so much information that we don't know where the problems are. Problems in stratified design can be in three different problem areas:

1. Interaction between layers

2. Implementation of one layer

3. Implementation of one function

We can zoom into one problem area with the right zoom level.

1. Global zoom level

At the global zoom level, we see the entire call graph we are interested in. This is the default view. It allows us to see everything, including interactions between layers.

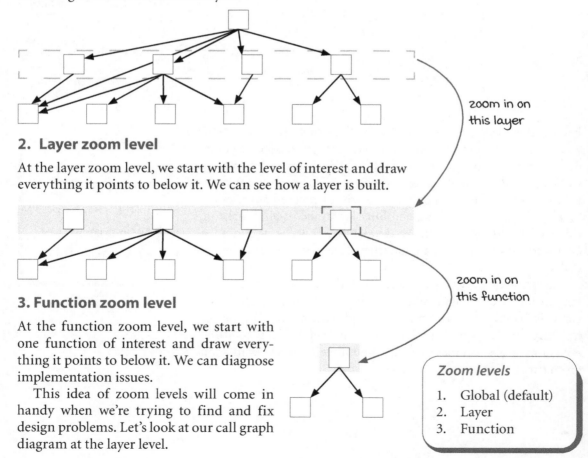

zoom in on this layer

2. Layer zoom level

At the layer zoom level, we start with the level of interest and draw everything it points to below it. We can see how a layer is built.

zoom in on this function

3. Function zoom level

At the function zoom level, we start with one function of interest and draw everything it points to below it. We can diagnose implementation issues.

This idea of zoom levels will come in handy when we're trying to find and fix design problems. Let's look at our call graph diagram at the layer level.

> *Zoom levels*
>
> 1. Global (default)
> 2. Layer
> 3. Function

At the layer zoom level, we compare arrows across functions

Here is our complete diagram (at the global zoom level):

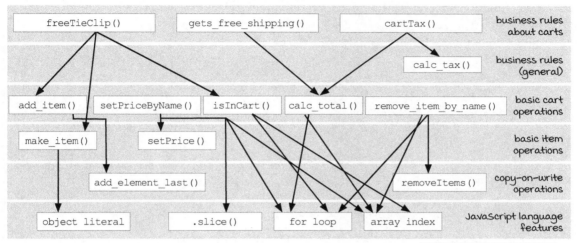

When we focus on a layer, we look at the functions in that layer plus all the functions they call directly. Let's focus on on the basic cart operations layer.

> **Zoom levels**
> 1. Global (default)
> 2. Layer
> 3. Function

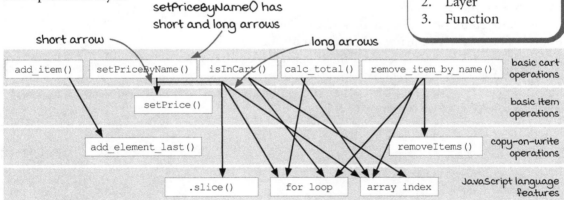

This diagram may look messy. But the parts that are messy—the arrows—are pure facts about our code. The messiness in the diagram reflects the messiness in our code. We're trying to gain perspectives on it that will let us tidy up.

In a straightforward implementation, all arrows would be about the same length. But here we see that some arrows are one layer long and some are three layers long. This is evidence that we are not working at the same level of detail across the entire layer.

Before we get into the solution, let's zoom into a single function. It's often easier to solve the problems there first.

> **Patterns**
> - ☐ **Straightforward implementations**
> - ☐ Abstraction barrier
> - ☐ Minimal interface
> - ☐ Comfortable layers

At the function zoom level, we compare arrows from one function

When we focus on a function, we look at the arrows coming from just one function. Here is the same graph zooming in on `remove_item_by_name()`. It draws that function and the functions and language features it uses.

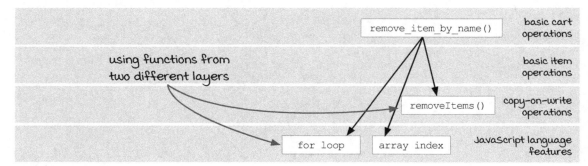

Even in this one function, we see that we are using things from two different layers. This is not a straightforward implementation.

In a straightforward implementation, at the extreme, all arrows from `remove_item_by_name()` would have the same length. How can we achieve that here?

The most common way is with intermediary functions. We want to shorten the two arrows that stretch all the way down to language features. If we insert a function that does the same job as the for loop and array index at the same level as the `removeItems()` operation, then all arrows would be the same length. It would wind up looking like this:

> **Patterns**
>
> ☑ **Straightforward implementations**
>
> ☐ Abstraction barrier
>
> ☐ Minimal interface
>
> ☐ Comfortable layers

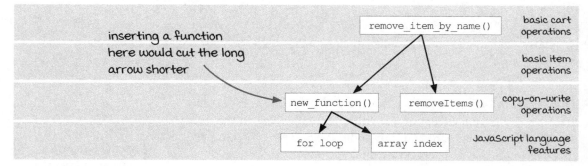

Luckily, that operation is the same as extracting the for loop into a new function, which we've already seen! This diagram is just another way to look at it.

> **Zoom levels**
>
> 1. Global (default)
> 2. Layer
> 3. Function

Extracting the for loop

We can extract the for loop from remove_item_by_name().
This for loop is doing a linear search through the array. And the
result is the index into the array where the item was found. So we'll
call the new function indexOfItem().

Before

```
function remove_item_by_name(cart, name) {
  var idx = null;
  for(var i = 0; i < cart.length; i++) {
    if(cart[i].name === name)
      idx = i;
  }
  if(idx !== null)
    return removeItems(cart, idx, 1);
  return cart;
}
```

extract the for
loop into a new
function

After

```
function remove_item_by_name(cart, name) {
  var idx = indexOfItem(cart, name);



  if(idx !== null)
    return removeItems(cart, idx, 1);
  return cart;
}

function indexOfItem(cart, name) {
  for(var i = 0; i < cart.length; i++) {
    if(cart[i].name === name)
      return i;
  }
  return null;
}
```

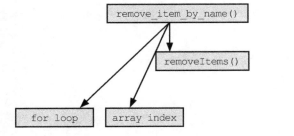

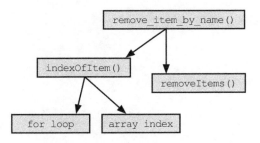

The implementation of remove_item_by_name() is easier
to read. And it shows in the diagram. indexOfItem() is on
a slightly higher layer than removeItems() because
removeItems() is more general. indexOfItem() knows about
the structure of the elements in the array. That is, it knows that
they are objects with a 'name' property. We will see in chapter 10
how to make a more general version of this same for loop.

    In the meantime, we've opened up a new possibility for reuse
with this function. Reuse tends to happen when you've got a good
layer structure, as we'll see in the next exercise.

It's your turn

`isInCart()` and `indexOfItem()` have very similar-looking code. Is this an opportunity for reuse? Can one be written in terms of the other?

```
function isInCart(cart, name) {
  for(var i = 0; i < cart.length; i++) {
    if(cart[i].name === name)
      return true;
  }
  return false;
}
```

```
function indexOfItem(cart, name) {
  for(var i = 0; i < cart.length; i++) {
    if(cart[i].name === name)
      return i;
  }
  return null;
}
```

Implement one in terms of the other and then draw the diagram for these functions down to for loops and array index.

 **Answer**

`indexOfItem()` and `isInCart()` have very similar code. `indexOfItem()` is more lower level than `isInCart()`. `indexOfItem()` returns the array index of an item, which can only be useful if the calling code knows the cart is an array. `isInCart()` returns a boolean. The calling code does not have to know the data structure.

Because `isInCart()` is higher level, it should be written in terms of the lower-level `indexOfItem()`.

Original

```
function isInCart(cart, name) {
  for(var i = 0; i < cart.length; i++) {
    if(cart[i].name === name)
      return true;
  }
  return false;
}

function indexOfItem(cart, name) {
  for(var i = 0; i < cart.length; i++) {
    if(cart[i].name === name)
      return i;
  }
  return null;
}
```

indexOfItem() has a similar for loop

Written in terms of each other

```
function isInCart(cart, name) {
```

call function in place of loop

```
  return indexOfItem(cart, name) !== null;
}

function indexOfItem(cart, name) {
  for(var i = 0; i < cart.length; i++) {
    if(cart[i].name === name)
      return i;
  }
  return null;
}
```

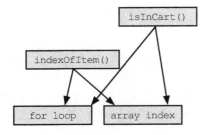

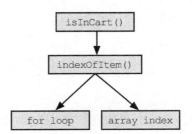

Our code is shorter because we are getting some reuse. And our code is stratifying into clearer layers. Both of those are a win.

But it is not always so clearly beneficial. Let's see another case of reuse on the next page.

It's your turn

If we look closely, setPriceByName() also has a very similar for loop inside of it as does indexOfItem().

```
function setPriceByName(cart, name, price) {        function indexOfItem(cart, name) {
  var cartCopy = cart.slice();
  for(var i = 0; i < cartCopy.length; i++) {          for(var i = 0; i < cart.length; i++) {
    if(cartCopy[i].name === name)                        if(cart[i].name === name)
      cartCopy[i] = setPrice(cartCopy[i], price);          return i;
  }                                                    }
  return cartCopy;                                     return null;
}                                                    }
```

Implement one in terms of the other and then draw the diagram for these functions down to for loops and array index.

 **Answer**

`indexOfItem()` and `setPriceByName()` have very similar code. `indexOfItem()` is more lower level than `setPriceByName()`.

<table>
<tr><th>Original</th><th>Written in terms of each other</th></tr>
</table>

Original

```
function setPriceByName(cart, name, price) {
  var cartCopy = cart.slice();
  for(var i = 0; i < cartCopy.length; i++) {

    if(cartCopy[i].name === name)

      cartCopy[i] =
        setPrice(cartCopy[i], price);
  }
  return cartCopy;
}

function indexOfItem(cart, name) {
  for(var i = 0; i < cart.length; i++) {
    if(cart[i].name === name)
      return i;
  }
  return null;
}
```

Written in terms of each other

```
function setPriceByName(cart, name, price) {
  var cartCopy = cart.slice(b);

  var i = indexOfItem(cart, name);

  if(i !== null)
    cartCopy[i] =
      setPrice(cartCopy[i], price);

  return cartCopy;
}

function indexOfItem(cart, name) {
  for(var i = 0; i < cart.length; i++) {
    if(cart[i].name === name)
      return i;
  }
  return null;
}
```

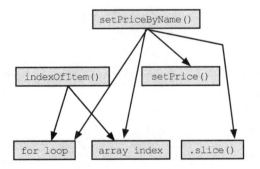

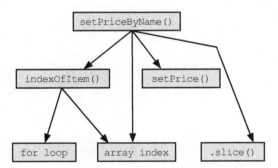

The code seems better (since we got rid of that for loop), but the graph doesn't look much better. Before, `setPriceByName()` was pointing to two different layers. It's still pointing to two. Wasn't stratifying our code supposed to help?

Counting the layers a function points to is sometimes a good indication of complexity, but in this case it is not a great sign. What we should focus on instead is that one of the longer arrows has been replaced—we have improved the design by removing one of the longer arrows. Now only two remain! And we can continue the same process and stratify more. Are we really taking full advantage of the layers we have? We'll see one way to improve this in the next exercise.

✎ It's your turn

In chapter 6, we developed a lot of functions for doing copy-on-write operations on arrays
and objects. One of them was called `arraySet()`, which would set the element at an
index with a copy-on-write discipline. It looks like it shares quite a lot with
`setPriceByName()`. Can `setPriceByName()` be written in terms of `arraySet()`?

```
function setPriceByName(cart, name, price) {      function arraySet(array, idx, value) {
  var cartCopy = cart.slice();                      var copy = array.slice();
  var idx = indexOfItem(cart, name);
  if(idx !== null)
    cartCopy[idx] =                                   copy[idx] =
      setPrice(cartCopy[idx], price);                   value;
  return cartCopy;                                  return copy;
}                                                 }
```

Implement `setPriceByName()` in terms of `arraySet()` and draw the diagram
for them.

 **Answer**

`indexOfItem()` and `setPriceByName()` have very similar code. `indexOfItem()` is more lower level than `setPriceByName()`.

Original

```
function setPriceByName(cart, name, price) {
  var cartCopy = cart.slice();
  var i = indexOfItem(cart, name);
  if(i !== null)
    cartCopy[i] =

      setPrice(cartCopy[i], price);
  return cartCopy;
}

function arraySet(array, idx, value) {
  var copy = array.slice();
  copy[idx] = value;
  return copy;
}
```

Written in terms of each other

```
function setPriceByName(cart, name, price) {

  var i = indexOfItem(cart, name);
  if(i !== null)

    return arraySet(cart, i,
      setPrice(cart[i], price));
  return cart;
}

function arraySet(array, idx, value) {
  var copy = array.slice();
  copy[idx] = value;
  return copy;
}
```

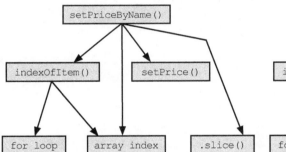 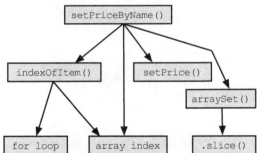

The code is better. We got rid of the long arrow to `.slice()`, replacing it with a shorter arrow to `arraySet()`. But now it looks like we're pointing to three different layers! Again, we should focus on the progress: We've replaced a longer arrow, which corresponds to another detail we can ignore.

However, it still feels like this function is not straightforward. This function is still pointing to that lowest layer by using array index. We should trust this feeling. It is a feeling many functional programmers have felt in the past, struggling to find some more general function to extract that will clarify the code. Feel free to give it a try. You may know how to get rid of that last arrow to array index.

We will leave this code for now. In the next chapter, we will apply the abstraction barrier principle to clarify it. In chapter 10, we will learn a technique to make it even more straightforward.

 **Brain break**

There's more to go, but let's take a break for questions

Q: **Is the design of** setPriceByName() **really getting better? It looks like the graph is getting more complicated, not more straightforward.**

A: That's a great question. It gets right at the difficulty with design. There is no formula for determining the best design. It is a complex combination of many factors, including how you use the code and the skill level of your developers. What these patterns can do is point at useful signals in the code or the call graph. And, ultimately, you have to settle on a design through iterative exploration and intuition.

Design is difficult, different programmers often disagree as to the best design, and design depends on the situation. It's important to be able to have a shared vocabulary to discuss design. And it's important to evaluate design choices in context. The exercise in this chapter and the next will help you hone your ability to evelute those choices.

Noodle on it

We can easily remove the array index by inserting a new function. Does that improve the design?

With array index

```
function setPriceByName(cart, name, price) {
  var i = indexOfItem(cart, name);
  if(i !== null) {
    var item = cart[i];
    return arraySet(cart, i,
      setPrice(item, price));
  }
  return cart;
}

function indexOfItem(cart, name) {
  for(var i = 0; i < cart.length; i++) {
    if(cart[i].name === name)
      return i;
  }
  return null;
}
```

Without array index

```
function setPriceByName(cart, name, price) {
  var i = indexOfItem(cart, name);
  if(i !== null) {
    var item = arrayGet(cart, i);
    return arraySet(cart, i,
      setPrice(item, price));
  }
  return cart;
}

function indexOfItem(cart, name) {
  for(var i = 0; i < cart.length; i++) {
    if(arrayGet(cart, i).name === name)
      return i;
  }
  return null;
}

function arrayGet(array, idx) {
  return array[idx];
}
```

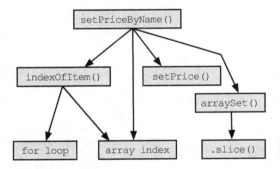

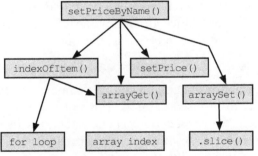

Instead of answering yes or no, list the situations where each design would be better. Complete the following sentences as a prompt:

Using array index is a better design when . . .

- my team is comfortable with arrays
-
-
-
-
-

Wrapping array index is a better design when . . .

- we need clearer layers
-
-
-
-

Pattern 1 Review: Straightforward implementation

Straightforward code solves a problem at a single level of detail

If we code without regard to design, we often have code that is hard to read and modify. But why is it so hard? Most often, the code is hard to read because you have to understand it at different levels of detail. There is a lot to understand to read the function. Straightforward implementations try to narrow the levels of detail you need to understand in order to read the code.

Stratified design helps us target a specific level of detail

While it's not an easy formula, we can train our sense of design to look out for these levels of detail with a variety of clues in the code. We can then make appropriate changes.

The call graph gives us a rich source of clues about levels of detail

The code itself gives us a lot of clues, but there's often too much to read at once to get a big picture view. A call graph can show us how many functions are defined in terms of each other. As we draw the graph, we can place functions at layers that correspond to their level of detail. Using the function signature, body, and call graph, we have a lot of information to help us write straightforward code.

Extracting out a function makes a more general function

One way to make a function more straightforward is to extract out a more general function that takes care of details we don't want to deal with at that level. The more general function is often easier to test, since it handles one specific detail. It also makes the code more readable through clearer code and appropriate naming.

More general functions are more reusable

As functions are extracted, it is common to find other places for them to be used. This is different from looking for "duplicate code." We extract out general functions in order to clarify an implementation. But it turns out that general functions are more generally useful than specific functions. There will be serendipitous reuse.

Patterns

☑ **Straightforward implementations**

☐ Abstraction barrier

☐ Minimal interface

☐ Comfortable layers

We don't hide the complexity

It is very easy to make any code *look* straightforward. We could hide unclear code in "helper functions." However, this is not stratified design. In stratified design, we want every layer to be straightforward. We can't just move the complex stuff out of our current layer. We want to find general functions at a lower level that are themselves straightforward, out of which we can build our software in a straightforward way.

Conclusion

In this chapter, we've learned how to visualize our code as a call graph and recognize distinct layers of abstraction. We've seen the first and most important pattern of stratified design, which asks us to find straightforward implementations. The layer structure helps us organize our code to build simple functions out of other simple functions. However, there is more to stratified design than that. We'll see three more patterns in the next chapter.

Summary

- Stratified design organizes code into layers of abstraction. Each layer helps us ignore different details.

- When implementing a new function, we need to identify what details are important to solving the problem. This will tell you what layer the function should be in.

- There are many clues that can help us locate functions in layers. We can look at the name, the body, and the call graph.

- The name tells us the intent of the function. We can group it with other functions with related intents.

- The body can tell us the details that are important to a function. These are clues as to where in the layer structure it goes.

- The call graph can show us that an implementation is not straightforward. If the arrows coming from it are of varying lengths, it's a good sign the implementation is not straightforward.

- We can improve the layer structure by extracting out more general functions. More general functions are on lower layers and are more reusable.

- The pattern of straightforward implementation guides us to build layers such that our functions are implemented in a clear and elegant way.

Up next . . .

The pattern of straightforward implementation is just the beginning of what the layer structure can reveal to us. In the next chapter, we'll go over three more patterns based on the layer structure of our code that will help us improve the reuse, maintenance, and testability of our software.

Stratified design: Part 2 | 9

In this chapter

- Learn to construct abstraction barriers to modularize code.

- Discover what to look for in a good interface (and how to find it).

- Know when design is good enough.

- Discover how stratified design helps maintenance, testing, and reuse.

In the last chapter, we learned how to draw call graphs and look for layers to help us organize our code. In this chapter, we continue deepening our understanding of stratified design and honing our design intuition with three more patterns. These patterns help us with the maintenance, testing, and reuse of our code.

201

Patterns of stratified design

Just as a reminder, we are looking at the practice of stratified design through the lenses of four patterns. We already covered pattern 1 in the last chapter. Because we've already got the fundamentals down, in this chapter we will cover the remaining three. Here they are again for reference.

Pattern 1: Straightforward implementation

The layer structure of stratified design should help us build straightforward implementations. When we read a function with a straightforward implementation, the problem the function signature presents should be solved at the right level of detail in the body. Too much detail is a code smell.

Pattern 2: Abstraction barrier

Some layers in the graph provide an interface that lets us hide an important implementation detail. These layers help us write code at a higher level and free our limited mental capacity to think at a higher level.

Pattern 3: Minimal interface

As our system evolves, we want the interfaces to important business concepts to converge to a small, powerful set of operations. Every other operation should be defined in terms of those, either directly or indirectly.

Pattern 4: Comfortable layers

The patterns and practices of stratified design should serve our needs as programmers, who are in turn serving the business. We should invest time in the layers that will help us deliver software faster and with higher quality. We don't want to add layers for sport. The code and its layers of abstraction should feel comfortable to work in.

We've already seen the fundamentals: drawing the call graph and looking for layers. Now let's dive right into pattern 2.

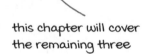

Patterns

- ✔ Straightforward implementations
- ☐ Abstraction barrier
- ☐ Minimal interface
- ☐ Comfortable layers

this chapter will cover the remaining three

Pattern 2: Abstraction barrier

The second pattern we will look at is called an *abstraction barrier*. Abstraction barriers solve a number of problems. One is clearly delegating responsibilities between teams.

Before abstraction barrier

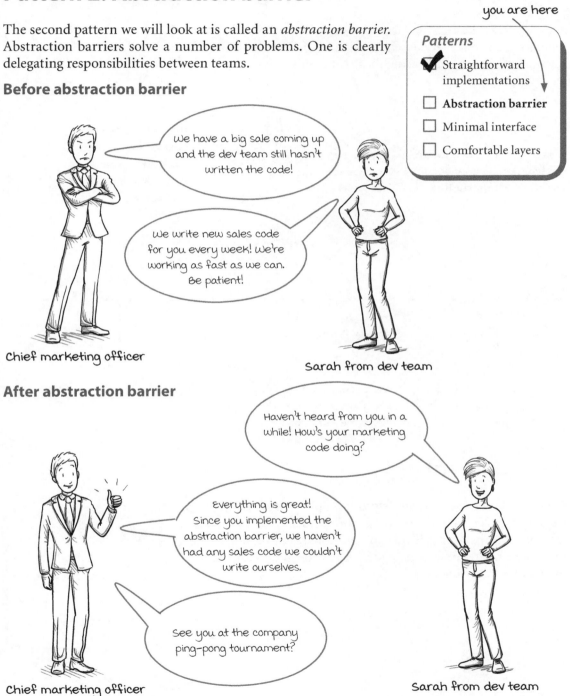

After abstraction barrier

Abstraction barriers hide implementations

An *abstraction barrier* is a layer of functions that hide the implementation so well that you can completely forget about how it is implemented even while using those functions.

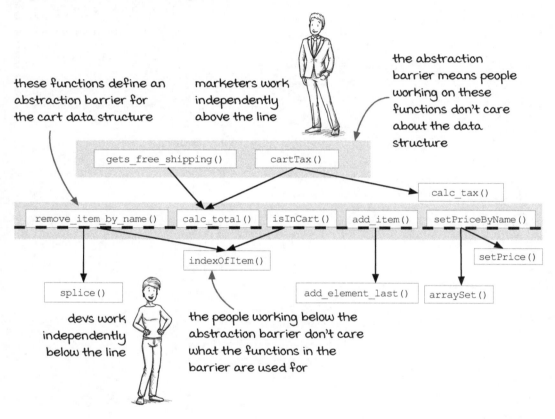

these functions define an abstraction barrier for the cart data structure

marketers work independently above the line

the abstraction barrier means people working on these functions don't care about the data structure

the people working below the abstraction barrier don't care what the functions in the barrier are used for

devs work independently below the line

Functional programmers strategically employ abstraction barriers because they let them think about a problem at a higher level. For instance, the marketing team can write and read functions having to do with marketing campaigns without dealing with the dirty work of for loops and arrays.

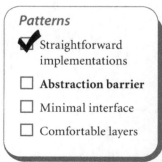

Patterns

☑ Straightforward implementations

☐ **Abstraction barrier**

☐ Minimal interface

☐ Comfortable layers

Ignoring details is symmetrical

I like the abstraction barrier because the names of functions make sense to our team.

We can write our own code and the dev team takes care of stuff we don't care about, like for loops.

I like the abstraction barrier because we aren't slowing down the marketing team.

And we're planning on a big implementation change and we won't even have to tell them, thanks to the barrier!

Chief marketing officer

Sarah from dev team

The abstraction barrier allows the marketing team to ignore details of the implementation. But there's a symmetrical "not caring." The dev team who implements the barrier doesn't have to care about the details of the marketing campaign code that uses the functions in the abstraction barrier. The teams can work largely independently, thanks to the power of the abstraction barrier.

You have likely encountered this with libraries or APIs that you have used. Let's say you're using a weather data API from a company called RainCo to make a weather app. Your job is to use the API to display it to the user. The RainCo team's job is to implement the weather data service. They don't care what your app does! The API is an abstraction barrier that clearly delineates the responsibilities.

The dev team is going to test the limits of the abstraction barrier by changing the underlying data structure of shopping carts. If the abstraction barrier is built correctly, the marketing team won't notice and their code won't have to change at all.

Patterns

✔ Straightforward implementations

☐ **Abstraction barrier**

☐ Minimal interface

☐ Comfortable layers

Swapping the shopping cart's data structure

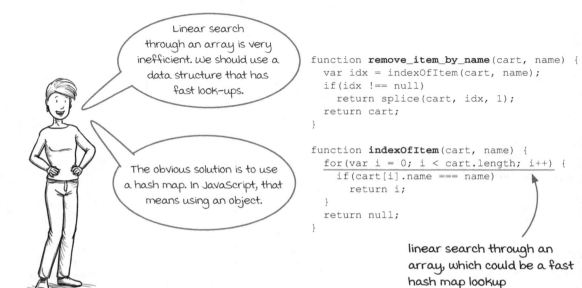

Linear search through an array is very inefficient. We should use a data structure that has fast look-ups.

The obvious solution is to use a hash map. In JavaScript, that means using an object.

Sarah from dev team

```
function remove_item_by_name(cart, name) {
  var idx = indexOfItem(cart, name);
  if(idx !== null)
    return splice(cart, idx, 1);
  return cart;
}

function indexOfItem(cart, name) {
  for(var i = 0; i < cart.length; i++) {
    if(cart[i].name === name)
      return i;
  }
  return null;
}
```

linear search through an array, which could be a fast hash map lookup

Sarah is onto something. We need to address the poor performance of linear search through arrays. We shouldn't hide the poor performance behind a clean interface.

The obvious thing to try is to use a JavaScript object (as a hash map) instead of an array. Adding to, removing from, and checking containment are all fast operations on a JavaScript object.

It's your turn

Which functions need to change to implement this change?

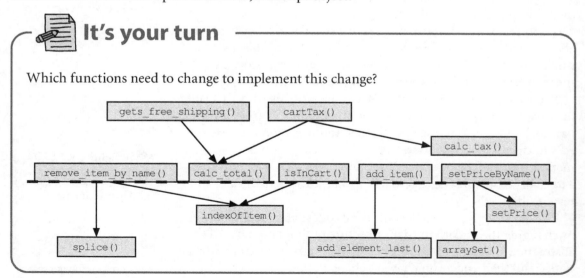

 **Answer**

Just the functions in the highlighted layer need to change. No other functions assume that the shopping cart is an array. These are the functions that create the abstraction barrier.

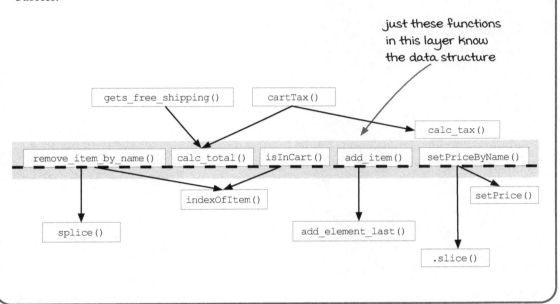

just these functions
in this layer know
the data structure

Re-implementing the shopping cart as an object

Re-implementing our shopping cart as a JavaScript object will make it more efficient and also more straightforward (yay pattern 1!). The object is a more appropriate data structure for random additions and removals.

Cart as array

```
function add_item(cart, item) {
  return add_element_last(cart, item);
}

function calc_total(cart) {
  var total = 0;

  for(var i = 0; i < cart.length; i++) {
    var item = cart[i];
    total += item.price;
  }
  return total;
}

function setPriceByName(cart, name, price) {
  var cartCopy = cart.slice();
  for(var i = 0; i < cartCopy.length; i++) {
    if(cartCopy[i].name === name)
      cartCopy[i] =
         setPrice(cartCopy[i], price);
  }
  return cartCopy;
}

function remove_item_by_name(cart, name) {
  var idx = indexOfItem(cart, name);
  if(idx !== null)
    return splice(cart, idx, 1);
  return cart;
}

function indexOfItem(cart, name) {
  for(var i = 0; i < cart.length; i++) {
    if(cart[i].name === name)
      return i;
  }
  return null;
}

function isInCart(cart, name) {
  return indexOfItem(cart, name) !== null;
}
```

Cart as object

```
function add_item(cart, item) {
  return objectSet(cart, item.name, item);
}

function calc_total(cart) {
  var total = 0;
  var names = Object.keys(cart);
  for(var i = 0; i < names.length; i++) {
    var item = cart[names[i]];
    total += item.price;
  }
  return total;
}

function setPriceByName(cart, name, price) {
  if(isInCart(cart, name)) {
    var item = cart[name];
    var copy = setPrice(item, price);
    return objectSet(cart, name, copy);
  } else {
    var item = make_item(name, price);
    return objectSet(cart, name, item);
  }
}

function remove_item_by_name(cart, name) {
  return objectDelete(cart, name);
}
```

this function doesn't make sense anymore, so it's gone

```
function isInCart(cart, name) {
  return cart.hasOwnProperty(name);
}
```

a built-in to know if an Object contains a key

Sometimes, unclear code is due to using the wrong data structure. Our code is smaller and cleaner—and more efficient. And the marketing department's code will still work unchanged!

The abstraction barrier lets us ignore details

What lets us change the data structure without changing all of the code that uses shopping carts?

We originally used an array to store the items in the shopping cart. We recognized that it was not efficient. We modified a handful of functions that operated on the shopping cart and completely swapped out the data structure it used. The marketing team didn't have to change their code. They didn't even have to know it happened! How did we manage that?

The reason we could swap out a data structure and only change five functions was because those functions define an abstraction barrier. Abstraction is just a fancy way of saying, "What details can I ignore?" We call a layer an abstraction barrier when all of the functions together in a layer let us ignore the same thing when working above that layer. It's a level of indirection that lets us ignore unwanted details.

Patterns

- ☑ Straightforward implementations
- ☐ **Abstraction barrier**
- ☐ Minimal interface
- ☐ Comfortable layers

these functions define an abstraction barrier for the cart data structure

the abstraction barrier means these functions don't care about the data structure

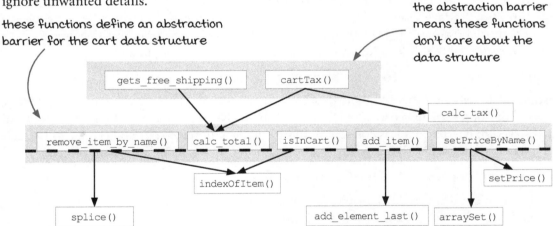

The abstraction barrier in this case means the functions above that layer don't need to know what the data structure is. They can use those functions exclusively and treat the implementation of the cart as a detail they don't care about, so much so that we can change from an array to an object and no function above the abstraction barrier notices.

Notice how there are no arrows that cross the dotted line. If a function above the line called splice() on a cart, for example, it would be violating the abstraction barrier. It would be using an implementation detail that it shouldn't care about. We would call it an incomplete abstraction barrier. The solution is to add a new function to complete the barrier.

When to use (and when *not* to use!) abstraction barriers

Abstraction barriers are useful in the design of our code, but they shouldn't be used everywhere. When should they be used?

1. To facilitate changes of implementation

In cases of high uncertainty about how you want to implement something, an abstraction barrier can be the layer of indirection that lets you change the implementation later. This property might be useful if you are prototyping something and you still don't know how best to implement it. Or perhaps you *know* something will change; you're just not ready to do it yet, like if you know you will want to get data from the server eventually, but right now you'll just stub it out.

> *Patterns*
> ☑ Straightforward
>   implementations
> ☐ **Abstraction barrier**
> ☐ Minimal interface
> ☐ Comfortable layers

However, this benefit is often a trap, so be careful. We often write a lot of code *just in case* something might change in the future. Why? To save writing other code! It's a silly practice to write three lines today to save three lines tomorrow (when tomorrow may never come); 99% of the time, the data structure never changes. The only reason it did in our example was that the team never stopped to think about efficiency until very late in development.

2. To make code easier to write and read

Abstraction barriers allow us to ignore details. Sometimes those details are bug magnets. Did we initialize the loop variables correctly? Did we have an off-by-one error in the loop exit condition? An abstraction barrier that lets you ignore those details will make your code easier to write. If you hide the right details, then less adept programmers can be productive when using it.

3. To reduce coordination between teams

Our development team could change things without talking with marketing first. And marketing could write simple marketing campaigns without checking in with development. The abstraction barrier allows teams on either side to ignore the details the other team handles. Thus, each team moves faster.

4. To mentally focus on the problem at hand

Now we get to the real prize of abstraction barriers. They let you think more easily about the problem you are trying to solve. Let's face it. We have limited mental capacity, and we have a lot of details to worry about. An abstraction barrier makes some details unimportant to the problem we are solving right now. It means we are less likely to make a mistake and less likely to get tired.

Pattern 2 Review: Abstraction barrier

Abstraction barrier is a very powerful pattern. It strongly decouples code above the barrier from code at and below the barrier. An abstraction barrier decouples by defining details that don't have to be considered on either side of the barrier.

Typically, the code above the barrier can ignore implementation details such as which data structure is used. In our example, the marketing code (above the barrier) doesn't have to care if the cart is an array or an object.

The code at or below the barrier can ignore the higher-level details like what the functions are being used for. The functions in the barrier can be used for anything, and they don't have to care. In our example, the code at the barrier doesn't care what the marketing campaign is all about.

All abstractions work like that: They define what code above and below doesn't have to care about. Any particular function could define the same details to ignore. The abstraction barrier just makes this definition very strongly and explicitly. It declares that no marketing code should ever have to know how the shopping cart is implemented. All of the functions in the abstraction barrier work together to make this possible.

We should be careful of the trap of "making future change easy." Abstraction barriers make change easy, but that's not why we should use them. They should be used strategically to reduce inter-team communication and help clarify messy code.

The key thing to remember about abstraction barriers is that it's all about ignoring details. Where is it useful to ignore details? What details can you help people ignore? Can you find a set of functions that, together, help you ignore the same details?

Patterns

- ✔ Straightforward implementations
- ✔ **Abstraction barrier**
- ☐ Minimal interface
- ☐ Comfortable layers

Our code is more straightforward

Touching base with pattern 1: Straightforward implementation

After changing out the data structure, most of our functions are now one-liners. The number of lines of code is not the important thing. What is important is that the solution is expressed at the correct level of generality and detail. One-liners typically don't have room to mix up levels, so they are a good sign.

```
function add_item(cart, item) {
  return objectSet(cart, item.name, item);
}

function gets_free_shipping(cart) {
  return calc_total(cart) >= 20;
}

function cartTax(cart) {
  return calc_tax(calc_total(cart));
}

function remove_item_by_name(cart, name) {
  return objectDelete(cart, name);
}

function isInCart(cart, name) {
  return cart.hasOwnProperty(name);
}
```

Two functions still have complex implementations:

```
function calc_total(cart) {
  var total = 0;
  var names = Object.keys(cart);
  for(var i = 0; i < names.length; i++) {
    var item = cart[names[i]];
    total += item.price;
  }
  return total;
}

function setPriceByName(cart, name, price) {
  if(isInCart(cart, name)) {
    var itemCopy = objectSet(cart[name], 'price', price);
    return objectSet(cart, name, itemCopy);
  } else {
    return objectSet(cart, name, make_item(name, price));
  }
}
```

We don't have all of the tools we need to make these functions more straightforward. We'll learn those tools in chapters 10 and 11. For now, we've got two more patterns to learn.

Pattern 3: Minimal interface

The third pattern we will look at to help guide our design sense is *minimal interface*. It asks us to consider where the code for new features belongs. By keeping our interfaces minimal, we avoid bloating our lower layers with unnecessary features. Let's see an example.

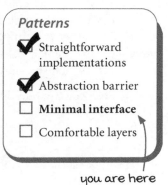

Patterns

☑ Straightforward implementations

☑ Abstraction barrier

☐ **Minimal interface**

☐ Comfortable layers

you are here

Marketing wants to give a discount for watches

The marketing department has a new campaign. They'd like to give anyone with a lot of items in their cart, along with a watch, a 10% discount.

Watch marketing campaign

> *If* the shopping cart's total is > $100
>   *and*
>   the shopping cart contains a watch
> *then*
>   they get a 10% discount.

implement this condition as a function that returns true or false

Your job is to implement the software to decide who gets this discount. Can you have it by Tuesday?

Chief marketing officer

Two choices for coding the marketing campaign

There are two ways we could implement this marketing campaign. The first is to implement it in the same layer as the abstraction barrier. The other is to implement it above the abstraction barrier. We can't implement it below the barrier because then marketing can't call it. Which should we choose?

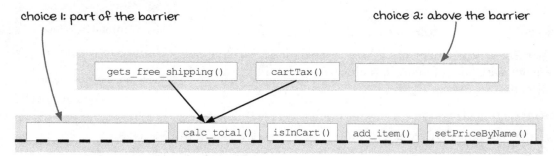

Choice 1: Part of the barrier

In the barrier layer, we can access the cart as a hash map. But we can't call any function in the same layer:

```
function getsWatchDiscount(cart) {
  var total = 0;
  var names = Object.keys(cart);
  for(var i = 0; i < names.length; i++) {
    var item = cart[names[i]];
    total += item.price;
  }
  return total > 100 && cart.hasOwnProperty("watch");
}
```

Choice 2: Above the barrier

Above the barrier, we can't treat it like a hash map. We have to go through the functions that define the barrier:

```
function getsWatchDiscount(cart) {
  var total    = calcTotal(cart);
  var hasWatch = isInCart("watch");
  return total > 100 && hasWatch;
}
```

 **Noodle on it**

Which do you think is better? Why?

Implementing the campaign above the barrier is better

Implementing the campaign above the barrier (choice 2) is better for many interrelated reasons. First of all, choice 2 is more straightforward than choice 1, so it wins on pattern 1. Choice 1 increases the amount of low-level code in the system.

Choice 1
```
function getsWatchDiscount(cart) {
  var total = 0;
  var names = Object.keys(cart);
  for(var i = 0; i < names.length; i++) {
    var item = cart[names[i]];
    total += item.price;
  }
  return total > 100 &&
    cart.hasOwnProperty("watch");
}
```

Choice 2
```
function getsWatchDiscount(cart) {
  var total    = calcTotal(cart);
  var hasWatch = isInCart("watch");
  return total > 100 && hasWatch;
}
```

Choice 1 doesn't technically violate the abstraction barrier. The arrows don't reach across any barriers. However, it violates the purpose behind the barrier. This function is for a marketing campaign, and the marketing team does not want to care about implementation details like for loops. Because choice 1 makes it part of the barrier, the dev team has to maintain it. The marketing team will need to talk to the dev team to change it. Choice 2 doesn't have these problems.

Straightforward implementations
- Choice 1
- ✔ Choice 2

But there is a subtler problem. The functions that make up the abstraction barrier are part of a contract between the marketing team and the development team. Adding a new function to the abstraction barrier increases the size of the contract. If anything needs to change there, the change will be more expensive because it requires renegotiating the terms of the contract. It's more code to understand. It is more details to keep in mind. In short, choice 1 dilutes the benefits of our abstraction barrier.

Abstraction barrier
- Choice 1
- ✔ Choice 2

The minimal interface pattern states that we should prefer to write new features at higher levels rather than adding to or modifying lower levels. Luckily, this marketing campaign is a really clear case and we don't need an extra function in the abstraction barrier layer. But there are many cases that are much muddier than this one. The minimal interface pattern guides us to solve problems at higher levels and avoid modifying lower levels. And the pattern applies to all layers, not just abstraction barriers.

Let's look at a more challenging example that will tempt even the best designers among us to make the wrong decision. Hold fast to pattern 3 as you turn the page.

Minimal interface
- Choice 1
- ✔ Choice 2

Marketing wants to log items added to the cart

The marketing team wants another feature. People are adding items to their carts, but then they abandon the carts without buying. Why? The marketing team wants more information to be able to answer the question so they can improve sales. Their request is to record a log of every time someone adds an item to the cart.

Patterns

- ✔ Straightforward implementations
- ✔ Abstraction barrier
- ☐ **Minimal interface**
- ☐ Comfortable layers

Can we log a record to a database? Once we have enough records, we can analyze it to answer our question.

Sure thing! The line of code for logging is easy. We just need to figure out where to put it.

Chief marketing officer

Jenna from dev team

Jenna creates the database table and codes up an action to save the record to the database. You call it like this:

```
logAddToCart(user_id, item)
```

Now we just need to put it somewhere so that it logs all of them. Jenna suggests putting it in the add_item() function, like this:

```
function add_item(cart, item) {
  logAddToCart(global_user_id, item);
  return objectSet(cart, item.name, item);
}
```

Is this where we should put it? Let's think about this like a designer. What are the advantages of putting it here? What are the disadvantages? Let's walk through the consequences together.

The design consequences of code location

Of course, Jenna's suggestion seems to make a lot of sense. We want to log a record every time a user adds an item to the cart, and `add_item()` is where that happens. It makes it easy to get that rule right because the function will do the logging for us. We won't have to remember. We can ignore that detail (the detail of logging) while we work above this layer.

However, there are serious, problematic consequences of logging inside of `add_item()`. For one, `logAddToCart()` is an action. If we call an action from inside `add_item()`, it becomes an action itself. And then everything that calls `add_item()` becomes an action by the spreading rule. That could have serious consequences for testing.

Because `add_item()` is a calculation, we were always allowed to use it wherever and whenever we wanted to. Here's an example:

```
function update_shipping_icons(cart) {
  var buttons = get_buy_buttons_dom();
  for(var i = 0; i < buttons.length; i++) {
    var button = buttons[i];
    var item = button.item;
    var new_cart = add_item(cart, item);
    if(gets_free_shipping(new_cart))
      button.show_free_shipping_icon();
    else
      button.hide_free_shipping_icon();
  }
}
```

we call add_item()
when the user didn't
add it to the cart

we definitely don't
want to log that!

`update_shipping_icons()` uses `add_item()`, even when the user hasn't added the item to the cart. This function gets called every time a product is displayed to the user! We don't want to log those as if the user added them to their cart.

Finally, and most importantly, we have such a nice, clean set of functions—an interface—to the shopping cart. We should cherish that. It serves our needs. It allows us to ignore the appropriate details. This change does not make the interface better. The call to `logAddToCart()` should really go above the abstraction barrier. Let's take a crack at that on the next page.

A better place to log adds to cart

We know two things for certain about the `logAddToCart()`
function: It is an action and it should go above our abstraction
barrier. But where should it go?

Again, this is a design decision, so there's no answer that's right
in all contexts. However, the function `add_item_to_cart()` is
a good choice. That's the click handler we put on the add to cart
button. That's the place where we are *sure* we are capturing the
intent of the user. It's also already an action. It also looks like a
dispatch of "here's everything that needs to happen when the user
adds an item to the cart." Calling `logAddToCart()` is just one
more thing to dispatch.

```
function add_item_to_cart(name, price) {
  var item = make_cart_item(name, price);
  shopping_cart = add_item(shopping_cart, item);
  var total = calc_total(shopping_cart);
  set_cart_total_dom(total);
  update_shipping_icons(shopping_cart);
  update_tax_dom(total);
  logAddToCart();
}
```

add to cart button
click handler

other actions that get
called when the user clicks

we can add it here along
with other stuff that
needs to happen when
users add items to cart

This isn't the best possible design, but it is the right place to call
this function for our particular design. Without completely rede-
signing our app, this is where it belongs. A better design would
require re-architecting the whole application.

We almost put this function in the wrong place, but we got
lucky. It's lucky we thought about the action spreading rule
and that we remembered that the call to `add_item()` is
`update_shipping_icons()`.

But we don't want to rely on luck for good design. We want a
principle that would have avoided this. That's what the pattern of
minimal interface gives us.

The pattern of minimal interface asks us to focus on the sense
of a clean, simple, and reliable interface and to use it as a proxy
for the unseen consequences in the rest of the code. The pattern
guides us to protect our interface from unnecessary changes or
expansion.

Pattern 3 Review: Minimal interface

We can think of the functions that define an abstraction barrier as an interface. They provide the operations through which we will access and manipulate a set of values. In stratified design, we find a dynamic tension between the completeness of the abstraction barrier and the pattern to keep it minimal.

There are many reasons to keep the abstraction barrier minimal:

1. If we add more code to the barrier, we have more to change when we change the implementation.

2. Code in the barrier is lower level, so it's more likely to contain bugs.

3. Low-level code is harder to understand.

4. More functions in an abstraction barrier mean more coordination between teams.

5. A larger interface to our abstraction barrier is harder to keep in your head.

Applying this pattern in practice means that if you can implement a function above a layer, using existing functions in that layer, you should. Think carefully about the purpose of the function and at what layer of abstraction it makes sense to implement it. In general, you should prefer higher layers on the graph.

Although the benefit of the minimal interface pattern is clearest in the case of abstraction barriers, it applies generally to all layers. In the ideal case, a layer should have as many functions as necessary, but no more. And, also ideally, the functions should not have to change, nor should you need to add functions later. The set should be complete, minimal, and timeless. This is the ideal to which the minimal interface pattern draws all layers.

Is this possible? Yes, we do see it happening, though not for every layer. We see the ideal achieved when we find a file of source code that has not been modified for years, yet the functions in it are used heavily throughout the codebase. This ideal is achievable at the lower layers of your call graph if they define a small set of operations that provide great power. But keep in mind that it is an ideal to strive toward, not a destination.

The key thing is to sharpen your sense of how well the functions in the layer serve their purpose. Do they do it well, with a small number of functions? Does your change really add to that purpose?

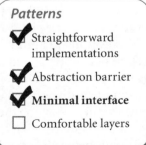

Patterns

✔ Straightforward implementations

✔ Abstraction barrier

✔ **Minimal interface**

☐ Comfortable layers

Pattern 4: Comfortable layers

The first three patterns have asked us to build our layers. They have given us guidance on how best to do that by striving for ideals. The fourth and final pattern, *comfortable layers*, asks us to consider the practical side.

It often feels really nice to build layers very tall. Look how powerful! Look at how few details I have to think about! However, it's rarely so easy to come up with robust layers of abstraction. Often, over time, we realize that an abstraction barrier we built was not so helpful after all. It wasn't complete. Or it was less convenient than not using it. We all have had the experience of building towers of abstractions too high. The exploration and subsequent failure is part of the process. It is hard to build very high.

It's also the case that abstraction can mean the difference between an impossible task and a possible one. Look at the JavaScript language, which provides a nice abstraction barrier over machine code. Who thinks about the machine instructions when they're coding in JavaScript? You can't! JavaScript does too much and there are too many differences between implementations. How did such a useful layer get devised and built? Thousands of person-years of work over many decades to build robust parsers, compilers, and virtual machines.

As programmers working in the industry, presented with a problem to solve in software, we don't have the luxury of such resources for finding and building great abstractions. They take too much time. The business can't afford to wait.

The comfort pattern gives us a practical test of when to stop striving for the other patterns (and also when to start again). We ask ourselves, "Are we comfortable?" If we are comfortable working in the code, we can relax on design. Let the for loops go unwrapped. Let the arrows grow long and the layers meld into one another.

However, if we are uncomfortable with the details we have to keep in our heads or with how unclean the code feels, start applying the patterns again. No codebase reaches the ideal. There is constant tension between design and the need for new features. Let comfort guide you on when to stop. Basically, you and your team live in this code. You have to make it meet your needs as programmers and the needs of the business.

We've finished the four patterns of stratified design. Let's summarize our patterns before we take a last look at the call graph to see how much information we can get from it.

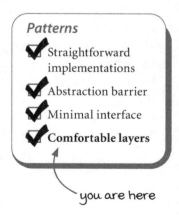

Patterns

☑ Straightforward implementations

☑ Abstraction barrier

☑ Minimal interface

☑ **Comfortable layers**

you are here

Patterns of stratified design

We've reached the end, so just for reference, here are the four patterns we studied in these two chapters.

Pattern 1: Straightforward implementation

The layer structure of stratified design should help us build straightforward implementations. When we read a function with a straightforward implementation, the problem the function signature presents should be solved at the right level of detail in the body. Too much detail is a code smell.

Pattern 2: Abstraction barrier

Some layers in the graph provide an interface that lets us hide an important implementation detail. These layers help us write code at a higher level and free our limited mental capacity to think at a higher level.

Pattern 3: Minimal interface

As our system evolves, we want the interfaces to important business concepts to converge to a small, powerful set of operations. Every other operation should be defined in terms of those, either directly or indirectly.

Pattern 4: Comfort

The patterns and practices of stratified design should serve our needs as programmers, who are in turn serving the business. We should invest time in the layers that will help us deliver software faster and with higher quality. We don't want to add layers for sport. The code and its layers of abstraction should feel comfortable to work in. If they do, we don't need to improve the design for the sake of it.

Now we will look at the call graph abstractly to see what it can tell us about reusability, testability, and changeability. We want to keep these factors in mind as we add code around the different layers.

222   Chapter **9** | *Stratified design: Part 2*

What does the graph show us about our code?

We have learned how to draw the call graph and to use it to help us improve our code. We spent a lot of time in the last chapter on how the graph can guide us to make our code more straightforward. We have also spent time learning other patterns for organizing the layers. But we haven't talked much about how the structure of the call graph itself can reveal a lot about our code.

The call graph structure shows which functions call what. It's pure facts. If we eliminate the names of the functions, we have an abstract view of just that structure.

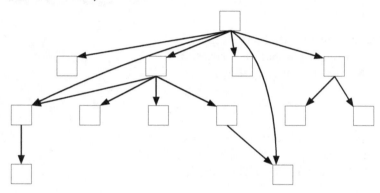

Believe it or not, this structure by itself can tell us a lot about three important nonfunctional requirements. *Functional requirements* are the things the software has to do work correctly. For example, it has to get the right answer when it does a tax calculation. *Nonfunctional requirements* (NFRs) are things like how testable, maintainable, or reusable the code is. These are often considered the main reasons for doing software design. They are often called *ilities*, as in testab*ility*, reusab*ility*, or maintainab*ility*. (No, I am not making this up.)

Let's look at what the structure of the call graph can tell us about these three NFRs:

1. *Maintainability*—What code is easiest to change when requirements change?

2. *Testability*—What is most important to test?

3. *Reusability*—What functions are easier to reuse?

By looking at just the structure of the call graph, without function names, we'll see how the position in the call graph largely determines these three important NFRs.

Code at the top of the graph is easier to change

Given an abstract call graph diagram (no function names), can we figure out what code is easiest to change? Knowing that, we'll know where we need to put the code that implements rapidly changing requirements (like business rules). We'll also know where to put the code that changes the least. If we put things in the right places, we can drastically reduce the cost of maintenance.

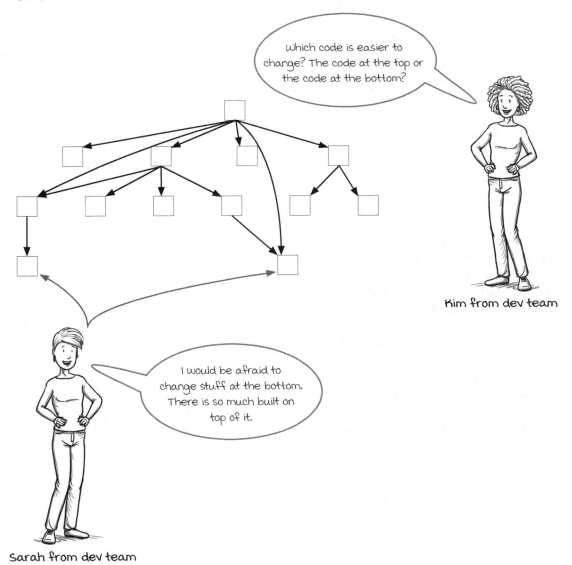

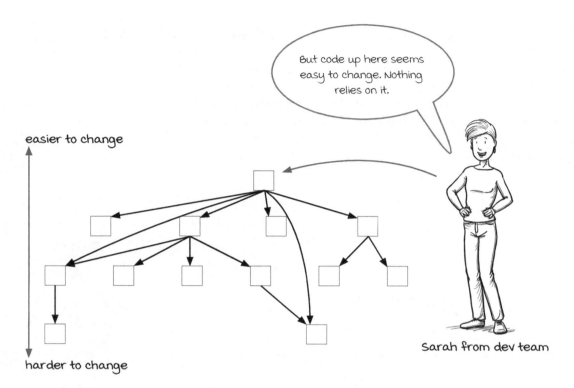

Sarah from dev team

Sarah is right. Code at the top of the graph is easier to change. If you change the function at the very top, you don't have to think about what else is calling it since nothing is calling it. It can completely change behavior without affecting any calling code.

Contrast that with functions at the bottom layer. Three levels of functions are relying on its behavior. If you change its external behavior, you change the behavior of everything on the path up to the top. That's why it's hard to change safely.

We want code at the bottom that we know implements timeless functions. That's why we find copy-on-write functions way at the bottom. They can be done once correctly and never changed. When we extract functions into a lower layer (pattern 1) or add functions at higher layers (pattern 3), we are stratifying code into layers of change.

> **The longer the path from the top to a function, the more expensive that function will be to change.**

> **If we put code that changes frequently near or at the top, our jobs will be easier. Build less on top of things that change.**

Testing code at the bottom is more important

Now let's see what this graph can tell us about which code is more important to test. We might think "we should test everything," but that doesn't always happen. If we can't test everything, what is the most important stuff we should test so that the time spent testing will pay off the most in the long term?

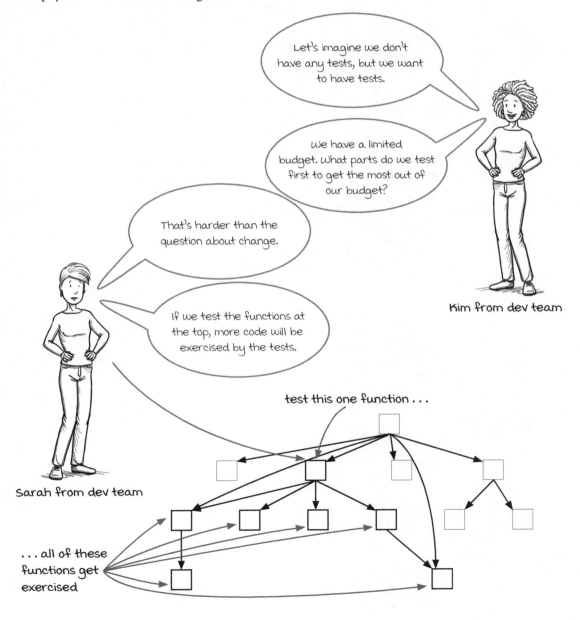

Let's imagine we don't have any tests, but we want to have tests.

We have a limited budget. What parts do we test first to get the most out of our budget?

Kim from dev team

That's harder than the question about change.

If we test the functions at the top, more code will be exercised by the tests.

Sarah from dev team

test this one function . . .

. . . all of these functions get exercised

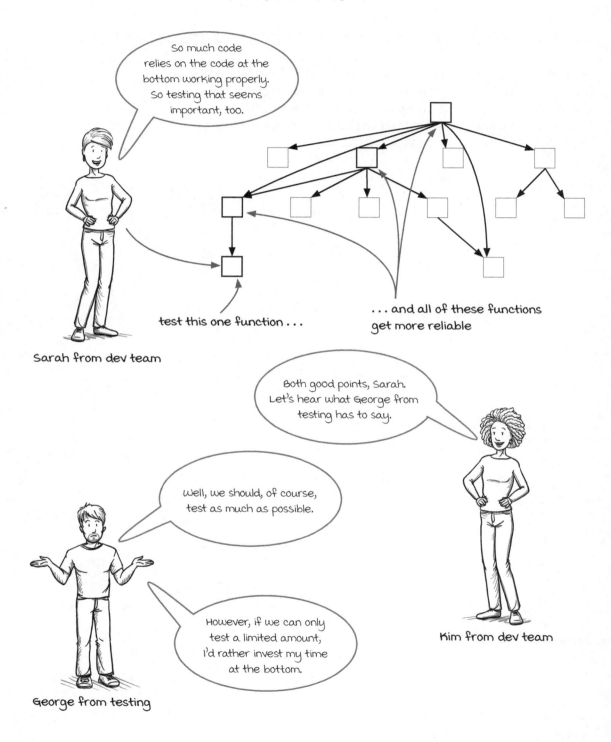

If we're doing it right, code at the top changes
more frequently than code at the bottom.

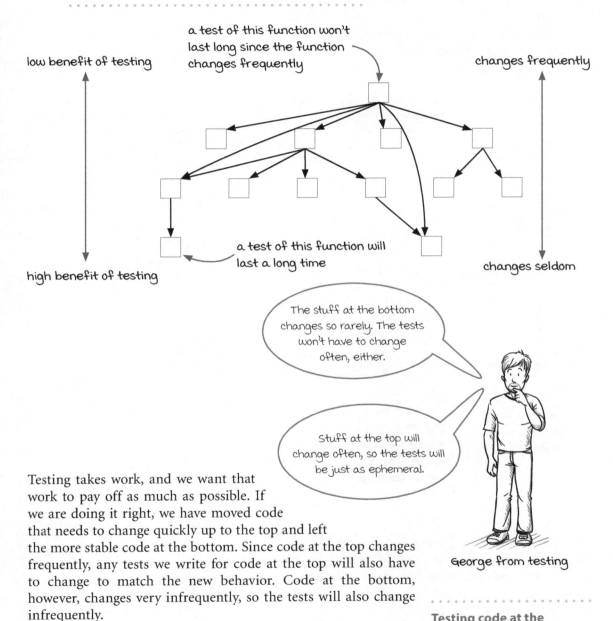

a test of this function won't
last long since the function
changes frequently

low benefit of testing

changes frequently

a test of this function will
last a long time

high benefit of testing

changes seldom

The stuff at the bottom
changes so rarely. The tests
won't have to change
often, either.

Stuff at the top will
change often, so the tests will
be just as ephemeral.

George from testing

Testing takes work, and we want that
work to pay off as much as possible. If
we are doing it right, we have moved code
that needs to change quickly up to the top and left
the more stable code at the bottom. Since code at the top changes
frequently, any tests we write for code at the top will also have
to change to match the new behavior. Code at the bottom,
however, changes very infrequently, so the tests will also change
infrequently.

Our patterns help us stratify code into layers of testability. As
we extract functions into lower layers or build functions in higher
layers, we are choosing how valuable their tests will be.

Testing code at the
bottom benefits you more
in the long run.

Code at the bottom is more reusable

We have seen that code at the top is easier to change and that code
at the bottom is more important to test. Which code is easier to
reuse? Reused code is code you didn't have to write, test, or change
twice. Code reuse saves time and money.

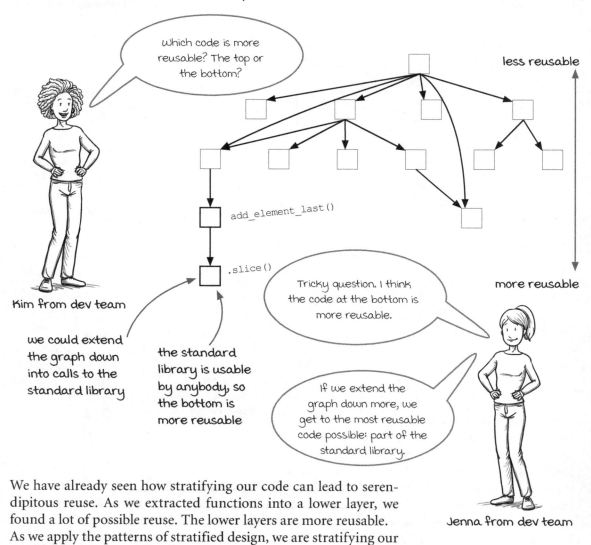

Which code is more
reusable? The top or
the bottom?

less reusable

add_element_last()

.slice()

Tricky question. I think
the code at the bottom is
more reusable.

more reusable

Kim from dev team

we could extend
the graph down
into calls to the
standard library

the standard
library is usable
by anybody, so
the bottom is
more reusable

If we extend the
graph down more, we
get to the most reusable
code possible: part of the
standard library.

Jenna from dev team

We have already seen how stratifying our code can lead to serendipitous reuse. As we extracted functions into a lower layer, we
found a lot of possible reuse. The lower layers are more reusable.
As we apply the patterns of stratified design, we are stratifying our
code into layers of reusability.

**The more code below a
function, the less reusable it is.**

Summary: What the graph shows us about our code

We've just seen that the call graph can tell us a lot about the nonfunctional requirements (NFRs) of our code. Let's review them and rephase them as rules of thumb.

Maintainability

Rule: *The fewer functions on the path to the top of the graph, the easier a function is to change.*

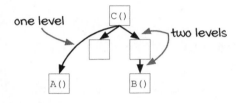

- A() is easier to change than B(). A() has one function above it. B() has two.
- C() is easiest of all to change because it has no functions above it.

Bottom line: *Put code that changes frequently near the top.*

Testability

Rule: *The more functions on the path to the top of the graph, the more valuable its tests will be.*

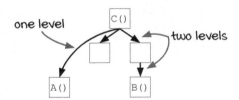

- It is more valuable to test B() than A() since more code relies on it, having two functions above it.

Bottom line: *Test code at the bottom more than code at the top.*

Reusability

Rule: *The fewer functions underneath a function, the more reusable it is.*

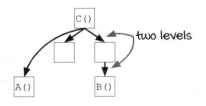

- A() and B() are about the same reusability. They each have no functions under them.
- C() would be the least reusable, since it has two levels of functions underneath it.

Bottom line: *Extract functions into lower layers to make them reusable.*

These properties emerge from the structure of our code. We should use these to find optimal layers for change, testing, and reuse. We'll see a very practical application of this in chapter 16 when we explore the onion architecture.

Conclusion

Stratified design is a technique for organizing our functions into layers of abstraction, where each function is implemented in terms of functions defined in the layers below it. We follow our intuitions to guide our code to a more comfortable system for solving our business's needs. The layer structure also shows us which code is more testable, changeable, and reusable.

Summary

- The pattern of abstraction barrier lets us think at a higher level. Abstraction barriers let us completely hide details.

- The pattern of minimal interface has us build layers that will converge on a final form. The interfaces for important business concepts should not grow or change once they have matured.

- The pattern of comfort helps us apply the other patterns to serve our needs. It is easy to over-abstract when applying these patterns. We should apply them with purpose.

- Properties emerge from the structure of the call graph. Those properties tell us where to put code to maximize our testability, maintainability, and reusability.

Up next . . .

This chapter marks the end of the first major leg of our journey. We have learned about actions, calculations, and data, and how they manifest in our code. We refactored quite a lot, yet there were some functions that resisted easy extractions. In the next chapter, we learn how to truly abstract the for loop. And so begins the next leg of the journey, in which code can be used like data.

Part 2

• •

First-class abstractions

Distinguishing actions, calculations, and data allowed us to learn many new skills. That distinction will continue to serve us. But we must learn a new skill to enter the next realm, where new skills await. The skill we need is the idea of first-class values, especially first-class functions. Once equipped with that new skill, we can learn a functional way to iterate. We can build complex calculations using chains of operations. We can discover a way to operate on deeply nested data. And we'll learn to control the ordering and repetition of actions to eliminate timing bugs. We'll finish the journey with two architectures that let us structure our services. These skills will be available once we learn about first-class values.

• •

In this chapter

- Discover the power of first-class values.

- Learn how to make first-class function versions of syntax.

- Learn to wrap syntax using higher-order functions.

- Apply two refactorings that use first-class and higher-order functions.

You are now in the waiting room to the second part of this book. This room contains a door labeled "first-class functions." This chapter will open that door and reveal a new world of powerful ideas related to first-class functions. What are first-class functions? What are they used for? How can we make them? All of these questions will be addressed in this chapter. We'll explore a small part of the vast array of uses for them in the rest of the chapters of this part.

In this chapter, we're going to learn a code smell and two refactorings that help us eliminate duplication and find better abstractions. We'll apply these new skills throughout this chapter and the whole of part 2 of this book. Don't worry about learning them on this page. This is just a summary. We'll learn each one as we need them in this chapter.

Code smell: *Implicit argument in function name*

This code smell identifies aspects of code that could be better expressed as first-class values. If you are referring to a value in the body of a function, and that value is named in the function name, this smell applies. The solution is the next refactoring.

 **Vocab time**

A *code smell* is a characteristic of a piece of code that might be a symptom of deeper problems.

Characteristics

1. There are very similar function implementations.

2. The name of the function indicates the difference in implementation.

Refactoring: *Express implicit argument*

When you have an implicit argument in the function name, how do you turn that into an actual argument to the function? This refactoring adds an argument to your function so that the value becomes first-class. This may let you better express the intent of the code and potentially eliminate duplication.

Steps

1. Identify the implicit argument in the name of the function.

2. Add explicit argument.

3. Use new argument in body in place of hard-coded value.

4. Update the calling code.

Refactoring: *Replace body with callback*

The syntax of a language is often not first-class. This refactoring allows you to replace the body (the part that changes) of a piece of code with a callback. You can then pass in the behavior in a first-class function. It is a powerful way to create higher-order functions from existing code.

Steps

1. Identify the before, body, and after sections.

2. Extract the whole thing into a function.

3. Extract the body section into a function passed as an argument to that function.

These three ideas are a good overview of the structure of the chapter. And they are going to be used in this and the next eight chapters.

Marketing still needs to coordinate with dev

The abstraction barrier that provided a nice API for the marketing team has been working, but not as well as predicted. Yes, they can mostly work without coordinating, but often the marketing team requests that the dev team add new functions to the API—stuff they can't do with the API as given. Here are some of the requests:

Search results: Showing 2,343 tickets from marketing to dev team

Feature request: A way to set the price of an item in the cart

set the price

Priority: URGENT!!!
We need this for our coupon sale next week.

 Requested by:
Chief marketing officer

 Owned by:
Jenna on dev team

Feature request: A way to set the quantity of an item in the cart

set the quantity

Priority: URGENT!!1!
We need this for our Super Saturday Special this week.

 Requested by:
Chief marketing officer

 Owned by:
Jenna on dev team

set the shipping

Feature request: A way to set the shipping of an item in the cart

Priority: DOUBLE URGENT!
This is necessary for the half-off shipping spectacular we have that starts TOMORROW!

 Requested by:
Chief marketing officer

 Owned by:
Jenna on dev team

all very similar requests that differ only in the field they set

There are many more like it, and they're not slowing down. All of the requests are very similar—even the code to solve them was similar. Wasn't the abstraction barrier supposed to prevent this? Before, the marketing team could just reach into the data structure. Now they are waiting again on the dev team. The abstraction barrier is clearly not working.

Code smell: *Implicit argument in function name*

The marketing team needs to be able to change items in the cart in order to implement their promotion, for example, by giving certain items free shipping or setting the price to zero. The dev team has diligently made functions to meet marketing's needs. But they all look very similar. Here are just four functions that are very similar indeed:

```
function setPriceByName(cart, name, price) {
  var item = cart[name];
  var newItem = objectSet(item, 'price', price);
  var newCart = objectSet(cart, name, newItem);
  return newCart;
}
```

```
function setQuantityByName(cart, name, quant) {
  var item = cart[name];‡
  var newItem = objectSet(item, 'quantity', quant);
  var newCart = objectSet(cart, name, newItem);
  return newCart;
}
```

these functions differ only by these strings

```
function setShippingByName(cart, name, ship) {
  var item = cart[name];
  var newItem = objectSet(item, 'shipping', ship);
  var newCart = objectSet(cart, name, newItem);
  return newCart;
}
```

```
function setTaxByName(cart, name, tax) {
  var item = cart[name];
  var newItem = objectSet(item, 'tax', tax);
  var newCart = objectSet(cart, name, newItem);
  return newCart;
}
```

the function name duplicates the string

the function name duplicates the string

just for reference, we defined objectSet() back in chapter 6; here's the definition again to refresh your memory

```
function objectSet(object, key, value) {
  var copy = Object.assign({}, object);
  copy[key] = value;
  return copy;
}
```

There's a big code smell in this code. Well, to be honest, there's a lot of odor coming out of these lines. The first and most noticeable is the duplication. These four functions are nearly identical. But a more subtle smell is that the main difference between them—the strings that determine the field—is also in the name of the function. It's as if the function name, or part of it, is an argument. That's why we call this *implicit argument in function name*. Instead of explicitly passing a value, it's "passed in" as part of the name.

 A sense of smell

There are two characteristics to the *implicit argument in function name smell*:

1. Very similar function implementations
2. Name of function indicates the difference in implementation

The function name difference is an implicit argument.

 Vocab time

A *code smell* is a characteristic of a piece of code that might be a symptom of deeper problems.

Chief marketing officer   Jenna from dev team   Kim from dev team

CMO: Code can smell?

Jenna: Well, sort of, yeah. It just means that there's something worth checking out in the code. It's not necessarily bad code, but maybe it hints at an underlying problem.

Kim: Yes! This code is definitely smelly. Look at all that duplication.

Jenna: Yeah, it's very similar code, alright. But I don't quite see how to get rid of the duplication. We need ways of setting the price and setting the quantity. Aren't those different?

Kim: The duplication is telling us that they're not *that* different. They only differ by that one string that names the field, like 'price,' 'quantity,' or 'tax.'

Jenna: Oh, I see! And that string is also in the name of the function.

Kim: Precisely. That's the code smell: Instead of passing the field name as an argument, it's part of the function name.

CMO: So you said there's a way to fix it?

Kim: Yes. There's a refactoring I know of that can replace all four of these functions with just one. It involves making the field name first-class.

CMO: First-class? Like on a train?

Kim: Ugh. I guess. It just means the field name becomes an argument. We'll define that later.

Refactoring: *Express implicit argument*

We can apply the refactoring called *express implicit argument* whenever we have an implicit argument as part of the name of the function. The basic idea is to turn the implicit argument into an explicit argument. That's what the word *express* means: Make the implicit explicit. Here are the steps:

1. Identify the implicit argument in the name of the function.
2. Add explicit argument.
3. Use new argument in body in place of hard-coded value.
4. Update the calling code.

Let's look at how we would refactor `setPriceByName()`, which can only set the price, into `setFieldByName()`, which can set any field of an item.

other argument gets more generic name

we add the explicit argument

price is the implicit argument in the name

Before

```
function setPriceByName(cart, name, price) {
  var item = cart[name];
  var newItem = objectSet(item, 'price', price);
  var newCart = objectSet(cart, name, newItem);
  return newCart;
}
```

After

```
function setFieldByName(cart, name, field, value) {
  var item = cart[name];
  var newItem = objectSet(item, field, value);
  var newCart = objectSet(cart, name, newItem);
  return newCart;
}
```

we use the new argument

```
cart = setPriceByName(cart, "shoe", 13);
cart = setQuantityByName(cart, "shoe", 3);
cart = setShippingByName(cart, "shoe", 0);
cart = setTaxByName(cart, "shoe", 2.34);
```

```
cart = setFieldByName(cart, "shoe", 'price', 13);
cart = setFieldByName(cart, "shoe", 'quantity', 3);
cart = setFieldByName(cart, "shoe", 'shipping', 0);
cart = setFieldByName(cart, "shoe", 'tax', 2.34);
```

update the calling code

we use single quotes for keys and double quotes for values. if it's both key and value (like for "shoe"), we use double quotes

This refactoring, applied to this code, replaces four existing functions with one generic one—and who knows how many functions won't have to be written because of the generic `setFieldByName()`.

What we've done is make the field name a first-class value. Previously, the field name was never exposed to the API clients except implicitly as part of the function names. Now, it is a value (a string in this case) that can be passed as an argument but also stored in a variable or in an array. That's what we mean by *first-class*. We can use the whole language to work with it. And making things first-class is the topic of this chapter.

You might think that using strings like this is unsafe. We'll discuss that in a few pages. For now, please just go with it!

 **Vocab time**

A *first-class value* can be used just like all of the other values in your language.

Chief marketing officer   Jenna from dev team   Kim from dev team

CMO: We won't have to file a ticket to set each field?

Jenna: That's right. Now, you can access any field you want. You just have to name it in a string and pass it in.

CMO: How will we know what fields are called what?

Kim: That's easy. We'll just make it part of the API specification. It will be part of the abstraction barrier.

CMO: Hmm . . . I'm starting to like this idea. But another question: What about if you add a new field to the spec for carts or items. What then?

Jenna: This new function should work with existing fields and new fields alike. If we add a new field, we'll have to tell you the name, but then you should be able to use all the functions you know about.

CMO: That sounds okay. It really sounds much easier for us.

Kim: It should be! We went from you needing to know a bunch of functions (plus requests for new ones!) to just one function and a handful of field names.

Old API surface

```
function setPriceByName(cart, name, price)

function setQuantityByName(cart, name, quant)

function setShippingByName(cart, name, ship)

function setTaxByName(cart, name, tax)

...
```

New API surface

```
function setFieldByName(cart, name, field, value)
```

```
'price'
'quantity'
'shipping'
'tax'
...
```

pass these things here

Recognize what is and what isn't first-class
JavaScript is littered with non-first-class things, and whatever language you use is probably littered with them, too

Think about what you can do with a number in JavaScript. You can pass it to a function. You can return it from a function. You can store it in a variable. You can make it an item in an array or a value in an object. And you can do the same with strings, booleans, arrays and objects. In JavaScript, like many languages, you can also do all of those things with functions (which we'll see shortly). These values are first-class because you can do all of those things with them.

Wait! I don't get what we just did.

George from testing

But the JavaScript language has a lot of things that are not first-class values. For instance, there is no way to refer to the + operator as a value you can assign to a variable. Nor can you pass * to a function. The arithmetic operators are not first-class in JavaScript.

And there's more! What is the value of an `if` keyword? Or the `for` keyword? They don't have values in JavaScript. That's what we mean when we say *they're not first-class*. That's not a judgment on the language. Almost all languages have things that are not first-class, but it's important to recognize what things are and how we can make something first-class when it isn't by default.

Here's what we did on the last page:

there's no way to refer to a piece of a name, so we made it an argument

```
function setPriceByName(cart, name, price)
function setFieldByName(cart, name, field, value)
```

There's no way to refer to a small piece of a function name as a value in JavaScript. That's not a first-class value. So we made it first-class by replacing it with a string argument. In JavaScript, we can use strings to access fields on objects. So that's what we did! And it gave us a little bit of power—enough to solve our problem.

We'll see this pattern throughout the chapter and the rest of part 2. We'll identify something that is not first-class and make it first-class, which will give us some new ability to solve our problem. It's an important technique in functional programming. Knowing this skill will open many doors to more sophisticated functional programming patterns.

> **Examples of non-first-class things in JavaScript**
>
> 1. Arithmetic operators
> 2. For loops
> 3. If statements
> 4. Try/catch blocks

> **Examples of things you can do with a first-class value**
>
> 1. Assign it to a variable.
> 2. Pass it as an argument to a function.
> 3. Return it from a function.
> 4. Store it in an array or object.

Will field names as strings lead to more bugs?

George worries that it will be easy to mess strings up. What if there's a typo in one of the strings?

OMG! Passing field names as strings?? That will be a bug festival worse than the time we left out that pizza over the winter holidays.

George from testing

That's a valid concern, but one that we've got covered. There are really two options: compile-time checks and run-time checks.

Compile-time checks usually involve a static type system. JavaScript doesn't have a static type system, but we can add one with something like TypeScript. TypeScript would allow us to check that the strings belong to a known set of valid fields. If we have a typo, the type checker will tell us before we even run our code.

Many languages have static type checking, and you should use it if you can to guarantee the correctness of the field names. For instance, in Java you could use an Enum type. In Haskell you could use a discriminated union. Every type system is different, so you'll have to determine the best way to use it with your team.

Run-time checks don't run at compile-time. They run every time your function runs. They can also check that the strings we pass in are valid. Since JavaScript doesn't have a static type system, we might choose this option. Here's what it can look like:

we can put any valid fields in here

```javascript
var validItemFields = ['price', 'quantity', 'shipping', 'tax'];

function setFieldByName(cart, name, field, value) {
  if(!validItemFields.includes(field))
    throw "Not a valid item field: " +
          "'" + field + "'.";
  var item = cart[name];
  var newItem = objectSet(item, field, value);
  var newCart = objectSet(cart, name, newItem);
  return newCart;
}
```

we defined objectSet() in Chapter 6

run-time checks are easy when fields are first-class

```javascript
function objectSet(object, key, value) {
  var copy = Object.assign({}, object);
  copy[key] = value;
  return copy;
}
```

 **Noodle on it**

JavaScript doesn't check field names or function names. Are George's concerns about using field name strings instead of accessor functions valid? Is it really worse to use strings?

Will first-class fields make the API hard to change?

Jenna is concerned that we are exposing an implementation detail of our entities by using first-class field names. The cart and item entities are objects with certain fields set, but they are defined below an abstraction barrier. By asking people above the abstraction barrier to pass in field names, aren't we breaking the abstraction barrier? Are we not exposing the internals? By putting field names in the API spec, we're essentially guaranteeing them forever.

I really like this idea because it will solve marketing's problems. But won't it be hard to change the API?

Jenna from dev team

It's true that we are guaranteeing them forever. But we are not exposing our implementation. If we change the names in the internal implementation, we can still support the names we guarantee. We can just swap them out.

Let's say we needed to change `'quantity'` to `'number'` for some reason. We don't want to break all of the existing code, so we still have to accept `'quantity'`. We can just swap it out ourselves:

```
var validItemFields = ['price', 'quantity', 'shipping', 'tax', 'number'];
var translations = { 'quantity': 'number' };

function setFieldByName(cart, name, field, value) {
  if(!validItemFields.includes(field))
    throw "Not a valid item field: '" + field + "'.";
  if(translations.hasOwnProperty(field))
    field = translations[field];
  var item = cart[name];
  var newItem = objectSet(item, field, value);
  var newCart = objectSet(cart, name, newItem);
  return newCart;
}
```

do a simple translation from old field name to new field name

 **Noodle on it**

The field names we are exposing now as strings were all being exposed in the function names. If the field names changed, the function name didn't have to. How is using strings different? And how is it the same?

This is possible because we have made the field first-class. A first-class field name means we can put it in an array, store it in an object, and generally apply the full power of the language to logic.

It's your turn

Here's an easy and silly one. Someone on the team has written the following functions that have the *implicit argument in function name* code smell. Apply the *express implicit argument* refactoring to remove the duplication.

```
function multiplyByFour(x) {
  return x * 4;
}

function multiplyBy12(x) {
  return x * 12;
}
```

```
function multiplyBySix(x) {
  return x * 6;
}

function multiplyByPi(x) {
  return x * 3.14159;
}
```

write your answer here

Steps

1. Identify implicit argument.
2. Add explicit argument.
3. Use new argument in body.
4. Update calling code.

don't worry about the calling code in this exercise

Answer

```
function multiply(x, y) {
  return x * y;
}
```

It's your turn

Here's one from the UI team. In the shopping cart view, there are buttons for increment-ing the quantity and the size of clothing items.

```
function incrementQuantityByName(cart, name) {
  var item = cart[name];
  var quantity = item['quantity'];
  var newQuantity = quantity + 1;
  var newItem = objectSet(item, 'quantity', newQuantity);
  var newCart = objectSet(cart, name, newItem);
  return newCart;
}
```

implicit arguments

```
function incrementSizeByName(cart, name) {
  var item = cart[name];
  var size = item['size'];
  var newSize = size + 1;
  var newItem = objectSet(item, 'size', newSize);
  var newCart = objectSet(cart, name, newItem);
  return newCart;
}
```

The field names ('quantity' and 'size') are part of the function names. Apply the *express implicit argument* refactoring to remove the duplication.

write your answer here

Steps

1. Identify implicit argument.
2. Add explicit argument.
3. Use new argument in body.
4. Update calling code.

don't worry about the calling code in this exercise

Answer

```
function incrementFieldByName(cart, name, field) {
  var item = cart[name];
  var value = item[field];
  var newValue = value + 1;
  var newItem = objectSet(item, field, newValue);
  var newCart = objectSet(cart, name, newItem);
  return newCart;
}
```

It's your turn

The dev team is starting to worry that people using the API will try to increment other fields they're not supposed to. For instance, you shouldn't increment the price or the name of the item! Add some run-time checks. Throw an error if the field name is not `'size'` or `'quantity'`. Run-time checks usually come at the beginning of a function, so put yours there.

```
function incrementFieldByName(cart, name, field) {
```

Write your answer here.

```
  var item = cart[name];
  var value = item[field];
  var newValue = value + 1;
  var newItem = objectSet(item, field, newValue);
  var newCart = objectSet(cart, name, newItem);
  return newCart;
}
```

Answer

```
function incrementFieldByName(cart, name, field) {
  if(field !== 'size' && field !== 'quantity')
    throw "This item field cannot be incremented: " +
          "'" + field + "'.";
  var item = cart[name];
  var value = item[field];
  var newValue = value + 1;
  var newItem = objectSet(item, field, newValue);
  var newCart = objectSet(cart, name, newItem);
  return newCart;
}
```

We will use a lot of objects and arrays

We are using hash maps to represent entities like shopping cart items because hash maps can easily represent properties and values, and JavaScript objects are a convenient way to do that. What you use in your language will differ, of course. If you're using Haskell, an algebraic data type might be best. If you're using Java, consider a hash map if you need first-class keys. Other OO languages make it easier to pass first-class accessors, like Ruby does. Every language does it differently and you'll have to use your judgment. But in JavaScript, you'll probably find that you're using a lot more objects than before.

> It seems like if we have first-class field names, we'll be using a lot of JavaScript objects in our code.

Kim from dev team

The important thing is that we're trying to treat data as data instead of wrapping each one in a custom interface. Bespoke interfaces allow one interpretation of data while prohibiting others. They are very specific to particular use cases. But those entities (carts and items) are very general. They are relatively low on the call graph. They are too low to be so specific as to have a custom API. We should use general-purpose structures like objects and arrays.

General entities like *item* and *cart* should be in general structures like objects and arrays.

specific

our entities are general and need to be reusable, so they should be in general-purpose formats like objects and arrays

general

An important advantage of data is that data can be interpreted in multiple ways. Limiting that by defining a limited API will make our data less powerful. We might not be able to predict what those future interpretations will be, but they will be useful when they are needed.

This is an important principle of a style called *data orientation*, which is a style we will be using in the code for this book. We still can add an optional interface with abstraction barriers as we saw in chapter 9.

 Vocab time

Data orientation is a style of programming that uses generic data structures to represent facts about events and entities.

Static versus dynamic typing

There is a long debate in software engineering: whether to check types at compile time or at run time. Languages that check the types at compile time are called *statically typed* languages. And those that don't check the types at compile time, yet still have a notion of run-time type checks, are called *dynamically typed* languages. The debate still gets very heated, even after many decades. And nowhere is the debate hotter than in the functional programming community.

The truth is that we don't have an answer. There are good arguments on both sides. This book can't really resolve this long-running issue. However, it is important to understand that the debate has two sides and nobody has clearly won yet. It isn't obvious, even after careful study, if one is better than the other for producing quality software. For example, some studies suggest getting a good night's sleep is more important for software quality than the difference between static and dynamic typing. (https://increment.com /teams/the-epistemology-of-software-quality/)

There's another issue to address, which is that this book uses JavaScript for examples. JavaScript is a dynamically typed language. But this should not be understood as an endorsement of dynamic typing—nor an endorsement of JavaScript. The most important reason this book uses it is that it is a popular language that can be understood by many people because of its familiar syntax. And it's good to use one without a static type system because type systems are a lot to learn at the same time as you're learning the functional programming paradigm.

However, there are other concerns. One thing that is often left out of the debate is that every type system is different. There are good static type systems and bad static type systems. Likewise, there are good dynamic type systems and bad dynamic type systems. Trying to compare them as groups doesn't make sense. Neither group is entirely better than the other group.

So what should you do? Choose a language you and your team are comfortable with. Then stop worrying about it and get some sleep.

It's all strings on the wire

You're right! We could have errors in our strings. But consider these arguments before you dismiss this notion outright.

Wait a second! Are you telling me we're just going to pass strings around? They could have anything in them. They could have typos!

Many dynamically typed programming languages do pass around what amount to strings that represent fields on data structures. Prominent examples include JavaScript, Ruby, Clojure, and Python. And, yes, they often have typos and other errors due to incorrect strings. It happens. However, many large businesses are built on those languages, with billions—if not trillions—of dollars relying on those systems functioning correctly. We can get by with strings.

Sarah from dev team

But this problem of strings goes much deeper than we often like to think. Our web browsers send JSON to the server. That JSON is just strings. The server will receive and parse it. The server hopes the message is well-formed JSON. If it is well formed, then we hope that the data structure is understandable.

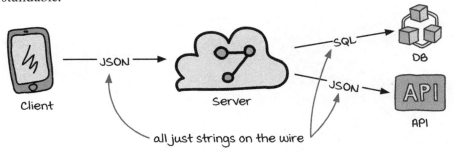

The same goes for the web server talking to the database. The web server has to serialize the commands to the database into a string that gets serialized over the wire. The database has to parse and interpret it. It's all strings on that wire, too. And even if there are types built into the data format, it's still just bytes—plenty of opportunity for typos or malicious behavior.

An API must check data at runtime as it enters the server from a client, even if it's a static language. All the static type system can do is guarantee that the code in one piece of the system is consistent with the assumptions you encode as types.

Does that mean you shouldn't use static types? No. Does it mean you should? No. You should just be aware that dynamic typing did not create this problem and static typing doesn't make it go away. We're seeing one downside of data: It requires interpretation.

First-class functions can replace any syntax

We mentioned before that there are lots of things in JavaScript that are not first-class. You can't assign the + operator to a variable. But you can make something equivalent to the + operator with a function.

```
function plus(a, b) {
  return a + b;
}
```

Functions are first-class values in JavaScript, so this essentially makes a first-class value out of the + operator. This may seem silly, since we could just write +, but we'll soon see many uses for a first-class addition function. Remember, making things first-class can give us power. We can use that power to solve problems.

It's your turn

Write first-class versions of the other arithmetic operators, *, −, and /. That is, wrap them in functions.

   *   −

   /

Answer

```
function times(a, b) {          function minus(a, b) {
  return a * b;                   return a - b;
}                               }

function dividedBy(a, b) {
  return a / b;
}
```

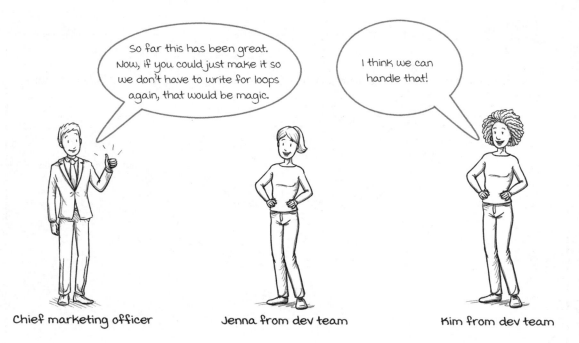

Chief marketing officer   **Jenna from dev team**   **Kim from dev team**

CMO: You can handle that? Because you know, we're marketers, not programmers. We get so many things wrong when we write for loops, it's not even funny.

Jenna: But how can we help you stop writing for loops? Wait, let me guess: We make the for loop first-class.

Kim: Yes and no. Yes, technically, we will make it first-class. But no, that's not how we'll help marketing. We will help them by making a function that takes a first-class function as an argument. In other words, we'll write a *higher-order function*.

CMO: Just so you know, I don't understand those words. First-class? Higher-order?

Kim: The two words are related. *First-class* means you can pass it as an argument. *Higher order* means the function takes another function as an argument. You can't have higher order functions without first-class functions.

CMO: Okay, I think I get it. I just want my people not to freak out over the for loop syntax. Can you make it so I don't have to write a for loop again?

Kim: Yeah! I know a refactoring that will basically let you do that. It's called *replace body with callback*.

Jenna: Wow! I'd love to see this!

 **Vocab time**

Higher-order functions take other functions as arguments or return functions as their return values.

For loop example: Eating and cleaning up

Let's look at two typical for loops that iterate through arrays. The first one has us prepare and eat our food. The second one has us clean all the dirty dishes.

Preparing and eating

```
for(var i = 0; i < foods.length; i++) {
  var food = foods[i];
  cook(food);
  eat(food);

}
```

Washing up

```
for(var i = 0; i < dishes.length; i++) {
  var dish = dishes[i];
  wash(dish);
  dry(dish);
  putAway(dish);
}
```

The purposes of these for loops are quite different, yet the code is very similar. We can't really call it duplication until we've made the code look exactly the same. Let's systematically make these two for loops as identical as possible. If we can make them identical, we can delete one of them. We won't skip any steps here, so if it's going too slow for you, feel free to skim it.

Let's start by highlighting everything that is the same:

```
for(var i = 0; i < foods.length; i++) {
  var food = foods[i];
  cook(food);
  eat(food);

}
```

```
for(var i = 0; i < dishes.length; i++) {
  var dish = dishes[i];
  wash(dish);
  dry(dish);
  putAway(dish);
}
```

these parts are identical, including the closing }

Our ultimate goal is to make all of the holes—the non-underlined parts—go away. The first thing we'll do is wrap them in functions. That will make things easier.

give them descriptive names

```
function cookAndEatFoods() {
  for(var i = 0; i < foods.length; i++) {
    var food = foods[i];
    cook(food);
    eat(food);

  }
}
```

```
function cleanDishes() {
  for(var i = 0; i < dishes.length; i++) {
    var dish = dishes[i];
    wash(dish);
    dry(dish);
    putAway(dish);
  }
}
```

```
cookAndEatFoods();
```

```
cleanDishes();
```

call the new functions so they still run

We're out of room here, so let's continue on the next page.

On the last page, we had just wrapped our for loops in functions. We named the functions after what they do. Here's what we had:

```
function cookAndEatFoods() {            function cleanDishes() {
  for(var i = 0; i < foods.length; i++) {  for(var i = 0; i < dishes.length; i++) {
    var food = foods[i];                    var dish = dishes[i];
    cook(food);                             wash(dish);
    eat(food);                              dry(dish);
  }                                         putAway(dish);
}                                         }
                                        }

cookAndEatFoods();                      cleanDishes();
```

these variables serve the same function but have different names

> **Attributes of implicit argument in function name** *smell*
> 1. Similar implementations
> 2. Difference cited in function name

One thing that pops out is that we are naming a local variable very specifically. In one we call it `food`, in the other `dish`. Names are arbitrary, so we can just rename that local to something generic:

```
function cookAndEatFoods() {            function cleanDishes() {
  for(var i = 0; i < foods.length; i++) {  for(var i = 0; i < dishes.length; i++) {
    var item = foods[i];                    var item = dishes[i];
    cook(item);                             wash(item);
    eat(item);                              dry(item);
  }                                         putAway(item);
}                                         }
                                        }

cookAndEatFoods();                      cleanDishes();
```

call these both "item"

> **Steps in express implicit argument refactoring**
> 1. Identify implicit argument.
> 2. Add explicit argument.
> 3. Use new argument in body.
> 4. Update calling code.

Now we can smell what we just learned about: *implicit argument in function name*. Notice how we are referring to *foods* in the function name and in the name of the array, likewise for *dishes*. Let's apply the express implicit argument refactoring:

change name to reflect that it is generic

```
function cookAndEatArray(array) {       function cleanArray(array) {
  for(var i = 0; i < array.length; i++) {  for(var i = 0; i < array.length; i++) {
    var item = array[i];                    var item = array[i];
    cook(item);                             wash(item);
    eat(item);                              dry(item);
  }                                         putAway(item);
}                                         }
                                        }

cookAndEatArray(foods);                 cleanArray(dishes);
```

add explicit array argument

pass the arrays in

We're getting close. We're out of room again. Let's go to the next page.

On the last page, we had just expressed the implicit arguments in the function names. Now both of the arrays can be called `array`. Here's what we had:

```
function cookAndEatArray(array) {              function cleanArray(array) {
  for(var i = 0; i < array.length; i++) {        for(var i = 0; i < array.length; i++) {
    var item = array[i];                           var item = array[i];
    cook(item);                                    wash(item);
    eat(item);                                     dry(item);
                                                   putAway(item);
  }                                              }
}                                              }

cookAndEatArray(foods);                        cleanArray(dishes);
```

We've just got one thing left, which is the body of the for loop. That's the only thing that differs. Because it's multiple lines, let's extract them as functions:

the only difference between these functions is the implicit argument in the name

```
function cookAndEatArray(array) {              function cleanArray(array) {
  for(var i = 0; i < array.length; i++) {        for(var i = 0; i < array.length; i++) {
    var item = array[i];                           var item = array[i];
    cookAndEat(item);                              clean(item);
  }                                              }
}                                              }
```

call our extracted functions

```
function cookAndEat(food) {                    function clean(dish) {
  cook(food);                                    wash(dish);
  eat(food);                                     dry(dish);
}                                                putAway(dish);
                                               }
```

the definitions of the extracted functions

```
cookAndEatArray(foods);                        cleanArray(dishes);
```

Now that the body is one named function, we've got a familiar smell again: *implicit argument in function name*! `cookAndEatArray()` calls `cookAndEat()`, while `cleanArray()` calls `clean()`. Let's apply the refactoring on the next page.

> **Attributes of implicit argument in function name** *smell*
>
> 1. Similar implementations
> 2. Difference cited in function name

On the last page, we had just identified the implicit argument in function name smell. We had two functions with similar implementations, and the difference between implementations was cited in the function name:

function names cite difference

```
function cookAndEatArray(array) {
  for(var i = 0; i < array.length; i++) {
    var item = array[i];
    cookAndEat(item);
  }
}

function cookAndEat(food) {
  cook(food);
  eat(food);
}


cookAndEatArray(foods);
```

```
function cleanArray(array) {
  for(var i = 0; i < array.length; i++) {
    var item = array[i];
    clean(item);
  }
}

function clean(dish) {
  wash(dish);
  dry(dish);
  putAway(dish);
}

cleanArray(dishes);
```

similar functions

> **Attributes of implicit argument in function name *smell***
> 1. Similar implementations
> 2. Difference cited in function name

Let's apply the refactoring!

rename to something generic

express the argument

express the argument

```
function operateOnArray(array, f) {
  for(var i = 0; i < array.length; i++) {
    var item = array[i];
    f(item);
  }
}

function cookAndEat(food) {
  cook(food);
  eat(food);
}


operateOnArray(foods, cookAndEat);
```

```
function operateOnArray(array, f) {
  for(var i = 0; i < array.length; i++) {
    var item = array[i];
    f(item);
  }
}

function clean(dish) {
  wash(dish);
  dry(dish);
  putAway(dish);
}

operateOnArray(dishes, clean);
```

use the new argument in body

add argument to calling code *add argument to calling code*

add argument to calling code

> **Steps in express implicit argument *refactoring***
> 1. Identify implicit argument.
> 2. Add explicit argument.
> 3. Use new argument in body.
> 4. Update calling code.

Now those two original pieces of code look identical. We've extracted every part that differs into the arguments. The parts that differ were just the array to operate on and the function to operate with. Let's keep talking about this on the next page.

On the last page, we had just finished making the two functions at the top identical. Here's what we had at the end of the last page:

```
function operateOnArray(array, f) {        function operateOnArray(array, f) {
  for(var i = 0; i < array.length; i++) {    for(var i = 0; i < array.length; i++) {
    var item = array[i];                       var item = array[i];
    f(item);                                   f(item);
  }                                          }
}                                          }
```

←— identical functions —→

```
function cookAndEat(food) {                function clean(dish) {
  cook(food);                                wash(dish);
  eat(food);                                 dry(dish);
}                                            putAway(dish);
                                           }
```

```
operateOnArray(foods, cookAndEat);         operateOnArray(dishes, clean);
```

The differences have been removed, so we can delete one of the definitions. Plus, in JavaScript, this function is traditionally called `forEach()`, so let's rename it that:

see how forEach() takes a function as argument? that means forEach() is a higher-order function

```
function forEach(array, f) {
  for(var i = 0; i < array.length; i++) {
    var item = array[i];
    f(item);
  }
}
```

```
function cookAndEat(food) {                function clean(dish) {
  cook(food);                                wash(dish);
  eat(food);                                 dry(dish);
}                                            putAway(dish);
                                           }
```

```
forEach(foods, cookAndEat);                forEach(dishes, clean);
```

`forEach()` takes an array and a function as arguments. Because it takes a function as an argument, it is a *higher-order function*.

We're done. That was a lot of steps, so let's see the before and after for our code on the next page.

 **Vocab time**

Higher-order functions take other functions as arguments or return functions as their return values.

We've just done a lot of refactoring steps over the last few pages. It's easy to lose track of where we started. It's easy to miss the big picture. Let's see the original and new versions. We'll look at the difference using an *anonymous function*:

Original

```
for(var i = 0; i < foods.length; i++) {
   var food = foods[i];
   cook(food);
   eat(food);

}

for(var i = 0; i < dishes.length; i++) {
   var dish = dishes[i];
   wash(dish);
   dry(dish);
   putAway(dish);
}
```

look at all the stuff we don't need anymore

Using `forEach()`

```
forEach(foods, function(food) {
   cook(food);
   eat(food);
});



forEach(dishes, function(dish) {
   wash(dish);
   dry(dish);
   putAway(dish);
});
```

anonymous functions

forEach() is the last for loop over arrays you'll ever have to write. It encapsulates that pattern we've all written so many times. Now we can use it just by calling forEach().

forEach() is a higher-order function. That's because it takes a function as an argument. The power of higher-order functions is in the ability to abstract over code. Before, you had to write the for loop code every time, because the part that changed was inside the for loop body. But by making it a higher-order function, we can pass in the code that differs in each for loop.

forEach() is an important function to learn. We'll spend all of chapter 12 on it and similar functions. But what we're talking about here is the process of how to create a higher-order function. The series of refactorings we just did is one way to achieve that. Here's what we did:

Vocab time

Anonymous functions are functions without names. They can be written *inline*—right where they are used.

1. Wrap code in functions.

2. Rename to be more generic.

3. Express implicit argument.

4. Extract function.

5. Express implicit argument.

That's a lot of steps. We want to be able to do it in one go. That's why there's a refactoring called *replace body with callback*. It's a shorter way to do what we just did. Let's start learning it on the next page. It will apply to the new logging system George is prototyping.

Refactoring: *Replace body with callback*

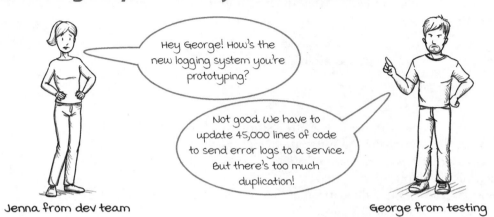

Jenna from dev team   George from testing

Jenna: That sounds bad.

George: Yeah. My carpal tunnel is acting up. We have to wrap thousands of lines in try/catch blocks so we can catch and send errors to **Snap Errors®**, the error logging service. It's not the typing I mind. The worst part is all the duplication: try/catch statements everywhere! Here's what the code looks like with the try/catch:

> **Snap Errors®**
>
> *To err is human, to Snap is divine.*
>
> **From Snap Errors API docs**
>
> `logToSnapErrors(error)`
>
> Send an `error` to the **Snap Errors®** service. The `error` should be an error thrown and caught in your code.

```
try {
  saveUserData(user);
} catch (error) {
  logToSnapErrors(error);
}
```

We tried wrapping it in a function, but we couldn't figure out how. You can't separate the catch from the try. It breaks the syntax, so they can't go in separate functions. We're desperate. Nothing seems to get rid of the duplication.

Jenna: Woah! What a coincidence! I was just learning a refactoring for doing just that. It's called *replace body with callback*.

George: I'm doubtful it will work, but I'm willing to try anything.

Jenna: I'd be happy to help, but I'm still learning it. It involves identifying the before and after code, which doesn't change, and also finding the body code, which does. Then we replace the body with a function.

George: Woah! Slow down! I still don't get it.

Jenna: We want to pass in a function as an argument, which represents the different code that needs to execute.

George: Okay, I think I'm seeing it now, but I'd sure like to see it in code.

George basically has spent the last few weeks prototyping try/catch blocks around important code. After all of his refinements, they look like this:

```
try {                              same catch        try {                the Snap Errors
  saveUserData(user);              everywhere          fetchProduct(productId);  API function
} catch (error) {                                    } catch (error) {
  logToSnapErrors(error);                              logToSnapErrors(error);
}                                                    }
```

And from the looks of it, he'll be writing similar try/catch statements with the same catch body for the next quarter. However, Jenna knows that *replace callback with body* is a good solution for eliminating this duplication.

The trick is to identify the pattern of before-body-after. Here's what it looks like for George's code:

```
try {                    before      try {
  saveUserData(user);    body          fetchProduct(productId);
} catch (error) {                    } catch (error) {
  logToSnapErrors(error); after         logToSnapErrors(error);
}                                    }
```

The before and after sections don't change with each instance. Both of the pieces of code have the exact same code in the before and after sections. However, they do have a part between the before and after sections that is different (the body section). We need to be able to vary that while reusing the before and after sections. Here's how we can do that:

before and after sections don't differ between instances. they form a "hole" that you slip the different code into

1. Identify the before, body, and after sections.   already done!

2. Extract the whole thing into a function.

3. Extract the body section into a function passed as an argument to that function.

We've already done step 1. Let's check out the next two steps on the next page.

 **Vocab time**

In the JavaScript world, functions passed as arguments are often called *callbacks*, but we also hear the same term outside of the JavaScript community. The function you are passing the callback to is expected to call the function. Other communities might call these *handler functions*. Experienced functional programmers are so used to passing functions as arguments, they often don't need a special name for them.

On the last page, we had already identified our before, body, and after sections. The next step is to extract the whole thing into a function. We'll call this one `withLogging()`.

Original

```
try {
  saveUserData(user);
} catch (error) {
  logToSnapErrors(error);
}
```

After function extraction

```
function withLogging() {
  try {
    saveUserData(user);
  } catch (error) {
    logToSnapErrors(error);
  }
}

withLogging();
```

call withLogging()
after we define it

By naming this extracted function, we'll now have a way to refer to it. The next step is to extract the body—the part that differs—into an argument:

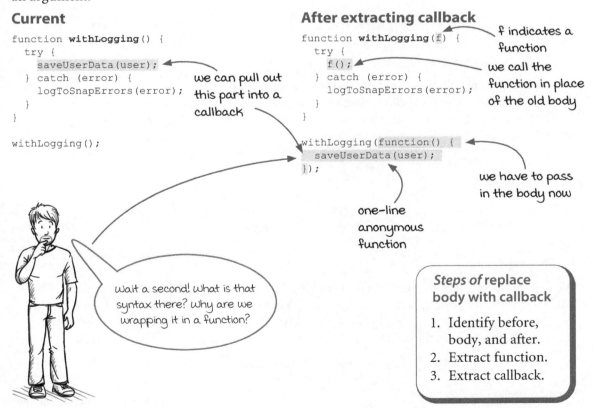

Current

```
function withLogging() {
  try {
    saveUserData(user);
  } catch (error) {
    logToSnapErrors(error);
  }
}

withLogging();
```

we can pull out
this part into a
callback

After extracting callback

```
function withLogging(f) {
  try {
    f();
  } catch (error) {
    logToSnapErrors(error);
  }
}

withLogging(function() {
  saveUserData(user);
});
```

f indicates a
function

we call the
function in place
of the old body

we have to pass
in the body now

one-line
anonymous
function

Wait a second! What is that syntax there? Why are we wrapping it in a function?

Steps of replace body with callback

1. Identify before, body, and after.
2. Extract function.
3. Extract callback.

That's two great questions! Let's take them on in the next couple of pages.

What is this syntax?

Here's the code we just wrote that George was confused by:

```
withLogging(function() { saveUserData(user); });
```

We'll see that it's just a normal way to define and pass a function.
There are three ways to define functions. Let's go over them.

1. Globally defined

We can define and name a function at the global level. This is the
typical way you define most functions. It lets you refer to the function later by name from pretty much anywhere else in the
program.

```
function saveCurrentUserData() {
  saveUserData(user);
}
```

define the function
globally

```
withLogging(saveCurrentUserData);
```

pass the function
by name

2. Locally defined

We can define and name a function inside of a local scope. That
function will have a name, but we won't be able to refer to it outside of the scope. This is useful if you need to refer to other values
in the local scope but still want a name for it.

this function is given
a name only in the
local scope

```
function someFunction() {
  var saveCurrentUserData = function() {
    saveUserData(user);
  };
  withLogging(saveCurrentUserData);
}
```

pass the
function by
name

3. Defined inline

We can define a function right where it is being used. That is, we
don't assign the function to a variable, so it doesn't have a name. We
call that an *anonymous function*. This is most useful for short functions that make sense in the context and only need to be used once.

```
withLogging(function() { saveUserData(user); });
```

this function has no name

define the function where
it is being used

And that's what we did on the last page. We wrote an anonymous
function inline. *Anonymous* means it has no name (because it
didn't need a name). *Inline* means we defined it where it was used.

Vocab time

An *inline function* is
defined where it is
used. For example, a
function might be
defined in the argu-
ment list.

Vocab time

An *anonymous func-
tion* is a function
without a name. That
usually happens
when we define the
function inline.

Why are we wrapping the code in a function?

Here's the code that George was confused by. His question was why we need to wrap `saveUserData(user)` in a function. Let's break it down and see how this lets us defer the execution of that code:

```
function withLogging(f) {
  try {
    f();                                    why wrap this line of code in a
  } catch (error) {                         function definition?
    logToSnapErrors(error);
  }
}

withLogging(function() { saveUserData(user); });
```

George has a small piece of code—saveUserData(user)— that he needs to run in a certain context—inside the try block. He could wrap the line of code in a try/catch. Or, instead, he could wrap it in a function definition. If he does that, the code won't be run right away. It will be "saved," like a fish stored in a block of ice. A function is a way of deferring the execution of code.

```
function() {
  saveUserData(user);                    this line won't be run until we
}                                        call the wrapping function
```

Because functions are first-class in JavaScript, we now have a bunch of options. We can give it a name by saving it to a variable. We can store it in a collection (array or object). Or we could pass it to a function. It's first-class.

Name it	**Collect it**	**Pass it**
`var f = function() {`	`array.push(function() {`	`withLogging(function() {`
`  saveUserData(user);`	`  saveUserData(user);`	`  saveUserData(user);`
`};`	`});`	`});`

In our case, we are passing it to a function. The function we pass it to can choose not to call it, can call it at a later time, and can set up a context and execute the deferred code inside it.

Choose not to call it	**Call it later**	**Call it in a new context**
`function callOnThursday(f) {`	`function callTomorrow(f) {`	`function withLogging(f) {`
`  if(today === "Thursday")`	`  sleep(oneDay);`	`  try {`
`    f();`	`  f();`	`    f();`
`}`	`}`	`  } catch (error) {`
only calls f()	waits one day	`    logToSnapErrors(error);`
on Thursday	before calling f()	`  }`
		`}`
		calls f() within try/catch

We're wrapping code in a function to defer its execution and execute it within the try/catch context that `withLogging()` sets up. `withLogging()` codifies the standard that George's team needs. However, we'll see a way to improve this later in the chapter.

 **Brain break**

There's more to go, but let's take a break for questions

Q: The *replace body with callback* refactoring seems really useful for eliminating certain kinds of duplication. But is it just for duplication?

A: Great question. In a sense, yes; it is all about eliminating duplication. It's the same for creating non-higher-order functions: They let you run code by naming the function instead of duplicating its body. Higher-order functions are the same, but they let you differ by code to execute (the callback) instead of just data.

Q: Why are you passing in functions? Why not pass in a regular data value?

A: Another excellent question. Imagine in our try/catch example that we passed in data (a "regular" argument) instead of a function argument. Our code would look like this:

```
function withLogging(data) {          passing in just the result of calling
  try {                               the function, not the function itself
    data;
  } catch (error) {
    logToSnapErrors(error);
  }
}
                                      notice the function is called outside
                                      of the context of the try/catch block
withLogging(saveUserData(user));
```

The question is, what if there is an error in `saveUserData()`? Will the try/catch surround it?

The answer is no. `saveUserData()` will run and throw an error before `withLogging()` is run. The try/catch is useless in that case.

The reason we are passing in a function is so that the code in that function can be run in a particular context. In this case, the context is inside the try/catch. In the case of `forEach()`, the context is the body of the for loop. Higher-order functions let us set up contexts for code defined elsewhere. The context becomes reusable because it's in a function.

Conclusion

This chapter introduced us to the ideas of *first-class values*, *first-class functions*, and *higher-order functions*. We are going to be exploring the potential of these ideas in the next chapters. After the distinction between actions, calculations, and data, the idea of higher-order functions opens up a new level of functional programming power. The second part of this book (the part you are reading now) is all about that power.

Summary

- First-class values are anything that can be stored in a variable, passed as an argument, and returned from functions. A first-class value can be manipulated by code.

- Many parts of a language are not first-class. We can wrap those parts in functions that do the same thing to make them first-class.

- Some languages have first-class functions that let you treat functions as first-class values. First-class functions are necessary for doing this level of functional programming.

- Higher-order functions are functions that take other functions as arguments (or that return a function). Higher-order functions let us abstract over varying behavior.

- *Implicit argument in function name* is a code smell where the difference between functions is named in the function name. We can apply *express implicit argument* to make the argument first-class instead of an inaccessible part of the function name.

- We can apply the refactoring called *replace body with callback* to abstract over behavior. It creates a first-class function argument that represents the behavioral difference between two functions.

Up next . . .

We've opened the door to the potential of higher-order functions. We will see many ways that these can help us, both in calculations and in actions. In the next chapter, we're going to continue applying the two refactorings we've learned to improve our code.

First-class functions: Part 2 | **11**

In this chapter

- Learn more applications of *replace body with callback*.

- Understand how returning functions from functions can give
functions superpowers.

- Get lots of practice writing higher-order functions to sharpen
your skills.

In the last chapter, we learned skills for creating higher-order functions. This chapter will deepen the learning as we apply those skills to more examples. We start by codifying our copy-on-write discipline. We then improve the logging system so it's not as much work.

One code smell and two refactorings

In the last chapter, we learned a code smell and two refactorings that help us eliminate duplication and find better abstractions. They let us create first-class values and higher-order functions. Just as a reminder, here they are again. We'll apply these new skills throughout the whole of part 2 of this book. Here they are again for reference.

Code smell: *Implicit argument in function name*

This code smell identifies aspects of code that could be better expressed as first-class values. If you are referring to a value in the body of a function, and that value is named in the function name, this smell applies. The solution is the next refactoring.

Characteristics

1. There are very similar function implementations.

2. The name of the function indicates the difference in implementation.

Refactoring: *Express implicit argument*

When you have an implicit argument in the function name, how do you turn that into an actual argument to the function? This refactoring adds an argument to your function so that the value becomes first-class. This may let you better express the intent of the code and potentially eliminate duplication.

Steps

1. Identify the implicit argument in the name of the function.

2. Add explicit argument.

3. Use new argument in body in place of hard-coded value.

4. Update the calling code.

Refactoring: *Replace body with callback*

The syntax of a language is often not first-class. This refactoring allows you to replace the body (the part that changes) of a piece of code with a callback. You can then pass in the behavior in a first-class function. It is a powerful way to create higher-order functions from existing code.

Steps

1. Identify the before, body, and after sections.

2. Extract the whole thing into a function.

3. Extract the body section into a function passed as an argument to that function.

We'll be iteratively applying these powerful skills so that they become second nature.

Refactoring copy-on-write

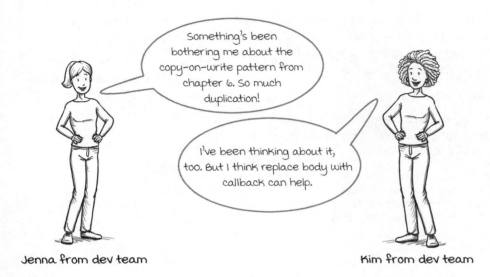

Jenna from dev team

Kim from dev team

Jenna:1 Really? I thought *replace body with callback* only worked with eliminating duplication in syntax like for loops and try/catch statements.

Kim: Well, it does help with those, as we've seen. But it can also work with other kinds of duplication—even the duplication of a coding discipline.

Jenna: Whoa! Nice! I'd love to see it.

Kim: Well, you know the first step.

Jenna: Right . . . identify the before, body, and after sections.

Kim: That's right. Once you have those, it's smooth sailing.

Jenna: The rules of copy-on-write are make a copy, modify the copy, return the copy. The thing that varies is how you modify. The other two are always the same for a given data structure.

Kim: Well, if it varies, it must be the body. And it's nestled between two unchanging sections, the before and after.

Jenna: This refactoring really does apply here!

Kim: Yep! We're running out of room on this page, so let's flip to the next one and get to it.

Steps of replace body with callback

1. Identify before, body, and after.
2. Extract function.
3. Extract callback.

Steps of copy-on-write

1. Make a copy.
2. Modify the copy.
3. Return the copy.

before

after

body

Refactoring copy-on-write for arrays

In chapter 6, we developed several copy-on-write routines for arrays. They all followed the basic pattern of make a copy, modify the copy, return the copy. Let's apply the *replace body with callback refactoring* to them to standardize the pattern.

> **Steps of copy-on-write**
>
> 1. Make a copy.
> 2. Modify the copy.
> 3. Return the copy.

1. Identify before, body, after

Here's just a few copy-on-write operations. We can see that they have very similar definitions. The copy, modify, return corresponds naturally to before, body, after.

```
function arraySet(array, idx, value) {        function push(array, elem) {
  var copy = array.slice();   ◄── before ──►   var copy = array.slice();
  copy[idx] = value;          ◄── body ────►   copy.push(elem);
  return copy;                ◄── after ───►   return copy;
}                                             }

function drop_last(array) {                   function drop_first(array) {
  var array_copy = array.slice(); ◄ before ►   var array_copy = array.slice();
  array_copy.pop();           ◄── body ────►   array_copy.shift();
  return array_copy;          ◄── after ───►   return array_copy;
}                                             }
```

Since the copying and returning are the same, let's focus on the first one, `arraySet()`. You could choose any of them.

> **Steps of replace body with callback**
>
> 1. Identify before, body, and after.
> 2. Extract function.
> 3. Extract callback.

2. Extract function

Our next step is to extract these three sections into a function. That function will contain the before and after code, so we can name it after the important part, which is copying arrays.

Original

```
function arraySet(array, idx, value) {
  var copy = array.slice();
  copy[idx] = value;
  return copy;
}
```

extract to a function

not defined in this scope

After function extraction

```
function arraySet(array, idx, value) {
  return withArrayCopy(array);
}

function withArrayCopy(array) {
  var copy = array.slice();
  copy[idx] = value;
  return copy;
}
```

not defined in this scope

That's the right way to do it, but we won't be able to run this code yet. Notice that `idx` and `value` are undefined in the scope of `withArrayCopy()`. Let's continue with the next step.

Our next step is to extract out the body into a callback. Let's do that on the next page.

On the last page, we started applying *replace body with callback* to the copy-on-write operations on arrays so that we could codify the discipline in code. We had just finished step 2 of *replace body with callback*. Here's the code we were left with:

```
function arraySet(array, idx, value) {
  return withArrayCopy(array);
}
```
the copy-on-write operation

```
function withArrayCopy(array) {
  var copy = array.slice();
  copy[idx] = value;
  return copy;
}
```
before
body
after
two variables not defined in this scope

> **Steps of replace body with callback**
> 1. Identify before, body, and after.
> 2. Extract function.
> 3. Extract callback.

We've done the second step correctly, but we won't be able to run this code yet. Notice that `idx` and `value` are undefined in the scope of `withArrayCopy()`. Let's continue with the next step.

3. Extract callback

Our next step is to extract the body into a callback. Because the callback will modify the array, we'll call it `modify`.

Current

```
function arraySet(array, idx, value) {
  return withArrayCopy(
    array

  );
}

function withArrayCopy(array) {
  var copy = array.slice();
  copy[idx] = value;
  return copy;
}
```

make the body an argument and pass it in

After extracting callback

```
function arraySet(array, idx, value) {
  return withArrayCopy(
    array,
    function(copy) {
      copy[idx] = value;
    });
}

function withArrayCopy(array, modify) {
  var copy = array.slice();
  modify(copy);
  return copy;
}
```
callback

And we're done! Let's compare the original to where we are after the refactoring on the next page.

On the last page, we completed the refactoring. Let's compare the code before the refactoring to where we ended up after the refactoring. Then we can discuss what this refactoring has done for us.

Before refactoring

```
function arraySet(array, idx, value) {
  var copy = array.slice();
  copy[idx] = value;
  return copy;
}
```

After refactoring

```
function arraySet(array, idx, value) {
  return withArrayCopy(array, function(copy) {
    copy[idx] = value;
  });
}
```

reusable function that standardizes the discipline

```
function withArrayCopy(array, modify) {
  var copy = array.slice();
  modify(copy);
  return copy;
}
```

Sometimes refactoring code and getting rid of duplication shortens the code. But not in this case. The duplicated code was already pretty short—just two lines. We did achieve a big benefit. We have codified and standardized the copy-on-write discipline for arrays. It no longer has to be written the same way all over the codebase. It's in one place.

We've also gained a new ability. In chapter 6, where we explored the copy-on-write discipline, we developed copy-on-write versions of basically all of the important array operations. However, what if we forgot one? The new `withArrayCopy()` function—the result of this refactoring—can handle any operation that modifies an array. For instance, what if we found a library with a faster way to sort? We can easily maintain our copy-on-write discipline and use this new sort routine.

> **Benefits we achieved**
>
> 1. Standardized discipline
> 2. Applied discipline to new operations
> 3. Optimized sequences of modifications

```
var sortedArray = withArrayCopy(array, function(copy) {
  SuperSorter.sort(copy);
});
```

the better sort routine that sorts in place

This benefit is huge. It even gives us an avenue for optimization. A series of copy-on-write operations will create a new copy for each operation. That can be slow and hog memory. `withArrayCopy()` gives us a way to optimize them by making one single copy.

Makes intermediate copies

```
var a1 = drop_first(array);
var a2 = push(a1, 10);
var a3 = push(a2, 11);
var a4 = arraySet(a3, 0, 42);
```

this code makes four copies of the array

Makes one copy

make one copy

```
var a4 = withArrayCopy(array, function(copy){
  copy.shift();
  copy.push(10);
  copy.push(11);
  copy[0] = 42;
});
```

make four modifications to the copy

Now we can re-implement all array copy-on-write functions using `withArrayCopy()`. In fact, that sounds like a good exercise.

It's your turn

We've just created a function called `withArrayCopy()` that codifies the copy-on-write discipline we learned in chapter 6. Following the example of `arraySet()`, rewrite `push()`, `drop_last()`, and `drop_first()`.

```
function withArrayCopy(array, modify) {
  var copy = array.slice();
  modify(copy);
  return copy;
}
```

Example

```
function arraySet(array, idx, value) {
  var copy = array.slice();
  copy[idx] = value;
  return copy;
}
```

```
function arraySet(array, idx, value) {
  return withArrayCopy(array, function(copy) {
    copy[idx] = value;
  });
}
```

write your answers here

```
function push(array, elem) {
  var copy = array.slice();
  copy.push(elem);
  return copy;
}
```

```
function drop_last(array) {
  var array_copy = array.slice();
  array_copy.pop();
  return array_copy;
}
```

```
function drop_first(array) {
  var array_copy = array.slice();
  array_copy.shift();
  return array_copy;
}
```

 **Answer**

Original

```
function push(array, elem) {
  var copy = array.slice();
  copy.push(elem);
  return copy;
}
```

Using withArrayCopy()

```
function push(array, elem) {
  return withArrayCopy(array, function(copy) {
    copy.push(elem);
  });
}
```

```
function drop_last(array) {
  var array_copy = array.slice();
  array_copy.pop();
  return array_copy;
}
```

```
function drop_last(array) {
  return withArrayCopy(array, function(copy) {
    copy.pop();
  });
}
```

```
function drop_first(array) {
  var array_copy = array.slice();
  array_copy.shift();
  return array_copy;
}
```

```
function drop_first(array) {
  return withArrayCopy(array, function(copy) {
    copy.shift();
  });
}
```

It's your turn

We just developed `withArrayCopy()`, which implements a copy-on-write discipline for arrays. Can you do the same for objects?

Here is the code for a couple of copy-on-write implementations:

```
function objectSet(object, key, value) {          function objectDelete(object, key) {
  var copy = Object.assign({}, object);             var copy = Object.assign({}, object);
  copy[key] = value;                                delete copy[key];
  return copy;                                      return copy;
}                                                  }
```

Write a function `withObjectCopy()` and use it to re-implement these two object copy-on-write functions.

write your answer here

Answer

```
function withObjectCopy(object, modify) {
  var copy = Object.assign({}, object);
  modify(copy);
  return copy;
}

function objectSet(object, key, value) {
  return withObjectCopy(object, function(copy) {
    copy[key] = value;
  });
}

function objectDelete(object, key) {
  return withObjectCopy(object, function(copy) {
    delete copy[key];
  });
}
```

 ## It's your turn

George just finished wrapping everything he needed to in `withLogging()`. It was a big task, but he's done. However, he sees another way he could make a more general version. The try/catch has two parts that vary, the body of the try and the body of the catch. We only let the body of the try vary. Could you help him adapt this refactoring to the case where it has two bodies that vary? In essence, George would like to write

```
tryCatch(sendEmail, logToSnapErrors)
```

instead of

```
try {
  sendEmail();
} catch(error) {
  logToSnapErrors(error);
}
```

Your task is to write `tryCatch()`.

Hint: It will be a lot like `withLogging()`, but with two function arguments.

write your answer here

Answer

```
function tryCatch(f, errorHandler) {
  try {
    return f();
  } catch(error) {
    return errorHandler(error);
  }
}
```

It's your turn

Just for fun, let's wrap another piece of syntax using the *replace body with callback* refactoring. This time, we will refactor an if statement. This might not be practical, but it's good practice. To make it easier, let's just do an if statement with no else. Here are two if statements to work with:

"test" clause   "then" clause

```
if(array.length === 0) {                     if(hasItem(cart, "shoes")) {
  console.log("Array is empty");               return setPriceByName(cart, "shoes", 0);
}                                            }
```

Use these two examples and the refactoring to write a function called when(). You should be able to use it like this:

"test" clause   "then" clause

```
when(array.length === 0, function() {        when(hasItem(cart, "shoes"), function() {
  console.log("Array is empty");               return setPriceByName(cart, "shoes", 0);
});                                           });
```

write your answer here

Answer

```
function when(test, then) {
  if(test)
    return then();
}
```

It's your turn

After writing the function called when() in the last exercise, a few people started using it—and loving it! They want a way to add an else statement. Let's rename the function from when() to IF() and add a new callback for the else branch.

"test" clause   "then" clause

```
IF(array.length === 0, function() {
  console.log("Array is empty");
}, function() {
  console.log("Array has something in it.");
});
```

"else" clause

```
IF(hasItem(cart, "shoes"), function() {
  return setPriceByName(cart, "shoes", 0);
}, function() {
  return cart; // unchanged
});
```

write your answer here

Answer

```
function IF(test, then, ELSE) {
  if(test)
    return then();
  else
    return ELSE();
}
```

Returning functions from functions

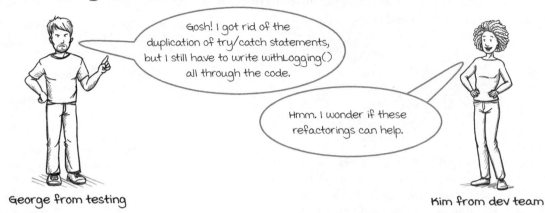

George: I hope they can help. We need to wrap code in a try/catch and send errors to **Snap Errors®**. We are taking some normal code and giving it the superpower. The superpower runs the code, catches any errors, and sends them to **Snap Errors®**. It's like putting on a superhero outfit that gives your code superpowers.

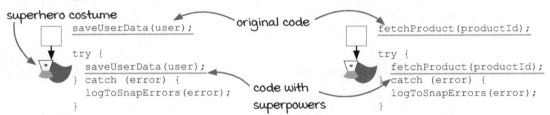

George: It works fine. But there are thousands of lines of code that need to be wrapped like that. Even after the refactoring we did before, I had to do it manually, one at a time.

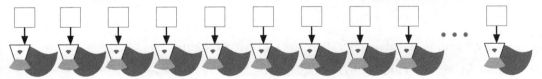

George: What would be nice is if we could write a function that just did it for me, so I wouldn't have to manually do it thousands of times.

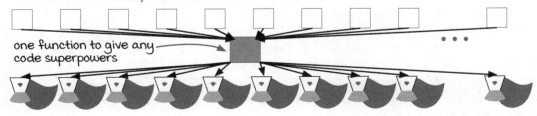

Kim: Well, let's just write it, then! It's just a higher-order function.

Let's review George's problem and the current prototype solution.

George needed to catch errors and log them to the Snap Errors®
service. Some snippets of code looked like this:

*these two snippets differ only
in one line; lots of duplication!*

```
try {                          try {
  saveUserData(user);            fetchProduct(productId);
} catch (error) {              } catch (error) {
  logToSnapErrors(error);        logToSnapErrors(error);
}                              }
```

*superhero costume
indicates superpowers*

George was going to have to write very similar try/catch blocks all
throughout the code—everywhere these functions were called. He
wanted to solve that duplication problem up front.

Here is what he and Jenna came up with:

```
function withLogging(f) {        this function encapsulates
  try {                          the repeated code
    f();
  } catch (error) {
    logToSnapErrors(error);
  }                                    using the code still
}                                      has lots of duplication;
                                       only difference is
```
                                       underlined part

Using this new function, the try/catch statements above are transformed into this.

```
withLogging(function() {           withLogging(function() {
  saveUserData(user);                fetchProduct(productID);
});                                });
```

Now we have a standard system. But there are still two problems:

1. We could still forget to log in some places.

2. We still have to manually write this code everywhere.

Even though there is much less code to duplicate, there is still
enough duplication to be annoying. We want to get rid of all of
the duplication.

What we really want is a thing to call that has all of the
functionality—the original functionality of the code *plus* the
superpower of catching and logging errors. We can write that,
but we want something that will write it for us automatically.
Let's see how on the next page.

Snap Errors®

*To err is human, to Snap is
divine.*

From Snap Errors API docs

`logToSnapErrors(error)`

Send an error to the **Snap
Errors®** service. The error
should be an error thrown and
caught in your code.

On the last page, we summarized where George's prototype is now and how it needs to improve. He could wrap any code in a standard way so that it logged errors consistently. Let's imagine what it would look like if we moved that functionality directly into a function. Luckily, we're dealing with a prototype, and we can make changes easily. We'll go back to the original code:

does the functionality plus the superpower (logging)

Original

```
try {                              try {
  saveUserData(user);               fetchProduct(productId);
} catch (error) {                  } catch (error) {
  logToSnapErrors(error);            logToSnapErrors(error);
}                                  }
```

Just to make things super clear, let's rename those functions to reflect that they don't do logging on their own:

change names to reflect that they don't log

Clearer names

```
try {                              try {
  saveUserDataNoLogging(user);      fetchProductNoLogging(productId);
} catch (error) {                  } catch (error) {
  logToSnapErrors(error);            logToSnapErrors(error);
}                                  }
```

We can wrap these snippets of code in functions with names that reflect that they *do* logging. This is also just for clarity.

we can call these functions and know that logging is happening

Functions that do logging

```
function saveUserDataWithLogging(user) {    function fetchProductWithLogging(productId) {
  try {                                       try {
    saveUserDataNoLogging(user);                fetchProductNoLogging(productId);
  } catch (error) {                           } catch (error) {
    logToSnapErrors(error);                     logToSnapErrors(error);
  }                                           }
}                                           }
```

but we still have lots of duplication in the bodies

We are wrapping these two functions that don't log with logging functionality. This way, any time we call the logging versions, we know the logging is happening. If we have these functions, we don't have to remember to wrap our code in try/catch blocks. And we only need to write a handful of these superpowered functions instead of wrapping thousands of calls to the no-logging versions.

But now we have new duplication. These two functions are very similar. We want a way to automatically make functions that look like this. Let's see that on the next page.

On the last page, we had two very similar functions. They did different things, but there was a lot of code in common. We want to deduplicate the code.

lots of duplication

```
function saveUserDataWithLogging(user) {
  try {
    saveUserDataNoLogging(user);
  } catch (error) {
    logToSnapErrors(error);
  }
}
```

```
function fetchProductWithLogging(productId) {
  try {
    fetchProductNoLogging(productId);
  } catch (error) {
    logToSnapErrors(error);
  }
}
```

Let's imagine for the moment that these functions didn't have names. We'll remove the names and make them anonymous. We will also rename the argument to something generic.

before
body
after

```
function(arg) {
  try {
    saveUserDataNoLogging(arg);
  } catch (error) {
    logToSnapErrors(error);
  }
}
```

```
function(arg) {
  try {
    fetchProductNoLogging(arg);
  } catch (error) {
    logToSnapErrors(error);
  }
}
```

Now we have a very clear case of before, body, and after. Let's apply our refactoring *replace body with callback*. But instead of adding a callback to this function, we'll do what we did originally and wrap it in a new function. Let's do it to the function on the left:

returns a function

takes function as argument

defer execution of superpower code by wrapping in function

```
function(arg) {

  try {
    saveUserDataNoLogging(arg);
  } catch (error) {
    logToSnapErrors(error);
  }

}
```

```
function wrapLogging(f) {
  return function(arg) {
    try {
      f(arg);
    } catch (error) {
      logToSnapErrors(error);
    }
  }
}
```

assign the return value to a variable to name it

call wrapLogging() with the function we want to transform

```
var saveUserDataWithLogging = wrapLogging(saveUserDataNoLogging);
```

Now, wrapLogging() takes a function f and returns a function that wraps f in our standard try/catch. We can take our non-logging versions and easily convert them to logging versions. We can give any function logging superpowers!

```
var saveUserDataWithLogging = wrapLogging(saveUserDataNoLogging);
var fetchProductWithLogging = wrapLogging(fetchProductNoLogging);
```

We have eliminated the duplication. Now we have an easy way to add standard logging behavior to any function. Let's review.

On the last page, we created a function that can wrap any function we want in our logging superpower. Let's look at the before and after:

Manual superpower

Automatic superpower

```
try {
  saveUserData(user);
} catch (error) {
  logToSnapErrors(error);
}
```

`saveUserDataWithLogging(user)`

imagine writing the try/catch and logging line a thousand times

Of course, a lot went on behind the scenes. We have a function that will give any function this same superpower:

```
function wrapLogging(f) {
  return function(arg) {
    try {
      f(arg);
    } catch (error) {
      logToSnapErrors(error);
    }
  }
}
```

And we can use that to define `saveUserDataWithLogging()` in terms of `saveUserData()`. Let's also visualize it:

```
var saveUserDataWithLogging = wrapLogging(saveUserData);
```

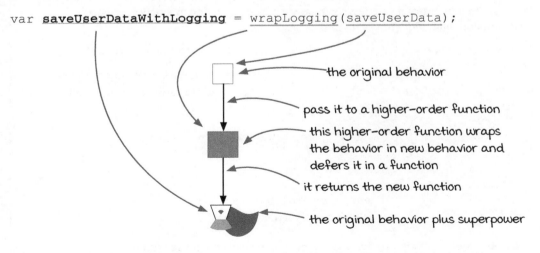

the original behavior

pass it to a higher-order function

this higher-order function wraps the behavior in new behavior and defers it in a function

it returns the new function

the original behavior plus superpower

Returning functions from functions lets us make function factories. They automate the creation of functions and codify a standard.

 **Brain break**

There's more to go, but let's take a break for questions

Q: **You're assigning the return value of that function to a variable, but I'm used to all functions being defined using the `function` keyword at the top level. Won't it be confusing?**

A: That's a good question. It does take a little bit of getting used to. But even without using this pattern, you were probably already using other signals to know which variables contain data and which contain functions. For instance, functions typically are named using verbs, while variables are named using nouns.

What you have to get used to is that there are different ways to define functions. Sometimes you define them directly with code you write; sometimes you define them as the return value from another function.

Q: **The function `wrapLogging()` took a function that worked on one argument. How can you make it so it works on more? And how can we get the return value from a function?**

A: Great questions. The return value is easy. Just add a return keyword to return it from the inner function. That will be the return value of the new function you're making.

Dealing with variable arguments in classic JavaScript could be kind of a pain. It is much easier in ES6, the new style of JavaScript. If you're using ES6, you should search for *rest arguments* and the *spread operator*. Other languages may have similar features.

However, it's not that difficult in practice, even in classic JavaScript, since JavaScript is very flexible with arguments if you pass too many or not enough. And in practice, we rarely have functions with more than a handful of arguments.

If you want to make wrapLogging() work for functions with up to nine arguments, you could do this:

```
function wrapLogging(f) {
  return function(a1, a2, a3, a4, a5, a6, a7, a8, a9) {
    try {
      return f(a1, a2, a3, a4, a5, a6, a7, a8, a9);
    } catch (error) {
      logToSnapErrors(error);
    }
  }
}
```

JavaScript will ignore unused arguments when you call it

just return from the inner function to get the return value out

There are other methods, but this one is simple to explain and doesn't require deeper understanding of JavaScript. Look up in your language how to apply functions to variable numbers of arguments.

It's your turn

Write a function that transforms the function you pass it into a function that catches and ignores all errors. If there is an error, just return `null`. Make it work on functions of at least three arguments.

Hint

- You normally ignore errors by wrapping code in a try/catch and doing nothing in the catch.

```
try {
  codeThatMightThrow();
} catch(e) {
  // ignore errors by doing nothing
}
```

write your answer here

Answer

```
function wrapIgnoreErrors(f) {
  return function(a1, a2, a3) {
    try {
      return f(a1, a2, a3);
    } catch(error) {  // error is ignored
      return null;
    }
  };
}
```

It's your turn

Write a function called makeAdder() that makes a function to add a number to another number. For instance,

```
var increment = makeAdder(1);        var plus10 = makeAdder(10);

> increment(10)                       > plus10(12)
11                                    22
```

write your answer here

Answer

```
function makeAdder(n) {
  return function(x) {
    return n + x;
  };
}
```

 **Brain break**

There's more to go, but let's take a break for questions

Q: It looks like there's a lot we can do by returning functions from higher-order functions. Can we write our whole program that way?

A: That's a great question. It is probably possible to write your whole program using nothing but higher-order functions. The better question, though, is whether you would want to.

Writing functions this way is more general. It is very easy to get carried away with the fun of writing higher-order functions. It tickles a center in our brain that makes us feel clever, like solving intricate puzzles. Good engineering is not about solving puzzles. It's about solving problems in effective ways.

The truth is, you should use higher-order functions for their strength, which is reducing the repetition we find in codebases. We loop a lot, so it's nice to have a higher-order function for getting those right (`forEach()`). We catch errors a lot, so something to do that in a standard way might also be helpful.

Many functional programmers do get carried away. There are entire books written about how to do the simplest things using only higher-order functions. But when you look at the code, is it really clearer than writing it the straightforward way?

You should explore and experiment. Try higher-order functions in lots of places for lots of purposes. Find new uses for them. Explore their limits. But do so outside of production code. Remember that the exploration is just for learning.

When you do come up with a solution using a higher-order function, compare it to the straightforward solution. Is it really better? Does it make the code clearer? How many duplicate lines of code are you really removing? How easy would it be for someone to understand what the code is doing? We mustn't lose sight of that.

Bottom line: These are powerful techniques, but they come at a cost. They're a little too pleasant to write, and that blinds us to the problem of reading them. Get good at them, but only use them when they really make the code better.

Conclusion

This chapter deepened the ideas of *first-class values*, *first-class functions*, and *higher-order functions*. We are going to be exploring the potential of these ideas in the next chapters. After the distinction between actions, calculations, and data, the idea of higher-order functions opens a new level of functional programming power. The second part of this book is all about that power.

Summary

- Higher-order functions can codify patterns and disciplines that otherwise we would have to maintain manually. Because they are defined once, we can get them right once and can use them many times.

- We can make functions by returning them from higher-order functions. The functions can be used just like normal by assigning them to a variable to give them a name.

- Higher-order functions come with a set of tradeoffs. They can remove a lot of duplication, but sometimes they cost readability. Learn them well and use them wisely.

Up next . . .

In the last chapter we saw a function called `forEach()` that let us iterate over arrays. In the next chapter, we will explore a functional style of iteration by expanding on that idea. We will learn three functional tools that capture common patterns of iteration over arrays.

In this chapter

- Learn the three functional tools, `map()`, `filter()`, and `reduce()`.

- Discover how to replace simple for loops over arrays with the functional tools.

- Derive implementations for the three functional tools.

Many functional languages come with a variety of powerful, abstract functions for dealing with collections of data. In this chapter, we're going to focus on three very common ones, namely `map()`, `filter()`, and `reduce()`. These tools form the backbones of many functional programs. They replace for loops as the workhorse of the functional programmer. Since looping over arrays is something we do a lot, these tools are extremely useful.

One code smell and two refactorings

In chapter 10, we learned a code smell and two refactorings that help us eliminate duplication and find better abstractions. They let us create first-class values and higher-order functions. Just as a reminder, here they are again. We'll apply these new skills throughout the whole of part 2 of this book. Here they are again for reference.

Code smell: *Implicit argument in function name*

This code smell identifies aspects of code that could be better expressed as first-class values. If you are referring to a value in the body of a function, and that value is named in the function name, this smell applies. The solution is the next refactoring.

Characteristics

1. There are very similar function implementations.

2. The names of the functions indicate the difference in implementation.

Refactoring: *Express implicit argument*

When you have an implicit argument in the function name, how do you turn that into an actual argument to the function? This refactoring adds an argument to your function so that the value becomes first-class. This may let you better express the intent of the code and potentially eliminate duplication.

Steps

1. Identify the implicit argument in the name of the function.

2. Add explicit argument.

3. Use new argument in body in place of hard-coded value.

4. Update the calling code.

Refactoring: *Replace body with callback*

The syntax of a language is often not first-class. This refactoring allows you to replace the body (the part that changes) of a piece of code with a callback. You can then pass in the behavior in a first-class function. It is a powerful way to create higher-order functions from existing code.

Steps

1. Identify the before, body, and after sections.

2. Extract the whole thing into a function.

3. Extract the body section into a function passed as an argument to that function.

We'll be iteratively applying these powerful skills so that they become second nature.

MegaMart is creating a communications team

To: MegaMart employees
From: MegaMart management

Hello!

We now have over 1 million customers. We need to send them emails.

- Marketing sends promotional emails.
- Legal sends emails relating to legal issues.
- Business development sends account emails.
- And more!

These emails have different purposes. But they have one thing in common: We need to send them to some customers and not others. That is a critical challenge we wish to face.

We estimate that there are hundreds of different subsets of customers we will need to send emails to. To adequately respond to this need, we are setting up a customer communications team. They will be responsible for writing and maintaining the code.

The team will consist of these people:

- Kim from the dev team
- John from marketing
- Harry from customer service

Starting immediately, if you have a need for customer data, send your requests to them.

Sincerely,
The Management

With no heads up to the new team members, this memo went out this morning. While the new team gets organized, requests are already coming in. Here's the first one:

Data request: Coupon email process		
We implemented this back in chapter 3, but now it's your job, so here it is.		Requested by: Chief marketing officer
		Owned by: Kim on dev team

John from marketing   Harry from customer service   Kim from dev team

Code from chapter 3

```
function emailsForCustomers(customers, goods, bests) {
  var emails = [];
  for(var i = 0; i < customers.length; i++) {
    var customer = customers[i];
    var email = emailForCustomer(customer, goods, bests);
    emails.push(email);
  }
  return emails;
}
```

it's a for loop, but we have forEach() now

John: You think you can improve this?

Harry: I don't know. It looks pretty simple already. It's already a calculation, not an action.

Kim: That's true. But imagine how many times we're going to have to write code just like this. You read the memo: hundreds of different subsets of customers.

John: Yeah! I don't think I can stay sane writing that many for loops.

Kim: I bet functional programming has an answer, but I don't know it yet. But just to get started, didn't we recently learn "the last for loop over arrays you'll ever need to write?" That should be applicable here.

Harry: You're right! Let's convert this for loop to a `forEach()`.

```
function emailsForCustomers(customers, goods, bests) {
  var emails = [];
  forEach(customers, function(customer) {
   var email = emailForCustomer(customer, goods, bests);
   emails.push(email);
  });
  return emails;
}
```

John from marketing   Harry from customer service   Kim from dev team

Converted to `forEach()`

```
function emailsForCustomers(customers, goods, bests) {
  var emails = [];
  forEach(customers, function(customer) {
    var email = emailForCustomer(customer, goods, bests);
    emails.push(email);
  });
  return emails;
}
```

Harry: That is much better! We got rid of a lot of repetitive junk.

John: Yes, but I would still go nuts if I have to write this same function a million times. I did not become a marketer so that my life could be a real-world *Groundhog Day*.

Kim: Wait! This looks a lot like something I was reading about. It's called `map()`.

John: `map()`? As in what you use to find what road to take?

Kim: No! Not that kind of map. `map()` is a function that transforms one array into another array of the same length. Notice how we're taking an array of customers and returning an array of emails? That's perfect for `map()`.

Harry: Hmm. I think I see it. Can you explain it again?

Kim: Okay. Just like `forEach()` is a higher-order function that loops through an array, `map()` is a higher-function that loops through an array. The difference is that `map()` returns a new array.

John: What's in the new array?

Kim: That's the beauty of it: The function you pass to it tells you what to put in the new array.

John: And that will make this code easier?

Kim: Yes! It will be shorter and clearer. I want to explain more, but I'll need a new page . . .

Deriving `map()` from examples

Let's look at some of the functions that the customer communications team now owns that match this same pattern:

```
function emailsForCustomers(customers, goods, bests) {
  var emails = [];
  forEach(customers, function(customer) {
    var email = emailForCustomer(customer, goods, bests);
    emails.push(email);
  });
  return emails;
}
```
before
body
after

```
function biggestPurchasePerCustomer(customers) {
  var purchases = [];
  forEach(customers, function(customer) {
    var purchase = biggestPurchase(customer);
    purchases.push(purchase);
  });
  return purchases;
}
```
body

```
function customerFullNames(customers) {
  var fullNames = [];
  forEach(customers, function(cust) {
    var name = cust.firstName + ' ' + cust.lastName;
    fullNames.push(name);
  });
  return fullNames;
}
```
before
body
after

```
function customerCities(customers) {
  var cities = [];
  forEach(customers, function(customer) {
    var city = customer.address.city;
    cities.push(city);
  });
  return cities;
}
```
body

> **Steps of replace body with callback**
>
> 1. Identify before, body, and after.
> 2. Extract function.
> 3. Extract callback.

Really, when you look at it closely, the only thing that differs is the code that generates the new elements of the array. We can do a standard *replace body with callback* like we saw in the last two chapters.

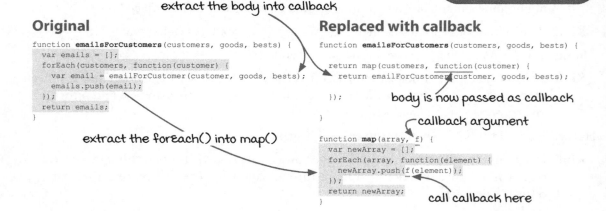

extract the body into callback

Original
```
function emailsForCustomers(customers, goods, bests) {
  var emails = [];
  forEach(customers, function(customer) {
    var email = emailForCustomer(customer, goods, bests);
    emails.push(email);
  });
  return emails;
}
```
extract the forEach() into map()

Replaced with callback
```
function emailsForCustomers(customers, goods, bests) {

  return map(customers, function(customer) {
    return emailForCustomer(customer, goods, bests);

  });

}
```
body is now passed as callback

callback argument
```
function map(array, f) {
  var newArray = [];
  forEach(array, function(element) {
    newArray.push(f(element));
  });
  return newArray;
}
```
call callback here

We've extracted a new function, called `map()`, that does the common iteration. This function is a common tool used by functional programmers. In fact, it is one of the three main functional tools because it is so useful. Let's spend a little bit more time looking at what it does.

Functional tool: map ( )

map() is one of three "functional tools" that do a ton of work for the functional programmer. The other two are filter() and reduce(), which we'll see shortly. Right now, let's take a look at map() a little more closely.

```
                    ┌ takes array and function
function map(array, f) {
  var newArray = [];          ← creates a new empty array
  forEach(array, function(element) {
    newArray.push(f(element));      calls f() to create a new element based
  });                               on the element from original array
  return newArray;
}                            adds the new element for each
  returns the new array      element in the original array
```

You could say that map() transforms an array of X (some group of values) into an array of Y (a different group of values). To do so, you need to pass in a function from X to Y—that is, a function that takes an X and returns a Y. map() turns a function that operates on a single value at a time into one that can operate on an entire array at a time.

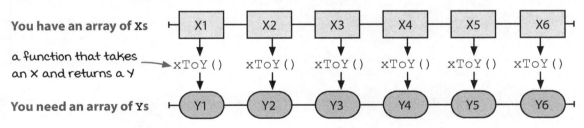

You have an array of Xs — X1 — X2 — X3 — X4 — X5 — X6 —

a function that takes an X and returns a Y → xToY()   xToY()   xToY()   xToY()   xToY()   xToY()

You need an array of Ys — Y1 — Y2 — Y3 — Y4 — Y5 — Y6 —

It is easiest to use map() when you pass it a calculation. If you do so, the expression calling map() will also be a calculation. If you pass map() an action, it will call the action once for every element in the array. In that case, the expression will be an action. Let's take a look at how we're using it in our example.

```
    pass map() an Array              pass map() a function that takes
    of customers                     a customer and returns an email
                        \            /
function emailsForCustomers(customers, goods, bests) {
  return map(customers, function(customer) {
    return emailForCustomer(customer, goods, bests);
  });
}
          returns an email calculated
          from the customer
```

how do you know to call this "customer"?

Wait! What's going on with the syntax there? Where is the name "customer" coming from?

```
function emailsForCustomers(customers, goods, bests) {
  return map(customers, function(customer) {
    return emailForCustomer(customer, goods, bests);
  });
}
```

Harry from
customer service

It's good that we talk about this. It's a very common stumbling block for people new to higher-order functions.

Let's walk through it one step at a time. `map()` takes two arguments: an array and a function.

Here we are passing `map()` an array that we expect to have customers in. JavaScript doesn't check the types, so it is possible that there's something else in there. However, we expect it to have only customers. A language that checks types would be able to guarantee that expectation. But if we trust our code, that array only has customers.

```
function emailsForCustomers(customers, goods, bests) {
  return map(customers, function(customer) {
    return emailForCustomer(customer, goods, bests);
  });
}
```

Vocab time

An *inline function* is a function that is defined where it is used instead of named and referred to later.

The function we pass it is an *inline, anonymous function*, which means we are defining it right in the place where it is used. When we define a function, we get to tell it what the names of the arguments are. We could name it anything. We could name it X or Y, or even `pumpkin`. But for clarity, we are calling it `customer`.

Vocab time

An *anonymous function* is a function without a name. That usually happens when we define the function inline.

```
function(X) {              function(Y) {              function(pumpkin) {
  return emailForCustomer(    return emailForCustomer(    return emailForCustomer(
    X, goods, bests            Y, goods, bests            pumpkin, goods, bests
  );                         );                          );
}                          }                           }
```

these are all equivalent functions

Why `customer`? Because `map()` is going to call this function with elements from the array we pass to it, one element at a time. Because we expect the array to only have customers in it, it makes sense to call it `customer`. It's singular because `map()` will call it with one element at a time.

Three ways to pass a function

Vocab time

An *inline function* is defined where it is used. For example, a function might be defined in the argument list.

There are three ways in JavaScript to pass a function to another function. Other languages might have more or fewer. JavaScript is pretty typical for languages with first-class functions.

Globally defined

We can define and name a function at the global level. This is the typical way you define most functions. It lets you refer to the function later by name from pretty much anywhere else in the program.

```
function greet(name) {
  return "Hello, " + name;
}
```
define the function with a name at one place in the program

refer to the function by name elsewhere. here we are passing it to map()

```
var friendGreetings = map(friendsNames, greet);
```

Locally defined

Vocab time

An *anonymous function* is a function without a name. That usually happens when we define the function inline.

We can define and name a function inside of a local scope. That function will have a name, but we won't be able to refer to it outside of the scope. This is useful if you need to refer to other values in the local scope but still want a name for it.

```
function greetEverybody(friends) {
  var greeting;
  if(language === "English")
    greeting = "Hello, ";
  else
    greeting = "Salut, ";

  var greet = function(name) {
    return greeting + name;
  };

  return map(friends, greet);
}
```
we're in the scope of this function

define the function with a name at one place in the scope

refer to the function by name in same scope

Defined inline

We can define a function right where it is being used. That is, we don't assign the function to a variable so it doesn't have a name. We call that an *anonymous function*, which is most useful for short functions that make sense in the context and only need to be used once.

define the function where it is being used

close the { from the function definition and close the (from the call to map()

```
var friendGreetings = map(friendsNames, function(name) {
  return "Hello, " + name;
});
```

Example: Email addresses of all customers

Let's look at a simple, yet typical, example of using `map()`. We need to generate an array of email addresses for all customers. We know we can get an array of all customers. This is the perfect use for `map()`.

We have: Array of <u>customers</u>

We want: Array of their <u>email addresses</u>

Function: Takes one <u>customer</u> and returns their <u>email address</u>

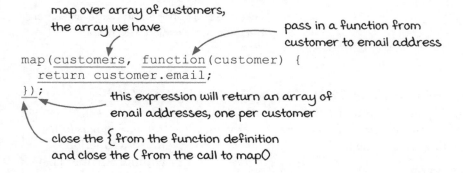

```
map(customers, function(customer) {
  return customer.email;
});
```

`map()` helps us apply a function to a whole array of values.

Careful, now!

`map()` is a very useful function. Functional programmers use it safely all the time. But it's very simple (and that's why we like it). Notice that it doesn't check at all what gets added to the returned array. What if the customer does not have an email and `customer.email` is `null` or `undefined`? That `null` will get put into the array.

This is the same problem we had before: If your language allows `null`s (like JavaScript does), then you might get `null`s sometimes. However, `map()` can multiply the problem since it will run the function over entire arrays. There are two solutions: Be mindful or use a language where `null` is impossible.

And if you do expect `null`s, but you want to get rid of them, the next tool, `filter()`, will help you with that.

It's your turn

One piece of code we'll need to write is useful during the holidays. We need to send out postcards to all of our customers. We need an object containing the first name, last name, and address of each customer. Using `map()`, write the code to generate this array of objects.

Givens

- `customers` is an Array of all customers
- `customer.firstName`, `customer.lastName`, and `customer.address` will give you the data you need

write your answer here

Answer

```
map(customers, function(customer) {
  return {
    firstName : customer.firstName,
    lastName  : customer.lastName,
    address   : customer.address
  };
});
```

Data request: A list of our best customers

We would like to email just our best and awesomest customers and ask them to buy more! That means everyone with three or more purchases.

Requested by:
Chief marketing officer

Owned by:
Kim on dev team

John from marketing

Harry from customer service

Kim from dev team

Harry: I wonder if we can use `map()` for this.

John: I doubt it. `map()` always gives you an array of the same length as you give it. This is asking for a subset of the customers—just the best ones.

Kim: You're right. Let's look at what this would look like as a `forEach()`:

```
function selectBestCustomers(customers) {
  var newArray = [];
  forEach(customers, function(customer) {
    if(customer.purchases.length >= 3)
      newArray.push(customer);
  });
  return newArray;
}
```

Harry: It's similar, but it's not a `map()`. `map()` didn't have a conditional.

John: Kim, you always know what patterns these things are. Any ideas?

Kim: In fact, I do recognize it now. This is a `filter()`. `filter()` is the second functional tool!

John: Second functional tool? Seems like a big coincidence to me.

Kim: That's what you get when you're a character in a book. Anyway, `filter()` is a higher-order function that lets you create a new array based on an existing array. But it lets you say what elements you want to keep in the new array, and which elements you skip.

Harry: I see! So we can call `filter()` and pass to it a function that selects only the best customers.

Kim: Bingo! Let's look at this on the next page.

Deriving `filter()` **from examples**

Let's look at some of the functions that the customer communications team now owns that match this same pattern:

```
function selectBestCustomers(customers) {
  var newArray = [];                         ← before
  forEach(customers, function(customer) {
    if(customer.purchases.length >= 3)
      newArray.push(customer);       ← body (test of
  });                                   if statement)
  return newArray;
}                                  ← after
```

```
function selectCustomersAfter(customers, date) {
  var newArray = [];
  forEach(customers, function(customer) {
    if(customer.signupDate > date)
      newArray.push(customer);        ← body (test of
  });                                    if statement)
  return newArray;
}
```

```
function selectCustomersBefore(customers, date) {
  var newArray = [];                         ← before
  forEach(customers, function(customer) {
    if(customer.signupDate < date)
      newArray.push(customer);       ← body (test of
  });                                   if statement)
  return newArray;
}                                  ← after
```

```
function singlePurchaseCustomers(customers) {
  var newArray = [];
  forEach(customers, function(customer) {
    if(customer.purchases.length === 1)
      newArray.push(customer);        ← body (test of
  });                                    if statement)
  return newArray;
}
```

The only thing that differs is the test expression of the if statement. That is the code that selects which elements get put into the new array. That will be the body. We can do a standard *replace body with callback*.

wrap the expression in a function and pass it as argument

Original

```
function selectBestCustomers(customers) {
  var newArray = [];
  forEach(customers, function(customer) {
    if(customer.purchases.length >= 3)
      newArray.push(customer);
  });
  return newArray;
}
```

extract the forEach() into filter()

Replaced with callback

```
function selectBestCustomers(customers) {
  return filter(customers, function(customer) {
    return customer.purchases.length >= 3;
  });
}
```

```
function filter(array, f) {
  var newArray = [];
  forEach(array, function(element) {
    if(f(element))
      newArray.push(element);
  });
  return newArray;
}
```

test expression now contained in callback

We've extracted a new function, called `filter()`, that does the common iteration. This function is a common tool used by functional programmers. It is the second of the three main functional tools because it is so useful.

Remember that the callback can be globally defined, locally defined, or defined inline. In this case, since it's short and clear, we define it inline.

Let's spend a little bit more time looking at what `filter()` does.

Three ways to define a function

1. Globally defined
2. Locally defined
3. Defined inline

Functional tool: `filter()`

`filter()` is the second of three "functional tools" that functional programmers rely on. The other two are `map()` and `reduce()`. We'll see `reduce()` shortly. Right now, let's look at `filter()` a little more closely:

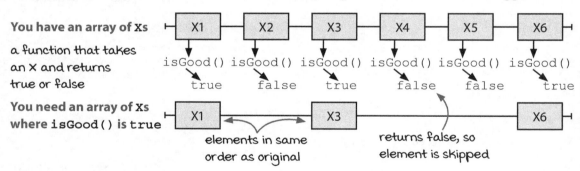

```
function filter(array, f) {                    takes array and function
  var newArray = [];                           creates a new empty array
  forEach(array, function(element) {
    if(f(element))                             calls f() to check if the element
      newArray.push(element);                  should go in the new array
  });                                          adds the original element
  return newArray;                             if it passes the check
}                    returns the
                     new array
```

You could say that `filter()` selects a subset of the elements of an array. If it's an array of X, it's still an array of X, but with potentially fewer elements. To do the selection, you need to pass in a function from X to `Boolean`—that is, a function that takes an X and returns `true` or `false` (or the equivalent). That function determines if each element stays (in the case of `true`) or goes (in the case of `false`). Functions that return `true` or `false` are often called *predicates*. The new array will have the elements in the same order as the original, but some could be skipped.

You have an array of Xs

a function that takes
an X and returns
true or false

**You need an array of Xs
where isGood() is true**

| X1 | X2 | X3 | X4 | X5 | X6 |

isGood() isGood() isGood() isGood() isGood() isGood()

true   false   true   false   false   true

| X1 | | X3 | | | X6 |

elements in same
order as original

returns false, so
element is skipped

Like with `map()`, it is easiest to call `filter()` with a calculation. `filter()` calls the function you pass it once for each element in the array. Let's look at how we're using it in our example:

Vocab time

Predicates are functions that return true or false. They are useful for passing to `filter()` and other higher-order functions.

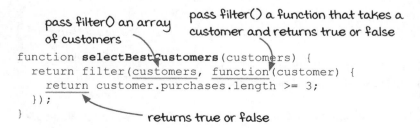

pass filter() an array
of customers

pass filter() a function that takes a
customer and returns true or false

```
function selectBestCustomers(customers) {
  return filter(customers, function(customer) {
    return customer.purchases.length >= 3;
  });
}                    returns true or false
```

Example: Customers with zero purchases

Let's look at a simple, yet typical, example of using `filter()`. We need to generate an array of all customers who haven't completed a purchase yet. This is the perfect use for `filter()`.

We have: Array of customers

We want: Array customers who have zero purchases

Function: Takes one customer and returns true if they have zero purchases

filter the array of customers,
the array we have

pass in a function that determines
if they have zero purchases

```
filter(customers, function(customer) {
  return customer.purchases.length === 0;
});
```

make sure we return
true or false from our
predicate; filter will keep
all of the customers where
the predicate returns true

this expression will return an array of customers
and all of those customers will have zero purchases

`filter()` helps us select a subset of values in an array, while maintaining their original order.

Careful, now!

A few pages ago we talked about how you might wind up with `null`s in your array when you run `map()` over it. Sometimes that's okay! But how do you get rid of those `null`s? Well, you can just filter them out.

```
var allEmails = map(customers, function(customer) {
  return customer.email;
});
```

the customer's email might be null; in that
case, there will be nulls in the array

```
var emailsWithoutNulls = filter(emailsWithNulls, function(email) {
  return email !== null;
});
```

we can filter out the nulls from the array,
leaving us with just the good emails

`map()` and `filter()` work well together. We'll spend a lot of time learning how to do more complex queries by combining `map()`, `filter()`, and `reduce()` in the next chapter.

It's your turn

The marketing department wants to run a small test. They want to arbitrarily select approximately one third of the customers and send them a different email from the rest. For marketing's purposes, it is good enough to use the user's ID and check if it's divisible by 3. If it is, they're in the test group. Your task is to write code to generate the test and non-test groups.

Givens

- `customers` is an array of all customers.

- `customer.id` will give you the user's ID.

- `%` is the remainder operator; `x % 3 === 0` checks if x is divisible by 3.

write your answer here

```
var testGroup =
```

```
var nonTestGroup =
```

Answer

```
var testGroup = filter(customers, function(customer) {
  return customer.id % 3 === 0;
});

var nonTestGroup = filter(customers, function(customer) {
  return customer.id % 3 !== 0;
});
```

Data request: A count of all purchases across all customers

We want to know how many purchases
have ever been made. Purchases are
stored as part of the customer record,
so we need a way to count them all.

Requested by:
Chief marketing officer

Owned by:
Kim on dev team

John from marketing

Harry from customer service

Kim from dev team

Harry: Wow, this one doesn't sound like `map()` or `filter()`. It's not returning an array at all.

John: You're right. This one wants a number. Kim, do you have another functional tool for us?.

Kim: I think so. Let's see what it looks like as a `forEach()`.

```
function countAllPurchases(customers) {
  var total = 0;
  forEach(customers, function(customer) {
    total = total + customer.purchases.length;
  });
  return total;
}
```

Harry: It's similar, but it's not a `map()` and it's not a filter.

John: This one is neat, though, because the previous total is used in the calculation of the next total.

Kim: Yes! This is `reduce()`, the third and final functional tool. `reduce()` is also a higher-order function, like the other two. But it's used to accumulate a value as it iterates over the array. In this case, we're accumulating a sum by adding. But accumulating can mean lots of different things—whatever you want, in fact.

Harry: Let me guess: The function you pass to `reduce()` tells you how to accumulate.

Kim: You got it! Let's look at it on the next page.

Deriving `reduce()` from examples

Let's look at some of the functions that the customer communications team now owns that match this same pattern.

```
function countAllPurchases(customers) {
  var total = 0;                                        before
  forEach(customers, function(customer) {
    total = total + customer.purchases.length;
  });                                    body (combining operation)
  return total;
}                                    after
```

```
function concatenateArrays(arrays) {
  var result = [];
  forEach(arrays, function(array) {
    result = result.concat(array);
  });                                    body
  return result;                         (combining
}                                        operation)
```

```
function customersPerCity(customers) {
  var cities = {};                                      before
  forEach(customers, function(customer) {
    cities[customer.address.city] += 1;
                                   body (combining operation)
  });
  return cities;
}                                    after
```

```
function biggestPurchase(purchases) {
  var biggest = {total:0};
  forEach(purchases, function(purchase) {
    biggest = biggest.total>purchase.total?
              biggest:purchase;
  });                          body (combining operation)
  return total;
}
```

In these examples, there are only two things that differ. The first is the initialization of the variable. The second is the calculation that computes the next value of the variable. The next value of the variable is based on the previous value of the variable and the current element of the array you're processing. There's some kind of combining operation that is different.

> **The next value is based on**
> 1. Current value
> 2. Current element of array

Original

```
function countAllPurchases(customers) {
  var total = 0;
  forEach(customers, function(customer) {
    total = total + customer.purchases.length;
  });
  return total;
}
```

extract the forEach() into reduce()

Replaced with callback

```
function countAllPurchases(customers) {
  return reduce(
    customers, 0, function(total, customer) {
      return total + customer.purchase.length;
    }
  );
}
```

initial value   callback function

```
function reduce(array, init, f) {
  var accum = init;
  forEach(array, function(element) {
    accum = f(accum, element);
  });
  return accum;
}
```

two arguments to callback

We've extracted a new function, called `reduce()`, that does the common iteration. This function is a common tool used by functional programmers. It is the third of the three main functional tools because it is so useful. Let's spend a little bit more time looking at what it does.

Functional tool: `reduce ( )`

`reduce ()` is the third of three "functional tools" that functional programmers rely on. The other two are `map ()` and `filter ()`. Let's look at `reduce ()` a little more closely.

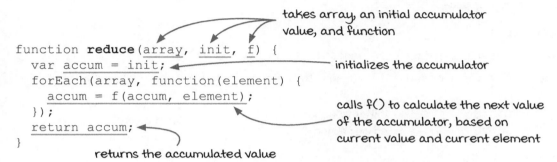

```
                                              takes array, an initial accumulator
                                              value, and function
function reduce(array, init, f) {
  var accum = init;                           initializes the accumulator
  forEach(array, function(element) {
    accum = f(accum, element);
  });                                         calls f() to calculate the next value
                                              of the accumulator, based on
  return accum;                               current value and current element
}
          returns the accumulated value
```

`reduce ()` accumulates a value while iterating over an array. Accumulating a value is kind of an abstract idea. It could take many concrete forms. For instance, adding things up is an accumulation. So is adding stuff to a hash map or concatenating strings. You get to decide what accumulation means by the function you pass in. The only restriction is that it is a computation that takes the current value of the accumulator and the current element of the iteration. That function's return value will be the new value of the accumulator.

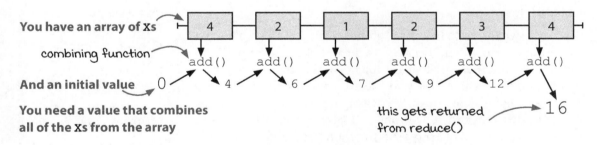

You have an array of Xs

combining function

And an initial value

You need a value that combines all of the Xs from the array

this gets returned from reduce()

The function you pass to `reduce ()` needs two arguments. It takes the current value of the accumulator and the current element of the array. The function should return a value of the same type as the first argument. Let's look at how we're using it in our example.

```
    pass reduce() an array of customers
                                    pass reduce() an initial value
function countAllPurchases(customers) {
  return reduce(                        pass reduce() a function of two
    customers, 0,                       arguments. it should return the
    function(total, customer) {         same type as the first argument
      return total + customer.purchase.length;
  });                                   returns the sum of the current total plus
}                                       the current customer's purchase count
```

Example: Concatenating strings

Let's look at a simple, yet typical, example of using reduce(). We
have an array of strings and we need to concatenate them together.
This is the perfect use for reduce().

We have: Array of strings

We want: One string that is the original strings concatenated ◄── *combining operation*

Function: Takes an accumulated string and the current string from the array to concatenate

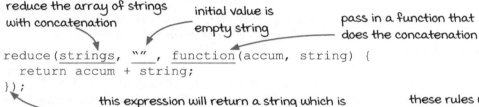

reduce the array of strings with concatenation   *initial value is empty string*   *pass in a function that does the concatenation*

```
reduce(strings, "" , function(accum, string) {
  return accum + string;
});
```

this expression will return a string which is the concatenation of all strings in the array

these rules will apply in this book, but different languages do it differently

reduce() helps us combine the elements in an array into a single
value, starting from an initial value.

Careful, now!

There are two things to be careful about with reduce(). The first
is the argument order. Because there are three arguments to
reduce(), and there are two arguments to the function you pass
to reduce(), it can be easy to mess up the order. In fact, the
reduce() equivalents in different languages will put the arguments in different orders. No one can agree! In this book we're
using the convention of array first, function last for all of the array
functions. With that rule, there's only one place for the initial
value to go—right in the middle.

> ***Argument order for functional tools in Grokking Simplicity***
>
> 1. Array first
> 2. Callback last
> 3. Other arguments (if any) in between

The second is how to determine the initial value. It depends on
the operation and the context. But it's the same answer as these
questions:

- **Where does the calculation start?** For instance, summing
  starts at zero, so that's the initial value for addition. But
  multiplying starts at 1, so that's the initial value for
  multiplication.

- **What value should you return if the array is empty?** In the
  case of an empty list of strings, concatenating them should
  be an empty string.

> ***How to find the initial value***
>
> 1. Where does the calculation start?
> 2. What should you return for empty array?
> 3. Is there a business rule?

It's your turn

The accounting department does a lot of adding and multiplying. Write them functions for adding up a list of numbers and for multiplying a list of numbers. Be careful with choosing the right initial value to pass to reduce().

```
// add up all numbers in the array
function sum(numbers) {



}

// multiply all numbers in the array
function product(numbers) {



}
```

write your answer here

Answer

```
function sum(numbers) {
  return reduce(numbers, 0, function(total, num) {
    return total + num;
  });
}

function product(numbers) {
  return reduce(numbers, 1, function(total, num) {
    return total * num;
  });
}
```

It's your turn

reduce() is very useful if you get clever with the accumulator function. Write two functions using reduce() for determining the smallest and largest numbers in an array without using Math.min() and Math.max().

Givens

- Number.MAX_VALUE is the largest number possible in JavaScript.

- Number.MIN_VALUE is the smallest number possible in JavaScript.

```
// return the smallest number in the array
// (or Number.MAX_VALUE if the array is empty)
function min(numbers) {




}

// return the largest number in the array
// (or Number.MIN_VALUE if the array is empty)
function max(numbers) {




}
```

write your answer here

Answer

```
function min(numbers) {
  return reduce(numbers, Number.MAX_VALUE, function(m, n) {
    if(m < n) return m;
    else      return n;
  });
}

function max(numbers) {
  return reduce(numbers, Number.MIN_VALUE, function(m, n) {
    if(m > n) return m;
    else      return n;
  });
}
```

It's your turn

One way to understand the functional tools is to figure out what they do at the extremes. Answer the following questions, which all have to do with one extreme or another:

1. What does map() return when you pass it an empty array?
    ```
    > map([], xToY)
    ```

2. What does filter() return when you pass it an empty array?
    ```
    > filter([], isGood)
    ```

3. What does reduce() return when you pass it an empty array?
    ```
    > reduce([], init, combine)
    ```

4. What does map() return if the function you pass to it just returns its argument?
    ```
    > map(array, function(x) { return x; })
    ```

5. What does filter() return if the function you pass to it always returns true?
    ```
    > filter(array, function(_x) { return true; })
    ```

6. What does filter() return if the function you pass to it always returns false?
    ```
    > filter(array, function(_x) { return false; })
    ```
    we prepend an underscore to
    indicate an unused argument

Answer

1. []
2. []
3. init
4. A shallow copy of array
5. A shallow copy of array
6. []

reduce() looks neat but it doesn't seem very useful. Not as useful as map() and filter().

It's interesting that you say that because reduce () is way more powerful. In fact, map () and filter () can be written in terms of reduce (), but not the other way around.

You can do a ton of stuff with reduce (). It's a tool that unlocks a whole lot of cool features you can write. We're not going to go into these in-depth now, but here's a list of things that reduce () will let you do.

Things you can do with reduce ()

Undo/redo

Undo and redo are two operations that are typically incredibly hard to implement correctly, especially if you didn't plan for them. If you imagine your current state as applying reduce () to a list of user interactions, undo just means removing the last interaction from the list.

Replaying user interaction for testing

Think about it: If your initial value is the initial state of the system, and your array is a sequence of user interactions, reduce () can combine all of those into a single value—which will be the current state.

Time-traveling debugger

Some languages will let you replay all of the changes up to a point. If something is behaving incorrectly, you can back up and examine the state at any point in time, fix the problem, then play it forward with the new code. It sounds like magic, but it's enabled by reduce ().

Audit trails

Sometimes you want to know the state of the system at a certain point in time, like when the legal department calls you to ask "What did we know as of December 31?" reduce () enables you to record the history so you'll not only know where you are, but also how you got there.

 **Language safari**

reduce () has different names in different languages. You may also see it called fold (). There are sometimes variations like foldLeft () and foldRight (), which indicate the direction in which you process the list.

314

Chapter **12** | *Functional iteration*

It's your turn

It was said that map() and filter() could be written in terms of reduce().
Try that yourself.

Answer

We can implement map() and filter() in many different ways. Here are two ways to
implement each. They are all calculations. One set uses non-mutable operations and the
other mutates the returned array at each step. The mutating one is much more efficient.
They are all still calculations, though, because it only mutates a local value, then doesn't
mutate it after returning it.

```
function map(array, f) {
  return reduce(array, [], function(ret, item) {
    return ret.concat(f([item]));
  });
}
```
using only non-mutating
operations (inefficient)

```
function map(array, f) {
  return reduce(array, [], function(ret, item) {
    ret.push(f(item));
    return ret;
  });
}
```
using mutating operations
(more efficient)

```
function filter(array, f) {
  return reduce(array, [], function(ret, item) {
    if(f(item)) return ret.concat([item]);
    else        return ret;
  });
}
```
using only non-mutating
operations (inefficient)

```
function filter(array, f) {
  return reduce(array, [], function(ret, item) {
    if(f(item))
      ret.push(item);
    return ret;
  });
}
```
using mutating operations
(more efficient)

It is important to see both of these implementations because we said earlier that the function you pass to reduce() should be a calculation. In the mutating operations, we have
violated this rule. However, we also can clearly see that in these functions, the mutation
only happens in a local context. We are sure map() and filter() are still calculations.
These examples show that the rules are more like guidelines. They should be followed by
default. Use caution and judgment when you violate them.

Three functional tools compared

`map()` Transform an array into a new array, applying a function to each element.

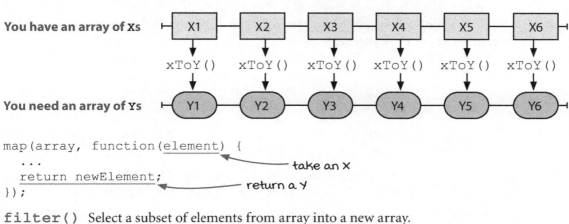

```
map(array, function(element) {
  ...
  return newElement;
});
```
— take an X
— return a Y

`filter()` Select a subset of elements from array into a new array.

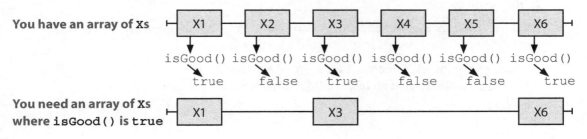

```
filter(array, function(element) {
  ...
  return true;
});
```
— be sure to return true or false

`reduce()` Combine the elements of an array into a final value.

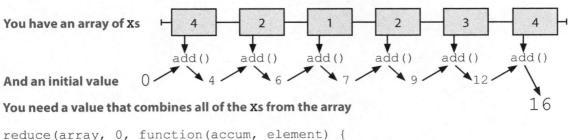

```
reduce(array, 0, function(accum, element) {
  ...
  return combine(accum, element);
});
```
— any combine() function you choose

Conclusion

Functional programming is filled with small, abstract functions that each do one thing well. Most commonly used are the three functional tools we saw in this chapter: map(), filter(), and reduce(). We've seen how they are easy to define and are extremely useful, yet they derive easily from common iteration patterns.

Summary

- The three most common functional tools are map(), filter(), and reduce(). Nearly every functional programmer uses them often.

- map(), filter(), and reduce() are essentially specialized for loops over arrays. They can replace those for loops and add clarity because they are special-purpose.

- map() transforms an array into a new array. Each element is transformed with the callback you specify.

- filter() selects a subset of elements from one array into a new array. You choose which elements are selected by passing in a predicate.

- reduce() combines elements of an array, along with an initial value, into a single value. It is used to summarize data or to build a value from a sequence.

Up next . . .

We've just learned some very powerful tools for operating on sequences of data. However, there are still some complex questions we can't answer about our customers. In the next chapter, we're going to learn how to chain our functional tools together into steps in a process. That will let us combine the powers of the three tools and transform our data in even more powerful ways.

Chaining functional tools | 13

In this chapter

- Learn to combine functional tools to do complex queries over data.

- Understand how to replace complex, existing for loops with chains of functional tools.

- Learn how to build data transformation pipelines to do work.

We've learned to use the functional tools in isolation to do the work we typically do with for loops over arrays. But as the computation gets more complex, a single functional tool can't do the job. In this chapter, we will learn how to express complex calculations as a series of steps called a *chain*. Each step is an application of a functional tool. By combining multiple functional tools together, we can build very complex computations, yet make sure that each step is simple and easy to read and write. This skill is very common among functional programmers. It shows how deep the power of functional tools can get.

The customer communications team continues

> ### Data request: Biggest purchases from our best customers
>
> We suspect that our most loyal customers also make the biggest purchases. We would like to know what the biggest purchase is for each of our best customers (three or more purchases).
>
>
> Requested by:
> Chief marketing officer
>
>
> Owned by:
> Kim on dev team

Here's a new request for the communications team.

John from marketing   Harry from customer service
Kim from dev team

Harry: This one seems more complicated.

John: Yeah. We need to get the biggest purchase, but only from the best customers. That sounds hard.

Kim: Yes, it's a little harder. But we know how to do each of the steps. We should be able to combine them to make this one query. When you combine multiple steps like that, it's called *chaining*.

John: I see! So what are the steps?

Harry: Well, I think we need to select the best customers, then select the biggest purchase from each.

Kim: That sounds like a filter, then a map. But how do we select the biggest purchase?

John: Earlier, we selected the biggest number. Maybe we could do something similar?

Kim: That makes sense. I'm not sure what that will look like yet, but I think we can do it when we get to it. Let's start building this query. We can use the output of one step as input to the next.

We need to find the biggest purchase for each of our best customers. We can break it down into a series of steps that we'll run in order.

1. Filter for only good customers (three or more purchases).

2. Map those to their biggest purchases.

Biggest purchases will likely be a `reduce()`, just like `max()` from page 310. First, we'll start by defining the function:

we will start with the signature

```
function biggestPurchasesBestCustomers(customers) {
```

Then we'll filter for just the best customers. We've done this already on page 301. This will be our first step in the chain:

step 1

```
function biggestPurchasesBestCustomers(customers) {
  var bestCustomers = filter(customers, function(customer) {
    return customer.purchases.length >= 3;
  });
```

Now we need to get the biggest purchase for each of those and put those into an array. We don't have a function for doing that yet, but we know that this will be a `map()`. Let's add that step to the chain:

step 1

step 2

```
function biggestPurchasesBestCustomers(customers) {
  var bestCustomers = filter(customers, function(customer) {
    return customer.purchases.length >= 3;
  });

  var biggestPurchases = map(bestCustomers, function(customer) {
    return ...;
  });
}
```

we know to use map(), but what do we return?

We know how to find the biggest number (page 310). We can adapt that easily to return the biggest purchase. That code used a `reduce()`, so we'll do something similar for step 2. We'll tackle that on the next page.

On the last page, we built the framework for step two, but we still haven't figured out what the callback for the map() step should look like. Here's where we left off:

```
function biggestPurchasesBestCustomers(customers) {
  var bestCustomers = filter(customers, function(customer) {        ← step 1
    return customer.purchases.length >= 3;
  });

  var biggestPurchases = map(bestCustomers, function(customer) {    ← step 2
    return ...;
  });                                            we know to use map(),
}                                                but what do we return?
```

We know how to find the biggest number (page 310). We can adapt that easily to return the biggest purchase. That code used a reduce(), so we'll do something similar here:

```
function biggestPurchasesBestCustomers(customers) {
  var bestCustomers = filter(customers, function(customer) {        ← step 1
    return customer.purchases.length >= 3;
  });
             use an empty purchase for the initial value for reduce()
  var biggestPurchases = map(bestCustomers, function(customer) {    ← step 2
    return reduce(customer.purchases, {total: 0}, function(biggestSoFar, purchase) {
      if(biggestSoFar.total > purchase.total)
        return biggestSoFar;
      else
        return purchase;
    });                                                 reduce() is in the callback for
  });              use reduce() to figure out          map() because we're finding
  return biggesetPurchases;  the biggest purchase      the biggest purchase for each
}                                                      customer
```

That will work, but it's a big beast of a function, with multiple nested callbacks. It's really hard to understand. Functions like these give chaining functional tools a bad reputation. Let's not leave it here. There is so much room for cleaning this up. Let's get started.

Here's the code we had from the last page. It works, but it's really hard to understand:

```
function biggestPurchasesBestCustomers(customers) {
  var bestCustomers = filter(customers, function(customer) {
    return customer.purchases.length >= 3;
  });

  var biggestPurchases = map(bestCustomers, function(customer) {
    return reduce(customer.purchases, {total: 0}, function(biggestSoFar, purchase) {
      if(biggestSoFar.total > purchase.total)
        return biggestSoFar;
      else
        return purchase;
    });
  });
  return biggesetPurchases;
}
```

nested callbacks are hard to read

Let's zoom in on that `reduce()` step and compare it to the `max()` function we wrote on page 310:

Find biggest purchase   *initialize with smallest possible*   **Find biggest number**

```
reduce(customer.purchases,
       {total: 0},
       function(biggestSoFar, purchase) {
         if(biggestSoFar.total > purchase.total)
           return biggestSoFar;
         else
           return purchase;
       });
```

return biggest   *compare*

```
reduce(numbers,
       Number.MIN_VALUE,
       function(m, n) {
         if(m > n)
           return m;
         else
           return n;
       });
```

The difference between them is that the code for biggest purchase has to compare the totals, while the regular `max()` can compare numbers directly. Let's extract that operation (getting the total) as a callback.

Original

```
reduce(customer.purchases,
       {total: 0},
       function(biggestSoFar, purchase) {
         if(biggestSoFar.total > purchase.total)
           return biggestSoFar;
         else
           return purchase;
       });
```

extract reduce() into maxKey()

With callback extracted

```
maxKey(customer.purchases, {total: 0},
       function(purchase) { return purchase.total; }
    );

function maxKey(array, init, f) {
  return reduce(array,
                init,
                function(biggestSoFar, element) {
                  if(f(biggestSoFar) > f(element)) {
                    return biggestSoFar;
                  else
                    return element;
                });
}
```

pass in callback saying how to compare values

We've just created a function `maxKey()` that finds the largest value from an array. It uses a function to determine what part of the value you should compare. Let's plug that back into our original function.

On the last page, we had just finished writing maxKey(), which finds the largest value in an array. Let's plug it into the code we had in the place of reduce():

```
function biggestPurchasesBestCustomers(customers) {
  var bestCustomers = filter(customers, function(customer) {         step 1
    return customer.purchases.length >= 3;
  });

  var biggestPurchases = map(bestCustomers, function(customer) {     step 2
    return maxKey(customer.purchases, {total: 0}, function(purchase) {
    return purchase.total;
  });
  });

  return biggestPurchases;
}
```

nested returns are hard to read

call maxKey() in place of reduce()

This code is pretty concise. We've extracted another functional tool (maxKey()) that helps us express our meaning that much better. reduce() is a low-level function, meaning it is very general. It means nothing more by itself than combining the values on an array. maxKey() is more specific. It means choosing the biggest value from an array.

It's your turn

max() and maxKey() are very similar, so in theory they should have very similar code. Consider these questions if you have to write one in terms of the other:

1. Which one would it be and why?

2. Write the code for both.

3. Draw the call graph for these two functions.

4. What does that say about which is more general?

(Answer on next page.)

Even though the code is very concise, it could be made more clear. While we're learning, we might as well keep improving this code to see what great functional chaining can look like. There are nested callbacks with nested return statements. The code does not explain very well what it does. There are two approaches we could take. We'll explore both, then compare them, in the next pages.

📝 Answer

1. `max()` should be written in terms of `maxKey()` because `maxKey()` is more general. `maxKey()` can find the largest value based on an arbitrary comparison, while `max()` can only compare directly.

2. We can write `max()` in terms of `maxKey()` by using the identity function, a function that returns its argument unchanged.

```
function maxKey(array, init, f) {
  return reduce(array,
                init,
                function(biggestSoFar, element) {
                  if(f(biggestSoFar) > f(element))
                    return biggestSoFar;
                  else
                    return element;
                });
}

function max(array, init) {
  return maxKey(array, init, function(x) {
    return x;
  });
}
```

tell maxKey() to compare the whole value unchanged

a function that returns its argument unchanged is called "identity"

3. Here is the call graph.

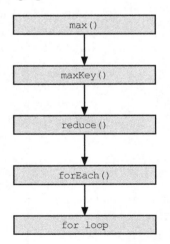

📚 Vocab time

The *identity function* is a function that returns its argument unchanged. It appears to do nothing, but it is useful for indicating just that: Nothing should be done.

4. Because `maxKey()` is below `max()`, `maxKey()` is necessarily more general than `max()`. That makes sense because `max()` is just a specialized version of `maxKey()`.

Clarifying chains, method 1: Name the steps

One way we can clarify the steps in our chains is by naming each
step. Here is the last code we saw:

```
function biggestPurchasesBestCustomers(customers) {
  var bestCustomers = filter(customers, function(customer) {          step 1
    return customer.purchases.length >= 3;
  });

  var biggestPurchases = map(bestCustomers, function(customer) {      step 2
    return maxKey(customer.purchases, {total: 0}, function(purchase) {
      return purchase.total;
    });
  });

  return biggestPurchases;
}
```

If we extracted a function for each higher-order function and
named it, it would look like this:

```
function biggestPurchasesBestCustomers(customers) {
  var bestCustomers    = selectBestCustomers(customers);            step 1
  var biggestPurchases = getBiggestPurchases(bestCustomers);        step 2
  return biggestPurchases;
}
```
steps are shorter and
dense with meaning
```
function selectBestCustomers(customers) {
  return filter(customers, function(customer) {
    return customer.purchases.length >= 3;
  });
}
```
higher-order functions
are called in named
functions to add context
```
function getBiggestPurchases(customers) {
  return map(customers, getBiggestPurchase);
}
```
we can extract
this higher-order
function as well
```
function getBiggestPurchase(customer) {
  return maxKey(customer.purchases, {total: 0}, function(purchase) {
    return purchase.total;
  });
}
```

That definitely does leave the function with the steps much clearer.
In addition, the two functions that implement the steps are clear as
well. However, this sweeps the unclear parts under the rug. The
callbacks are still defined as inline functions and so cannot be
reused. And are these new functions reusable at all? We know the
key to reuse is to make small functions that appear low on the call
graph. Aren't there smaller functions we could break this into?

  The answer is that, yes, the second method addresses those
issues. Let's see it on the next page.

Clarifying chains, method 2: Naming the callbacks

The other way to clarify our chains is to name the callbacks. Let's revert the code back to how it was before we named the steps:

```
function biggestPurchasesBestCustomers(customers) {
  var bestCustomers = filter(customers, function(customer) {          step 1
    return customer.purchases.length >= 3;
  });

  var biggestPurchases = map(bestCustomers, function(customer) {       step 2
    return maxKey(customer.purchases, {total: 0}, function(purchase) {
      return purchase.total;
    });
  });

  return biggestPurchases;
}
```

This time, instead of extracting and naming the steps, we will extract and name the *callbacks*:

```
function biggestPurchasesBestCustomers(customers) {
  var bestCustomers     = filter(customers, isGoodCustomer);          step 1
  var biggestPurchases = map(bestCustomers, getBiggestPurchase);      step 2
  return biggestPurchases;
}

function isGoodCustomer(customer) {
  return customer.purchases.length >= 3;
}

function getBiggestPurchase(customer) {
  return maxKey(customer.purchases, {total: 0}, getPurchaseTotal);
}

function getPurchaseTotal(purchase) {
  return purchase.total;
}
```

callbacks are named

steps are still short and meaningful

By extracting and naming the callbacks, we've created more reusable functions. We know they are reusable because they have less under them in the call graph. And intuitively, they must be more reusable. For instance, isGoodCustomer() works on a single customer, while selectBestCustomers() only works on an array of customers. You can always apply isGoodCustomer() to an array with filter().

Let's look at the two of them together for comparison on the next page.

Clarifying chains: Two methods compared

We've seen two methods for clarifying chains of functional tools. Let's compare the resulting code and discuss:

Method 1: Naming steps

```
function biggestPurchasesBestCustomers(customers) {
  var bestCustomers    = selectBestCustomers(customers);
  var biggestPurchases = getBiggestPurchases(bestCustomers);
  return biggestPurchases;
}

function selectBestCustomers(customers) {
  return filter(customers, function(customer) {
    return customer.purchases.length >= 3;
  });
}

function getBiggestPurchases(customers) {
  return map(customers, getBiggestPurchase);
}

function getBiggestPurchase(customer) {
  return maxKey(customer.purchases, {total: 0}, function(purchase) {
    return purchase.total;
  });
}
```

Method 2: Naming callbacks

```
function biggestPurchasesBestCustomers(customers) {
  var bestCustomers    = filter(customers, isGoodCustomer);
  var biggestPurchases = map(bestCustomers, getBiggestPurchase);
  return biggestPurchases;
}

function isGoodCustomer(customer) {
  return customer.purchases.length >= 3;
}

function getBiggestPurchase(customer) {
  return maxKey(customer.purchases, {total: 0}, getPurchaseTotal);
}

function getPurchaseTotal(purchase) {
  return purchase.total;
}
```

In general, method 2 results in clearer, more reusable code since the callbacks are more reusable than the calls to the higher-order functions. It also removes a level of nesting since the callbacks now have names instead of being inline.

Of course, this all depends on the syntax and semantics of the language you are using. Functional programmers will try both of these methods and compare the results to ultimately decide which code to use.

Example: Emails of customers who have made one purchase

Let's look at a simple, yet typical, example of functional tool chaining. The marketing team wants to send out a special email to entice first-time customers with a special offer.

We have: Array of customers

We want: Email address of those customers who have exactly one purchase

Plan:

1. Filter for customers with one purchase

2. Map over customers for emails

define a new variable containing the result of the filtering

```
var firstTimers = filter(customers, function(customer) {
  return customer.purchases.length === 1;
});
```

use that variable as the argument to the next step

```
var firstTimerEmails = map(firstTimers, function(customer) {
  return customer.email;
});
```

the last variable will have the answer you are looking for

If you want to make it more compact by extracting and naming callback functions, it would look like this:

```
var firstTimers      = filter(customers, isFirstTimer);
var firstTimerEmails = map(firstTimers, getCustomerEmail);

function isFirstTimer(customer) {
  return customer.purchases.length === 1;
}

function getCustomerEmail(customer) {
  return customer.email;
}
```

these would likely be defined elsewhere and be reusable

It's your turn

Marketing would like to know which customers have made at least one purchase over $100 *AND* two or more purchases total. People who meet both criteria are known as *big spenders*. Your task is to write that function as a chain of functional tools. Please make it clean and readable.

```
function bigSpenders(customers) {
```

write your answer here

```
}
```

Answer

```
function bigSpenders(customers) {
  var withBigPurchases       = filter(customers, hasBigPurchase);
  var with2OrMorePurchases = filter(withBigPurchases, has2OrMorePurchases);
  return with2OrMorePurchases;
}

function hasBigPurchase(customer) {
  return filter(customer.purchases, isBigPurchase).length > 0;
}

function isBigPurchase(purchase) {
  return purchase.total > 100;
}

function has2OrMorePurchases(customer) {
  return customer.purchases.length >= 2;
}
```

It's your turn

Virtually all departments want to average an array of numbers at some point. Write a function that computes the average.

> **Hint:** The average is the sum divided by the count.
> **Hint:** You can use `reduce()` for the sum.

```
function average(numbers) {
```

write your answer here

```
}
```

Answer

```
function average(numbers) {
  return reduce(numbers, 0, plus) / numbers.length;
}

function plus(a, b) {
  return a + b;
}
```

It's your turn

We need to compute the average purchase total for each customer. You can assume average() exists from the last page.

```
function averagePurchaseTotals(customers) {
```

write your answer here

```
}
```

Answer

```
function averagePurchaseTotals(customers) {
  return map(customers, function(customer) {
    var purchaseTotals = map(customer.purchases, function(purchase) {
      return purchase.total;
    });
    return average(purchaseTotals);
  });
}
```

Yes, both `filter()` and `map()` create new arrays, and potentially add many items to them, each time they are called. This can be inefficient, but most of the time it is not a problem. These arrays are created and garbage-collected very quickly. You'd be surprised how fast modern garbage collectors are.

> Wait a second. Isn't this very inefficient? We're creating a new array any time we call map() or filter().

Jenna from dev team

But it's a fact that sometimes it's not efficient enough. Luckily, `map()`, `filter()`, and `reduce()` can be optimized very easily without dropping back down to for loops. The process of optimizing a chain of `map()`, `filter()`, and `reduce()` calls is called *stream fusion*. Let's see how it works.

If you have two `map()` calls in a row, you can combine them into one step. Here is an example:

Two `map()` steps in a row

```
var names       = map(customers, getFullName);
var nameLengths = map(names, stringLength);
```

Equivalent as a single `map()` step

```
var nameLengths = map(customers, function(customer) {
  return stringLength(getFullName(customer));
});
```

combine both operations into a single operation

These two pieces of code get the same answer, but the one on the right does it in one `map()` step without a garbage array.

We can do something similar with `filter()`. Two `filter()` steps in a row are like performing a logical AND with two booleans.

Two `filter()` steps in a row

```
var goodCustomers = filter(customers, isGoodCustomer);
var withAddresses = filter(goodCustomers, hasAddress);
```

Equivalent as a single `filter()` step

```
var withAddresses = filter(customers, function(customer) {
  return isGoodCustomer(customer) && hasAddress(customer);
});
```

use && to combine both predicates

Again, this gets the same result with less garbage.

Finally, `reduce()` can do a lot of the work itself. It can take on a lot more of the processing. For example, if you have a `map()` followed by a `reduce()`, you can do this:

`map()` step followed by `reduce()` step

```
var purchaseTotals = map(purchases, getPurchaseTotal);
var purchaseSum    = reduce(purchaseTotals, 0, plus);
```

Equivalent as a single `reduce()` step

```
var purchaseSum = reduce(purchases, 0, function(total, purchase) {
  return total + getPurchaseTotal(purchase);
});
```

do the operations inside the callback to reduce()

Because we're avoiding the call to `map()`, we don't have any intermediate arrays to garbage-collect. Again, this is an optimization. It will only make a difference if that is the bottleneck. In most cases, it is much clearer to do things in multiple steps, since each step will be clear and readable.

Refactoring existing for loops to functional tools

Up until now, we've seen many examples of how to write new chains for the functional tools from descriptions of the requirements. But sometimes we have existing for loops in our code that we want to refactor. How can we do that?

Strategy 1: Understand and rewrite

The first strategy is simply to read the for loop, figure out what it does, then forget the implementation. Now, you can do what we've just done for the examples we've already seen in this chapter: Just figure it out again as a series of steps.

Strategy 2: Refactor from clues

Though you can often understand a piece of code well enough, sometimes you can't. In that case, we can pick apart the existing for loop and turn it into chains of functional tools. Let's work through an example.

Here is an example code snippet with a nested for loop:

```
var answer = [];                                    answer is an array, presumably
                                                    built up in the loop
var window = 5;
                                                    outer loop goes through
for(var i = 0; i < array.length; i++) {            every element of array
  var sum   = 0;
  var count = 0;                                    inner loop loops through
  for(var w = 0; w < window; w++) {                a small range, 0–4
    var idx = i + w;
    if(idx < array.length) {                       calculate a new index
      sum   += array[idx];
      count += 1;
    }                                              accumulate some values
  }
  answer.push(sum/count);                          add a value to the answer array
}
```

Even without fully understanding what this code does, we can begin to break it down. There are many clues in the code that we can pick up on.

The strongest clue is that we are adding one element to the answer array for each element in the original array. That's a strong indication that we want a map(). That's the outer loop. The inner loop is like a reduce(). It's looping over something and combining elements into a single answer.

That inner loop is as good a place to start as any. However, what is it looping over? Let's take a closer look on the next page.

Tip 1: Make data

We know that doing multiple map() and filter() steps in a row often creates intermediate arrays that are used and then immediately discarded. When writing a for loop, the data we loop over is often not realized in an array. For instance, we might use a for loop to count to 10. Each time through the loop, i is a different number. But those numbers were never stored in an array. This tip suggests we put that data into an array so that we can use our functional tools on it.

> **Refactoring tips**
>
> 1. **Make data.**
> 2. Operate on whole array.
> 3. Take many small steps.

Here's the code from the last page:

```
var answer = [];

var window = 5;

for(var i = 0; i < array.length; i++) {
  var sum   = 0;
  var count = 0;
  for(var w = 0; w < window; w++) {        w will be 0 to window – 1; those numbers
    var idx = i + w;                       are never stored in an array
    if(idx < array.length) {               idx will be i to i + window –1; those numbers
      sum   += array[idx];                 are never stored in an array
      count += 1;
    }                                      the small range of values from array
  }                                        is never stored in its own array
  answer.push(sum/count);
}
```

The inner loop is looping through a small range of elements in array. So we ask ourselves, what if that data were in its own array, and we looped through that instead?

Well, it turns out that this is just the array's own .slice() method. .slice() makes an array of elements from a subsequence inside the array. Let's replace that:

```
var answer = [];

var window = 5;

for(var i = 0; i < array.length; i++) {
  var sum   = 0;
  var count = 0;
  var subarray = array.slice(i, i + window);    put subset into its own array
  for(var w = 0; w < subarray.length; w++) {
    sum   += subarray[w];
    count += 1;                                 then we can loop over it
  }                                             with standard for loop
  answer.push(sum/count);
}
```

Tip 2: Operate on whole array at once

Now that we've built that subarray, we are looping over an entire
array. That means we can use map(), filter(), or reduce() on
it, because those tools operate on whole arrays. Let's look at the
code from the last page to see how we can replace this loop.

Refactoring tips

1. Make data.
2. **Operate on whole array.**
3. Take many small steps.

```
var answer = [];

var window = 5;

for(var i = 0; i < array.length; i++) {
  var sum   = 0;
  var count = 0;
  var subarray = array.slice(i, i + window);
  for(var w = 0; w < subarray.length; w++) {
    sum   += subarray[i];
    count += 1;
  }
  answer.push(sum/count);
}
```

*standard for loop
over subarray*

*combining values from subarray
into sum and count*

dividing them to get an average

In this case, the code is combining elements from the subarray
into a sum and a count, and then dividing them. Sounds like an
average to me! We know how to do that since we wrote it on
page 329. It's just a reduce(). We could either write the code
again here or call our existing average function. Let's just call the
existing average() function. We wrote it to be reused, after all.

```
var answer = [];

var window = 5;

for(var i = 0; i < array.length; i++) {
  var subarray = array.slice(i, i + window);
  answer.push(average(subarray));
}
```

*this for loop doesn't use the element
from the array; instead, the loop
index is used in the body*

*we have entirely replaced
the inner loop with .slice()
and a call to average()*

Looking good! Now we've got one for loop left. It's looping through
the entire array, which suggests using map(). But this for loop is
not using the current element in the array, so we can't replace it
directly. Remember, the callback to map() only gets the current
element. Instead, this for loop's index i is being used to slice out
a subarray. We can't replace this directly with map(). There is a
solution, but we need a new page.

 **Noodle on it**

We used to have a for
loop, now we don't.
Where did it go?

Tip 3: Take many small steps

Our original code was doing a lot. We've gotten it down to something very manageable. But we suspect there's a hidden `map()` in there. We're looping through an entire array and generating a new array with the same number of elements. Here's our code from the last page:

```
var answer = [];

var window = 5;

for(var i = 0; i < array.length; i++) {
  var subarray = array.slice(i, i + window);
  answer.push(average(subarray));
}
```

use the loop index to create a subarray

The trouble is that we want to loop over the *indices*, not the values of the array. The indices will let us slice into our original array, creating subarrays or "windows." It may be hard (or impossible) to loop over the indices in the one step we already have. So let's do it in many small steps. First, since we need the indices, why don't we just generate them as an array (tip 1)? Then we can operate on the whole array of indices with a functional tool (step 2). Let's do that now:

```
var indices = [];

for(var i = 0; i < array.length; i++)
  indices.push(i);
```

create the indices in a small step

Note that we're adding a step! Now we can convert the for loop into a `map()` over those indices:

```
var indices = [];

for(var i = 0; i < array.length; i++)
  indices.push(i);

var window = 5;

var answer = map(indices, function(i) {
  var subarray = array.slice(i, i + window);
  return average(subarray);
});
```

map over the indices array

the callback will be called with each index in turn

The new step, generating an array of numbers, let's replace a for loop with a `map()`. Now we are doing two things inside the callback to `map()`. Let's see about splitting that up.

Tip 3: Take many small steps

Let's look at what we have from the last page:

```
var indices = [];
for(var i = 0; i < array.length; i++)
  indices.push(i);

var window = 5;

var answer = map(indices, function(i) {
  var subarray = array.slice(i, i + window);
  return average(subarray);
});
```

we're doing two things, creating a subarray and calculating the average

We're doing two things in the callback to map(). We're making a subarray and we're averaging it. Clearly this could be two separate steps:

```
var indices = [];
for(var i = 0; i < array.length; i++)
  indices.push(i);

var window = 5;

var windows = map(indices, function(i) {
  return array.slice(i, i + window);
});

var answer = map(windows, average);
```

step 1, create subarrays

step 2, average subarrays

The last thing to do is to extract the loop that generates indices into a helper function. It will certainly be useful later.

```
function range(start, end) {
  var ret = [];
  for(var i = start; i < end; i++)
    ret.push(i);
  return ret;
}
```

the range() function will be useful later

```
var window = 5;

var indices = range(0, array.length);
var windows = map(indices, function(i) {
  return array.slice(i, i + window);
});
var answer = map(windows, average);
```

generate the indices using range()

step 1, create indices

step 2, create subarrays

step 3, average subarrays

We've replaced all the for loops with a chain of functional tools. Now let's review.

Refactoring tips

1. Make data.
2. Operate on whole array.
3. **Take many small steps.**

Comparing functional to imperative code

We're done! Let's see how far we've come:

Original imperative code

```
var answer = [];

var window = 5;

for(var i = 0; i < array.length; i++) {
  var sum   = 0;
  var count = 0;
  for(var w = 0; w < window; w++) {
    var idx = i + w;
    if(idx < array.length) {
      sum   += array[idx];
      count += 1;
    }
  }
  answer.push(sum/count);
}
```

Code using functional tools

```
var window = 5;

var indices = range(0, array.length);
var windows = map(indices, function(i) {
  return array.slice(i, i + window);
});
var answer = map(windows, average);
```

Plus a reusable tool

```
function range(start, end) {
  var ret = [];
  for(var i = start; i < end; i++)
    ret.push(i);
  return ret;
}
```

We started with code that had nested loops, index calculations, and local mutable variables. We ended up with a three-step process where each step is clear. Actually, we can write the steps in English.

Moving Average

1. Given a list of numbers, you generate a "window" around each number.

2. Then you calculate the average of each window.

The steps in the code correspond closely to the steps in the algorithm description. Plus the functional version has spun off the `range()` helper function. Functional programmers use this function all the time.

 **Noodle on it**

Where in the call graph does this `range()` function go? Does that position indicate that it would be easily

1. Reused?

2. Tested?

3. Maintained?

Summary of chaining tips

We've seen three tips in the past few pages to help us refactor for loops into chains of three functional tools. Here are those tips again, with some other tips thrown in for good measure.

Make data

The functional tools work best when they work over an entire array of data. If you find the for loop is working over a subset of the data, try to break that data out into its own array. Then `map()`, `filter()`, and `reduce()` can make short work of it.

Operate on the whole array

Ask yourself, "How could I process this whole array uniformly, as a single operation, instead of iteratively as in a for loop?" `map()` transforms every element. `filter()` keeps or removes every element. `reduce()` combines every element. Make a bold move and process the whole thing.

Many small steps

When the algorithm starts to feel like too much to do at once, a counterintuitive move is to do it in two or more steps. Can more steps really make it easier to think about? Yes! Because each step is much simpler. Ask yourself what small step will get you closer to the goal.

Bonus: Replace conditionals with `filter()`

Conditionals embedded in for loops often skip elements of the array. Why not filter those out as a step before hand?

Bonus: Extract helper functions

`map()`, `filter()`, and `reduce()` are not all of the functional tools. They're just the most commonly used. There are many more, and you'll probably discover a lot yourself. Extract them, give them a good name, and use them!

Bonus: Experiment to improve

Some people are really good at finding elegant and clear ways of solving problems using functional tools. How did they get that way? They tried lots of things. They practiced. They challenged themselves to find new ways to combine them.

It's your turn

Here's some code from the MegaMart codebase. Your job is to turn it into a chain of functional tools. Please note that there is more than one way to do it.

```
function shoesAndSocksInventory(products) {
  var inventory = 0;
  for(var p = 0; p < products.length; p++) {
    var product = products[p];
    if(product.type === "shoes" || product.type === "socks") {
      inventory += product.numberInInventory;
    }
  }
  return inventory;
}
```

write your answer here

Answer

```
function shoesAndSocksInventory(products) {
  var shoesAndSocks = filter(products, function(product) {
    return product.type === "shoes" || product.type === "socks";
  });
  var inventories = map(shoesAndSocks, function(product) {
    return product.numberInInventory;
  });
  return reduce(inventories, 0, plus);
}
```

Debugging tips for chaining

Working with higher-order functions can get very abstract, and therefore it can be hard to understand when things go wrong. Here are some tips.

Keep it concrete

It's easy to forget what your data looks like, especially a few steps into a pipeline. Be sure to use clear names in your code so that you don't lose track of what's what. Variable names like x and a keep things short, but they have no meaning. Use names to your advantage.

Print it out

Even experienced functional programmers lose track of what data they've got. So what do they do? They insert a print statement between two steps, and then they run the code. It's a good reality check to make sure each step is working as expected. Pro tip: For really complex chains, add one step at a time and check the result before you add the next.

Flow your types

Each functional tool has a really concise type. Yes, even if you're in an untyped language like JavaScript, the functional tools still have types. They're just not checked by the compiler. Use this to your advantage and mentally trace the types of the values as they flow through the chain.

For instance, you know map() returns a new array. What's in it? Well, whatever type the callback returns.

What about filter()? The result array is the same type as the argument.

And reduce()? The resulting value is the same type as the return of your callback—which is the same type as the initial value.

With that in mind, you can walk through each step in your mind, figuring out what type each step generates. That will help you understand the code and debug problems.

Many other functional tools

There are many other functional tools that programmers commonly use. `map()`, `filter()`, and `reduce()` are simply the most common. You'll find that the standard libraries of functional languages are full of these things. It's worth your time to scroll through their documentation for inspiration. Here are just a few:

pluck()

Tired of writing callbacks for `map()` that just pull out a field? `pluck()` is your answer:

```
function pluck(array, field) {
  return map(array, function(object) {
    return object[field];
  });
}
```

Usage

```
var prices = pluck(products, 'price');
```

Variation

```
function invokeMap(array, method) {
  return map(array, function(object) {
    return object[method]();
  });
}
```

concat()

`concat()` unnests arrays inside of an array. It removes that one pesky level of nesting:

```
function concat(arrays) {
  var ret = [];
  forEach(arrays, function(array) {
    forEach(array, function(element) {
      ret.push(element);
    });
  });
  return ret;
}
```

Usage

```
var purchaseArrays = pluck(customers, "purchases");
var allPurchases = concat(purchaseArrays);
```

Variation

```
function concatMap(array, f) {
  return concat(map(array, f));
}
```

also called mapcat() or flatmap() in some languages

frequenciesBy() and groupBy()

Counting and grouping are invaluable. These functions return objects (hash maps):

```
function frequenciesBy(array, f) {
  var ret = {};
  forEach(array, function(element) {
    var key = f(element);
    if(ret[key]) ret[key] += 1;
    else         ret[key]  = 1;
  });
  return ret;
}

function groupBy(array, f) {
  var ret = {};
  forEach(array, function(element) {
    var key = f(element);
    if(ret[key]) ret[key].push(element);
    else         ret[key] = [element];
  });
  return ret;
}
```

Usage

```
var howMany = frequenciesBy(products, function(p) {
  return p.type;
});
> console.log(howMany['ties'])
4


var groups = groupBy(range(0, 10), isEven);
> console.log(groups)
{
  true:  [0, 2, 4, 6, 8],
  false: [1, 3, 5, 7, 9]
}
```

Where to find functional tools

Functional programmers find that knowing more tools multiplies their effectiveness. For instance, a Clojurist knows functions that could help them solve problems in JavaScript. Because those functions are easy to write, they write them first in JavaScript, then implement the solution using them. Peruse the following sources and borrow the best tools from other languages.

Lodash: Functional tools for JavaScript

Lodash is a JavaScript library that many people call "JavaScript's missing standard library." It is chock full of abstract operations on data. Each of them is simple enough to implement in a handful of lines. Plenty of inspiration there!

- Lodash documentation (https://lodash.com/docs)

Laravel Collections • Functional tools for PHP

Laravel has some great functional tools for working with the built-in PHP arrays. Many people swear by them. If you'd like to see an example of functional tools that make the built-in collections better than the original, check it out.

- Laravel collections documentation
  (https://laravel.com/docs/collections#available-methods)

Clojure standard library

The Clojure standard library is full of functional tools. The biggest problem is that there are so many of them. The official documentation is just a flat, alphabetical list, but I recommend ClojureDocs. It has a page with them organized.

- ClojureDocs quick reference
  (https://clojuredocs.org/quickref#sequences)
- Official docs
  (https://clojure.github.io/clojure/clojure.core-api.html)

Haskell Prelude

For a view of how short and concise the functional tools can be, be sure to check out Haskell's Prelude. Though not as complete as other languages, it does contain a lot of great gems. And if you can read type signatures, you'll get a clear understanding of how these work. It includes type signatures, implementations, a nice explanation, and a couple of examples for each function.

- Haskell Prelude
  (http://www.cse.chalmers.se/edu/course/TDA555/tourofprelude.html)

JavaScript conveniences

It's worth stating again: Even though we're using JavaScript for the examples in this book, this is not a book about functional programming in JavaScript. In fact, the examples you've read are a bit harder than what you would find in the typical JavaScript codebase.

Why are they harder? Because JavaScript makes map(), filter(), and reduce() much more convenient than what we've done here. For one, the functions are built in. You don't have to write them yourself. Two, they're methods on arrays, so you can call them more easily.

This book's implementation

```
var customerNames = map(customers, function(c) {
  return c.firstName + " " + c.lastName;
});
```

JavaScript's built-in tools

```
var customerNames = customers.map(function(c) {
  return c.firstName + " " + c.lastName;
});
```

JavaScript has .map() method on class array

Now, because they're methods on arrays, that means you can use method chaining instead of assigning them to intermediate variables. So the code for moving average from page 337 could be written differently. Some people prefer it:

This book's implementation

```
var window = 5;

var indices = range(0, array.length);
var windows = map(indices, function(i) {
  return array.slice(i, i + window);
});
var answer = map(windows, average);
```

With method chaining

```
var window = 5;

var answer =
  range(0, array.length)
    .map(function(i) {
      return array.slice(i, i + window);
    })
    .map(average);
```

you can line up the dots with methods

Next, JavaScript has a lot of fancy syntax for defining inline functions. It makes it much shorter and easier to use map(), filter(), and reduce(). For instance, the previous code can become even more terse:

```
var window = 5;

var answer =
  range(0, array.length)
    .map(i => array.slice(i, i + window))
    .map(average);
```

=> arrow syntax makes callbacks shorter and clearer

And, finally, JavaScript's map() and filter() also pass in the index of the element instead of just the element like we've been looking at. Can you believe that makes moving average a one-liner? We can even throw in the definition of average() as another one-liner:

```
var window  = 5;
var average = array => array.reduce((sum, e) => sum + e, 0) / array.length;
var answer  = array.map((e, i) => array.slice(i, i + window)).map(average);
```

current index is second argument after current element

If you're using JavaScript, there has never been a better time for functional programming.

Java streams

In Java 8, a new set of features was introduced to facilitate functional programming. There was a lot of new stuff, and we can't go into it all. Let's highlight three features relevant to functional tools.

Lambda expressions

Lambda expressions let you write what appear to be inline functions. (They really get turned into anonymous classes by the compiler.) But regardless of how they are implemented, they have a lot to like about them: They are *closures* (they refer to variables in scope) and they make a lot of what we've done in this chapter possible.

Functional interfaces

Java interfaces with a single method are called *functional interfaces*. Any functional interface can be instantiated with a lambda expression. What's more, Java 8 comes with a bunch of predefined functional interfaces, fully generic, that essentially give you a typed functional language. There are four functional interface groups to mention because they correspond to the callback types of the three functional tools from the last chapter and `forEach()`:

- **Function:** A function of one argument that returns a value—perfect for passing to `map()`

- **Predicate:** A function of one argument that returns `true` or `false`—perfect for passing to `filter()`

- **BiFunction:** A function of two arguments that returns a value—perfect for passing to `reduce()` if the first argument's type matches the return type

- **Consumer:** A function of one argument that doesn't return a value—perfect for passing to `forEach()`

Stream API

The Stream API is Java's answer to functional tools. Streams are constructed from data sources (such as arrays or collections) and have a variety of methods for processing them with functional tools, including `map()`, `filter()`, `reduce()`, and many more. Streams have a lot to like about them: They don't modify their data sources, they chain well, and they are efficient because they fuse streams automatically.

`reduce()` **for building values**

Until now, we've seen many examples of using reduce() to summarize data. We take a collection of data and combine all elements
into a single value. For example, we saw how to write a sum or an
average using reduce(). While that is an important use,
reduce() is more powerful than simple summarization.

Another use for reduce() is for building a value. Here's a scenario. Let's say we lost the user's shopping cart. Luckily, we have
logged all of the items the user has added to their cart in an array.
It looks like this:

*we have an array of
all items the user has
added to their cart*

```
var itemsAdded = ["shirt", "shoes", "shirt", "socks", "hat", ....];
```

Knowing this information, can we build the current state of the
shopping cart? And remember: We have to keep track of duplicates
by incrementing the quantity.

This is the perfect use for reduce(). It's iterating over an array
and combining its elements into a single value. In this case, the
single value is the shopping cart.

Let's build this code one step at a time. First, let's set up our call
to reduce(). We know the first argument is the list of items. The
second argument is our initial value. Shopping carts start out
empty, and we use an object to represent the cart, so we'll pass in
an empty object.

We also know the signature of the function we pass it. It needs
to return a cart, so that's the same type as the first argument. And
the array contains item names, so that's the second argument:

👆 **Tip:** ─────────

Set up the call to the
functional tool
before you fill in the
body of the callback.

```
var shoppingCart = reduce(itemsAdded, {}, function(cart, item) {
```

Now all we have to do is fill in this function. What should it do?

Let's take it in two cases. The easy case is when the cart does not
contain the item:

*for this example, let's
assume we can look up
the price given the name*

```
var shoppingCart = reduce(itemsAdded, {}, function(cart, item) {
  if(!cart[item])
    return add_item(cart, {name: item, quantity: 1, price: priceLookup(item)});
```

The harder case is when we already have the item in the cart. Let's
handle that, and then we're done!

```
var shoppingCart = reduce(itemsAdded, {}, function(cart, item) {
  if(!cart[item])
    return add_item(cart, {name: item, quantity: 1, price: priceLookup(item)});
  else {
    var quantity = cart[item].quantity;
    return setFieldByName(cart, item, 'quantity', quantity + 1);
  }
});
```

*increment the
quantity of the item*

We're done. Let's discuss it on the next page.

We just used `reduce()` to build a shopping cart from a list of items the user added. Here's where we left off on the last page:

```
var shoppingCart = reduce(itemsAdded, {}, function(cart, item) {
  if(!cart[item])
    return add_item(cart, {name: item, quantity: 1, price: priceLookup(item)});
  else {
    var quantity = cart[item].quantity;
    return setFieldByName(cart, item, 'quantity', quantity + 1);
  }
});
```

The function we pass to `reduce()` is very useful. In fact, we may want to promote it to the shopping cart's abstraction barrier by making it part of the API. It takes a cart and an item and returns a new cart with that item added, including handling if the item is already in the cart.

```
var shoppingCart = reduce(itemsAdded, {}, addOne);

function addOne(cart, item) {
  if(!cart[item])
    return add_item(cart, {name: item, quantity: 1, price: priceLookup(item)});
  else {
    var quantity = cart[item].quantity;
    return setFieldByName(cart, item, 'quantity', quantity + 1);
  }
}
```

just extracting and naming the callback

this function is extremely useful

The meaning of this code is pretty profound, so we should dwell on it a little more. It means that we can build the shopping cart at any time just by recording what items the user adds. We don't have to maintain the shopping cart object all the time. We can regenerate it any time we want from the log.

It's an important technique in functional programming. Imagine recording the items the user adds to the cart in an array. How do you implement undo? You just pop the last item out of the array. We won't get to it in this book. Look up *event sourcing* for a lot more information.

For now, though, we should go deeper into this example to reinforce some helpful hints.

One thing that the adding to cart example did not handle was removing items. How can we handle both adding and removing? Let's turn the page and find out.

Getting creative with data representation

On the last page, we used `reduce()` to build a shopping cart from a list of items added. Here's the code:

```
var itemsAdded = ["shirt", "shoes", "shirt", "socks", "hat", ....];

var shoppingCart = reduce(itemsAdded, {}, addOne);

function addOne(cart, item) {
  if(!cart[item])
    return add_item(cart, {name: item, quantity: 1, price: priceLookup(item)});
  else {
    var quantity = cart[item].quantity;
    return setFieldByName(cart, item, 'quantity', quantity + 1);
  }
}
```

This is great, but we also want to allow the user to remove items. What if instead of just storing the names of the items, we also stored whether they were added or removed, like so:

```
var itemOps = [['add', "shirt"], ['add', "shoes"], ['remove', "shirt"],
               ['add', "socks"], ['remove', "hat"], ....];
```

notice the 'remove' here

each pair has an operation and an item

Now we can handle the two cases, *add* and *remove*.

```
var shoppingCart = reduce(itemOps, {}, function(cart, itemOp) {
  var op = itemOp[0];
  var item = itemOp[1];
  if(op === 'add')    return addOne(cart, item);
  if(op === 'remove') return removeOne(cart, item);
});
function removeOne(cart, item) {
  if(!cart[item])
    return cart;
  else {
    var quantity = cart[item].quantity;
    if(quantity === 1)
      return remove_item_by_name(cart, item);
    else
      return setFieldByName(cart, item, 'quantity', quantity - 1);
  }
}
```

we switch on the operation and call the appropriate function

do nothing if it's not in the cart

if the quantity is 1, we need to get rid of the item

otherwise we decrement

We can now regenerate the shopping cart given a list of adds and removes recorded from the user's actions. There's an important technique we just used: We're augmenting the data. We represented an operation as a piece of data—in this case, an array with the name of the operation and its "argument." This is a common functional programming technique, and it will help you build better chains of functional tools. When you're chaining, think about whether augmenting the data you are returning would help a later step in the chain.

 **It's your turn**

The Annual Ecommerce Softball Tournament is coming up and MegaMart needs to send a team to defend their title. We need to develop a roster (i.e., choose who will play what positions). Every employee has been evaluated by a professional coach who recommended a position and gave them a score of how good they were.

You have a list of those recommendations. They are already sorted by score, best score first:

```
var evaluations = [{name: "Jane", position: "catcher", score: 25},
                   {name: "John", position: "pitcher", score: 10},
                   {name: "Harry", position: "pitcher", score: 3},
                   ...];
```

The roster should look like this:

```
var roster = {"pitcher": "John",
             "catcher": "Jane",
             "first base": "Ellen",
             ...};
```

Your task is to write the code to build the roster, given the evaluations.

write your answer here

 **Answer**

```
var roster = reduce(evaluations, {}, function(roster, eval) {
  var position = eval.position;
  if(roster[position]) // already filled the position
    return roster;      // so do nothing
  return objectSet(roster, position, eval.name);
});
```

It's your turn

The Annual Ecommerce Softball Tournament is coming up and MegaMart needs to send a team to defend their title. We need to evaluate the employees to see what position they are best suited for. Are they good at throwing? Pitcher! Are they good at catching? Catcher! We have a function called `recommendPosition()`, provided by a professional softball coach, that takes an employee, runs a battery of tests, and returns a recommendation.

Here's an example:

```
> recommendPosition("Jane")
"catcher"
```

You are given a list of employee names. Your job is to augment the list into a recommendation record that contains the employee's name and their recommended position. Jane's will look like this:

```
{
  name: "Jane",
  position: "catcher"
}
```

Now go for it: Take that list of employee names and turn it into a list of recommendation records using `recommendPosition()`.

```
var employeeNames = ["John", "Harry", "Jane", ...];

var recommendations =
```

write your answer here

Answer

```
var recommendations = map(employeeNames, function(name) {
  return {
    name: name,
    position: recommendPosition(name)
  };
});
```

It's your turn

The Annual Ecommerce Softball Tournament is coming up and MegaMart needs to send a team to defend their title. We need to maximize our chance of winning, so we need to know which players are the best at their recommended positions. Luckily, the professional coach we hired has another function, `scorePlayer()`, which takes an employee's name and recommended position and returns a numeric score. The higher the score, the better the player.

```
> scorePlayer("Jane", "catcher")
25
```

You are given a list of recommendation records. Your job is to augment those records with a score that you get from `scorePlayer()`. It should look like this:

```
{
  name: "Jane",
  position: "catcher",
  score: 25
}
```

Now go for it: Take that list of recommendation records and augment it:

```
var recommendations = [{name: "Jane", position: "catcher"},
                       {name: "John", position: "pitcher"},
                       ...];

var evaluations =
```

write your answer here

Answer

```
var evaluations = map(recommendations, function(rec) {
  return objectSet(rec, 'score', scorePlayer(rec.name, rec.position));
});v
```

It's your turn

The Annual Ecommerce Softball Tournament is coming up and MegaMart needs to send a team to defend their title. We've done three pieces of work in the last three exercises. Now let's put it all together into a chain! Your task is to go all the way from a list of employee names to a roster in one chain.

Other than your answers from the last three exercises, you will also need the following:

- `sortBy(array, f)`, which returns a copy of `array` with its elements sorted according to the return values of `f` (use it to sort by score)

- `reverse(array)`, which returns a copy of `array` with the elements in the reverse order

Get to it! The tournament is this weekend!

```
var employeeNames = ["John", "Harry", "Jane", ...];
```

write your answer here

Answer

```
var recommendations = map(employeeNames, function(name) {
  return {
    name: name,
    position: recommendPosition(name)
  };
});

var evaluations = map(recommendations, function(rec) {
  return objectSet(rec, 'score', scorePlayer(rec.name, rec.position));
});

var evaluationsAscending = sortBy(evaluations, function(eval) {
  return eval.score;
});

var evaluationsDescending = reverse(evaluationsAscending);

var roster = reduce(evaluations, {}, function(roster, eval) {
  var position = eval.position;
  if(roster[position]) // already filled the position
    return roster;      // so do nothing
  return objectSet(roster, position, eval.name);
});
```

Line up those dots

Functional tool chaining can really play to a programmer's itch for clean formatting. There is something about seeing a clean line of vertical dots that pleases the eye. But it's not just eye candy. A long line of vertical dots means you're using the functional tools together well. The longer the line, the more steps you're using and the more your code is like a pipeline with input data coming in at the top and output data coming out of the bottom.

Just for fun, here are some examples of what it can look like. We'll use the moving average example from this chapter.

ES6

```
function movingAverage(numbers) {
  return numbers
          .map((_e, i) => numbers.slice(i, i + window))
          .map(average);
}
```

Classic JavaScript with Lodash

```
function movingAverage(numbers) {
  return _.chain(numbers)
          .map(function(_e, i) { return numbers.slice(i, i + window); })
          .map(average)
          .value();
}
```

Java 8 Streams

```
public static double average(List<Double> numbers) {
  return numbers
          .stream()
          .reduce(0.0, Double::sum) / numbers.size();
}

public static List<Double> movingAverage(List<Double> numbers) {
  return IntStream
          .range(0, numbers.size())
          .mapToObj(i -> numbers.subList(i, Math.min(i + 3, numbers.size())))
          .map(Utils::average)
          .collect(Collectors.toList());
}
```

C#

```
public static IEnumerable<Double> movingAverage(IEnumerable<Double> numbers) {
  return Enumerable
          .Range(0, numbers.Count())
          .Select(i => numbers.ToList().GetRange(i, Math.Min(3, numbers.Count() - i)))
          .Select(l => l.Average());
}
```

Conclusion

In this chapter we saw how we can combine the functional tools from the last chapter. We combine them into multi-step processes called *chains*. Each step in the chain is a simple operation that transforms the data to be one bit closer to the desired result. We also learned how to refactor existing for loops into chains of functional tools. Finally, we saw how powerful `reduce()` can be. All of these techniques are very common among functional programmers. They form the basis of a mind-set that sees computation as data transformation.

Summary

- We can combine functional tools into multi-step chains. Their combination allows us to express very complex computations over data in small, clear steps.

- One perspective of chaining is that the functional tools form a query language, much like SQL. Chaining functional tools lets you express complex queries over arrays of data.

- We often have to make new data or augment existing data to make subsequent steps possible. Look for ways of representing implicit information as explicit data.

- There are many functional tools. You will find them as you refactor your code. You can also find inspiration for them in other languages.

- Functional tools are making their way into languages that are traditionally not considered functional, like Java. Use them where they are appropriate.

Up next . . .

We've just learned some very powerful patterns for operating on sequences of data. However, we still have trouble working with nested data. The more nested it is, the harder it is to work with. We will develop some more functional tools, using higher-order functions, to help us manipulate deeply nested data.

In this chapter

- Build higher-order functions that operate on values stored in hash maps.

- Learn to easily operate on deeply nested data with higher-order functions.

- Understand recursion and how to do it safely.

- Understand when to apply abstraction barriers to deep, nested entities.

We've learned several useful functional tools that operate over arrays. In this chapter, we're going to derive and use functional tools that operate on objects as hash maps. These tools allow you to operate on deeply nested maps, which we often find as we build more complex data structures together. Without the tools, operating on nested data in an immutable way is very awkward. But with the tools, we are free to nest as deeply as we like, which gives us the freedom to structure our data however we see fit. These higher-order functions are very common in functional languages.

Higher-order functions for values in objects

We're still happy with the higher-order functions! But we have found some repetition we'd like help with.

Sure thing! What have you got?

Chief marketing officer   Jenna from dev team   Kim from dev team

CMO: Well, we've been using your higher-order functions and they've really helped clean up our code.

Jenna: Great!

CMO: Yes! Truly great. We've actually done a lot of cleanup using the refactorings that you showed us a couple of chapters ago. But now we're doing all of these operations that must be higher-order functions, and we just can't figure out how.

Jenna: Ah, okay. Can you tell me more?

CMO: Sure. We're trying to modify the values that are nested inside an item object. We've got lots of operations that increment or decrement the size or the quantity. But somehow we can't get past the duplication. I will have to show you how we got to where we are.

Jenna: It sounds like you're looking for a higher-order function that deals with data in objects. We've just worked with higher-order functions that operate on data in arrays. It sounds really useful to be able to operate on values stored in objects as well.

Kim: Okay, let's dive in. There isn't much room here, so let's jump onto the next page.

Making the field name explicit

The marketing team started applying the refactorings from chapter 10 on their own. Here's what they came up with. They started with similar functions like this:

naming quantity field

naming size field

```
function incrementQuantity(item) {
  var quantity = item['quantity'];
  var newQuantity = quantity + 1;
  var newItem = objectSet(item, 'quantity', newQuantity);
  return newItem;
}
```

```
function incrementSize(item) {
  var size = item['size'];
  var newSize = size + 1;
  var newItem = objectSet(item, 'size', newSize);
  return newItem;
}
```

First, they recognized that they were naming the field in the function name. We called that the *implicit argument in function name* code smell. All of these operations were referring to the field name in their names. They eliminated that smell with the *express implicit argument* refactoring, which we have used a lot in the last few chapters.

make field explicit argument

Original with smell

```
function incrementQuantity(item) {
  var quantity = item['quantity'];
  var newQuantity = quantity + 1;
  var newItem = objectSet(item, 'quantity', newQuantity);
  return newItem;
}
```

After expressing argument

```
function incrementField(item, field) {
  var value = item[field];
  var newValue = value + 1;
  var newItem = objectSet(item, field, newValue);
  return newItem;
}
```

That's great. It eliminated a lot of duplication. But after doing that for a few different operations (increment, decrement, double, halve, and so on), things are starting to look like duplicates again. Here are some examples:

operation named in function name

```
function incrementField(item, field) {
  var value = item[field];
  var newValue = value + 1;
  var newItem = objectSet(item, field, newValue);
  return newItem;
}
```

```
function decrementField(item, field) {
  var value = item[field];
  var newValue = value - 1;
  var newItem = objectSet(item, field, newValue);
  return newItem;
}
```

operation named in function name

```
function doubleField(item, field) {
  var value = item[field];
  var newValue = value * 2;
  var newItem = objectSet(item, field, newValue);
  return newItem;
}
```

```
function halveField(item, field) {
  var value = item[field];
  var newValue = value / 2;
  var newItem = objectSet(item, field, newValue);
  return newItem;
}
```

These functions are all very similar. They differ only in the operation they perform. But if we look closely, we see the same *implicit argument in function name* code smell. Each of these functions names the operation. Luckily we can just apply the *express implicit argument* refactoring again. Let's turn the page and see.

Deriving `update()`

Here is the code from the last page. Notice that we've got four very
similar functions. They each differ by what operation they do on
the value. And that operation is called out in the name. We would
like to remove that duplication and derive a functional tool that
handles updating an object for us.

```
function incrementField(item, field) {
  var value = item[field];
  var newValue = value + 1;
  var newItem = objectSet(item, field, newValue);
  return newItem;
}
```

```
function decrementField(item, field) {
  var value = item[field];
  var newValue = value - 1;
  var newItem = objectSet(item, field, newValue);
  return newItem;
}
```

```
function doubleField(item, field) {
  var value = item[field];
  var newValue = value * 2;
  var newItem = objectSet(item, field, newValue);
  return newItem;
}
```
before
body
after

```
function halveField(item, field) {
  var value = item[field];
  var newValue = value / 2;
  var newItem = objectSet(item, field, newValue);
  return newItem;
}
```

We can pull two refactorings off at the same time. We can make
this implicit argument explicit with *express implicit argument*. But
that argument will be a function, which will carry out the operation. So it will also be like *replace body with callback*. Let's see what
this looks like on the first function in the previous code:

```
function incrementField(item, field) {
  var value = item[field];
  var newValue = value + 1;
  var newItem = objectSet(item, field, newValue);
  return newItem;
}
```
extract into its own function

```
function incrementField(item, field) {
  return updateField(item, field, function(value) {
    return value + 1;
  });
}
```
pass in modify function

```
function updateField(item, field, modify) {
  var value = item[field];
  var newValue = modify(value);
  var newItem = objectSet(item, field, newValue);
  return newItem;
}
```

Now all of those operations have been condensed into one higher-
order function. You pass in the difference in behavior, which is the
operation to perform on the desired field, as a callback. We typically don't need to call out the fact that we're specifying the field,
so we usually call it `update()`.

```
function update(object, key, modify) {
  var value     = object[key];
  var newValue  = modify(value);
  var newObject = objectSet(object, key, newValue);
  return newObject;
}
```
get
modify
set

`update()` lets us modify a value contained in an object. We give
it the object, the key where the value lives, and the function for
modifying it. It follows a copy-on-write discipline because it is
built on `objectSet()`, which also follows that discipline. Let's
see how you might use this on the next page.

Using `update()` to modify values

Let's say we have an employee and we want to give her a 10% raise. We need to update her record:

```
var employee = {
  name: "Kim",
  salary: 120000
};
```

We have a function called `raise10Percent()` that takes a salary and returns it raised by 10%:

```
function raise10Percent(salary) {
  return salary * 1.1;
}
```

We can apply this to the employee record using `update()`. We know that the salary is located under the salary key:

```
> update(employee, 'salary', raise10Percent)

{
  name: "Kim",
  salary: 132000
}
```

`update()` allows us to apply `raise10Percent()` inside the context of the `employee` object (hash map). `update()` takes an operation that acts on a specific kind of value (here, the salary) and applies it directly to a hash map containing that value under a certain key. You might say it applies a function to a value in a nested context.

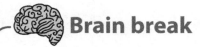 **Brain break**

There's more to go, but let's take a break for questions

Q: Does `update()` **modify the original hash map?**

A: No, `update()` doesn't modify the original hash map. It uses the copy-on-write discipline we learned in chapter 6. `update()` returns a modified copy of the hash map you pass it.

Q: If it doesn't modify the original, what use is it?

A: Good question. As we saw in chapter 6, we can use functions to represent change over time by swapping in the return values from the `update()` function. Here's an example:

```
var employee = {
  name: "Kim",
  salary: 120000
};

employee = update(employee, salary, raise10Percent);
```

swap out the old value
for the new value

We are separating the calculation (computing the raise) from the action (modifying state).

Refactoring: *Replace get, modify, set with update()*

We just applied two refactorings at the same time: (1) *express implicit argument* and (2) *replace body with callback*. However, we can use a more direct process. Here's the before and after code:

Before refactoring

```
function incrementField(item, field) {
  var value = item[field];            get
  var newValue = value + 1;           modify
  var newItem = objectSet(item, field, newValue);
  return newItem;                            set
}
```

After refactoring

```
function incrementField(item, field) {
  return update(item, field, function(value) {
    return value + 1;
  });
}
```

Notice how on the left we're completing three steps:

1. Get the value out of the object.

2. Modify the value.

3. Set the new value on the object (using copy-on-write).

If we are doing those three operations on the same key, we can replace it with a single update() call. We pass the object, the key whose value will be modified, and the calculation that modifies:

Steps of *replace get, modify, set with* **update()**

There are really two steps to this refactoring.

1. Identify the get, modify, and set.

2. Replace the code with a call to update(), passing the modify operation as a callback.

Step 1: Identify get, modify, and set

```
function halveField(item, field) {     get
  var value = item[field];             modify
  var newValue = value / 2;                   set
  var newItem = objectSet(item, field, newValue);
  return newItem;
}
```

Step 2: Replace with call to update()

```
function halveField(item, field) {
  return update(item, field, function(value) {
    return value / 2;
  });                              modify operation
}                                  passed as callback
```

The *replace get, modify, set with* update() refactoring is very useful since we are often working with nested objects.

Functional tool: `update()`

`update()` is another important functional tool. The functional tools we learned in the last chapters operated on arrays, but this one operates on objects (treated as hash maps). Let's look at it more closely:

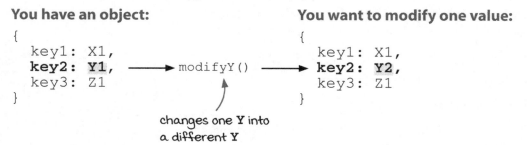

```
function update(object, key, modify) {
  var value = object[key];
  var newValue = modify(value);
  var newObject = objectSet(object, key, newValue);
  return newObject;
}
```

takes the object, the location of the value (key), and the modify operation

get

modify

set

returns the modified object (copy-on-write)

`update()` let's us take a function that operates on a single value and apply it in place inside of an object. It only changes one value under one key, so it's a very surgical operation:

You have an object: **You want to modify one value:**

```
{                                          {
  key1: X1,                                  key1: X1,
  key2: Y1,       ──→ modifyY() ──→          key2: Y2,
  key3: Z1                                   key3: Z1
}                                          }
```

changes one Y into a different Y

`update()` needs three things: (1) the object to modify, (2) the key for where to find the value to modify, and (3) the function to call to modify the value. Make sure the function you pass to `update()` is a calculation. It will take one argument (the current value) and return the new value. Let's look at how we're using it in our example:

pass update() an object (the item)

pass update() the field for the value to modify

pass update() the function that modifies the value

```
function incrementField(item, field) {
  return update(item, field, function(value) {
    return value + 1;
  });
}
```

returns the value incremented by one

Visualizing values in objects

Let's take another more visual look at the update() operation.
Let's imagine we have an item object that looks like this:

Code

```
var shoes = {
  name: "shoes",
  quantity: 3,
  price: 7
};
```

we will visualize this object with this diagram

Equivalent diagram

```
shoes
  name: "shoes"
  quantity: 3
  price: 7
```

And we want to run this code, which is supposed to double the quantity:

```
> update(shoes, 'quantity', function(value) {
  return value * 2; // double the number
});
```

We will go step-by-step through the code for update():

Step #   Code

```
      function update(object, key, modify) {
1.      var value = object[key];                              get
2.      var newValue = modify(value);                         modify
3.      var newObject = objectSet(object, key, newValue);     set
        return newObject;
      }
```

Step 1: Get the value from the object at key

quantity

```
shoes
  name: "shoes"
  quantity: 3
  price: 7
```

3

Step 2: Call modify() on the value to produce a new value

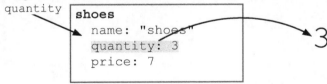

modify()
x * 2

3   6

Step 3: Create a modified copy

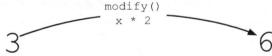

objectSet()

6

```
shoes
  name: "shoes"
  quantity: 3
  price: 7
```

```
shoes copy
  name: "shoes"
  quantity: 6
  price: 7
```

It's your turn

We have a function called `lowercase()` that will convert a string to lowercase. Users have an email address under the `'email'` key. Using `update()`, modify the `user` record by applying `lowercase()` to their email.

```
var user = {                          make this string lowercase
  firstName: "Joe",
  lastName: "Nash",    ◄──────
  email: "JOE@EXAMPLE.COM",
                                                   write your answer here
  ...
};
```

Answer

```
> update(user, 'email', lowercase)

{
  firstName: "Joe",
  lastName: "Nash",
  email: "joe@example.com",
  ...
}
```

It's your turn

The user interface team wants to encourage big purchases. They think a 10x button that multiplies the quantity by 10 will help. Write a function, using `update()`, that multiplies the current quantity of an item by 10. An example item is given:

```
var item = {
  name: "shoes",
  price: 7,
  quantity: 2,
  ...
};

function tenXQuantity(item) {
```

multiply this by 10

write your answer here

Answer

```
function tenXQuantity(item) {
  return update(item, 'quantity', function(quantity) {
    return quantity * 10;
  });
}
```

✎ It's your turn

For the following questions, we're going to use this data structure:

```
var user = {
  firstName: "Cindy",
  lastName: "Sullivan",
  email: "cindy@randomemail.com",
  score: 15,
  logins: 3
};
```

Givens
- increment() adds one
- decrement() subtracts one
- uppercase() converts a string to uppercase

1. What is the value of the following code?
```
> update(user, 'score', increment).score
```

write your answers here

2. What is the value of the following code?
```
> update(user, 'logins', decrement).score
```

3. What is the value of the following code?
```
> update(user, 'firstName', uppercase).firstName
```

✎ Answer

```
1.
> update(user, 'score', increment).score
16

2.
> update(user, 'logins', decrement).score
15

3.
> update(user, 'firstName', uppercase).firstName
"CINDY"
```

since we're updating "logins", the score doesn't change

CMO: Yeah. `update()` seems to work well with data inside an object. But we've got objects inside of objects over here. Sometimes three objects deep!

Jenna: Wow, can you show us what that looks like?

CMO: Yeah. Here's our code for incrementing the size of a shirt:

```
var shirt = {
  name: "shirt",
  price: 13,                    nesting an object inside an object
  options: {
    color: "blue",             have to dig out the options object
    size: 3
  }
};
```

```
function incrementSize(item) {
  var options = item.options;                          get
  var size = options.size;                             get
  var newSize = size + 1;                              modify
  var newOptions = objectSet(options, 'size', newSize);    set
  var newItem = objectSet(item, 'options', newOptions);    set
  return newItem;
}                              objectSet() on both on the way out
```

Kim: Oh! I see what you mean. You've got a get, get, modify, set, set. It doesn't exactly match our refactoring.

CMO: Is there anything we can do?

Jenna: Let's not give up hope just yet. I think there is an update hidden in there. We will be able to apply the refactoring after all.

Visualizing nested updates

Here is the definition of the function dealing with the nested `options` object that the CMO showed us on the last page. We need to deeply understand what it is doing. Let's step through it line-by-line:

Step #   **Code**

```
     function incrementSize(item) {                      get
1.      var options    = item.options;                   get
2.      var size       = options.size;
3.      var newSize    = size + 1;           modify
4.      var newOptions = objectSet(options, 'size', newSize);     set
5.      var newItem    = objectSet(item, 'options', newOptions);  set
        return newItem;
     }
```

Step 1: Get the value from the object at the key

options

```
shirt
  name: "shirt"
  price: 13
  options
    color: "blue"
    size: 3
```

```
options
  color: "blue"
  size: 3
```

Step 2: Get the value from the object at the key

size

```
options
  color: "blue"
  size: 3
```

3

Step 3: Produce the new value

size + 1

3   4

Step 4: Create a modified copy

objectSet()

4

```
options
  color: "blue"
  size: 3
```

```
options copy
  color: "blue"
  size: 4
```

Step 5: Create a modified copy

objectSet()

```
options copy
  color: "blue"
  size: 4
```

```
shirt
  name: "shirt"
  price: 13
  options
    color: "blue"
    size: 3
```

```
shirt copy
  name: "shirt"
  price: 13
  options copy
    color: "blue"
    size: 4
```

Applying `update()` to nested data

Now that we've visualized it, let's see how we can refactor this to
use `update()`. Here's the code we have now:

```
function incrementSize(item) {
  var options = item.options;                      ← get         a get, modify,
  var size = options.size;                      ← get            set nested inside
  var newSize = size + 1;                      ← modify
  var newOptions = objectSet(options, 'size', newSize);      ← set
  var newItem = objectSet(item, 'options', newOptions);      ← set
  return newItem;
}
```

We have a refactoring called *replace get, modify, set with* `update()`
that we would like to use. We need to identify a series of get, modify, set operations. Can we apply it here?

In fact, we can! Right in the middle, there is a series of get, modify, set sandwiched between a get at the top and a set at the bottom.
Let's apply the refactoring to those three statements in the middle:

> **Steps for replace
> get, modify, set with
> `update()`**
>
> 1. Identify get,
>   modify, and set.
> 2. Replace with
>   `update()`,
>   passing modify as
>   callback.

Original

get, modify, set to
replace with update()

```
function incrementSize(item) {
  var options = item.options;
  var size = options.size;
  var newSize = size + 1;
  var newOptions = objectSet(options, 'size', newSize);
  var newItem = objectSet(item, 'options', newOptions);
  return newItem;
}
```

Refactored

```
function incrementSize(item) {
  var options = item.options;      ← get
                                      modify
  var newOptions = update(options, 'size', increment);
  var newItem = objectSet(item, 'options', newOptions);
  return newItem;                      ← set
}
```

now we have get,
modify, set again

That's pretty straightforward. But now look! We have converted
the middle get, modify, set into a modify. The `update()` call is
modifying the options. So we have another get, modify, set to
apply the refactoring to. Let's do it.

Refactored once

```
function incrementSize(item) {       ← get    ← modify
  var options = item.options;
  var newOptions = update(options, 'size', increment);
  var newItem = objectSet(item, 'options', newOptions);
  return newItem;                      ← set
}
```

Refactored twice   replace with update()

```
function incrementSize(item) {
  return update(item, 'options', function(options) {
    return update(options, 'size', increment);
  });
}
```

inner update() is the callback
to the outer update()

This is an important realization: We can nest the updates to work
on nested objects. As we nest calls to `update()`, we are working
on a deeper level of nested objects. Let's continue to develop this
idea on the next page.

Deriving `updateOption()`

We just wrote some code that did an update inside an update. We can generalize that operation to a function called `update2()`:

```
function incrementSize(item) {
  return update(item, 'options', function(options) {
    return update(options, 'size', increment);
  });
}
```
← nested updates

the nested data
we operated on

```
var shirt = {
  name: "shirt",
  price: 13,
  options: {
    color: "blue",
    size: 3
  }
};
```
← size is nested
under options

Notice that we are calling `update()` twice and the `size` data is nested twice (we go through two objects to get to it). You'll find that you will have to nest the `update()` calls as deeply as your data is nested.

That's an important point, and we will get to it in just a moment, but let's work on this function we just wrote. We notice two smells that we've smelled before. Actually, it's the same smell twice:

```
function incrementSize(item) {
  return update(item, 'options', function(options) {
    return update(options, 'size', increment);
  });
}
```
referring to an implicit argument in
the function name again! twice even!

> **Steps in express implicit argument *refactoring***
>
> 1. Identify implicit argument.
> 2. Add explicit argument.
> 3. Use new argument in body.
> 4. Update calling code.

We've got two implicit arguments, so let's make them explicit. We can do them one at a time. First is the `'size'`:

With implicit option argument

```
function incrementSize(item) {
  return update(item, 'options', function(options) {
    return update(options, 'size', increment);
  });
}
```

With explicit option argument

```
function incrementOption(item, option) {
  return update(item, 'options', function(options) {
    return update(options, option, increment);
  });
}
```

With implicit modify argument

```
function incrementOption(item, option) {
  return update(item, 'options', function(options) {
    return update(options, option, increment);
  });
}
```

With explicit modify argument

```
function updateOption(item, option, modify) {
  return update(item, 'options', function(options) {
    return update(options, option, modify);
  });
}
```

Great! This function takes the item (object), the name of the option, and the function that modifies the option.

```
function updateOption(item, option, modify) {
  return update(item, 'options', function(options) {
    return update(options, option, modify);
  });
}
```
the smell has returned! we are
still naming the implicit argument
in the function name

It's the same smell again! This time, the implicit argument is `'options'`, and it's named in the function name. Let's tackle that on the next page.

Deriving `update2()`

On the last page, we finished expressing two implicit arguments. That refactoring revealed a third implicit argument. If we refactor just one more time, we'll derive a very general tool called update2(). Here's the code again:

we are naming this field name in the function name. it could be an argument

```
function updateOption(item, option, modify) {
  return update(item, 'options', function(options) {
    return update(options, option, modify);
  });
}
```

Let's apply that refactoring a third time. This refactoring will make the function more general, so we'll change the names to reflect how general it is as we go:

since this function is more generic, we rename arguments to be generic

With implicit argument

```
function updateOption(item, option, modify) {
  return update(item, 'options', function(options) {
    return update(options, option, modify);
  });
}
```
the 2 means nested twice

With explicit argument

```
function update2(object, key1, key2, modify) {
  return update(object, key1, function(value1) {
    return update(value1, key2, modify);
  });
}
```
make this an explicit argument

Wow. That's very general now. We can call it update2() because it works on any objects nested in objects (values two levels deep). That's why it needs two keys.

Just to be sure, let's try to reimplement incrementSize() using it. Here's the data structure we were working on:

```
var shirt = {
  name: "shirt",
  price: 13,
  options: {
    color: "blue",
    size: 3
  }
};
```
we wanted to increment this value along the path 'options', 'size'

> **Steps in express implicit argument *refactoring***
>
> 1. Identify implicit argument.
> 2. Add explicit argument.
> 3. Use new argument in body.
> 4. Update calling code.

And here's the original implementation alongside the reimplementation using update2():

Original

```
function incrementSize(item) {
  var options = item.options;
  var size = options.size;
  var newSize = size + 1;
  var newOptions = objectSet(options, 'size', newSize);
  var newItem = objectSet(item, 'options', newOptions);
  return newItem;
}
```

Using `update2()`

```
function incrementSize(item) {

  return update2(item, 'options', 'size', function(size) {
    return size + 1;
  });
}
```

update2() takes care of all of the get, get, modify, set, set that you would have to write yourself. This is all getting a bit abstract, so let's visualize it on the next page.

Visualizing `update2()` on nested objects

On the last page, we derived a function called `update2()` that will modify a value nested twice within objects. That's a mouthful! Let's see what that looks like in a picture.

    We are incrementing the size option. To do so, we need to follow a path through nested objects. Starting with the item, we step into the object at the `'options'` key, then finally the value at the `'size'` key. Collectively, the list of keys is called the *path*. We use it to locate the desired value inside of a nested object.

    Here is the code we would like to run:

Vocab time

The sequence of keys for locating a value in nested objects is called a *path*. The path has one key for each level of nesting.

```
> return update2(shirt, 'options', 'size', function(size) {
    return size + 1;
  });
```
incrementing the value   *the path to the desired value*

And here is the item we would like to modify. Notice that the options object is nested inside:

```
var shirt = {
  name: "shirt",
  price: 13,
  options: {
    color: "blue",
    size: 3
  }
};
```

```
shirt
  name: "shirt"
  price: 13
  options
    color: "blue"
    size: 3
```

And here is the item we would like to modify. Notice that the options object is nested inside:

On the way in (two gets)

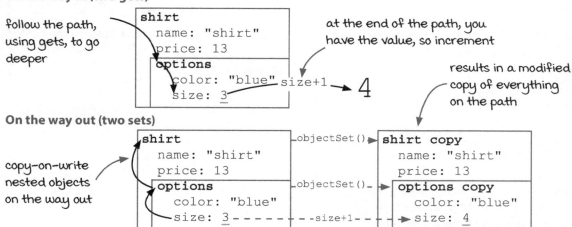

follow the path, using gets, to go deeper

```
shirt
  name: "shirt"
  price: 13
  options
    color: "blue" size+1
    size: 3
```
at the end of the path, you have the value, so increment

results in a modified copy of everything on the path

4

On the way out (two sets)

copy-on-write nested objects on the way out

```
shirt
  name: "shirt"
  price: 13
  options
    color: "blue"
    size: 3
```
— objectSet() →
```
shirt copy
  name: "shirt"
  price: 13
  options copy
    color: "blue"
    size: 4
```
— objectSet() —
- - - size+1 - - -

Chief marketing officer   Jenna from dev team   Kim from dev team

CMO: No, it's not bad. Well, it's just that we usually deal with items that are in the cart. Not always, but often.

Jenna: And?

CMO: That example is changing an option inside the options object, which is inside the item object. But the item object is inside of the cart object.

```
var cart = {
  shirt: {
    name: "shirt",
    price: 13,
    options: {
      color: "blue",
      size: 3
    }
  }
}
```

```
cart
  shirt
    name: "shirt"
    price: 13
    options
      color: "blue"
      size: 3
```

three levels of nesting

items are nested inside the cart object

Jenna: Oh! I see. There's one more level of nesting.

CMO: That's right. The function is called incrementSizeByName(). Does that mean we'll need an update3()?

Kim: We don't need it, but it might be useful. Let's see what we can do with what we already have. I think we can just add one level to what we've already got. Let's turn the page and get started.

Writing `incrementSizeByName()` **four ways**

The CMO is talking about modifying item options while they are in the cart. That's three levels of nesting. Let's explore four different ways to solve this problem. Specifically, the CMO wants to increment the size option for an item in the cart, given its name, with a function called `incrementSizeByName()`. This function takes a cart and the name of an item and increments the size option of that item. How do we write that function?

Option 1: using `update()` and `incrementSize()`

We need to operate on an item nested inside the cart. `update()` will modify a value nested in the cart and we can apply `incrementSize()` to the item:

```
function incrementSizeByName(cart, name) {
  return update(cart, name, incrementSize);
}
```

very straightforward way to use what we already have

Option 2: using `update()` and `update2()`

We could inline the implementation of `incrementSize()` and use `update2()`:

```
function incrementSizeByName(cart, name) {
  return update(cart, name, function(item) {
    return update2(item, 'options', 'size', function(size) {
      return size + 1;
    });
  });
}
```

inlining the call to incrementSize()
nests update2() inside update()

Option 3: using `update()`

We can inline `update2()`, which is two nested calls to `update()`.

```
function incrementSizeByName(cart, name) {
  return update(cart, name, function(item) {
    return update(item, 'options', function(options) {
      return update(options, 'size', function(size) {
        return size + 1;
      });
    });
  });
}
```

let's inline until it's just calls to update()

 **Noodle on it**

Which of these four options do you prefer? Why? Are any of the options totally off the table? Why? We will discuss this soon.

Option 4: writing it manually as gets, modify, and sets

We can inline `update()` into gets, modifies, and sets:

```
function incrementSizeByName(cart, name) {
  var item      = cart[name];
  var options   = item.options;
  var size      = options.size;
  var newSize   = size + 1;
  var newOptions = objectSet(options, 'size', newSize);
  var newItem   = objectSet(item, 'options', newOptions);
  var newCart   = objectSet(cart, name, newItem);
  return newCart;
}
```

get, get, get
modify
set, set, set

Deriving `update3()`

We're going to derive `update3()`. We've done something like this several times now, so we should be able to go through it pretty quickly. Let's start with option 2 from the last page, apply *express implicit argument*, and get a definition of `update3()`. We'll do it all in one go:

implicit arguments

Option 2

```
function incrementSizeByName(cart, name) {
  return update(cart, name, function(item) {
    return update2(item, 'options', 'size',
      function(size) { return size + 1; });
  });
}
```

extract to update3()

update3() is just an update2() nested in an update()

Refactored

```
function incrementSizeByName(cart, name) {
  return update3(cart,
    name, 'options', 'size',
    function(size) { return size + 1; });
}
```

three-part path

```
function update3(object, key1, key2, key3, modify) {
  return update(object, key1, function(object2) {
    return update2(object2, key2, key3, modify);
  });
}
```

`update3()` nests an `update2()` inside of an `update()`. The `update()` makes it go one level deeper than the `update2()` goes, for a total of four levels.

> ***Steps in* express implicit argument *refactoring***
>
> 1. Identify implicit argument.
> 2. Add explicit argument.
> 3. Use new argument in body.
> 4. Update calling code.

 **It's your turn**

The marketing team needs update4() and update5(). Write them for them.

we could really use update4() and update5(), too!

Chief marketing officer

write your answers here

 **Answer**

```
function update4(object, k1, k2, k3, k4, modify) {
  return update(object, k1, function(object2) {
    return update3(object2, k2, k3, k4, modify);
  });
}

function update5(object, k1, k2, k3, k4, k5, modify) {
  return update(object, k1, function(object2) {
    return update4(object2, k2, k3, k4, k5, modify);
  });
}
```

Deriving `nestedUpdate()`

We've just derived update3(), and we recognized the pattern that would let us quickly write update4() and update5(). But if the pattern is so clear, surely there is a way to capture it in a function. Before we get asked to derive update6() through update21(), let's start working on nestedUpdate(), which works with any number of nesting levels.

Let's start by picking apart the pattern:

```
function update3(object, key1, key2, key3, modify) {
  return update(object, key1, function(value1) {
    return update2(value1, key2, key3, modify);
  });
}          X       X - 1
```

```
function update4(object, key1, key2, key3, key4, modify) {
  return update(object, key1, function(value1) {
    return update3(value1, key2, key3, key4, modify);
  });
}          X       X - 1
```

The pattern is simple: We define updateX() as an updateX-1() nested inside an update(). The update() uses the first key, then passes the rest of the keys, in order, and modify to updateX-1(). What would this pattern look like for update2()? We already have update2(), but let's ignore that for now:

```
function update2(object, key1, key2, modify) {
  return update(object, key1, function(value1) {
    return update1(value1, key2, modify);
  });
}
```
the 2 in the name indicates two keys and call update1()

What would update1() look like? X-1 would be 0, so

```
function update1(object, key1, modify) {
  return update(object, key1, function(value1) {
    return update0(value1, modify);
  });
}
```
the 1 in the name indicates one key and call update0()

update0() will break the pattern because it is different in two ways. First, there are no keys, so we can't call update() with the first key, since there is no first key. Second, X-1 would be -1, which doesn't make sense for a path length.

Intuitively, update0() means we are nested zero objects deep. There are zero gets and zero sets, just the modify. In other words, we have the value we are looking for, so we should just apply the modify() function:

```
function update0(value, modify) {
  return modify(value);
}
```
the 0 in the name indicates zero keys

> **Attributes of implicit argument in function name smell**
> 1. Similar implementations
> 2. Difference cited in function name

Now, so far, this has been a pretty dry derivation. Sorry! But here's the cool thing: Our code smell has shown up again! We've got an *implicit argument in function name*. The numbers in the function name always match the number of arguments. Let's tackle this on the next page.

On the last page, we noticed the pattern with the `updateX()` functions. But in particular, we identified the *implicit argument in function name* smell. That's great, because we have a refactoring that can remove that smell, *express implicit argument*.

Let's look at `update3()` as an example. How do we make the 3 an explicit argument?

```
                         ✗            ┌─ X keys
function update3(object, key1, key2, key3, modify) {
  return update(object, key1 function(value1) {
    return update2(value1, key2, key3, modify);
  });              ↖─ X–1      ↖ leave off first key
}
```

We could easily just add an argument called depth:

explicit depth argument ─┐   depth corresponds
                         ↓   to number of keys
```
function updateX(object, depth, key1, key2, key3, modify) { ◄─┐
  return update(object, key1, function(value1) {              note that this
    return updateX(value1, depth-1, key2, key3, modify);      function won't work
  });
}         └─ recursive call  └─ pass depth–1   └─ one fewer keys
```

That does make the argument explicit, but that creates a new problem: How do we make sure the depth and the number of keys correspond? A separate depth parameter will probably lead to bugs down the line. However, it does give a clue: We need to maintain the *order* and the *number of keys*. That indicates a clear data structure: arrays. What if we pass the keys in as an array? The depth parameter will be the length. Here is the signature:

```
function updateX(object, keys, modify) {    ┌─ array of keys
```

We'll follow the same pattern as before. We call `update()` with the first key, then pass the rest of the keys to `updateX()`. The rest of the keys will be of length X–1:

```
                    ┌─ use first key for call to update()
function updateX(object, keys, modify) {
  var key1 = keys[0];              ┌─ omit first key in
  var restOfKeys = drop_first(keys);   recursive call
  return update(object, key1, function(value1) {
    return updateX(value1, restOfKeys, modify);
  });
}
```

That's great! This will be able to replace all of the `updateX()` functions except `update0()`, which had a different pattern. Let's look at `update0()` on the next page.

Vocab time

A *recursive function* is a function that is defined in terms of itself. A recursive function will have a *recursive call* where the function calls itself.

we'll see more about recursion in a few pages. let's finish the function first

Here's what we've got for updateX() so far:

```
function updateX(object, keys, modify) {
  var key1 = keys[0];
  var restOfKeys = drop_first(keys);
  return update(object, key1, function(value1) {
    return updateX(value1, restOfKeys, modify);
  });
}
```

what happens when there are no keys?

It can replace update1(), update2(), and update3() (and presumably update4, 5, 6, ...()) because they all followed the same pattern. But update0() was different. It didn't call update() at all. It just called modify(), the callback. How can we incorporate this?

```
function update0(value, modify) {
  return modify(value);
}
```

the definition of update0() is different from the others

it's not recursive

Well, we have to make a special case for zero. We know we have zero keys if the length of the keys array is zero. In that case, we'll just call modify(). Otherwise, we do what is in updateX(). Let's do it:

Without handling zero

```
function updateX(object, keys, modify) {


  var key1 = keys[0];
  var restOfKeys = drop_first(keys);
  return update(object, key1, function(value1) {
    return updateX(value1, restOfKeys, modify);
  });
}
```

Handling zero handle zero case

```
function updateX(object, keys, modify) {
  if(keys.length === 0)
    return modify(object);
  var key1 = keys[0];
  var restOfKeys = drop_first(keys);
  return update(object, key1, function(value1) {
    return updateX(value1, restOfKeys, modify);
  });
}
```

not recursive

recursive call

Now we have a version of updateX() that works for any number of keys. We can use it to apply a modify() function to a value at any depth in nested objects. We only have to know the keys to follow into each object to find the value.

updateX() is typically called nestedUpdate(). Let's rename it on the next page.

 **Vocab time**

A *base case* in recursion is a case with no recursive call that stops the recursion. Each recursive call should make progress toward the base case.

On the last page, we finished deriving a complete updateX() that
works for any depth of nested data, including zero. Data nested
zero layers in is modified directly.

We don't typically call this updateX(). A better name would
be nestedUpdate(). It takes an object, a path of keys to follow
into the nesting of the objects, and a function to call on the value
once it is found. It then makes modified copies of all the levels on
the way out:

```
function nestedUpdate(object, keys, modify) {
  if(keys.length === 0)
    return modify(object);                    ← base case (path of zero length)
  var key1 = keys[0];
  var restOfKeys = drop_first(keys);          ← make progress toward
  return update(object, key1, function(value1) {   base case (by dropping
    return nestedUpdate(value1, restOfKeys, modify);  one path element)
  });
}                        ← recursive case
```

nestedUpdate() works on paths of any length, including zero,
but also as deep as you could imagine. It is *recursive*, meaning it is
defined in terms of itself. Functional programmers use recursion a
little more than other programmers. This concept is a deep one,
and we should spend at least a couple of pages really understanding how it works.

 ## Brain break

There's more to go, but let's take a break for questions

Q: How can a function call itself?

A: That's a good question. A function can call any function it wants to, including itself. If it does call itself, it's called *recursive*. *Recursion* is the general idea of functions calling themselves. The nestedUpdate() function we just wrote is recursive:

```
function nestedUpdate(object, keys, modify) {
  if(keys.length === 0)
    return modify(object);
  var key1 = keys[0];
  var restOfKeys = drop_first(keys);
  return update(object, key1, function(value1) {
    return nestedUpdate(value1, restOfKeys, modify);
  });
}
```
— calls itself

Q: What's the point of recursion? It seems hard to understand.

A: Great question. Recursion can be hard to wrap our minds around, even with lots of experience. Recursion works really well for dealing with nested data. You'll recall that we defined deepCopy() recursively (see page 160) for this very reason. When dealing with nested data, we often treat each level in a similar way. Each call to the recursive function peels off one level of nesting, then dives in to do the same operation again at the next level.

Q: Can't we just use iteration? For loops are easier to understand.

A: For loops are very often easier to understand than recursion. You should write the code that most clearly represents your intentions. However, in this case, recursion is clearer. Recursion takes advantage of the function call stack that keeps track of the argument values and return locations of function calls. In order to do this with a for loop, we would need to manage our own stack. JavaScript's stack does what we need without having to worry about push and pop operations.

Q: Isn't recursion dangerous? Can't it go into infinite loops or blow the stack?

A: Yes! Recursion can go into an infinite loop just like iterative loops. Sometimes, depending on the recursive call and the language, it can loop so much it runs out of stack space. If everything is working correctly, we shouldn't go that deep into the stack. But getting things to work correctly with recursion requires getting a few things right. It is not hard once you learn the tricks. In fact, let's look at the anatomy of safe recursion.

The anatomy of safe recursion

Just like for and while loops can go into infinite loops, recursion can also go into an infinite loop.
If we follow a few best practices, we won't have any problems:

1. Base case

If we want our recursion to stop, we need a *base case*. The base case is where the recursion stops.
It doesn't include any recursive call, so the recursion will end there:

```
function nestedUpdate(object, keys, modify) {
  if(keys.length === 0)
    return modify(object);                    base case
  var key1 = keys[0];                         no recursive call
  var restOfKeys = drop_first(keys);
  return update(object, key1, function(value1) {
    return nestedUpdate(value1, restOfKeys, modify);
  });
}
```

The base case is usually easy to check for. It often occurs that when your argument is an empty
array, a countdown goes to zero, or you found what you're looking for. In those cases, your work
is clear. The base case is usually the easiest case to write.

2. Recursive case

A recursive function needs at least one *recursive case*. The recursive case is where the recursive
call happens:

```
function nestedUpdate(object, keys, modify) {
  if(keys.length === 0)
    return modify(object);                    restOfKeys is one
  var key1 = keys[0];                          shorter (progress)
  var restOfKeys = drop_first(keys);
  return update(object, key1, function(value1) {
    return nestedUpdate(value1, restOfKeys, modify);
  });                                          recursive call
}
```

3. Progress toward the base case

When you make the recursive call, you need to make sure that at least one of the arguments is
"smaller." That is, it's at least one step closer to the base case. For instance, if your base case is the
empty array, then we need to remove an element from the array each time.

If each recursive call is one step closer, then eventually you will reach the base case and the
recursion will stop. The worst you could do is to make a recursive call with the same arguments
you were passed. That is sure to make an infinite loop.

Let's visualize this function's behavior to better understand it.

Visualizing `nestedUpdate()`

This is all getting very abstract, so let's visually step through a call
to nestedUpdate(). We'll do it for a nesting level of three, where
previously we would have called update3().

   We are going to run this code that increments the size of an
item in a cart:

```
> nestedUpdate(cart, ["shirt", "options", "size"], increment)
```

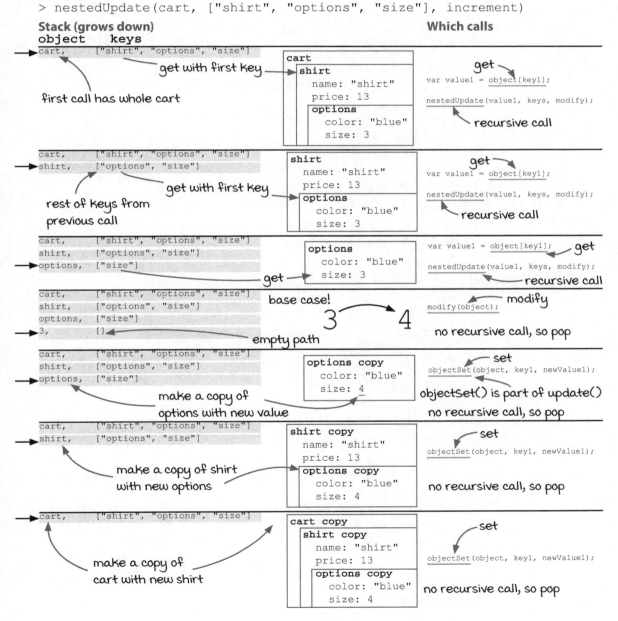

The superpower of recursion

For loops are great. We've used them so far whenever we've needed to work through arrays. Even our functional tools for arrays are implemented in terms of for loops. However, this time is different because we are dealing with nested data.

I still don't get why recursion works better than a for loop here.

When we iterated through an array, we processed the array in order, starting from the beginning. We added an element to the end of the resulting array as we visited each element:

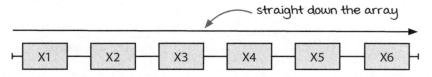

straight down the array

| X1 | X2 | X3 | X4 | X5 | X6 |

In contrast, when we operate on nested data, we have to do gets on the way down the levels, then modify the final value, then do sets on the way back up. Those sets make copies (because they are copy-on-write sets).

Jenna from dev team

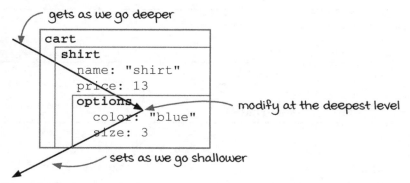

gets as we go deeper

```
cart
  shirt
    name: "shirt"
    price: 13
    options
      color: "blue"
      size: 3
```

modify at the deepest level

sets as we go shallower

The nesting of gets, modify, and sets mirrors the nesting of our data. We can't nest this way without recursion and the call stack.

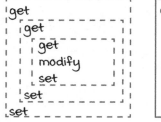

```
get
  get
    get
    modify
    set
  set
set
```

```
cart
  shirt
    options
      size
```

Noodle on it

How would you write `nestedUpdate()` using a loop (for or while)? Give it a shot!

It's your turn

On page 374, we saw four ways to write `incrementSizeByName()`. Your task is to write it a fifth way, using `nestedUpdate()`.

```
function incrementSizeByName(cart, name) {
```

write your answer here

Answer

```
function incrementSizeByName(cart, name) {
  return nestedUpdate(cart, [name, 'options', 'size'],
                      function(size) {
                        return size + 1;
                      });
}
```

Design considerations with deep nesting

This is a very common complaint. You use nestedUpdate() to access deeply nested data using a long path of keys. It's hard to remember all of the intermediate objects and what keys you can expect in each. It's most clear when you're dealing with an API and you can't control the data model.

nestedUpdate() is great. But when I read the code later, it's hard to remember what keys I can use.

Kim from dev team

callback

```
httpGet("http://my-blog.com/api/category/blog", function(blogCategory) {
  renderCategory(nestedUpdate(blogCategory, ['posts', '12', 'author', 'name'], capitalize));
});
```

nested object   *long path of keys*   *modification function*

In this code, we see a simplified example. We are fetching the "blog" category from the blog's API, which returns JSON, which we handle in the callback. In the callback, we capitalize the name of the author of the 12th blog post in the "blog" category. It's a contrived example, but it shows the problem clearly. When we come back three weeks later to read this code, how much stuff do we have to understand? Here's a list:

too much to fit!

user.name
posts[12]
post.author
category.posts

1. The category has posts under the 'posts' key.

2. You can access an individual post record by ID.

3. The post has a user record under the 'author' key.

4. The user record has the name under the 'name' key.

You'll find that for each level of nesting, there is a whole new data structure to load into your mind in order to understand the path. That's what makes it hard to remember what keys you have. Each intermediate object has a different set of keys that are expected, and none of this is obvious when looking at the path for nestedUpdate().

So what's the solution? Luckily, we already talked about the solution when discussing stratified design, specifically in chapter 9. When there is too much to think about, one way to address it is with an abstraction barrier. Abstraction barriers allow us to ignore details. Let's see what that looks like on the next page.

 Reminder

An *abstraction barrier* is a layer of functions that hide the implementation so well that you can completely forget about how it is implemented, even while using those functions.

Abstraction barriers on deeply nested data

On the last page, we saw how deeply nested data often brings with it a high cognitive load. We have to keep one data structure in our head per nesting level. The key is to reduce the number of data structures we have to understand in order to do the same work. We can do that with abstraction barriers. That means creating functions that use those data structures and giving the functions meaningful names. We should be moving toward this anyway as our understanding of the data involved stabilizes.

What if we made a function that could modify a category's post given the post's ID?

clear name

```
function updatePostById(category, id, modifyPost) {
  return nestedUpdate(category, ['posts', id], modifyPost);
}
```

structural detail of category is hidden from code above the barrier

you can use this function without knowing how posts are stored in a category

leaves knowledge of structure of post to callback

Now we can make an operation to modify a post's author:

clear name

```
function updateAuthor(post, modifyUser) {
  return update(post, 'author', modifyUser);
}
```

modifyUser knows how to handle users

use this function without knowing how the author is stored in a post

If we want to take this further, we could make an operation to capitalize any user's name:

clear name

```
function capitalizeName(user) {
  return update(user, 'name', capitalize);
}
```

lets you ignore the key

Now we can put them all together:

everything is tied together here

```
updatePostById(blogCategory, '12', function(post) {
  return updateAuthor(post, capitalizeUserName);
});
```

Is this better? Yes, for two reasons. First, there are three things to keep in your head instead of four. That helps tremendously. Second, the names of the operations make the individual things easier to load into your head. We know categories have posts already. Now we don't have to remember the keys where they are stored. The same is true with the author. We know the post has one. Now we don't have to know where it is.

A summary of our use of higher-order functions

In chapter 10, we first learned the idea of higher-order functions, which simply means functions that take other functions as arguments and/or return functions as return values.

We've seen quite a few uses for them. Now is a good time to list those uses to see just how useful the idea is.

Replace for loops over arrays

`forEach()`, `map()`, `filter()`, and `reduce()` are higher-order functions that let us operate effectively over arrays. We saw how we could chain them to build complex calculations.

• See pages 257, 294, 301, and 306.

Operate effectively on nested data

Changing a value nested deeply requires making copies of data along the path to the value you want to modify. We developed `update()` and `nestedUpdate()`, both higher-order functions, that let us surgically apply an operation to a particular value, regardless of how deeply nested it is.

• See pages 358 and 380.

Apply a copy-on-write discipline

Our copy-on-write discipline had a lot of duplicated code. We copied, modified, then returned. `withArrayCopy()` and `withObjectCopy()` were a way to apply any operation (the callback) in a context of a copy-on-write discipline. It's a great example of codifying a discipline into code.

• See pages 271 and 275.

Codify our try/catch logging policy

We built a function called `wrapLogging()` that could take any function and return a function that does the same thing that catches and logs errors. It was an example of a function that transforms the behavior of another function.

• See page 282.

Conclusion

In the last chapters, we applied two refactorings to arrive at our three main functional tools for operating on arrays of data. In this chapter, we learned how to apply the same refactorings to operations on nested data. We used recursion to work on data nested arbitrarily deep. We discussed the design implications of having such powerful operations on data and how to avoid the problems that power brings.

Summary

- `update()` is a functional tool that implements a common pattern. It lets you modify a value inside of an object without manually pulling the value out and setting it back in.

- `nestedUpdate()` is a functional tool that operates on deeply nested data. It is very useful for modifying a value when you know the path of keys to where it is located.

- Iteration (loops) can often be clearer than recursion. But recursion is clearer and easier when operating on nested data.

- Recursion can use the function call stack to keep track of where it left off before calling itself. This lets a recursive function's structure mirror the structure of nested data.

- Deep nesting can lead to difficulty of understanding. When you operate on deeply nested data, you often have to remember all of the data structures and their keys along the path.

- You can apply abstraction barriers to key data structures so that you don't have as much to remember. This can make working with deep structures easier.

Up next . . .

Now that we have a good grasp of first-class values and higher-order functions, we are going to begin applying them to one of the hardest parts of modern programming: distributed systems. Whether we like it or not, much software today has a frontend and a backend component, at the very least. Sharing resources like data between the frontend and backend can get complicated. By using the ideas of first-class values and higher-order functions, we can get a handle on them. See you in the next chapter.

In this chapter

- Learn how to draw timeline diagrams from code.

- Understand how to read timeline diagrams to find bugs.

- Discover how to improve code design by reducing resources
  shared between timelines.

In this chapter, we will start using timeline diagrams to represent sequences of actions over time. They help us understand how our software runs. They are particularly useful in a distributed system, like when a web client talks to a web server. Timeline diagrams help us diagnose and predict bugs. We can then develop a solution.

There's a bug!

MegaMart support is getting a lot of phone calls about the shopping cart showing the wrong total. The customers add stuff to their cart, it tells them it will cost $X, but when they check out, they are charged $Y. That's no good, and the customers are not happy. Let's see if we can debug this for them.

We can't reproduce it when we click through slowly

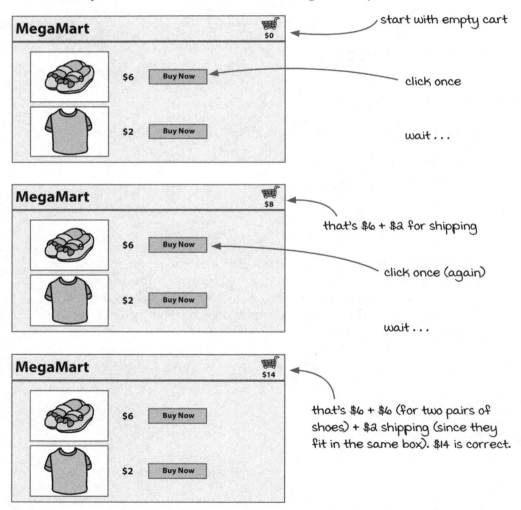

The slow clickthrough seems to work. But clicking things quickly will result in a different outcome. Let's check it out.

Now we can try to click twice fast

Customers told us the bug happened when they clicked quickly

We can reproduce the bug by clicking on the buy button twice very quickly. Let's see that:

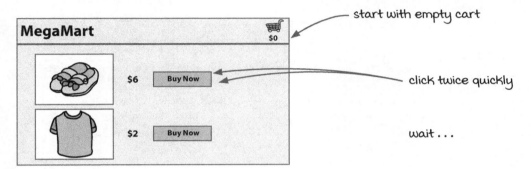

start with empty cart

click twice quickly

wait . . .

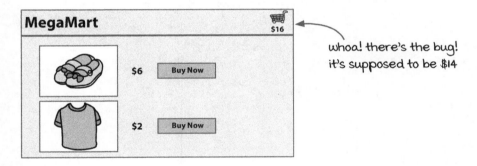

whoa! there's the bug!
it's supposed to be $14

We tested it a few more times and got a variety of results

We ran the same scenario (add shoes twice fast) several times. We got these answers:

- $14   the correct answer
- $16
- $22

 ## Noodle on it

It looks like the speed of the clicks is causing a problem. What do you think is happening?

Let's read the code to understand the bug

Here is the relevant code from the add-to-cart buttons:
`add_item_to_cart()` is the handler function called when the
button is pressed.

this function is run when the user clicks add to cart

```
function add_item_to_cart(name, price, quantity) {
  cart = add_item(cart, name, price, quantity);
  calc_cart_total();
}
```

read and write to cart global variable

```
function calc_cart_total() {
  total = 0;
  cost_ajax(cart, function(cost) {
    total += cost;
    shipping_ajax(cart, function(shipping) {
      total += shipping;
      update_total_dom(total);
    });
  });
}
```

AJAX request to products API
callback when request is complete
AJAX request to sales API
callback when sales API answers
add them up and show in DOM

It's also useful to see the traditional use case diagram. Notice that
the code talks to two different APIs sequentially:

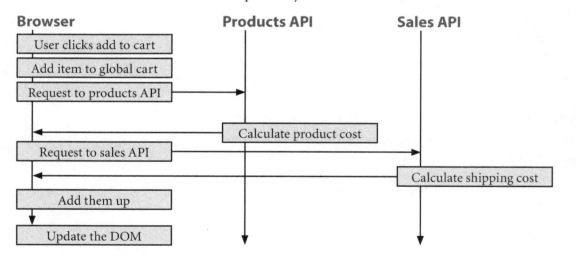

Unfortunately, both the code and the use case diagrams look correct. And, in fact, the behavior of the system is correct if you add
one item to the cart and wait a while before you add the next. We
need a way to understand how the system operates when you don't
wait—when two things are running at the same time. Let's look at
timeline diagrams on the next page, which show us just that.

The timeline diagram shows what happens over time

Following, you can see a timeline diagram showing two clicks that occur very quickly. A *timeline* is a sequence of actions. A *timeline diagram* graphically represents a sequence of actions over time. When put side by side, we can see how the actions can interact and interfere with each other.

Vocab time

A *timeline* is a sequence of actions over time. There can be multiple timelines running at the same time in your system.

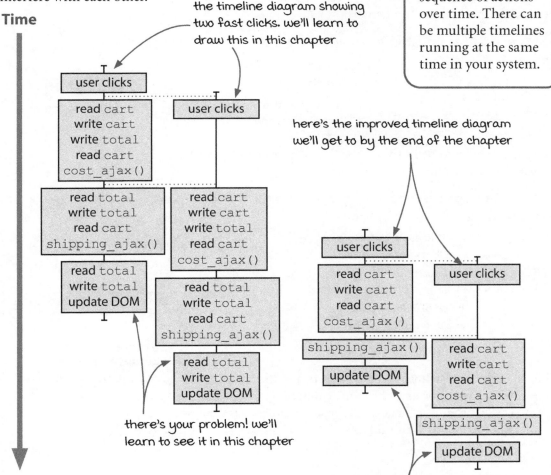

Believe it or not, the diagram on the left clearly shows the problem that causes the incorrect behavior. In this chapter, we're going to learn how to draw timeline diagrams from code. We're going to learn how to read the diagram to see issues with timing. And we're going to fix this bug (mostly!) using some of the principles of timelines.

There's a lot to learn, and the angry customers won't wait! So let's get started learning to draw these diagrams.

The two fundamentals of timeline diagrams

Timeline diagrams show two main things: what actions will run in sequence and what will run in parallel. By visualizing those two things, we can get a good understanding of how our code will run—whether correctly or incorrectly. These two fundamental rules will guide us to translate our code into timeline diagrams. Let's look at these two fundamentals.

1. If two actions occur in order, put them in the same timeline

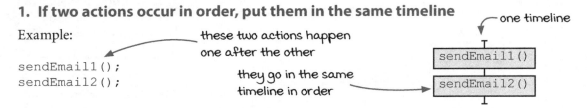

Only actions need to be in timelines. Calculations can be left out because they don't depend on when they are run.

2. If two actions can happen at the same time or out of order, they belong in separate timelines

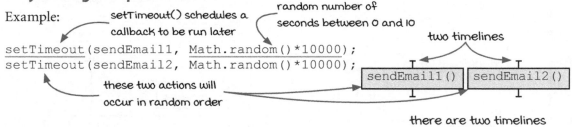

We have different timelines when actions run in different threads, processes, machines, or asynchronous callbacks. In this case, we have two asynchronous callbacks. Because the timeout is random, we don't know which will run first.

Summary

1. Actions either run sequentially or in parallel.

2. Sequential actions go in one timeline, one after the other.

3. Parallel actions go in multiple timelines side-by-side.

Once you can apply these rules, translating code is just a matter of understanding how the code runs over time.

It's your turn

Here's some code that handles dinner. Draw the timeline diagram that corresponds to it. Each of the functions that `dinner()` calls is an action.

```
function dinner(food) {
  cook(food);
  serve(food);
  eat(food);
}
```

draw your diagram here

Answer

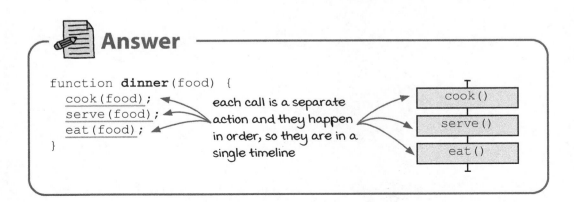

It's your turn

Here's some code for three people eating dinner separately. Each happens as an asynchronous callback—dinner() is run when a button is clicked. Finish the timeline diagram that corresponds to three fast button clicks.

```
function dinner(food) {
  cook(food);
  serve(food);
  eat(food);
}

button.addEventListener('click', dinner);
```

we use dotted lines to show that the clicks happen in different timelines but not simultaneously

finish the timeline diagram for three clicks here

Click 1   Click 2   Click 3

 **Answer**

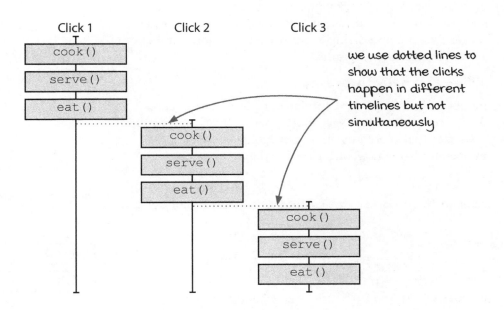

we use dotted lines to show that the clicks happen in different timelines but not simultaneously

Two tricky details about the order of actions

It's important to identify every action and to understand what order they are executed in. Every language has its own execution details, and JavaScript is no different. We've already seen this in part 1, but it's worth emphasizing again because it's going to be very important in timeline diagrams.

1. ++ and += are really three steps

Two operators in JavaScript (and similar languages like Java, C, C++, and C#, among others) are very short to write. But their brevity hides the fact that there are three steps going on. Here's the increment operator being used on a global variable:

```
total++;
```
this single operator
does three steps

This increments the variable `total`. However, it's just a shortcut for this:

```
var temp = total;        read (action)
temp = temp + 1;         addition (calculation)
total = temp;            write (action)
```

here's the diagram

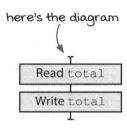

That's three steps. First, it reads `total`, then it adds one to it, then it writes `total` back. If `total` is a global variable, then steps 1 and 3 are actions. The second step, adding one, is a calculation, so it doesn't go on the diagram. This means that when you diagram `total++` or `total+=3`, you will have to diagram two different actions, the read and the write.

2. Arguments are executed before the function is called

If you call a function with an argument, the argument is executed before the function you're passing it to. That defines the order of execution that needs to show up in the timeline diagram. Here's an example where we are logging (action) the value of a global variable (action):

```
console.log(total)
```

the diagram for
both is the same

This code logs a global variable total. To see the order clearly, we can convert it to equivalent code:

```
var temp = total;
console.log(temp);
```

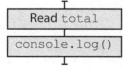

This clearly shows that the read to the total global variable goes first. It's very important to get all of the actions onto the diagram and in the right order.

Drawing the add-to-cart timeline: Step 1

We just learned the two main things that a timeline diagram shows—what is sequential and what is parallel. Now let's draw the diagram for our add-to-cart code. There are three steps to drawing a timeline diagram:

1. Identify the actions.

2. Draw each action, whether sequential or parallel.

3. Simplify using platform-specific knowledge.

1. Identify the actions

We'll just underline all of the actions. We can ignore calculations:

```
function add_item_to_cart(name, price, quantity) {
    cart = add_item(cart, name, price, quantity);
    calc_cart_total();
}

function calc_cart_total() {
    total = 0;
    cost_ajax(cart, function(cost) {
        total += cost;
        shipping_ajax(cart, function(shipping) {
            total += shipping;
            update_total_dom(total);
        });
    });
}
```

reading and writing global variables

read cart then call cost_ajax()

read total then write total

Actions
1. Read `cart`.
2. Write `cart`.
3. Write `total = 0`.
4. Read `cart`.
5. Call `cost_ajax()`.
6. Read `total`.
7. Write `total`.
8. Read `cart`.
9. Call `shipping_ajax()`.
10. Read `total`.
11. Write `total`.
12. Read `total`.
13. Call `update_total_dom()`.

That's 13 actions in this short section of code. We should also be aware that this has two asynchronous callbacks. One callback is passed to `cost_ajax()` and the other is passed to `shipping_ajax()`. We haven't seen how to draw callbacks yet. Let's put this code aside (remember, we just finished step 1) and come back to it after we've learned how to draw callbacks.

Asynchronous calls require new timelines

We've just seen that asynchronous callbacks happen in a new timeline. It's important to understand how that works, which is why you'll find a few pages describing the plumbing of JavaScript's asynchronous engine. You should read those pages if you're interested. Here, I'm just going to talk about why we're using the dotted lines.

Here's some illustrative code that saves the user and the document and manages loading spinners for them:

```
saveUserAjax(user, function() {          ── save the user to the server (ajax)
  setUserLoadingDOM(false);              ── hide user loading spinner
});
setUserLoadingDOM(true);                 ── show user loading spinner
saveDocumentAjax(document, function() {  ── save the document to the server (ajax)
  setDocLoadingDOM(false);               ── hide document
});                                          loading spinner
setDocLoadingDOM(true);        show document
                               loading spinner
```

This code is really interesting because the individual lines of code are executed in an order that is different from how they're written. Let's walk through the first two steps of diagramming for this code to get a timeline diagram.

First, we underline all of the actions. We'll assume that user and document are local vars, so reading them is not an action:

```
saveUserAjax(user, function() {
  setUserLoadingDOM(false);
});
setUserLoadingDOM(true);
saveDocumentAjax(document, function() {
  setDocLoadingDOM(false);
});
setDocLoadingDOM(true);
```

> **Three steps to diagramming**
> 1. Identify actions.
> 2. Draw each action.
> 3. Simplify.

Actions
1. saveUserAjax()
2. setUserLoadingDOM(false)
3. setUserLoadingDOM(true)
4. saveDocumentAjax()
5. setDocLoadingDOM(false)
6. setDocLoadingDOM(true)

Step 2 is to actually draw it. We'll step through the creation together over the next few pages. But here is what it will look like when we're done. If you understand it, you can skip ahead.

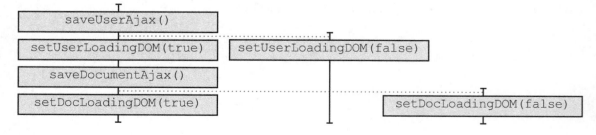

Different languages, different threading models

JavaScript uses a single-threaded, asynchronous model. Whenever you have a new asynchronous callback, it creates a new timeline. But many platforms don't use this same threading model. Let's go over this threading model and some other common ways that threading works in languages.

We have asynchronous callbacks in JavaScript. What if I'm in a language without them?

Jenna from dev team

Single-threaded, synchronous

Some languages or platforms do not allow multiple threads by default. For instance, PHP runs this way if you don't import the threading library. Everything happens in order. When you do any kind of input/output, your whole program blocks while waiting for it to complete. Although it limits what you can do, those limits make reasoning about the system very easy. Your one thread means one timeline, but you can still have other timelines if you contact a different computer, like you would with an API. Those timelines can't share memory, so you eliminate a huge class of shared resources.

Single-threaded, asynchronous

JavaScript has one thread. If you want to respond to user input, read files, or make network calls (any kind of input/output), you use an asynchronous model. Typically, this means that you give it a callback that will be called with the result of the input/output operation. Because the input/output operation can take an unknown amount of time, the callback will be called at some uncontrollable, unknown time in the future. That's why doing an asynchronous call creates a new timeline.

Multi-threaded

Java, Python, Ruby, C, and C# (among many others) allow multi-threaded execution. Multi-threaded is the most difficult to program because it gives you almost no constraints for ordering. Every new thread creates a new timeline. Languages in these categories allow unlimited interleaving between threads. To get around that, you need to use constructs like locks, which prevent two threads from running code protected by the lock at the same time. It gives you some control over ordering.

Message-passing processes

Erlang and Elixir have a threading model that allows for many different processes to run simultaneously. Each process is a separate timeline. The processes don't share any memory. Instead, they must communicate using messages. The unique thing is that processes choose which message they will process next. That's different from method calls in Java or other OO languages. The actions of individual timelines do interleave, but because they don't share any memory, they usually don't share resources, which means you don't have to worry about the large number of possible orderings.

Building the timeline step-by-step

We've seen the final result of building the timeline, but it will be good to step through creating it one line of code at a time. Here's our code again, and the actions that are in it:

```
1 saveUserAjax(user, function() {
2   setUserLoadingDOM(false);
3 });
4 setUserLoadingDOM(true);
5 saveDocumentAjax(document, function() {
6   setDocLoadingDOM(false);
7 });
8 setDocLoadingDOM(true);
```

Actions
1. saveUserAjax()
2. setUserLoadingDOM(false)
3. setUserLoadingDOM(true)
4. saveDocumentAjax()
5. setDocLoadingDOM(false)
6. setDocLoadingDOM(true)

JavaScript, in general, is executed top to bottom, so let's start at the top with line 1. It's easy. It needs a fresh timeline because none exist yet in the diagram:

> **Three steps to diagramming**
> 1. Identify actions.
> 2. Draw each action.
> 3. Simplify.

```
1 saveUserAjax(user, function() {
```

```
        saveUserAjax()
```

Next up, line 2 is part of a callback. That callback is asynchronous, which means it will be called sometime in the future when the request completes. It needs a new timeline. We also draw a dotted line to show that the callback will be called after the ajax function. That makes sense because we can't have the response come back before the request is sent.

```
2   setUserLoadingDOM(false);
```

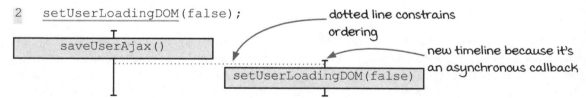

Line 3 doesn't have any actions on it, so we move onto line 4. It executes setUserLoadingDOM(true). But where does it go? Since it's not in a callback, it happens in the original timeline. Let's put it there, right after the dotted line:

```
4 setUserLoadingDOM(true);
```

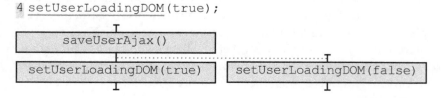

We've already managed to draw half of the actions onto the diagram. Here's the code, actions, and diagram for reference:

```
1 saveUserAjax(user, function() {
2   setUserLoadingDOM(false);
3 });
4 setUserLoadingDOM(true);
5 saveDocumentAjax(document, function() {
6   setDocLoadingDOM(false);
7 });
8 setDocLoadingDOM(true);
```

Actions
1. saveUserAjax()
2. setUserLoadingDOM(false)
3. setUserLoadingDOM(true)
4. saveDocumentAjax()
5. setDocLoadingDOM(false)
6. setDocLoadingDOM(true)

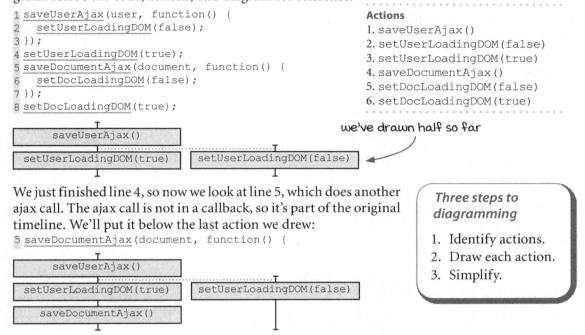

we've drawn half so far

We just finished line 4, so now we look at line 5, which does another ajax call. The ajax call is not in a callback, so it's part of the original timeline. We'll put it below the last action we drew:

```
5 saveDocumentAjax(document, function() {
```

Three steps to diagramming

1. Identify actions.
2. Draw each action.
3. Simplify.

It is part of an asynchronous callback, which creates a new timeline that will start sometime in the future, when the response comes back. We don't know when that will be, because networks are unpredictable. The diagram captures that uncertainty with a new timeline:

```
6   setDocLoadingDOM(false);
```

new timeline captures ordering uncertainty

Line 8 has the last action. It's in the original timeline:

```
8 setDocLoadingDOM(true);
```

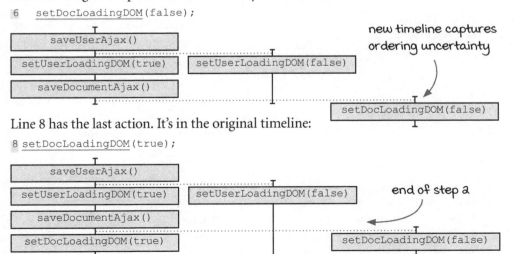

end of step 2

We've completed step 2 for this code. We will do step 3 later. For now, let's go back to our add-to-cart code and finish step 2.

Drawing the add-to-cart timeline: Step 2

A few pages ago, we identified all of the actions in this code. We also noted that there were two asynchronous callbacks. It's time for step 2: Draw the actions on a diagram. Here's what we had when we left off after identifying the actions:

> **Three steps to diagramming**
>
> 1. Identify actions.
> 2. Draw each action.
> 3. Simplify.

```
function add_item_to_cart(name, price, quantity) {
  cart = add_item(cart, name, price, quantity);
  calc_cart_total();
}

function calc_cart_total() {
  total = 0;
  cost_ajax(cart, function(cost) {
    total += cost;
    shipping_ajax(cart, function(shipping) {
      total += shipping;
      update_total_dom(total);
    });
  });
}
```

Actions

1. Read `cart`.
2. Write `cart`.
3. Write `total = 0`.
4. Read `cart`.
5. Call `cost_ajax()`.
6. Read `total`.
7. Write `total`.
8. Read `cart`.
9. Call `shipping_ajax()`.
10. Read `total`.
11. Write `total`.
12. Read `total`.
13. Call `update_total_dom()`.

2. Draw each action, whether sequential or parallel

Now that we have all the actions, our next step is to draw them, in order, on the diagram. Remember, ajax callbacks, of which we have two, require new timelines.

all 13 actions are on the diagram

cost_ajax() is ajax, so the callback is called on a new timeline

shipping_ajax() is also ajax, so new timeline

You can walk through the steps yourself to draw this diagram. We can check a few things: (1) All of the actions we identified (there were 13) are on the diagram, and (2) each asynchronous callback (there were two) resulted in a new timeline.

Before we move onto step 3, we'll focus on what this diagram is telling us.

Timeline diagrams capture the two kinds of sequential code

There are two ways that code can execute sequentially. Normally, any action can interleave between any two other actions in another timeline. However, in some circumstances, we can prevent interleaving. For example, in JavaScript's threading model, synchronous actions don't interleave. We'll see more ways to prevent interleaving later.

That gives us our two kinds of sequential code. The timeline diagram can capture both.

Code that can be interleaved

Any amount of time can pass between two actions. We represent each action with a box. The time between them is represented with a line. We can draw the line to be short or long, depending on how much time it takes, but however long you draw it, it means the same thing: There is an unknown amount of time that may pass between action 1 and action 2.

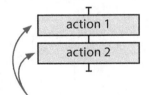

unknown amount of time may pass between these, and actions from other timelines may interleave

These two timelines will execute differently. The timeline on the left might interleave, meaning an action 3 (not shown) may run between action 1 and action 2. In the timeline on the right, this is impossible.

The timeline on the left (interleavable actions) has two boxes, while the timeline on the right only has one box. Shorter timelines are easier to manage. We'd like fewer boxes rather than more.

We haven't put multiple actions into one box yet. We usually do that in step 3, which we haven't gotten to. But we will soon! There's just a little bit more to learn about what the diagram is telling us.

Code that cannot be interleaved

Two actions run one after the other, and something is making it so that nothing can be run in between. What's causing it? It could be due to the runtime or because of some clever programming (we'll learn some of that later). We draw the actions in the same box.

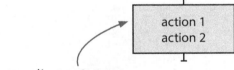

these actions occur one after the other with no possibility of interleaving

Vocab time

Actions on different timelines may *interleave* if they can occur between each other. This happens when multiple threads run at the same time.

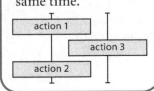

Timeline diagrams capture the uncertain ordering of parallel code

In addition to representing sequential code, timeline diagrams express the uncertainty of ordering among parallel code.

Parallel code is represented by timelines drawn side by side. But just because they are side by side does not mean action 1 and action 2 will run at the same time. Actions in parallel timelines can run in three orders. In general, all three are possible.

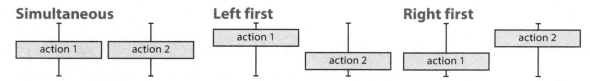

When we read a timeline diagram, we have to see these three orders, regardless of how long the lines are and how the actions line up. The following diagrams all mean the same thing, even though they look different:

these three diagrams represent the same thing

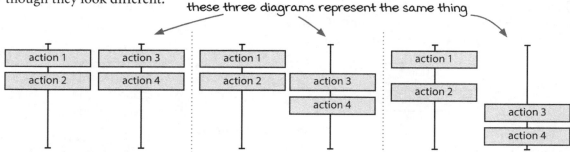

Being able to see these as the same is an important skill for reading timeline diagrams. You need to be able to imagine the *possible orderings*—especially those that may be problematic. We may draw diagrams differently to highlight one ordering, just for clarity.

Two timelines with one box each can run in three possible orderings. As timelines get longer or you get more timelines, the number of possible orderings goes up very quickly.

Like interleavings, the possible orderings are also dependent on your platform's threading model. It's also important to capture this in your timeline diagram, which we'll do in step 3.

 **Vocab time**

Multiple timelines can run in different ways, depending on timing. The ways that timelines can run are known as *possible orderings*. A single timeline has one possible ordering.

Principles of working with timelines

When we work with timelines, there are a few principles that guide us to improve our code so that it's easier to understand and work with. Remember, one reason systems are hard is because of the number of possible orderings you have to account for. Although these five principles always apply, in this chapter we're focusing on the first three. We'll see the others in chapters 16 and 17.

1. Fewer timelines are easier

The easiest system has a single timeline. Every action happens immediately after the action before it. However, in modern systems, we have to deal with multiple timelines. Multiple threads, asynchronous callbacks, and client-server communication all have multiple timelines.

Every new timeline dramatically makes the system harder to understand. If we can reduce the number of timelines (t in the formula on the right), it will help tremendously. Unfortunately, we often can't control how many timelines we have.

Formula for number of possible orderings

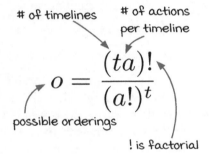

2. Shorter timelines are easier

Another lever we have is to reduce the number of steps in each timeline. If we can eliminate steps (decrease a in the formula on the right), we can reduce the number of possible orderings dramatically.

3. Sharing fewer resources is easier

If two steps on different timelines don't share resources, the order between them doesn't matter. It doesn't reduce the number of possible orderings, but it reduces the number of possible orderings that you have to consider. When looking at two timelines, you really only have to consider the steps that share resources across timelines.

4. Coordinate when resources are shared

If we eliminate as many shared resources as we can, we will still be left with some resources that we can't get rid of. We need to ensure that the timelines share these resources in a safe way. That means ensuring they take turns in the right order. Coordinating between timelines means eliminating possible orderings that don't give us the right result.

5. Manipulate time as a first-class concept

The ordering and proper timing of actions is difficult. We can make this easier by creating reusable objects that manipulate the timeline. We'll see examples of those in the next couple of chapters.

In this and the next few chapters, we're going to apply these principles to eliminate bugs and make our code easier to get right.

JavaScript's single-thread

JavaScript's threading model reduces the size of the problems of timelines sharing resources. Because JavaScript has only one main thread, most actions do not need separate boxes on the timeline. Here's an example. Imagine this Java code:

```java
int x = 0;

public void addToX(int y) {
  x += y;
}
```

In Java, if I have a variable shared between two threads, doing the += operation is actually three steps:

1. Read the current value.

2. Add a number to it.

3. Store the new value back.

+ is a calculation, so it doesn't need to be on the timeline. That means that two threads running the addToX() method at the same time can interleave in multiple ways, resulting in different possible answers. Java's threading model works that way.

However, JavaScript only has one thread. So it doesn't have this particular problem. Instead, in JavaScript, when you have the thread, it's yours for as long as you keep using it. That means you can read and write as much as you want with no interleaving. In addition, no two actions can run at the same time.

When you're doing standard imperative programming, like reading and writing to shared variables, there are no timelines to worry about.

However, once you introduce an asynchronous call into the mix, you've reintroduced the problem. Asynchronous calls are run by the runtime at an unknown time in the future. That means the lines between the boxes can stretch and contract. In JavaScript, it is important to know whether you are doing synchronous or asynchronous operations.

- JavaScript has one thread.

- Synchronous actions, like modifying a global variable, cannot be interleaved between timelines.

- Asynchronous calls are run by the runtime at an unknown time in the future.

- No two synchronous actions can run simultaneously.

+ is a calculation (it doesn't matter when it is run), so we don't need it on the timeline

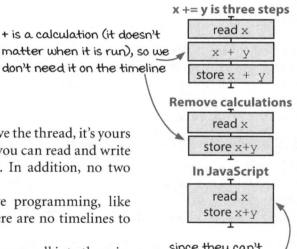

x += y is three steps

| read x |
| x + y |
| store x + y |

Remove calculations

| read x |
| store x+y |

In JavaScript

| read x
store x+y |

since they can't be interleaved in JavaScript, we can put them in the same box

JavaScript's asynchronous queue

The browser's JavaScript engine has a queue, called the *job queue*, which is processed by the *event loop*. The event loop takes one job off of the queue and runs it to completion, then takes the next job and runs it to completion, and loops like that forever. The event loop is run in a single thread, so no two jobs are run at the same time.

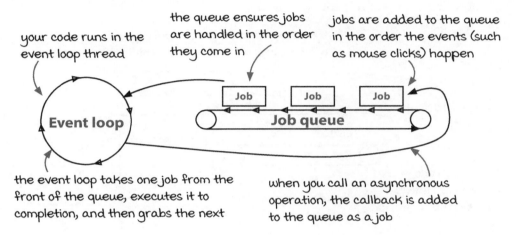

your code runs in the event loop thread

the queue ensures jobs are handled in the order they come in

jobs are added to the queue in the order the events (such as mouse clicks) happen

Event loop

Job **Job** **Job**

Job queue

the event loop takes one job from the front of the queue, executes it to completion, and then grabs the next

when you call an asynchronous operation, the callback is added to the queue as a job

What is a job?

The jobs on the job queue have two parts: the event data and the callback to handle that event. The event loop will call the callback with the event data as the only argument. Callbacks are just functions that define what should be executed by the event loop. The event loop just runs them with the event data as the first argument.

What puts jobs on the queue?

Jobs are added to the queue in response to events. Events are things like mouse clicks, typing on the keyboard, or AJAX events. If you put "click" callback function on a button, the callback function and event data (data about the click) are added to the queue. Because we can't predict mouse clicks or other events, we say they arrive *unpredictably*. The job queue brings some sanity back.

What does the engine do while there are no jobs?

Sometimes there are no jobs to process. The event loop might sit idle and save power, or it might use the time for maintenance like garbage collection. It's up to the browser developers.

AJAX and the event queue

AJAX is a term for browser-based web requests. It stands for *Asynchronous JavaScript And XML*. Yes, it's a silly acronym. And we're not always using XML. But the term stuck. In the browser, we often communicate with the server using AJAX.

In this book, functions that make AJAX requests will have an `_ajax` suffix on them. That way, you know that the functions are asynchronous.

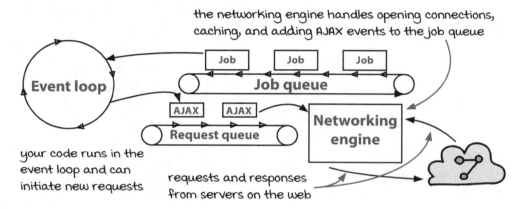

the networking engine handles opening connections, caching, and adding AJAX events to the job queue

your code runs in the event loop and can initiate new requests

requests and responses from servers on the web

When you initiate an AJAX request in JavaScript, behind the scenes, your AJAX request is added to a queue to be processed by the networking engine.

After adding it to the queue, your code continues to run. It won't wait for the request in any way—that's where the *asynchronous* in AJAX comes in. Many languages have synchronous requests, which do wait for the request to complete before continuing. Because the network is chaotic, responses come back out of order, so the AJAX callbacks will be added to the job queue out of order.

If it doesn't wait for the request, how do you get the response?

You can register callbacks for various events on the AJAX request. Remember, a callback is just a function that will be called when an event fires.

Throughout the life of the request, many events are fired by the networking engine. There are two events that are particularly common to use: `load` and `error`. `load` is called when the response has been completely downloaded. `error` is when something goes wrong. If you register callbacks for those two events, you'll be able to run code when the request is finished.

- AJAX stands for Asynchronous JavaScript And XML.

- AJAX is how we make web requests from JavaScript in the browser.

- Responses are handled asynchronously by callbacks.

- Responses come back out of order.

A complete asynchronous example

Here's a simple page from the MegaMart site. Let's look at all the steps to get the buy button to add items to the cart.

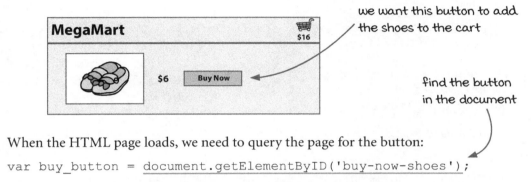

we want this button to add the shoes to the cart

find the button in the document

When the HTML page loads, we need to query the page for the button:

```
var buy_button = document.getElementByID('buy-now-shoes');
```

Then we need to set a callback for clicks to this button:

initiate an ajax request

define a callback for 'click' events on the button

```
buy_button.addEventListener('click', function() {
  add_to_cart_ajax({item: 'shoes'}, function() {
    shopping_cart.add({item: 'shoes'});
    render_cart_icon();
    buy_button.innerHTML = "Buy Now";
  });
  buy_button.innerHTML = "loading";
});
```

this callback will be run when the ajax completes

sometime later, when the ajax request is complete, we update the UI again

immediately after initiating the request, change the button to say "loading"

Sometime later, the user clicks the button, which adds a job to the queue. The event loop will work its way through jobs in the queue until it gets to that click event job. It will call the callback we registered.

The callback adds an AJAX request to the request queue, which will be consumed by the networking engine sometime later. Then the callback changes the button text. That's the end of the callback, so the event loop takes the next job off the queue.

Later, the AJAX request completes, and the networking engine adds a job to the queue with the callback we registered. The callback makes its way to the front of the queue, and then it is run. It updates the shopping cart, renders the cart icon, and sets the button text back to what it was.

The timeline of this example

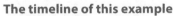
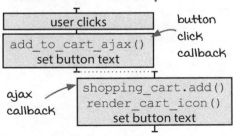

button click callback

ajax callback

Simplifying the timeline

We've finished step 2 of diagramming timelines. Now that we understand how our platform runs, we can simplify it in step 3. Here's what we had:

```
1 saveUserAjax(user, function() {
2   setUserLoadingDOM(false);
3 });
4 setUserLoadingDOM(true);
5 saveDocumentAjax(document, function() {
6   setDocLoadingDOM(false);
7 });
8 setDocLoadingDOM(true);
```

Actions

1. saveUserAjax()
2. setUserLoadingDOM(false)
3. setUserLoadingDOM(true)
4. saveDocumentAjax()
5. setDocLoadingDOM(false)
6. setDocLoadingDOM(true)

We're now starting step 3. This is where we simplify the diagram with knowledge of the threading model of our platform. Since all three of these timelines are running in JavaScript in the browser, we can apply our knowledge of the browser's runtime to this diagram. In JavaScript, this boils down to two simplifying steps:

> **Three steps to diagramming**
>
> 1. Identify actions.
> 2. Draw each action.
> 3. Simplify.

1. Consolidate all actions on a single timeline.

2. Consolidate timelines that end by creating one new timeline.

We have to perform these steps in order. Let's turn the page and get to it.

On the last page, we had this diagram. Remember, this is the end of step 2. We have a complete diagram. Now we can simplify it in step 3:

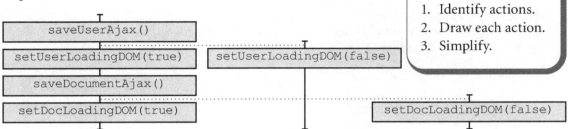

In JavaScript, we have two simplifying steps we can perform thanks to the single-threaded runtime:

1. Consolidate all actions on a single timeline.

2. Consolidate timelines that end by creating one new timeline.

Let's go through these two now.

1. Consolidate all actions on a single timeline

Since JavaScript runs in a single thread, actions on a single timeline can't be interleaved. A timeline runs to completion before any other timeline is started. If we have dotted lines, they are moved to the end of the timeline.

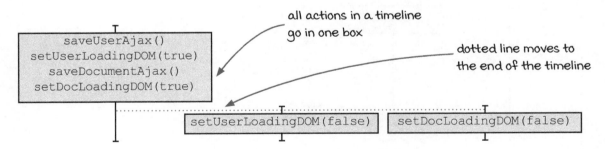

We can see how the JavaScript runtime simplifies the execution of code by eliminating lots of possible orderings.

2. Consolidate timelines that end by creating one new timeline

Because the first timeline ends by creating two new timelines, this rule doesn't apply. We'll see it apply in our add-to-cart code. But that means we're done with this one!

 **It's your turn**

Here's the code and diagram we used in a previous exercise. Since this is running in JavaScript, we have two simplification steps to do. Perform the first step where you consolidate actions. Assume cook(), serve(), and eat() are synchronous actions.

```
function dinner(food) {
  cook(food);
  serve(food);
  eat(food);
}
```

just do this step

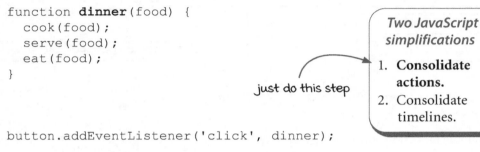

Two JavaScript simplifications

1. **Consolidate actions.**
2. Consolidate timelines.

```
button.addEventListener('click', dinner);
```

simplify this diagram

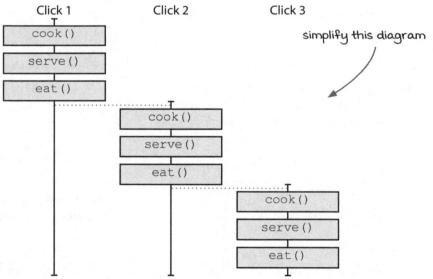

 **Answer**

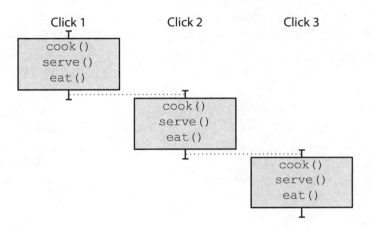

It's your turn

Here's the code and diagram we used in the previous exercise. Since this is running in JavaScript, we have two simplification steps to do. Perform the second step where you consolidate timelines. Assume cook(), serve(), and eat() are synchronous actions.

```
function dinner(food) {
  cook(food);
  serve(food);
  eat(food);
}
```

just do this step

> **Two JavaScript simplifications**
> 1. Consolidate actions.
> 2. **Consolidate timelines.**

```
button.addEventListener('click', dinner);
```

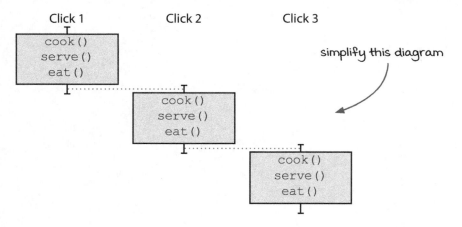

simplify this diagram

 **Answer**

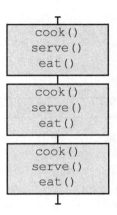

Reading our finished timeline

Before we move on, let's look at what this timeline we just finished
is telling us:

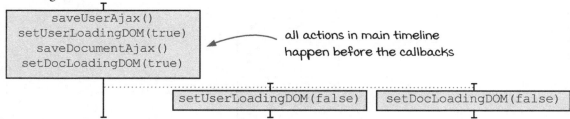

Remember, timeline diagrams show what possible orderings the
actions can take. By understanding those orderings, we can know
if our code will do the right thing. If we can find an ordering that
won't give the right result, we've found a bug. And if we can show
that all orderings give us the right result, we know our code is
good.

There are two kinds of orderings: certain and uncertain. Let's
look at the certain ones first. Because all of the actions on the main
timeline (on the left) are in a single timeline, we know that these
actions will happen in order. Further, because of the dotted line,
we know the main timeline will complete before the others run.

Now let's look at the uncertain orderings. Notice that the two
callback timelines have different orderings. As we saw before, there
are three possible orderings of one action in two timelines. Let's
look at them again:

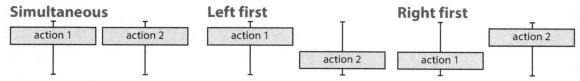

In JavaScript, simultaneous actions are impossible since there is
only one thread. So, we have two possible orderings, depending on
which ajax response comes back first:

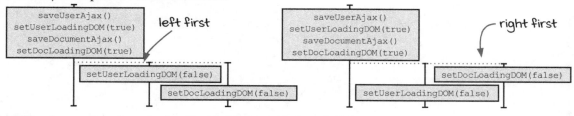

We're always showing the loading spinner, and then hiding it, in
that order. That's good, so this code doesn't have timing issues.

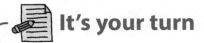 **It's your turn**

Here is a timeline diagram with three actions in JavaScript. List the possible orderings that this diagram indicates. You can draw them if you want to.

A		B
		C

write your answer here ↓

 **Answer**

1. A B C
2. B A C
3. B C A

Simplifying the add-to-cart timeline diagram: Step 3

Alright, folks! We've been waiting for step 3 for a while. We can now apply it to our add-to-cart timeline. Here's the result of step 2:

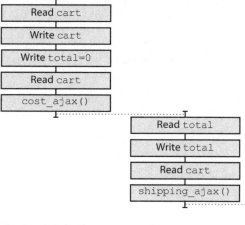

Because we're still in JavaScript in the browser, we're going to use the same two simplification steps we just used.

1. Consolidate all actions on a single timeline.

2. Consolidate timelines that end by creating one new timeline.

We have to perform these steps in order or it won't work right.

1. Consolidate all actions on a single timeline

Again, JavaScript runs in a single thread. No other thread will interrupt the current timeline, so there's no possibility of interleaving between these timelines. We can put all actions in a single timeline into a single box per timeline:

> **Two JavaScript simplifications**
> 1. Consolidate actions.
> 2. Consolidate timelines.

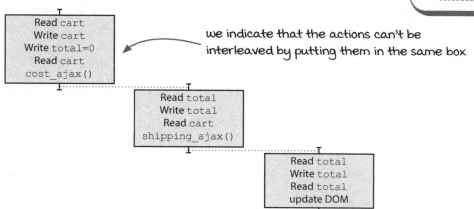

we indicate that the actions can't be interleaved by putting them in the same box

Here's where we were after consolidating all actions on a timeline into a single box on the last page:

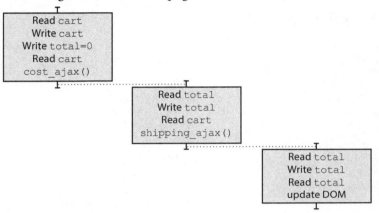

Now we can do the second simplification.

2. Consolidate timelines that end by creating one new timeline

Each timeline in our diagram ends by starting a new timeline. Each timeline ends with an ajax call where the callback continues the work. We can consolidate these three timelines into a single timeline:

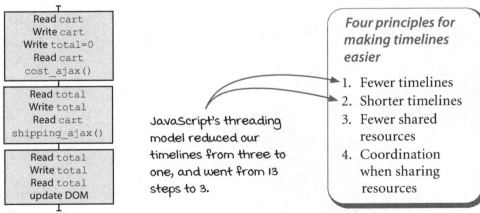

JavaScript's threading model reduced our timelines from three to one, and went from 13 steps to 3.

Four principles for making timelines easier

1. Fewer timelines
2. Shorter timelines
3. Fewer shared resources
4. Coordination when sharing resources

Note that we can't go back to step 1 at this point and put these all into one box. We have to leave it like this. Why? Because the separate boxes capture the possible interleaving that existed when they were shown on separate timelines.

This representation captures our intuition of callback chains—especially that they feel like a single timeline. It's also easier to draw. And that's the end of the three steps!

Review: Drawing the timeline (steps 1–3)

Let's see how far we've come. Our first step was identifying the actions in our code. There were 13:

```
function add_item_to_cart(name, price, quantity) {
  cart = add_item(cart, name, price, quantity);
  calc_cart_total();
}

function calc_cart_total() {
  total = 0;
  cost_ajax(cart, function(cost) {
    total += cost;
    shipping_ajax(cart, function(shipping) {
      total += shipping;
      update_total_dom(total);
    });
  });
}
```

Actions

1. Read `cart`.
2. Write `cart`.
3. Write `total = 0`.
4. Read `cart`.
5. Call `cost_ajax()`.
6. Read `total`.
7. Write `total`.
8. Read `cart`.
9. Call `shipping_ajax()`.
10. Read `total`.
11. Write `total`.
12. Read `total`.
13. Call `update_total_dom()`.

The second step was drawing the initial diagram. We captured two things in the timeline: whether the next action to draw was sequential or parallel. Sequential actions go in the same timeline. Parallel actions go in a new timeline:

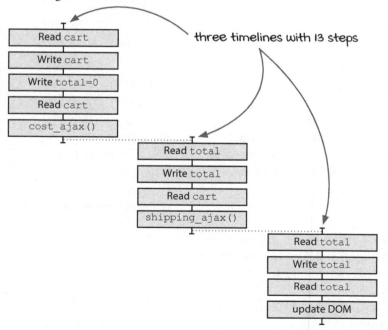

three timelines with 13 steps

> **Three steps to diagramming**
>
> 1. Identify actions.
> 2. Draw each action.
> 3. Simplify.

> **Four principles for making timelines easier**
>
> 1. Fewer timelines
> 2. Shorter timelines
> 3. Fewer shared resources
> 4. Coordination when sharing resources

The third step was simplification. Let's review it on the next page.

On the last page we had completed a review of step 2:

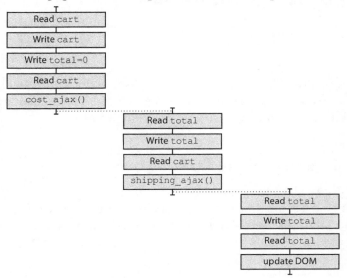

Three steps to diagramming

1. Identify actions.
2. Draw each action.
3. Simplify.

The third and last step was to simplify our timeline using knowledge of our platform. Since it runs in the browser in JavaScript, we applied two steps. JavaScript's single-threaded model allowed us to put every action in a single timeline into a single box. Then we could convert callbacks that continue the computation after an asynchronous action into a single timeline. The uncertainty of timing and the possibility of interleaving are captured in the diagram with multiple boxes.

Two JavaScript simplifications

1. Consolidate actions.
2. Consolidate timelines.

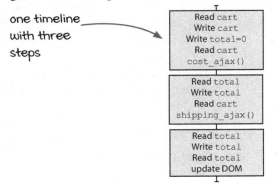

one timeline with three steps

Four principles for making timelines easier

1. Fewer timelines
2. Shorter timelines
3. Fewer shared resources
4. Coordination when sharing resources

The fact that we could simplify three timelines with 13 actions into a single, three-step timeline shows how much JavaScript's threading model helps simplify things. However, the diagram also shows that it doesn't completely eliminate the problem. Asynchronous actions still require separate boxes. On the next page, we'll see how this diagram lets us diagnose the bug we discovered.

Summary: Drawing timeline diagrams

Here is the skill of drawing timeline diagrams in a nutshell.

Identify actions

Every action goes on the timeline diagram. You should dig into composite actions until you have identified the atomic actions such as reading and writing to variables. Be careful with operations that look like one action but that are actually multiple actions, such as ++ and +=.

Draw actions

Actions can execute in two ways: in sequence or in parallel.

Actions that execute in sequence—one after the other

If actions occur in order, put them on the same timeline. This usually happens when two actions occur on subsequent lines. Sequential actions also occur in other execution semantics such as left-to-right argument evaluation order.

Actions that execute in parallel—simultaneous, left first, or right first

If they can happen at the same time or out of order, put them on separate timelines. These can occur for various reasons, including these:

- Asynchronous callbacks

- Multiple threads

- Multiple processes

- Multiple machines

Draw each action and use dotted lines to indicate constrained order. For instance, an ajax callback cannot occur before the ajax request. A dotted line can show that.

Simplify the timeline

The semantics of the particular language you are using might constrain the orderings further. We can apply those constraints to the timeline to help us understand it better. Here are general guidelines that apply to any language:

- If two actions cannot be interleaved, combine them into a single box.

- If one timeline ends and starts another, consolidate them into a single timeline.

- Add dotted lines when order is constrained.

Reading timelines

Actions in different timelines, in general, can occur in three different orders: simultaneous, left first, and right first. Evaluate the orders as impossible, desirable, or undesirable.

Timeline diagrams side-by-side can reveal problems

As we saw before, the steps the code takes to update the cart total look right for a single click to the button. The button only has a bug when we click it twice quickly. To see that situation, we have to put the timeline side by side with itself:

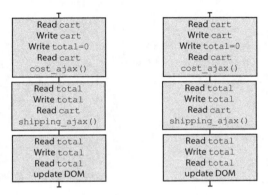

This shows that the two timelines, one for each click, can interleave with each other. There's just one more touch-up we have to do. Since the original step on the timelines will be handled in order (the event queue guarantees that), we can adjust this slightly. We'll add a dotted line to show that the second timeline can't start until after the first step of the first timeline is done:

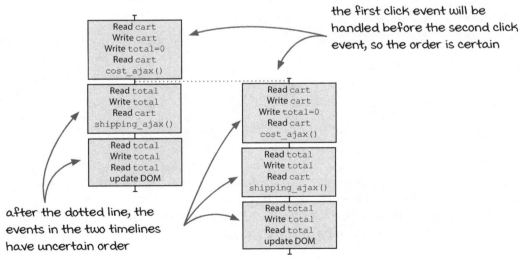

the first click event will be handled before the second click event, so the order is certain

after the dotted line, the events in the two timelines have uncertain order

It may not seem like it now, but this diagram is screaming with problems. By the end of the chapter, you should be able to see it yourself.

Two slow clicks get the right result

Now that we've got our diagram set up for two clicks, let's stretch out the lines between steps to emphasize different interleavings. Let's first look at the easy interleaving that always gets the right result—two slow clicks.

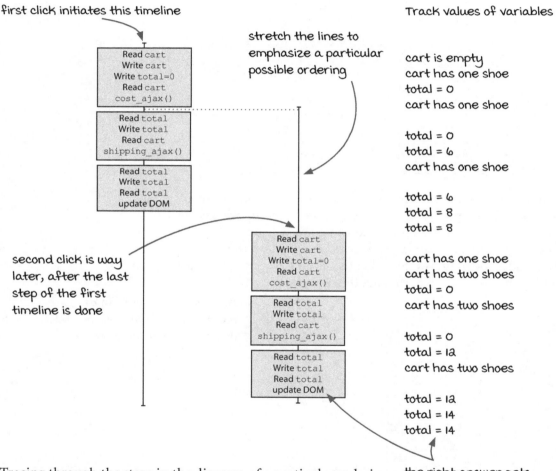

first click initiates this timeline

stretch the lines to emphasize a particular possible ordering

Track values of variables

Read cart
Write cart
Write total=0
Read cart
cost_ajax()

cart is empty
cart has one shoe
total = 0
cart has one shoe

Read total
Write total
Read cart
shipping_ajax()

total = 0
total = 6
cart has one shoe

Read total
Write total
Read total
update DOM

total = 6
total = 8
total = 8

second click is way later, after the last step of the first timeline is done

Read cart
Write cart
Write total=0
Read cart
cost_ajax()

cart has one shoe
cart has two shoes
total = 0
cart has two shoes

Read total
Write total
Read cart
shipping_ajax()

total = 0
total = 12
cart has two shoes

Read total
Write total
Read total
update DOM

total = 12
total = 14
total = 14

the right answer gets written to the DOM

Tracing through the steps in the diagram of a particular ordering shows how things play out. In this case, everything works out great. Now let's see if we can find a possible ordering that produces the wrong answer, $16, which we saw in the real system.

Two fast clicks can get the wrong result

We just saw an easy case where the second click happens after the first timeline is done. Let's see if we can find an ordering where it gets the wrong answer. We'll track the variables' values on the right:

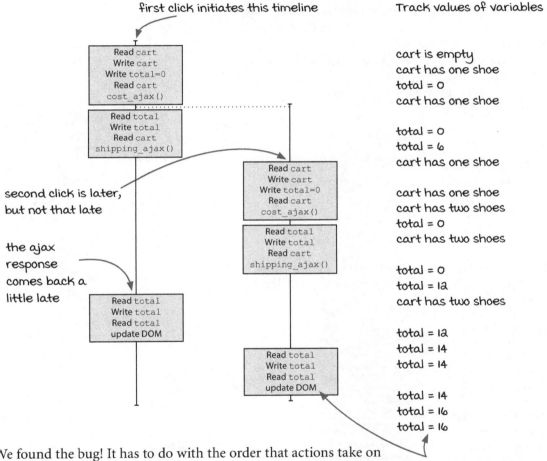

first click initiates this timeline

Track values of variables

Read cart	cart is empty
Write cart	cart has one shoe
Write total=0	total = 0
Read cart	cart has one shoe
cost_ajax()	

Read total	total = 0
Write total	total = 6
Read cart	cart has one shoe
shipping_ajax()	

second click is later, but not that late

Read cart	cart has one shoe
Write cart	cart has two shoes
Write total=0	total = 0
Read cart	cart has two shoes
cost_ajax()	

the ajax response comes back a little late

Read total	total = 0
Write total	total = 12
Read cart	cart has two shoes
shipping_ajax()	

Read total	total = 12
Write total	total = 14
Read total	total = 14
update DOM	

Read total	total = 14
Write total	total = 16
Read total	total = 16
update DOM	

the wrong answer gets written to the DOM

We found the bug! It has to do with the order that actions take on the click handler timelines. Since we can't control the interleaving of the steps, sometimes it happens this way, and sometimes it happens one of the other ways.

These two relatively short timelines can generate 10 possible orderings. Which ones are correct? Which ones are incorrect? We could do the work and trace through them, but most timelines are much longer. They can generate hundreds, thousands, or millions of possible orderings. Looking at each one of them is just not possible. We need a better way to guarantee that our code will work. Let's fix this code and make it easier to get it right.

Timelines that share resources can cause problems

We can remove problems by not sharing resources

We've got a pretty solid understanding of the timelines and our code. What in particular is causing the problem? In this case, the problem is caused by sharing resources. Both timelines are using the same global variables. They're stepping all over each other when they run interleaved.

Let's underline all of the global variables in the code.

```
function add_item_to_cart(name, price, quantity) {
  cart = add_item(cart, name, price, quantity);
  calc_cart_total();
}
function calc_cart_total() {
  total = 0;
  cost_ajax(cart, function(cost) {
    total += cost;
    shipping_ajax(cart, function(shipping) {
      total += shipping;
      update_total_dom(total);
    });
  });
}
```

global variables

Actions sharing the total global variable have a

Actions sharing the cart global variable have a

Actions sharing the DOM have a

Then, for clarity, we can annotate the timeline steps with information about which steps use which global variables:

if two steps share a resource, the order between them is important

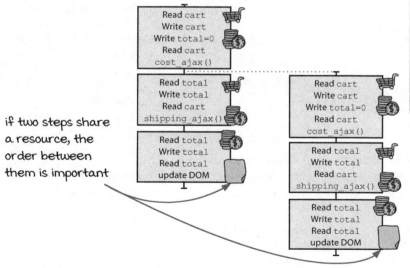

That's a lot of sharing of resources! Every step reads and writes to total, which can cause bugs. If things happen in the wrong order, they could definitely mess with each other. Let's start with the total global variable and convert it to a local one.

Converting a global variable to a local one

The global variable `total` does not need to be shared

There is no reason to use a global variable for the total. The easiest improvement is to use a local variable instead.

1. Identify the global variable we would like to make local

```
function calc_cart_total() {
  total = 0;
  cost_ajax(cart, function(cost) {
    total += cost;
    shipping_ajax(cart, function(shipping) {
      total += shipping;
      update_total_dom(total);
    });
  });
}
```

the total might not be zero here. another timeline could write to it before the callback is called

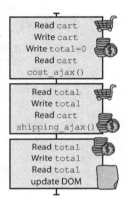

2. Replace the global variable with a local variable

```
function calc_cart_total() {
  var total = 0;
  cost_ajax(cart, function(cost) {
    total += cost;
    shipping_ajax(cart, function(shipping) {
      total += shipping;
      update_total_dom(total);
    });
  });
}
```

use a local variable instead

now reads and writes to total don't have an effect outside of the function, so they are not actions. only actions need to appear in timelines

it really shortens and simplifies the timeline

Well, that was easy! We got a lot of bang for converting `total` to a local variable. Our timeline still has three steps, so there are still 10 possible orderings. However, more of the orderings will be correct because they aren't using the same global variable `total`.

But we still use the `cart` global variable. Let's take care of that.

Converting a global variable to an argument

Remember the principle that stated fewer implicit inputs to an action were better? Well, it applies to timelines, too. This timeline uses the `cart` global variable as an implicit input. We can eliminate this implicit input and make the timelines share less in one go! The process is the same as for eliminating inputs to actions: Replace reads to global variables with an argument.

1. Identify the implicit input

```
function add_item_to_cart(name, price, quantity) {
  cart = add_item(cart, name, price, quantity);
  calc_cart_total();
}
function calc_cart_total() {
  var total = 0;
  cost_ajax(cart, function(cost) {
    total += cost;
    shipping_ajax(cart, function(shipping) {
      total += shipping;
      update_total_dom(total);
    });
  });
}
```

these two reads could read different values if cart is changed between reads

Read cart
Write cart
Read cart
cost_ajax()

Read cart
shipping_ajax()

update DOM

we still have one step that uses the cart global

2. Replace the implicit input with an argument

```
function add_item_to_cart(name, price, quantity) {
  cart = add_item(cart, name, price, quantity);
  calc_cart_total(cart);
}
function calc_cart_total(cart) {
  var total = 0;
  cost_ajax(cart, function(cost) {
    total += cost;
    shipping_ajax(cart, function(shipping) {
      total += shipping;
      update_total_dom(total);
    });
  });
}
```

add the cart as an argument

these reads are not to the global variable anymore

Read cart
Write cart
Read cart
cost_ajax()

shipping_ajax()

update DOM

We still have the one step that uses the global variable cart, but remember, the second timeline is constrained to run after the first step (hence the dotted line), so these first steps that use the cart will always run in order. They can't interfere with each other. We're going to use this property a lot throughout the rest of the book. It gives us a way to safely use global mutable state even in the presence of multiple timelines.

There's still a bug in this code. We're still sharing the DOM as a resource. We can't just get rid of it because we need to manipulate the DOM. We'll learn how to share resources in the next chapter.

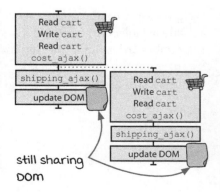

Read cart
Write cart
Read cart
cost_ajax()

shipping_ajax()
update DOM

Read cart
Write cart
Read cart
cost_ajax()

shipping_ajax()
update DOM

still sharing DOM

Brain break

There's more to go, but let's take a break for questions

Q: **We just eliminated all of the global variables from** `calc_cart_total()`. **Doesn't that mean it's a calculation?**

A: Good question. The answer is no. `calc_cart_total()` still performs several actions. For one, it contacts the server twice. Those are definitely actions. Finally, it updates the DOM, which is an action.

However, by removing the reads and writes to global variables, it is certainly more like a calculation. And that's a good thing. Calculations don't depend at all on when they are run. But this function depends less on when it is run than it used to. It hasn't crossed the line, but it is closer to it.

In the next few pages, we are going to move the DOM update from inside this function to outside, moving it even closer to the line and making it more reusable.

Q: **We've had to talk about the JavaScript threading model, AJAX, and the JavaScript event loop quite a lot. Are you sure this isn't a book about JavaScript?**

A: Yes, I'm sure. This is a book about functional programming, for any language. However, just to make sure we all understand what's happening, I've had to explain some of the inner workings of JavaScript.

I had to pick a language, and JavaScript is actually a great language for teaching functional programming for a number of reasons. One of them is that JavaScript is very popular. If I had chosen Java or Python, I would have had to teach some of their inner workings as well.

I've worked hard not to make JavaScript a distraction from the functional programming ideas. Try to see past the language and look at the reasoning that is happening.

It's your turn

Mark the following statements as true or false:

1. Two timelines can share resources.

2. Timelines that share resources are safer than timelines that don't share resources.

3. Two actions on the same timeline should avoid using the same resource.

4. You don't need to draw calculations on the timeline.

5. Two actions on the same timeline can happen in parallel.

6. JavaScript's single threaded model means you can ignore timelines.

7. Two actions in different timelines can occur simultaneously, left first, or right first.

8. A way to eliminate a shared global variable is to use arguments and local variables.

9. Timeline diagrams help us understand the possible orderings our software can run in.

10. Timelines that share resources can cause timing problems.

Answer

1. T, 2. F, 3. F, 4. T, 5. F, 6.F, 7. T, 8. T, 9. T, 10. T

Making our code more reusable

Accounting wants to be able to use `calc_cart_total()` without modifying a DOM. They want the total that is calculated as a number they can use in other calculations, not as an update to the DOM.

But we can't return the total as a return value from `calc_cart_total()`. It's not available until the two asynchronous calls are completed. How can we get the value out? That is, how can we make this implicit output into a return value when using asynchronous calls?

In chapters 4 and 5, we saw how to extract implicit outputs into return values. The DOM modification is an implicit output, but it's done in an asynchronous callback. We can't use a return value. So what's the solution? More callbacks!

> I know the folks in accounting are going to want to use this function. Can we make it more reusable?

Jenna from dev team

. . . .
When using asynchronous calls, we convert outputs into callbacks.
. . . .

Since we can't return the value we want, we'll have to pass it to a callback function. At the moment, after we finish calculating the total, we pass total to `update_total_dom()`. We'll extract that using *replace body with callback*:

> *Steps of* replace body with callback
>
> 1. Identify before, body, and after.
> 2. Extract function.
> 3. Extract callback.

it's already in a function, so we don't need to do this

right now, we pass total to update_total_dom()

Original

```
function calc_cart_total(cart) {
  var total = 0;
  cost_ajax(cart, function(cost) {
    total += cost;
    shipping_ajax(cart, function(shipping) {
      total += shipping;
      update_total_dom(total);
    });
  });
}

function add_item_to_cart(name, price, quant) {
  cart = add_item(cart, name, price, quant);
  calc_cart_total(cart);
}
```

body

With extracted callback

```
function calc_cart_total(cart, callback) {
  var total = 0;
  cost_ajax(cart, function(cost) {
    total += cost;
    shipping_ajax(cart, function(shipping) {
      total += shipping;
      callback(total);
    });
  });
}

function add_item_to_cart(name, price, quant) {
  cart = add_item(cart, name, price, quant);
  calc_cart_total(cart, update_total_dom);
}
```

replace with a callback argument

pass update_total_dom() as the callback

Now we have a way of getting the total once it is completely calculated. We can do what we want with it, including writing it to the DOM or using it for accounting purposes.

Principle: In an asynchronous context, we use a final callback instead of a return value as our explicit output

We can't return values from asynchronous calls. Asynchronous calls return immediately, but the value won't be generated until later, when the callback is called. You can't get a value out in the normal way, as you would with synchronous functions.

The way to get a value out in asynchronous calls is with a callback. You pass a callback as an argument, and you call that callback with the value you need. This is standard JavaScript asynchronous programming.

When doing functional programming, we can use this technique to extract actions from an asynchronous function. With a synchronous function, to extract an action we returned a value instead of calling the action within the function. We then call the action with that value one level up in the call stack. With asynchronous functions, we instead pass in the action as the callback.

Let's look at two functions, one synchronous, one asynchronous, that otherwise do the same thing:

> **Synchronous functions**
> • Return a value the caller can use.
> • Extract actions by returning values passed as the arguments to actions.

> **Asynchronous functions**
> • Call a callback with a result at some point in the future.
> • Extract actions by passing the action in as a callback.

Original synchronous function

```
function sync(a) {
    ...
    action1(b);
}
```

Original asynchronous function

```
function async(a) {
    ...
    action1(b);
}
```

synchronous and asynchronous functions may look similar at first

```
function caller() {
    ...
    sync(a);
}
```

```
function caller() {
    ...
    async(a);
}
```

the way they are called will look similar

Extracted action

```
function sync(a) {
    ...
    return b;
}
```

Extracted action

```
function async(a, cb) {
    ...
    cb(b);
}
```

synchronous uses a return value: asynchronous uses a callback

```
function caller() {
    ...
    action1(sync(a));
}
```

```
function caller() {
    ...
    async(a, action1);
}
```

synchronous's caller uses the return value to call action: asynchronous's caller passes action as callback

 **Brain break**

There's more to go, but let's take a break for questions

Q: Why can't we return a value from an asynchronous function? I thought all functions could have return values.

> **A:** Well, technically, you can. But you can't use it in the normal way. Here's an example:

```
function get_pets_ajax() {
  var pets = 0;
  dogs_ajax(function(dogs) {
    cats_ajax(function(cats) {
      pets = dogs + cats;
    });
  });
  return pets;
}
```

the callback passed to dogs_ajax() and the callback passed to cats_ajax() won't run until after the network responses come in. pets won't be set until then

returns immediately, before ajax requests are finished

What does this function return? It returns whatever is in the pets variable, but that will always be zero. So, yes, it is returning a value, but not the thing you're trying to calculate here.

What is happening is that `get_pets_ajax()` is calling `dogs_ajax()`, which sends the request to the network engine and immediately returns. The next statement is a return statement, so that happens. Sometime later, when the ajax request is completed, a completion event (called load) will be put on the job queue. And sometime after that, the event loop will pull it off the queue and call the callback.

Technically, you can return a value, but it has to be something that you have calculated in synchronous code. Anything done asynchronously can't use a return because it's run in another iteration of the event loop. The call stack will be empty at that point. In asynchronous code, result values need to be passed to a callback.

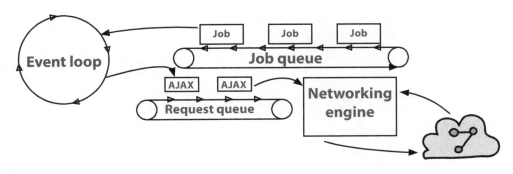

It's your turn

Here is some code for doing the dishes. It uses global variables and writes to the DOM to indicate how many dishes are done. Refactor it to eliminate implicit inputs and outputs. It should use arguments and local variables, and it should call a callback instead of writing to the DOM.

```
var plates = ...;
var forks  = ...;
var cups   = ...;
var total  = ...;

function doDishes() {
  total = 0;
  wash_ajax(plates, function() {
    total += plates.length;
    wash_ajax(forks, function() {
      total += forks.length;
      wash_ajax(cups, function() {
        total += cups.length;
        update_dishes_dom(total);
      });
    });
  });
}

doDishes();
```

write your answer here

Answer

```
var plates = ...;
var forks  = ...;
var cups   = ...;

function doDishes(plates, forks, cups, callback) {
  var total = 0;
  wash_ajax(plates, function() {
    total += plates.length;
    wash_ajax(forks, function() {
      total += forks.length;
      wash_ajax(cups, function() {
        total += cups.length;
        callback(total);
      });
    });
  });
}

doDishes(plates, forks, cups, update_dishes_dom);
```

Conclusion

In this chapter, we learned how to draw timeline diagrams and read them to discover bugs. We simplified the timelines using our knowledge of the JavaScript threading model, which shortened the timelines and reduced the number of timelines. We applied the principle of reducing shared resources to eliminate a bug.

Summary

- Timelines are sequences of actions that can run simultaneously. They capture what code runs in sequence and what runs in parallel.

- Modern software often runs with multiple timelines. Each computer, thread, process, or asynchronous callback adds a timeline.

- Because actions on timelines can interleave in ways we can't control, multiple timelines result in many different possible orderings. The more orderings, the harder it is to understand whether your code will always lead to the right result.

- Timeline diagrams can show how our code runs sequentially and in parallel. We use the timeline diagrams to understand where they can interfere with each other.

- It's important to understand your language's and platform's threading model. For distributed systems, understanding how things run sequentially and in parallel in your system is key.

- Shared resources are a source of bugs. By identifying and removing resources, we make our code work better.

- Timelines that don't share resources can be understood and executed in isolation. That wipes out a mental burden you no longer have to carry.

Up next . . .

We've still got that one shared resource, the DOM. Two add-to-cart timelines will both try to write different values to the DOM. We can't get rid of that resource because we need to show the user their total. The only way to share the DOM safely is by coordinating between the timelines. We'll see that in the next chapter.

Sharing resources between timelines | 16

In this chapter

- Learn how to diagnose bugs due to sharing resources.

- Understand how to create a resource-sharing primitive that can allow resources to be shared safely.

In the last chapter, we learned about timelines and how to reduce the number of resources they share. Timelines that don't share any resources are ideal, but sometimes you need to share resources. In that case, you need to make sure they share them in a safe way. In this chapter, we will see how we can create reusable pieces of code called *concurrency primitives* that will let us share resources.

Principles of working with timelines

Here are the principles again as a reminder. In the last chapter, we worked through principles 1–3, showing how they help ensure correctness. In this chapter, we will be applying principle 4. We have a resource that is shared between timelines, and we'll build a reusable way to coordinate the timelines so they share it safely.

1. Fewer timelines are easier

Every new timeline dramatically makes the system harder to understand. If we can reduce the number of timelines (t in the formula on the right), it will help tremendously. Unfortunately, we often can't control how many timelines we have.

2. Shorter timelines are easier

If we can eliminate steps in our timelines (decrease a in the formula on the right), we can reduce the number of possible orderings dramatically.

3. Sharing fewer resources is easier

When looking at two timelines, you really only have to consider the steps that share resources across timelines, which effectively reduces the number of steps on your diagram, and hence the number of possible orderings.

4. Coordinate when resources are shared

If we eliminate as many shared resources as we can, we will still be left with some resources that we can't get rid of. We need to ensure that the timelines share these resources in a safe way. That means ensuring that they take turns in the right order. Coordinating between timelines means reducing the number of possible orderings. In the process, we eliminate possible orderings that don't give us the right result while making the analysis easier. We can use inspiration from real-world coordination techniques to develop our own reusable ways to coordinate.

5. Manipulate time as a first-class concept

The ordering and proper timing of actions is difficult. We can make this easier by creating reusable objects that manipulate the timeline. We'll see examples of those in the next chapter.

Let's start applying principle 4 to our shopping cart, which still has a bug.

Formula for number of possible orderings

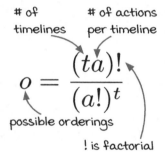

# of timelines   # of actions per timeline

$$o = \frac{(ta)!}{(a!)^t}$$

possible orderings

! is factorial

The shopping cart still has a bug

At the end of the last chapter, this was the timeline diagram we had. This timeline diagram clearly shows a bug. You might not be able to see it, but an expert functional programmer would. By the end of the chapter, you should see it, too. You will also know how to fix the bug.

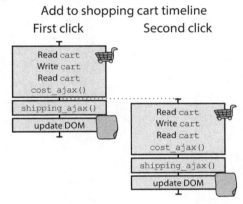

The bug has to do with the shared DOM resource. If two actions don't share resources, we don't need to care what order they happen in. Any of the three orders would give the same answer. But when they do share resources, we have to be concerned with what order they run in. Both timelines share the DOM, so there are potential problems.

Here are the three possible orderings of the two DOM updates:

> **Possible orderings**
>
> 1. Simultaneous
> 2. Left first
> 3. Right first

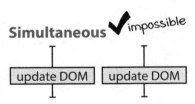

Simultaneous ✔ *impossible*

The JavaScript threading model makes simultaneous execution impossible, so we can rule it out. However, other threading models may have to consider this possibility.

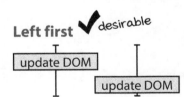

Left first ✔ *desirable*

This is the desired behavior. We want the second DOM update to overwrite the first one, because the second one has more up-to-date information.

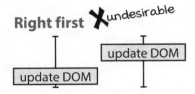

Right first ✘ *undesirable*

This is incorrect behavior. We don't want the total for the first item in the cart to overwrite the total for the second item. But nothing prevents this from happening!

If the DOM update for the second click happens before the DOM update for the first click, then old data will be overwritten by new data. Let's take a look at how this manifests on the next page.

With the same user input—adding the same items to the cart in
the same order—this timeline can show two different results:

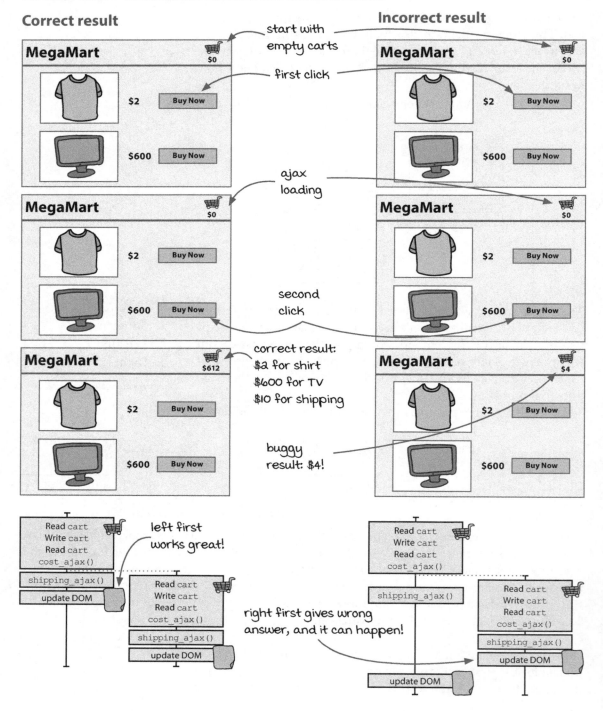

Correct result

Incorrect result

start with
empty carts

first click

ajax
loading

second
click

correct result:
$2 for shirt
$600 for TV
$10 for shipping

buggy
result: $4!

left first
works great!

right first gives wrong
answer, and it can happen!

We need to guarantee the order of the DOM updates

We want the DOM updates to occur in a certain order, but the nature of timelines such that the order of things on two different timelines does not guarantee itself. We need to force an order to these updates. In effect, we want to make the *right first* order impossible.

How can we ensure that we update the DOM in the correct order? The two clicks don't even know about each other.

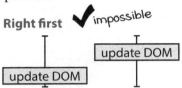

Jenna from dev team

We need to ensure that the DOM updates happen in the same order as the clicks come in. But when the update DOM actions occur is out of anyone's control. They happen when the network request completes, which depends on a lot of factors outside of our control. We need a way to coordinate the usage of the DOM so that the updates always happen in the same order as the clicks.

We often coordinate usage of shared resources in the real world without even thinking about it. That real-world coordination can serve as inspiration for how timelines can coordinate. One way we make sure things happen in order in the real world is to use a queue.

Queues are data structures where items are removed in the same order they are added. That means if we add items as the user clicks, we can then remove the items in that same order. Queues are often used to coordinate multiple actions across timelines to maintain a certain order.

The queue will become a shared resource. But it is made to be shared safely. Then we take them off the queue and do them in order. All tasks will be done in the same timeline, which further maintains the order.

Vocab time

A *queue* is a data structure where items are removed in the same order they are added.

tasks are taken off in same order as they are put in

worker loops through all tasks

tasks are done in one timeline, so they will always be done in order

three clicks result in three tasks added to queue

Clicks add to queue

items added in same order as clicks

queue is shared resource

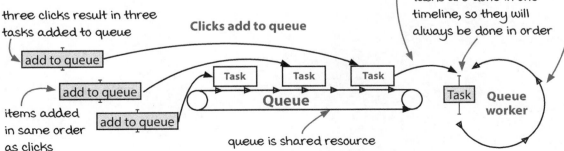

 **It's your turn**

In the following list, circle all of the things that could be a problematic resource shared between two timelines:

1. Global variables

2. DOM

3. Calls to a calculation

4. Shared local variables

5. Immutable values

6. The database

7. Calls to an API

Answer

The following can be problematic if shared between timelines: 1, 2, 4, 6, 7.

Building a queue in JavaScript

JavaScript does not have a queue data structure, so we have to build one

A queue is a data structure, but when we use it to coordinate time-lines, we call it a *concurrency primitive*. It's a small piece of reusable functionality that helps share resources.

Your language might already have built-in concurrency primitives. JavaScript doesn't have many, so it's the perfect vehicle for learning how to build our own. We'll see why building our own can be good soon.

Right now, we need to figure out what task our queue is going to do, and what work will go directly in the click handler.

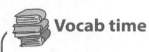

Vocab time

A *concurrency primitive* is a piece of reusable functionality that helps share resources across timelines.

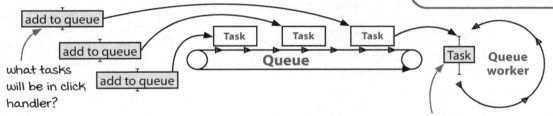

We can actually figure this out by starting from the current click handler's diagram:

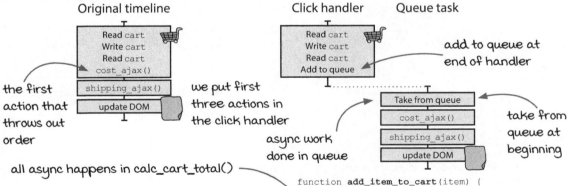

```
function add_item_to_cart(item) {
  cart = add_item(cart, item);
  calc_cart_total(cart, update_total_dom);
}
```

We want to include as much as we can in the click handler that doesn't maintain order. `cost_ajax()` is the first action that throws out order (since it's asynchronous), so we include everything up until then.

This luckily corresponds to the `calc_cart_total()` function. If we weren't so lucky, we'd have to move things around (without changing the order).

```
function calc_cart_total(cart, callback) {
  var total = 0;
  cost_ajax(cart, function(cost) {
    total += cost;
    shipping_ajax(cart, function(shipping) {
      total += shipping;
      callback(total);
    });
  });
}
```

Replace the work with adding to the queue

Our current code does everything in a single timeline. We'd like to move the work into another timeline. We'll start by replacing the work with a single action: adding the item to a queue.

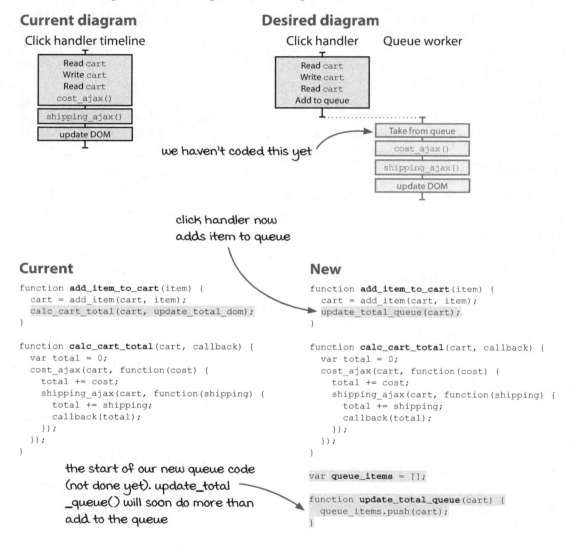

Current diagram

Click handler timeline

```
Read cart
Write cart
Read cart
cost_ajax()
```
```
shipping_ajax()
```
```
update DOM
```

Desired diagram

Click handler   Queue worker

```
Read cart
Write cart
Read cart
Add to queue
```

we haven't coded this yet

```
Take from queue
```
```
cost_ajax()
```
```
shipping_ajax()
```
```
update DOM
```

click handler now
adds item to queue

Current

```
function add_item_to_cart(item) {
  cart = add_item(cart, item);
  calc_cart_total(cart, update_total_dom);
}

function calc_cart_total(cart, callback) {
  var total = 0;
  cost_ajax(cart, function(cost) {
    total += cost;
    shipping_ajax(cart, function(shipping) {
      total += shipping;
      callback(total);
    });
  });
}
```

the start of our new queue code
(not done yet). update_total
_queue() will soon do more than
add to the queue

New

```
function add_item_to_cart(item) {
  cart = add_item(cart, item);
  update_total_queue(cart);
}

function calc_cart_total(cart, callback) {
  var total = 0;
  cost_ajax(cart, function(cost) {
    total += cost;
    shipping_ajax(cart, function(shipping) {
      total += shipping;
      callback(total);
    });
  });
}
```

```
var queue_items = [];
```

```
function update_total_queue(cart) {
  queue_items.push(cart);
}
```

Our queue is simple. It's just an array at the moment. Adding an item to the queue is as simple as adding an item to the end of the array.

Do the work on the first item in the queue

Now that our items are being added to the end of the queue, we can initiate the work. To do that, we need to pull the item at the beginning of the queue (to maintain order) and start the work:

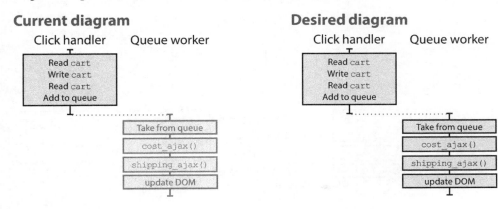

Current diagram

Click handler — Queue worker

Read cart
Write cart
Read cart
Add to queue

Take from queue
cost_ajax()
shipping_ajax()
update DOM

Desired diagram

Click handler — Queue worker

Read cart
Write cart
Read cart
Add to queue

Take from queue
cost_ajax()
shipping_ajax()
update DOM

Current

```javascript
function add_item_to_cart(item) {
  cart = add_item(cart, item);
  update_total_queue(cart);
}

function calc_cart_total(cart, callback) {
  var total = 0;
  cost_ajax(cart, function(cost) {
    total += cost;
    shipping_ajax(cart, function(shipping) {
      total += shipping;
      callback(total);
    });
  });
}

var queue_items = [];
```

pull the first item off the array and add it to the cart

```javascript
function update_total_queue(cart) {
  queue_items.push(cart);
}
```

start running the worker after adding an item

New

```javascript
function add_item_to_cart(item) {
  cart = add_item(cart, item);
  update_total_queue(cart);
}

function calc_cart_total(cart, callback) {
  var total = 0;
  cost_ajax(cart, function(cost) {
    total += cost;
    shipping_ajax(cart, function(shipping) {
      total += shipping;
      callback(total);
    });
  });
}

var queue_items = [];

function runNext() {
  var cart = queue_items.shift();
  calc_cart_total(cart, update_total_dom);
}
```

setTimeout() adds a job to the JavaScript event loop

```javascript
function update_total_queue(cart) {
  queue_items.push(cart);
  setTimeout(runNext, 0);
}
```

We are doing items in order, but nothing is stopping us from adding two items at the same time. Remember we'd like to completely order all items. That means only one item can be added at a time. Let's tackle that on the next page.

Prevent a second timeline from running at the same time as the first

Our code does not prevent two timelines from interleaving. We'd like to have one run at a time. Let's prevent two from interleaving by keeping track of whether something is already running:

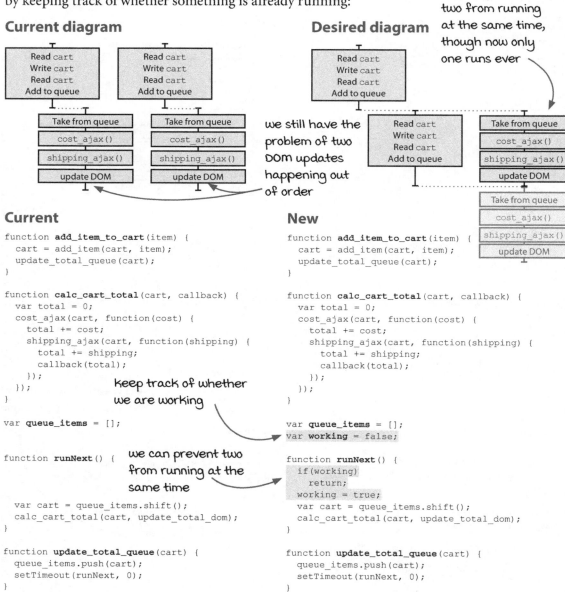

we can prevent two from running at the same time, though now only one runs ever

Current diagram

Desired diagram

we still have the problem of two DOM updates happening out of order

Current

```
function add_item_to_cart(item) {
  cart = add_item(cart, item);
  update_total_queue(cart);
}

function calc_cart_total(cart, callback) {
  var total = 0;
  cost_ajax(cart, function(cost) {
    total += cost;
    shipping_ajax(cart, function(shipping) {
      total += shipping;
      callback(total);
    });
  });
}

var queue_items = [];

function runNext() {



  var cart = queue_items.shift();
  calc_cart_total(cart, update_total_dom);
}

function update_total_queue(cart) {
  queue_items.push(cart);
  setTimeout(runNext, 0);
}
```

keep track of whether we are working

we can prevent two from running at the same time

New

```
function add_item_to_cart(item) {
  cart = add_item(cart, item);
  update_total_queue(cart);
}

function calc_cart_total(cart, callback) {
  var total = 0;
  cost_ajax(cart, function(cost) {
    total += cost;
    shipping_ajax(cart, function(shipping) {
      total += shipping;
      callback(total);
    });
  });
}

var queue_items = [];
var working = false;

function runNext() {
  if(working)
    return;
  working = true;
  var cart = queue_items.shift();
  calc_cart_total(cart, update_total_dom);
}

function update_total_queue(cart) {
  queue_items.push(cart);
  setTimeout(runNext, 0);
}
```

We are preventing two timelines from running at the same time, but only one item will ever be added to the cart. We will need to fix that by starting the next item when we finish with the current one.

Modify the callback to `calc_cart_total()` to start the next item

We send `calc_cart_total()` a new callback. This one will record that it's done (`working = false`) and run the next task:

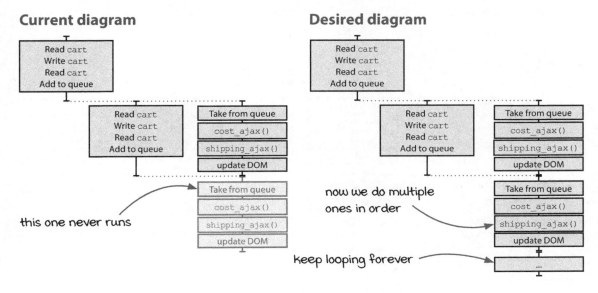

Current diagram

Desired diagram

this one never runs

now we do multiple ones in order

keep looping forever

Current

```
var queue_items = [];
var working = false;

function runNext() {
  if(working)
    return;
  working = true;
  var cart = queue_items.shift();
  calc_cart_total(cart, update_total_dom);
}

function update_total_queue(cart) {
  queue_items.push(cart);
  setTimeout(runNext, 0);
}
```

indicate we're done working and start the next item

New

```
var queue_items = [];
var working = false;

function runNext() {
  if(working)
    return;
  working = true;
  var cart = queue_items.shift();
  calc_cart_total(cart, function(total) {
    update_total_dom(total);
    working = false;
    runNext();
  });
}

function update_total_queue(cart) {
  queue_items.push(cart);
  setTimeout(runNext, 0);
}
```

We've essentially created a loop (though it is asynchronous). It will loop through all items in the list. But there's a problem: We don't stop if the list is empty! Let's address that.

Stop going through items when there are no more

Our queue worker loop basically runs off the end of the queue. Calling `queue_items.shift()` will return `undefined`. We don't want to try to add that to the cart.

Current diagram

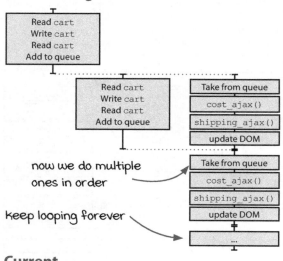

Desired diagram

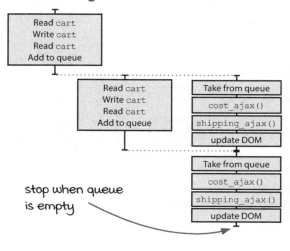

Current

```
var queue_items = [];
var working = false;

function runNext() {
  if(working)
    return;


  working = true;
  var cart = queue_items.shift();
  calc_cart_total(cart, function(total) {
    update_total_dom(total);
    working = false;
    runNext();
  });
}

function update_total_queue(cart) {
  queue_items.push(cart);
  setTimeout(runNext, 0);
}
```

stop if we have no items left

New

```
var queue_items = [];
var working = false;

function runNext() {
  if(working)
    return;
  if(queue_items.length === 0)
    return;
  working = true;
  var cart = queue_items.shift();
  calc_cart_total(cart, function(total) {
    update_total_dom(total);
    working = false;
    runNext();
  });
}

function update_total_queue(cart) {
  queue_items.push(cart);
  setTimeout(runNext, 0);
}
```

And now we have a working queue! This queue will let users click as many times as they want, as quickly as they can, and it will always process all of the clicks in order.

One last thing before we take a break: We've introduced two global variables. Global variables are problematic, so we should eliminate them.

Wrap the variables and functions in a function scope

We are using two global mutable variables. Let's wrap those up, and the functions that access them, within a new function we'll call `Queue()`. Since we are only expecting client code to call `update_total_queue()`, we'll return that from the function, save it to a variable, and use it:

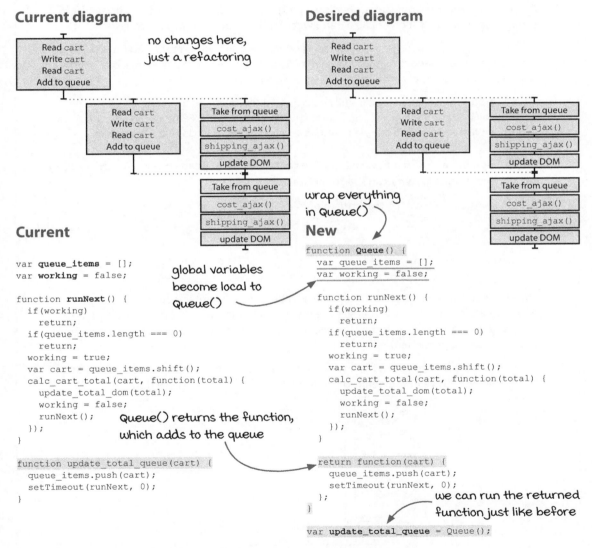

Current diagram

| Read cart |
| Write cart |
| Read cart |
| Add to queue |

no changes here, just a refactoring

| Read cart |
| Write cart |
| Read cart |
| Add to queue |

| Take from queue |
| `cost_ajax()` |
| `shipping_ajax()` |
| update DOM |

| Take from queue |
| `cost_ajax()` |
| `shipping_ajax()` |
| update DOM |

Desired diagram

| Read cart |
| Write cart |
| Read cart |
| Add to queue |

| Read cart |
| Write cart |
| Read cart |
| Add to queue |

| Take from queue |
| `cost_ajax()` |
| `shipping_ajax()` |
| update DOM |

| Take from queue |
| `cost_ajax()` |
| `shipping_ajax()` |
| update DOM |

Current

```
var queue_items = [];
var working = false;

function runNext() {
  if(working)
    return;
  if(queue_items.length === 0)
    return;
  working = true;
  var cart = queue_items.shift();
  calc_cart_total(cart, function(total) {
    update_total_dom(total);
    working = false;
    runNext();
  });
}

function update_total_queue(cart) {
  queue_items.push(cart);
  setTimeout(runNext, 0);
}
```

global variables become local to Queue()

Queue() returns the function, which adds to the queue

wrap everything in Queue()

New

```
function Queue() {
  var queue_items = [];
  var working = false;

  function runNext() {
    if(working)
      return;
    if(queue_items.length === 0)
      return;
    working = true;
    var cart = queue_items.shift();
    calc_cart_total(cart, function(total) {
      update_total_dom(total);
      working = false;
      runNext();
    });
  }

  return function(cart) {
    queue_items.push(cart);
    setTimeout(runNext, 0);
  };
}

var update_total_queue = Queue();
```

we can run the returned function just like before

By wrapping the variables in a function scope, we are ensuring that nothing can modify them outside of the small amount of code within the function. It also lets us make multiple queues, although they all do the same thing (add items to the cart).

 **Brain break**

There's more to go, but let's take a break for questions

Q: Isn't that a lot of mutation for a functional programming approach?

A: That's a really great question. Functional programming doesn't dictate any particular coding habits. Instead, it gives you a framework for thinking through your choices.

In this case, `update_total_queue()` is an action. It is a shared resource tied up with order and the number of times we call it. FP tells us that we need to pay extra close attention to actions—certainly more than we pay to calculations.

What's important is that we've carefully constructed the queue to be shareable. Any timeline can call `update_total_queue()` and it will be predictable. FP helps us tame our actions. If we need to add a couple of mutable values in order to do that, that's okay.

Q: Why do you have to add `runNext()` to the callback? If you need to call `runNext()` after `calc_cart_total()`, why can't it go on the next line?

A: You're asking why we did this instead of this

```
calc_cart_total(cart, function(total) {          calc_cart_total(cart, update_total_dom);
  update_total_dom(total);                          working = false;
  working = false;                                  runNext();
  runNext();
});
```

The answer is that `calc_cart_total()` is asynchronous. It contains steps that will be done some time in the future. Namely, the responses to the two ajax calls will be added to the event queue and processed by the event loop after some time. Meanwhile, some other events are being processed.

If we call `runNext()` right after it, it will start the next item while the ajax requests are in flight. That won't give us the behavior we want. Such is the way of JavaScript.

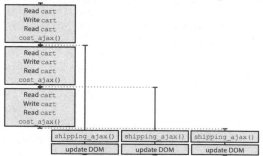

Q: That was a lot of work to get two timelines to share a resource. Is there an easier way?

A: Developing the queue carefully did take quite a few steps. However, notice that it's not that much code. And most of this code will be reusable.

Principle: Use real-world sharing as inspiration

We humans share resources all the time. We do it rather naturally. The trouble is that computers don't know how to share. We have to explicitly program in the sharing.

We chose to build a queue because people use queues all the time to share resources. We queue up to share a bathroom. We get in line at the bank. We share a food truck by waiting in line.

Queues are very common but won't work for everything. They also have some downsides, like forcing you to wait. There are other ways people share resources that don't have the same downsides:

- **Locks on bathroom** doors enable a one-person-at-a-time discipline.

- **Public libraries** (book pools) allow a community to share many books.

- **Blackboards** allow one teacher (one writer) to share information with an entire class (many readers).

We can use all of these and more when we need to program share-able resources. What's more, the constructs we write can be reusable, as we'll see in the next few pages.

 **Noodle on it**

Can you think of any other ways we share resources in the real world? Make a list. Think about how they work.

Making the queue reusable

Extracting the done() function

We would like to make this a 100% reusable queue. Right now, it can only add things to the shopping cart. But with the help of *replace body with callback*, we can separate the queue's looping code (calling runNext()) from the work we want the queue to do (calling calc_cart_total()).

Current

```
function Queue() {
  var queue_items = [];
  var working = false;

  function runNext() {
    if(working)
      return;
    if(queue_items.length === 0)
      return;
    working = true;
    var cart = queue_items.shift();

    calc_cart_total(cart, function(total) {
      update_total_dom(total);



      working = false;
      runNext();
    });
  }

  return function(cart) {
    queue_items.push(cart);
    setTimeout(runNext, 0);
  };
}

var update_total_queue = Queue();
```

extract two lines into a new function

body

New

```
function Queue() {
  var queue_items = [];
  var working = false;

  function runNext() {
    if(working)
      return;
    if(queue_items.length === 0)
      return;
    working = true;
    var cart = queue_items.shift();
    function worker(cart, done) {
      calc_cart_total(cart, function(total) {
        update_total_dom(total);
        done(total);
      });
    }
    worker(cart, function() {
      working = false;
      runNext();
    });
  }

  return function(cart) {
    queue_items.push(cart);
    setTimeout(runNext, 0);
  };
}

var update_total_queue = Queue();
```

done is the name of the callback

extract cart local to argument as well

done() is a callback that continues the work of the queue timeline. It sets working to false so that the next time through, it won't return early. Then it calls runNext() to initiate the next iteration. Now that worker() is isolated, let's extract it into an argument to Queue().

Extracting the custom worker behavior

Our queue right now is specific to adding items to the cart. We may in the future want to make a generic queue that is not specific and that we can reuse for many different operations. We can do another extract function argument refactoring to remove the custom code and pass it to the queue when it is created:

add a new argument, the function that does the work

Current

```
function Queue() {
  var queue_items = [];
  var working = false;

  function runNext() {
    if(working)
      return;
    if(queue_items.length === 0)
      return;
    working = true;
    var cart = queue_items.shift();
    function worker(cart, done) {
      calc_cart_total(cart, function(total) {
        update_total_dom(total);
        done(total);
      });
    }
    worker(cart, function() {
      working = false;
      runNext();
    });
  }

  return function(cart) {
    queue_items.push(cart);
    setTimeout(runNext, 0);
  };
}
```

```
var update_total_queue = Queue();
```

New

```
function Queue(worker) {
  var queue_items = [];
  var working = false;

  function runNext() {
    if(working)
      return;
    if(queue_items.length === 0)
      return;
    working = true;
    var cart = queue_items.shift();



    worker(cart, function() {
      working = false;
      runNext();
    });
  }

  return function(cart) {
    queue_items.push(cart);
    setTimeout(runNext, 0);
  };
}

function calc_cart_worker(cart, done) {
  calc_cart_total(cart, function(total) {
    update_total_dom(total);
    done(total);
  });
}
```

```
var update_total_queue = Queue(calc_cart_worker);
```

We've made a generic queue! Everything inside the Queue() function is generic. The nongeneric stuff is passed in as an argument. Let's take a moment to reflect on what we've done.

Accepting a callback for when the task is complete

Our programmers need one more feature, which is the ability to pass in a callback that will be called when our task is done. We can store both the data for the task and the callback in a small object. This is what we will push onto the queue:

> Hey, the queue is cool, but I really need a callback for when the task has been finished.

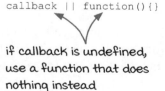

Current

```
function Queue(worker) {
  var queue_items = [];
  var working = false;

  function runNext() {
    if(working)
      return;
    if(queue_items.length === 0)
      return;
    working = true;
    var cart = queue_items.shift();
    worker(cart, function() {
      working = false;
      runNext();
    });
  }

  return function(cart) {
    queue_items.push(cart);



    setTimeout(runNext, 0);
  };
}

function calc_cart_worker(cart, done) {
  calc_cart_total(cart, function(total) {
    update_total_dom(total);
    done(total);
  });
}

var update_total_queue = Queue(calc_cart_worker);
```

pass the worker just the data

push both the data and the callback onto the array

New

```
function Queue(worker) {
  var queue_items = [];
  var working = false;

  function runNext() {
    if(working)
      return;
    if(queue_items.length === 0)
      return;
    working = true;
    var item = queue_items.shift();
    worker(item.data, function() {
      working = false;
      runNext();
    });
  }

  return function(data, callback) {
    queue_items.push({
      data: data,
      callback: callback || function(){}
    });
    setTimeout(runNext, 0);
  };
}

function calc_cart_worker(cart, done) {
  calc_cart_total(cart, function(total) {
    update_total_dom(total);
    done(total);
  });
}

var update_total_queue = Queue(calc_cart_worker);
```

Jenna from dev team

We are using a JavaScript idiom to give a default value to `callback`. `callback` may be `undefined`, which could happen if we don't pass a second argument. We want to be able to run the callback unconditionally, so we use this idiom to replace an undefined callback with a function that does nothing.

    We are now storing the callback, but we're not calling it yet. Let's do that on the next page.

`callback || function(){}`

if callback is undefined, use a function that does nothing instead

Calling the callback when the task is complete

On the last page, we started accepting and storing the callback along with the data for the task. Now we need to start calling the callback when the task is done:

Queue() is very generic, so the variable names are generic as well

Current

```
function Queue(worker) {
  var queue_items = [];
  var working = false;

  function runNext() {
    if(working)
      return;
    if(queue_items.length === 0)
      return;
    working = true;
    var item = queue_items.shift();
    worker(item.data, function() {
      working = false;

      runNext();
    });
  }

  return function(data, callback) {
    queue_items.push({
      data: data,
      callback: callback || function(){}
    });
    setTimeout(runNext, 0);
  };
}

function calc_cart_worker(cart, done) {
  calc_cart_total(cart, function(total) {
    update_total_dom(total);
    done(total);
  });
}

var update_total_queue = Queue(calc_cart_worker);
```

New

```
function Queue(worker) {
  var queue_items = [];
  var working = false;

  function runNext() {
    if(working)
      return;
    if(queue_items.length === 0)
      return;
    working = true;
    var item = queue_items.shift();
    worker(item.data, function(val) {
      working = false;
      setTimeout(item.callback, 0, val);
      runNext();
    });
  }

  return function(data, callback) {
    queue_items.push({
      data: data,
      callback: callback || function(){}
    });
    setTimeout(runNext, 0);
  };
}

function calc_cart_worker(cart, done) {
  calc_cart_total(cart, function(total) {
    update_total_dom(total);
    done(total);
  });
}

var update_total_queue = Queue(calc_cart_worker);
```

we allow done() to accept an argument

set up asynchronous call to item.callback

pass val to the callback

cart will get the item data; we call done() when we're done

here we know the specifics of what we're doing, so we use specific variable names

Notice that in the code for Queue(), we refer to item.data and val. These are very generic names because we don't know what the Queue() will be used for. However, in the code for calc_cart_worker(), we refer to the same values as cart and total (respectively) because we do know the task. Variable names need to reflect the level of detail we are working at.

Now our queue is incredibly reusable. It totally orders all tasks that go through it and lets the timeline continue once it's done. Let's take a few pages to reflect on what we've built.

It's a higher-order function that gives an action new powers

We built a function called `Queue()` that takes a function as an
argument and returns a new function.

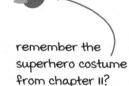

remember the
superhero costume
from chapter 11?

We've made a higher-order function that takes a function that creates a timeline and makes it so that only one version of that timeline runs at the same time.

   `Queue()` turns a timeline like this

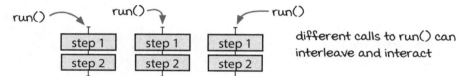

different calls to run() can
interleave and interact

into something like this:

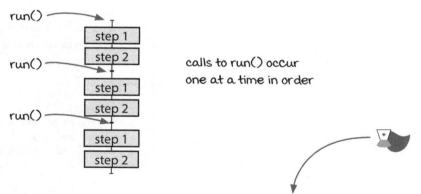

calls to run() occur
one at a time in order

In other words, `Queue()` gives actions the <u>superpower</u> of *guaranteeing order.*

   Maybe instead of calling it `Queue()`, we should call it
`linearize()` because that's what it's doing. It's linearizing the
calls to the action. It uses a queue internally, but that's just an
implementation detail.

   `Queue()` is a *concurrency primitive.* It is a piece of reusable code
that can help multiple timelines run correctly. Concurrency primitives usually work by limiting the possible orderings in some way.
If you eliminate the orderings that are undesirable, you can guarantee the code will run in one of the desirable orderings.

Vocab time

A *concurrency
primitive* is a piece of
reusable functional-
ity that helps share
resources across
timelines.

Analyzing the timeline

Harry is right. Luckily, timeline diagrams are made for this. Here is our timeline diagram. We can highlight the shared resources with icons again.

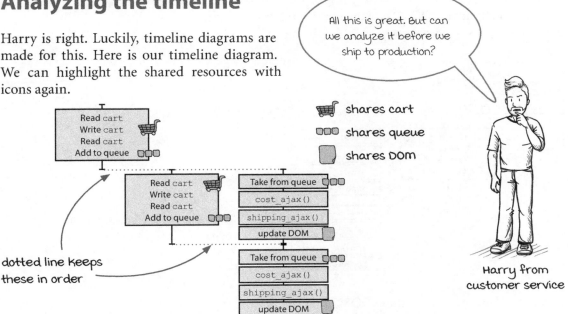

dotted line keeps
these in order

Harry from
customer service

Let's go through the three resources one at a time to make sure they happen in the correct order. Remember, we only have to compare carts with carts, DOMs with DOMs, and queues with queues. If they don't share a resource, it doesn't matter what relative order the actions happen in.

Let's start with the cart global variable. There are two uses of it, one in each click handler timeline. Each time a person clicks the add to cart button, the shopping cart global variable is accessed three times. However, these are all done synchronously in the same box. We need to ask whether two of these steps running in different timelines can get out of order. Technically, we don't have to look at all three orderings because the dotted line tells us that only one ordering is possible. But let's do it just for good measure:

Simultaneous ✔impossible

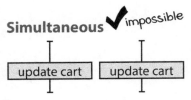

The JavaScript threading model makes simultaneous execution impossible, so we can rule it out. However, other threading models may have to consider this possibility.

Left first ✔desirable

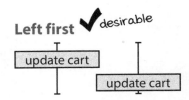

This is desirable behavior. The two click handlers are run in the same order as the clicks.

Right first ✔impossible

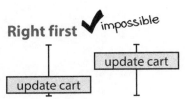

This is undesirable behavior, but it cannot happen because of the dotted line. The dotted line represents the ordering of UI events in the event queue, which maintains order. The click handlers happen in the same order as clicks.

Shopping cart looks good. Let's move onto the DOM.

We just saw that the shopping cart resources are shared correctly. Now let's look at the DOM, which was the reason we built this queue in the first place:

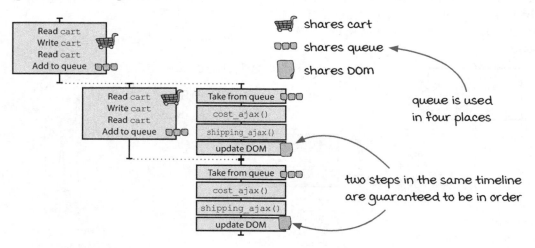

Because we've moved all of these DOM updates to a single timeline by using a queue, they cannot happen out of order. They will happen in the same order as the clicks on the add to cart button. We don't even need to check their orderings because they are in the same timeline. Actions in a single timeline are always done in order.

The final shared resource is the queue. This one is being used in four different steps! Let's look at it on the next page.

On the last page, we saw that the DOM updates will always happen in the correct order. However, now we have what seems to be a bigger problem. The queue is being shared between four different steps across three timelines. Let's see how we can analyze it. First, we'll eliminate the easy cases:

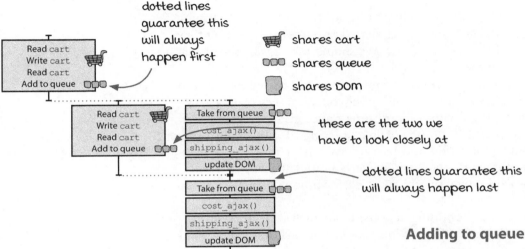

Adding to queue

```
queue_items.push({
  data: data,
  callback: callback
});
```

Taking from queue

```
queue_items.shift();
```

According to our diagram, one of our adds to the queue will come before everything else dealing with the queue. Also, one of the takes from the queue will come after everything else dealing with the queue. The dotted lines tell us that.

That just leaves the two in the middle. We have to check that the orders they can happen in are either desirable or impossible:

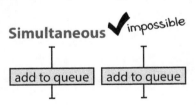

Simultaneous ✔ impossible

The JavaScript threading model makes simultaneous execution impossible, so we can rule it out. However, other threading models may have to consider this possibility.

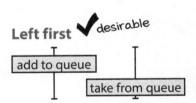

Left first ✔ desirable

This is desirable behavior. If one timeline happens to add to the queue before another timeline takes from the queue, that's okay. The order of items will be maintained.

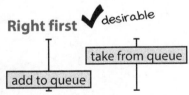

Right first ✔ desirable

This is also desirable behavior. We can take an existing item from the queue, then add another one later with no problem. The order of items is still maintained.

We can't guarantee that either of the actions will occur before the other. But that's okay! Both of the orderings will lead to the same correct result. The queue concurrency primitive guarantees that.

Principle: Analyze the timeline diagram to know if there will be problems

The biggest benefit of timeline diagrams is that they make timing problems obvious. You can see shared resources and whether they will occur in the wrong order. We should take advantage of that and draw out the diagram.

This is necessary because timing bugs are incredibly hard to reproduce. They're not obvious in the code, and they could pass all of the tests. Even with tests running hundreds of times, we may never reproduce all of the possible orderings. However, once you put it into production and have thousands or millions of users running the code, the improbable is bound to happen eventually. Timeline diagrams make it clear without having to go to production.

If you're programming actions, it is worth it to draw out the timeline diagram. It's a flexible tool for understanding how your software might operate, including all of the possible orderings.

Making the queue skip

Yeah, Sara is right. The way we implemented the queue, the worker will run each task to completion before moving on to the next. This can get really slow. Imagine if someone clicks the add to cart button four times really fast. We only need the last total to show up in the DOM. But our queue will process all four, one at a time. With two AJAX requests each, we could be talking about a whole second before we see the most up-to-date total.

> Sure, it happens in the right order, but it will be super slow!

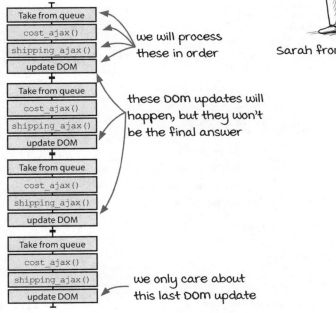

Sarah from dev team

the queue after clicking four times quickly

we will process these in order

these DOM updates will happen, but they won't be the final answer

we only care about this last DOM update

We would like to do better. One thing we notice is that we only really need the last item in the queue. The others will be immediately overwritten as soon as the next item finishes. What if we could drop items that will be overwritten anyway? We can do that with one small modification to our current queue code.

The current queue runs each task to completion before starting the next. We would like to make it skip work when new work comes in:

Normal Queue

```
function Queue(worker) {
  var queue_items = [];
  var working = false;

  function runNext() {
    if(working)
      return;
    if(queue_items.length === 0)
      return;
    working = true;
    var item = queue_items.shift();
    worker(item.data, function(val) {
      working = false;
      setTimeout(item.callback, 0, val);
      runNext();
    });
  }

  return function(data, callback) {
    queue_items.push({
      data: data,
      callback: callback || function(){}
    });

    setTimeout(runNext, 0);
  };
}

function calc_cart_worker(cart, done) {
  calc_cart_total(cart, function(total) {
    update_total_dom(total);
    done(total);
  });
}

var update_total_queue =
  Queue(calc_cart_worker);
```

Dropping Queue

rename to DroppingQueue

```
function DroppingQueue(max, worker) {
  var queue_items = [];
  var working = false;
```

pass the max # of tasks to keep

```
  function runNext() {
    if(working)
      return;
    if(queue_items.length === 0)
      return;
    working = true;
    var item = queue_items.shift();
    worker(item.data, function(val) {
      working = false;
      setTimeout(item.callback, 0, val);
      runNext();
    });
  }

  return function(data, callback) {
    queue_items.push({
      data: data,
      callback: callback || function(){}
    });
    while(queue_items.length > max)
      queue_items.shift();
    setTimeout(runNext, 0);
  };
}
```

keep dropping items from the front until we are under or at max

```
function calc_cart_worker(cart, done) {
  calc_cart_total(cart, function(total) {
    update_total_dom(total);
    done(total);
  });
}

var update_total_queue =
  DroppingQueue(1, calc_cart_worker);
```

drop all but one

With this change, now our `update_total_queue` will never grow longer than one unprocessed item, no matter how many we add or how fast we add them. The user will have to wait for at most two of the round trips to the server instead of all of them.

This was a very small change to our queue code, resulting in a better behavior for our use case. Both queues are common enough that we will probably want to keep them around. What's important is that we can use these queues as reusable concurrency primitives for other resources we need to share.

It's your turn

One problem with implementing a save document button is that if you have a slow network, your save_ajax() calls could overwrite each other. Here you'll see a timeline diagram showing the problem. Use the dropping queue to solve this problem.

```
var document = {...};

function save_ajax(document, callback) {...}

saveButton.addEventListener('click', function() {
  save_ajax(document);
});
```

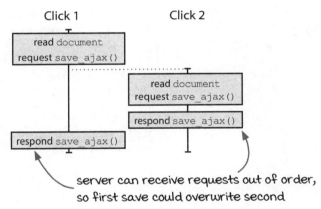

server can receive requests out of order,
so first save could overwrite second

write your answer here

Answer

```javascript
var document = {...};

function save_ajax(document, callback) {...}

var save_ajax_queued = DroppingQueue(1, save_ajax);

saveButton.addEventListener('click', function() {
  save_ajax_queued(document);
});
```

Click 1	Click 2	Queue

Click 1
```
read document
add to queue
```

Click 2
```
read document
add to queue
```

Queue
```
read queue
request save_ajax()
```
```
respond save_ajax()
```
```
read queue
request save_ajax()
```
```
respond save_ajax()
```

saves occur in order of clicking

Conclusion

In this chapter, we diagnosed a resource-sharing issue. Updating the DOM has to happen in a certain order. Once we found the problem, we solved it by building a queue. After a bit of work, the queue turned out to be a highly reusable higher-order function.

Summary

- Timing issues are hard to reproduce and often pass our tests. Use timeline diagrams to analyze and diagnose timing issues.

- When you have a resource-sharing bug, look to the real world for inspiration for how to solve it. People share stuff all the time, very often with no problems. Learn from people.

- Build reusable tools that help you share resources. They are called concurrency primitives, and they make your code clearer and simpler.

- Concurrency primitives often take the form of higher-order functions on actions. Those higher-order functions give the actions superpowers.

- Concurrency primitives don't have to be difficult to write yourself. Take small steps and refactor and you can build your own.

Up next . . .

We've seen how to diagnose resource-sharing issues and solve them with a custom concurrency primitive. In the next chapter, we'll see how to coordinate two timelines so that they can work together to solve a problem.

In this chapter

- Learn how to create a primitive to coordinate multiple timelines.

- Learn how functional programmers manipulate the two important aspects of time, ordering and repetition.

In the last chapter, we learned to diagnose resource-sharing bugs and created a *concurrency primitive* to share resources safely. Sometimes, multiple timelines need to work together when there's no explicit resource they are sharing. In this chapter, we will build a concurrency primitive that will help timelines coordinate and eliminate incorrect possible orderings.

Principles of working with timelines

Here are the principles again as a reminder. In the last two chapters, we worked through principles 1–4, showing how they help ensure correctness. In this chapter, we will be applying principle 5. We need to begin thinking of time itself as something to command.

1. Fewer timelines are easier

Every new timeline dramatically makes the system harder to understand. If we can reduce the number of timelines (t in the formula on the right), it will help tremendously. Unfortunately, we often can't control how many timelines we have.

Formula for number of possible orderings

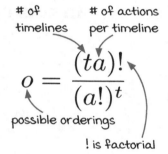

$$o = \frac{(ta)!}{(a!)^t}$$

# of timelines

# of actions per timeline

possible orderings

! is factorial

2. Shorter timelines are easier

If we can eliminate steps in our timelines (decrease a in the formula on the right), we can reduce the number of possible orderings dramatically.

3. Sharing fewer resources is easier

When looking at two timelines, you really only have to consider the steps that share resources across timelines, which effectively reduces the number of steps on your diagram, and hence the number of possible orderings.

4. Coordinate when resources are shared

Coordinating between timelines means reducing the number of possible orderings. In the process, we eliminate possible orderings that don't give us the right result while making the analysis easier.

5. Manipulate time as a first-class concept

The ordering and proper timing of actions is difficult. We can make it easier by creating reusable objects that manipulate the timeline. The important aspects of time itself—the ordering of calls and repetition of calls—can be directly manipulated.

Every language has an implicit model of time. But this model of time is often not the model we need to solve our problem. In functional programming, we can create a new model of time that better fits our problem.

Let's apply principle 5 to our shopping cart, which now has a new bug!

🐞 There's a bug!

It's been a few weeks since the shopping cart queue we saw in the
last chapter was deployed. Since then, there has been a big push for
user interface speed. Anything that slows down the shopping cart
or add to cart buttons has been aggressively optimized. And now
there's a bug.

The bug is that, even with just one item, sometimes we see the
wrong total. Let's see if we can reproduce it:

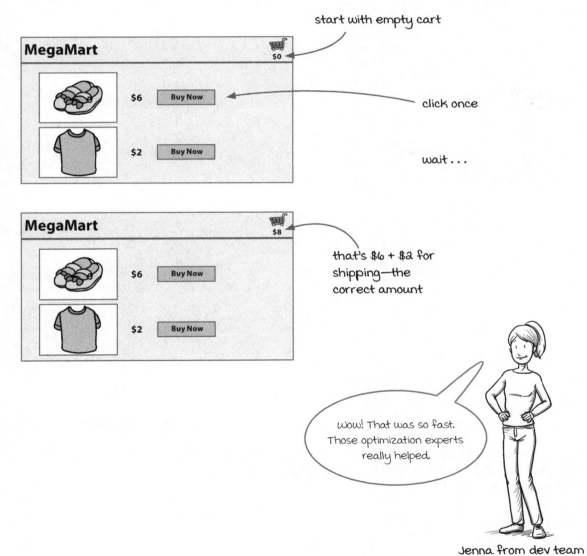

start with empty cart

click once

wait . . .

that's $6 + $2 for
shipping—the
correct amount

Wow! That was so fast.
Those optimization experts
really helped.

Jenna from dev team

Here's what it looks like when it doesn't work right:

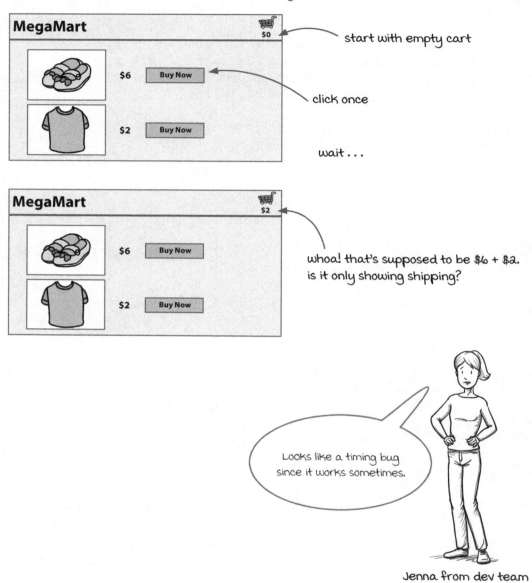

And this is just for adding one item to the cart. It's also broken for multiple items added quickly. But we won't demonstrate that. Let's fix the single case first.

How the code was changed

It was working just fine before all of the optimizations. Now it sometimes fails even when adding a single item. Let's see the code from the last chapter and compare it to what is there now, after the speed optimizations:

Before optimizations (working)

```
function add_item_to_cart(item) {
  cart = add_item(cart, item);
  update_total_queue(cart);
}

function calc_cart_total(cart, callback) {
  var total = 0;
  cost_ajax(cart, function(cost) {
    total += cost;

    shipping_ajax(cart, function(shipping) {
      total += shipping;
      callback(total);
    });
  });
}

function calc_cart_worker(cart, done) {
  calc_cart_total(cart, function(total) {
    update_total_dom(total);
    done(total);
  });
}

var update_total_queue =
  DroppingQueue(1, calc_cart_worker);
```

After optimizations (not working)

```
function add_item_to_cart(item) {
  cart = add_item(cart, item);
  update_total_queue(cart);
}

function calc_cart_total(cart, callback) {
  var total = 0;
  cost_ajax(cart, function(cost) {
    total += cost;
  });
  shipping_ajax(cart, function(shipping) {
    total += shipping;
    callback(total);
  });
}

function calc_cart_worker(cart, done) {
  calc_cart_total(cart, function(total) {
    update_total_dom(total);
    done(total);
  });
}

var update_total_queue =
  DroppingQueue(1, calc_cart_worker);
```

it looks like they moved a closing brace and parenthesis

It looks like they moved a closing brace and parenthesis. That makes the shipping_ajax() call happen immediately instead of in the cost_ajax() callback. Of course, this would be faster, since the two ajax requests are made at the same time. However, it has obviously caused a bug.

Let's draw the timeline diagram so we can see what's going on.

Identify actions: Step 1

On the last page, we saw the difference in the code. A simple movement of code out of a callback has made it faster but introduced a bug. Let's identify the actions:

```
function add_item_to_cart(item) {
  cart = add_item(cart, item);
  update_total_queue(cart);          the actions are
}                                    underlined in the code

function calc_cart_total(cart, callback) {
  var total = 0;
  cost_ajax(cart, function(cost) {
    total += cost;
  });
  shipping_ajax(cart, function(shipping) {
    total += shipping;
    callback(total);
  });

}

function calc_cart_worker(cart, done) {
  calc_cart_total(cart, function(total) {
    update_total_dom(total);
    done(total);
  });
}

var update_total_queue = DroppingQueue(1, calc_cart_worker);
```

> **Three steps to diagramming**
> 1. Identify actions.
> 2. Draw each action.
> 3. Simplify.

We want to be extra careful when we create this timeline diagram, so we're going to count the total variable even though it's local. You'll recall from a couple of chapters ago that we could eliminate the local variable total from our diagrams because all access to total was in a single timeline. However, now multiple timelines share access to it. We don't know if it's being shared safely (we'll soon see that it's not). It's very important when drawing a diagram of code to completely start over with zero assumptions. You can always simplify it again in step 3.

Let's get to step 2.

Draw each action: Step 2

We just identified all of the actions in the code as part of step 1. Let's move on to step 2, where we start to draw each action. Remember, we're completely starting over. We're not keeping any of the assumptions we could make before. We'll optimize again in step 3.

Three steps to diagramming

1. Identify actions.
2. Draw each action.
3. Simplify.

```
1 function add_item_to_cart(item) {
2   cart = add_item(cart, item);
3   update_total_queue(cart);
4 }
5
6 function calc_cart_total(cart, callback) {
7   var total = 0;
8   cost_ajax(cart, function(cost) {
9     total += cost;
10  });
11  shipping_ajax(cart, function(shipping) {
12    total += shipping;
13    callback(total);
14  });
15 }
16
17 function calc_cart_worker(cart, done) {
18   calc_cart_total(cart, function(total) {
19     update_total_dom(total);
20     done(total);
21   });
22 }
23
24 var update_total_queue = DroppingQueue(1, calc_cart_worker);
```

Actions

1. Read cart.
2. Write cart.
3. Read cart.
4. Call update_total_queue().
5. Initialize total = 0.
6. Call cost_ajax().
7. Read total.
8. Write total.
9. Call shipping_ajax().
10. Read total.
11. Write total.
12. Read total.
13. Call update_total_dom().

Let's get started with the drawing. Because we've had some practice, we'll do the actions in small chunks instead of one at a time:

```
2   cart = add_item(cart, item);
3   update_total_queue(cart);
```

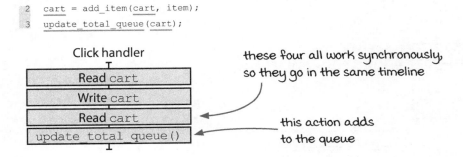

these four all work synchronously, so they go in the same timeline

this action adds to the queue

On the last page, we started drawing the timeline diagram. Let's continue. We had gotten through line 3:

```
1 function add_item_to_cart(item) {
2   cart = add_item(cart, item);
3   update_total_queue(cart);
4 }
5
6 function calc_cart_total(cart, callback) {
7   var total = 0;
8   cost_ajax(cart, function(cost) {
9     total += cost;
10  });
11  shipping_ajax(cart, function(shipping) {
12    total += shipping;
13    callback(total);
14  });
15 }
16
17 function calc_cart_worker(cart, done) {
18   calc_cart_total(cart, function(total) {
19     update_total_dom(total);
20     done(total);
21   });
22 }
23
24 var update_total_queue = DroppingQueue(1, calc_cart_worker);
```

Actions

1. Read `cart`.
2. Write `cart`.
3. Read `cart`.
4. Call `update_total_queue()`.
5. Initialize `total = 0`.
6. Call `cost_ajax()`.
7. Read `total`.
8. Write `total`.
9. Call `shipping_ajax()`.
10. Read `total`.
11. Write `total`.
12. Read `total`.
13. Call `update_total_dom()`.

> **Three steps to diagramming**
>
> 1. Identify actions.
> 2. Draw each action.
> 3. Simplify.

The next chunk is this bit of code:

```
7    var total = 0;
8    cost_ajax(cart, function(cost) {
9      total += cost;
10   });
```

remember, += is a read and a write

Click handler	Queue	`cost_ajax()` callback
Read `cart`		
Write `cart`		
Read `cart`		
`update_total_queue()`		

this runs in the queue, so it's a new timeline

Initialize `total`
`cost_ajax()`

this runs in an ajax callback, so it goes in a new timeline

Read `total`
Write `total`

We've worked through two chunks of code, and we managed to diagram eight actions. There are still three more. Let's do them in two chunks:

```
1 function add_item_to_cart(item) {
2   cart = add_item(cart, item);
3   update_total_queue(cart);
4 }
5
6 function calc_cart_total(cart, callback) {
7   var total = 0;
8   cost_ajax(cart, function(cost) {
9     total += cost;
10   });
11   shipping_ajax(cart, function(shipping) {
12     total += shipping;
13     callback(total);
14   });
15 }
16
17 function calc_cart_worker(cart, done) {
18   calc_cart_total(cart, function(total) {
19     update_total_dom(total);
20     done(total);
21   });
22 }
23
24 var update_total_queue = DroppingQueue(1, calc_cart_worker);
```

Actions

1. Read `cart`.
2. Write `cart`.
3. Read `cart`.
4. Call `update_total_queue()`.
5. Initialize `total = 0`.
6. Call `cost_ajax()`.
7. Read `total`.
8. Write `total`.
9. Call `shipping_ajax()`.
10. Read `total`.
11. Write `total`.
12. Read `total`.
13. Call `update_total_dom()`.

> ***Three steps to diagramming***
>
> 1. Identify actions.
> 2. Draw each action.
> 3. Simplify.

Now we address the call to `shipping_ajax()`:

```
11   shipping_ajax(cart, function(shipping) {
12     total += shipping;
13     callback(total);
14   });
```

We've got one action left, the call to `update_total_dom()`. There's no more room here, so let's handle it on the next page.

We've worked through 12 of the 13 actions on our list. We've got just one left:

```
1 function add_item_to_cart(item) {
2   cart = add_item(cart, item);
3   update_total_queue(cart);
4 }
5
6 function calc_cart_total(cart, callback) {
7   var total = 0;
8   cost_ajax(cart, function(cost) {
9     total += cost;
10  });
11  shipping_ajax(cart, function(shipping) {
12    total += shipping;
13    callback(total);
14  });
15 }
16
17 function calc_cart_worker(cart, done) {
18   calc_cart_total(cart, function(total) {
19     update_total_dom(total);
20     done(total);
21   });
22 }
23
24 var update_total_queue = DroppingQueue(1, calc_cart_worker);
```

update_total_dom() is part of the callback passed to calc_cart_total()

Actions
1. Read cart.
2. Write cart.
3. Read cart.
4. Call update_total_queue().
5. Initialize total = 0.
6. Call cost_ajax().
7. Read total.
8. Write total.
9. Call shipping_ajax().
10. Read total.
11. Write total.
12. Read total.
13. Call update_total_dom().

That callback is called in the callback to shipping_ajax(), so it goes in that timeline:

```
18   calc_cart_total(cart, function(total) {
19     update_total_dom(total);
20     done(total);
21   });
```

Three steps to diagramming
1. Identify actions.
2. Draw each action.
3. Simplify.

Two JavaScript simplifications
1. Consolidate actions.
2. Consolidate timelines.

update_total_dom() runs as part of the callback to shipping_ajax()

We've now managed to diagram all of the actions we've identified in the code. We can now apply our two simplifying rules that apply to JavaScript code.

Simplify the diagram: Step 3

We've drawn all 13 actions. We're ready to optimize. You will recall that we had two simplifying steps that the JavaScript threading model allowed us to apply in order.

JavaScript threading model simplification steps

1. All actions on a single timeline go into a single box.

2. Consolidate timelines that end by creating one new timeline.

These two steps will, we hope, reduce the cognitive burden of understanding this diagram. Here is the unsimplified diagram:

> **Three steps to diagramming**
>
> 1. Identify actions.
> 2. Draw each action.
> 3. Simplify.
>
> **Two JavaScript simplifications**
>
> 1. Consolidate actions.
> 2. Consolidate timelines.

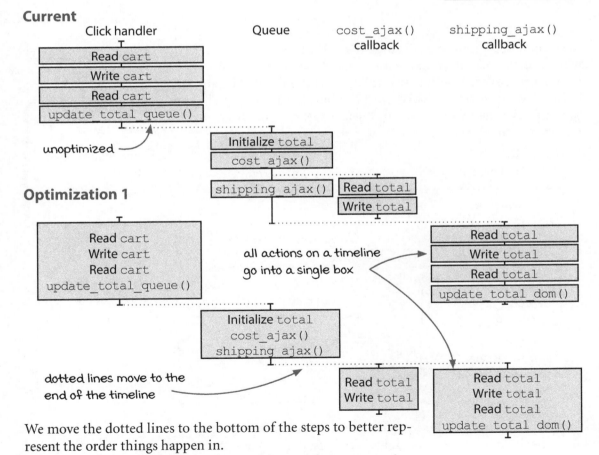

We move the dotted lines to the bottom of the steps to better represent the order things happen in.

The problem may already be clear at this stage, but we are going to continue with the full process of simplification.

We've done the first simplifying step. Now let's proceed to the second. Here's our diagram after doing the first step:

Optimization 1

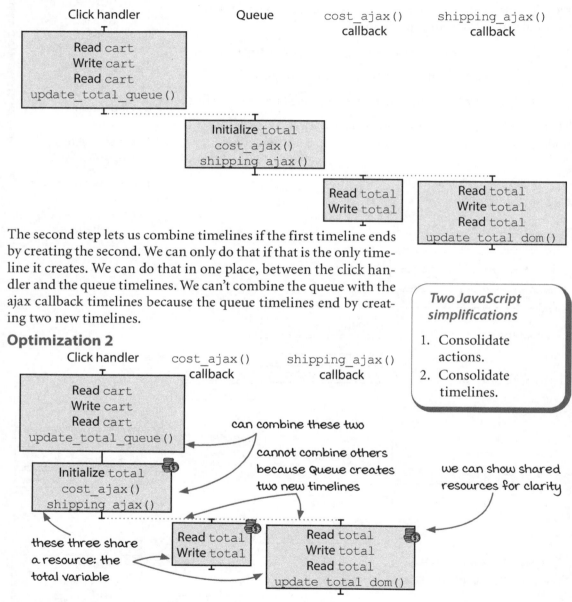

The second step lets us combine timelines if the first timeline ends by creating the second. We can only do that if that is the only timeline it creates. We can do that in one place, between the click handler and the queue timelines. We can't combine the queue with the ajax callback timelines because the queue timelines end by creating two new timelines.

Optimization 2

> ### *Two JavaScript simplifications*
> 1. Consolidate actions.
> 2. Consolidate timelines.

Now that we've finished the simplification, we can see what timeline steps share resources. The only shared resource is the total variable. Even though it is a local variable, three different timelines access it. Let's look at that more closely on the next page.

Possible ordering analysis

On the last page, we completed the timeline diagram and identified `total` as the only resource shared between timelines.

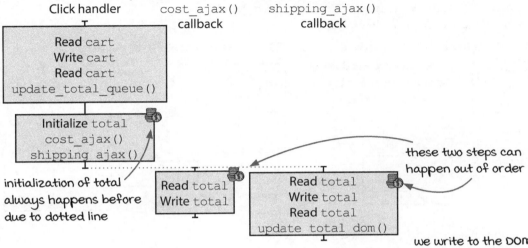

Let's analyze the three orderings of these two callbacks and see if any are problematic:

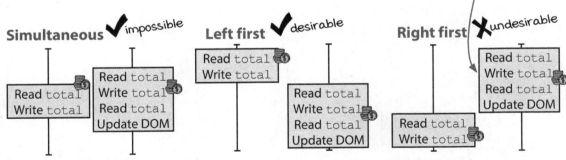

The JavaScript threading model makes simultaneous execution impossible, so we can rule it out. However, other threading models may have to consider this possibility.

This is desirable behavior. The DOM update happens after all of the numbers (cost plus shipping) have been combined into the `total` variable.

This is undesirable behavior. We update the DOM before we receive the response from `cost_ajax()`. It's the bug!

We see that our two callbacks can run in an undesirable order. It is possible that the `shipping_ajax()` callback runs after the `cost_ajax()` callback, even though the requests are initiated in the right order. That's our bug!

Let's see why this incorrect code can be faster before we fix it.

Why this timeline is faster

The aggressive optimization led to the bug that we saw on the last page. We saw why it works sometimes but fails at other times. Let's see if we can understand why this code is faster than the old code using their respective timeline diagrams:

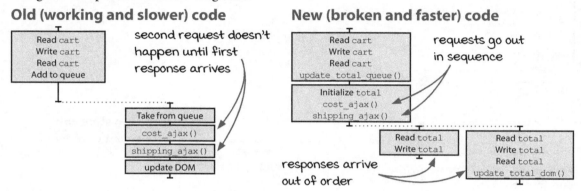

Let's imagine that `cost_ajax()` takes three seconds to respond and `shipping_ajax()` takes four seconds to respond. That's probably high for simple web requests, but let's use those numbers. What do the two timelines say is the minimum time the user will have to wait before the DOM is updated? Let's answer the question graphically:

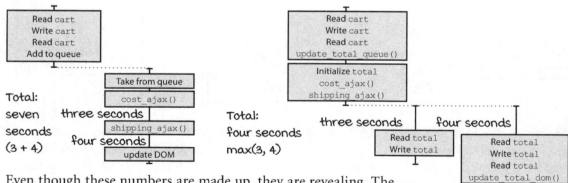

Even though these numbers are made up, they are revealing. The timeline on the left waits for two responses in *sequence*. That means we add the times. The timeline on the right waits for the two responses in *parallel*. That means we take the bigger of the two. That makes it finish faster.

But, of course, the faster timeline is broken. Is there a way to get the speed benefit of parallel responses without faulty behavior? Yes! We'll use another concurrency primitive to help coordinate the timelines so that the work always happens in the right order.

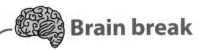 **Brain break**

There's more to go, but let's take a break for questions

rare, but if you have thousands of users per day, it could happen

Q: In the timeline, we are definitely sending `cost_ajax` before `shipping_ajax`. Why would `shipping_ajax` sometimes come back first?

A: That's a great question. There are many things that could happen to make requests come back out of order. It's impossible to list them all since there are so many reasons. However, here are some possibilities:

1. `cost_ajax` has a larger response payload, taking longer to download.

2. The server handling `cost_ajax` is busier than the shipping API server.

3. A phone in a moving car changes cell towers as `cost_ajax` is sent, causing a delay. `shipping_ajax` is sent on a single tower, so it's faster.

There is so much chaos on the network between any one computer and the server (and back!) that anything could happen.

Q: These analyses are really tedious. Do we really have to do all of these steps and draw all of these timelines?

A: That's a serious concern. The answer is yes, but you get much faster. As you get better at them, you'll do most of the analysis in your head. You won't have to draw them all. We are doing each step just to show our work. But as you get better with them, skipping steps is fine.

Waiting for both parallel callbacks

Our goal is simple: We want the ajax responses to come back in parallel, but we want to wait for both of them before writing to the DOM. If we write to the DOM after one is finished, but before the other, we get the wrong answer. We need what we see on the right:

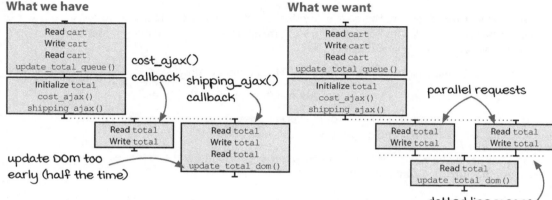

The diagram on the right shows how we can achieve our goal. We see that the two responses are still handled in parallel. They can happen in any order. Only after both responses have been handled do we finally update the DOM. The two callbacks wait for each other to finish. On the diagram, we represent the waiting with a dotted line.

We call the dotted line a *cut*. Like the dotted lines we've already been using, they guarantee a certain ordering. Unlike the dotted lines we've seen, cuts are drawn through the ends of multiple timelines. A cut on a timeline says everything above the cut happens before everything after it.

Cutting gives us serious leverage. A cut divides all participating timelines into before and after sections. We can analyze timelines before the cut separately from timelines after the cut. There is no way for actions after the cut to interleave with actions above the cut. Cutting severely lessens the number of possible orderings and thus decreases the complexity of the application.

In this case, we have two callback timelines that need to coordinate to calculate the final total. Each timeline has a number to combine into the total. These two timelines are working together on the same shared resource (the `total` local variable). The timelines need to coordinate so that once the total is read, it can be written to the DOM.

We can build a concurrency primitive that makes cuts. Let's go!

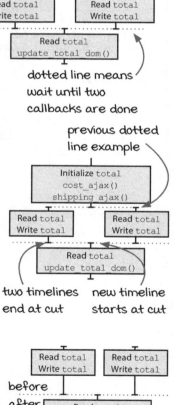

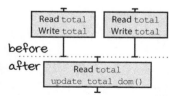

A concurrency primitive for cutting timelines

We want to write a simple, reusable primitive that allows multiple timelines to wait for each other, even if the timelines end in different orders. If we have one, we will be able to ignore that things happen in different orders and simply care when they are all finished. That way, we can prevent the race condition.

The underlying metaphor of the primitive follows the principle of taking inspiration from the real world. In the real world, if you and your friend are both working on separate things, you can agree to wait for each other, regardless of who finishes first. Then you can both take lunch together. We want a primitive that lets timelines finish in different orders and only continue when all timelines have finished. We'll do that on the next page.

 **Vocab time**

A *race condition* occurs when the behavior depends on which timeline finishes first.

In languages that have multiple threads, we would have to use some kind of atomic update so that the threads could share mutable state. However, we can take advantage of JavaScript's single thread and implement the primitive with a simple variable as long as we access it synchronously. We'll create a function. Every timeline will call that function when it's done. Every time the function is called, we increment the number of times it has been called. Then, when the last function calls it, it will call a callback:

# of timelines to wait for

the callback to execute when they are all done

```
function Cut(num, callback) {
    var num_finished = 0;
    return function() {
        num_finished += 1;
        if(num_finished === num)
            callback();
    };
}
```

initialize the count to zero

the returned function is called at the end of each timeline

each time function is called, we increment the count

when the last timeline finishes, we call the callback

A simple example

wait for three calls to done(), then print a message

```
var done = Cut(3, function() {
    console.log("3 timelines are finished");
});

done();
done();
done();

console=> "3 timelines are finished"
```

num_finished = 0

num_finished = 1
num_finished = 2
num_finished = 3

after third call to done(), the message is printed

We've got our primitive; let's put it into our add to cart code.

Reminder

JavaScript has one thread. A timeline runs to completion before other timelines begin. Cut() takes advantage of this fact to safely share a mutable variable. Other languages would need to use locks or other coordination mechanisms so timelines can coordinate.

Using Cut() in our code

We've got our Cut() concurrency primitive, and we need to use it in our add to cart code. Luckily, the required change is fairly minimal. There are two things to figure out:

1. What scope to store Cut()

2. What the callback for Cut() is

1. What scope to store Cut()

We need to call done() at the end of each callback. That suggests we create the Cut() in the scope of calc_cart_total(), where both callbacks are created.

2. What the callback for Cut() is

Inside of calc_cart_total(), we have already separated the callback that should happen after the total is calculated. Typically, this will be update_total_dom(), but it could be anything. We'll just pass that callback through to Cut(). Here is the result:

Before

```
function calc_cart_total(cart, callback) {
  var total = 0;



  cost_ajax(cart, function(cost) {
    total += cost;

  });
  shipping_ajax(cart, function(shipping) {
    total += shipping;
    callback(total);
  });
}
```

With Cut()

```
function calc_cart_total(cart, callback) {
  var total = 0;
  var done = Cut(2, function() {
    callback(total);
  });
  cost_ajax(cart, function(cost) {
    total += cost;
    done();
  });
  shipping_ajax(cart, function(shipping) {
    total += shipping;
    done();
  });
}
```

Timeline diagram

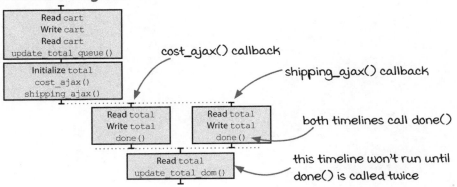

 **Brain break**

There's more to go, but let's take a break for questions

Q: Does `Cut()` **really work?**

A: Good question. `Cut()` does work, but we should emphasize one more discipline: You really do need to call `done()` at the end of a timeline. If you call it before the end, the timeline can continue on after the call to `done()`, which is not intended. It's best to avoid that situation, because it can be confusing. The rule is to call `done()` at the end of the timelines you want to cut.

Q: But `Cut()` **is so little code. Can something this useful be so easy?**

A: Great question. Let me phrase it this way: Can something that isn't simple be so reusable? We're implementing a very simple situation. If five friends want to go to lunch together, they wait in the hotel lobby until there are five of them ready to go. You just have to count up to five. And that's all `Cut()` does—it counts to a certain number, then calls a function.

Q: Wouldn't it be better to use something else, like Promises?

A: Good point. There are many concurrency primitives already implemented out there. Each language has its own. Experienced JavaScript programmers will be familiar with Promises, and in particular `Promise.all()`, which does something very similar to this.

If you know an existing primitive that will solve your problem, you should use it. However, the purpose of this book is not to teach JavaScript, but instead to teach functional programming. You should feel empowered, in any language, to use these principles to face your own software challenges. If a primitive doesn't exist, feel free to implement it.

Uncertain ordering analysis

On the last few pages we used the concurrency primitive on our add to cart. It seems to give us the best of both worlds: parallel execution (faster loads) with correct behavior (all orders are good).

Well, we hope! Let's analyze our timeline to make sure we get the best of both worlds. Here's the timeline we had:

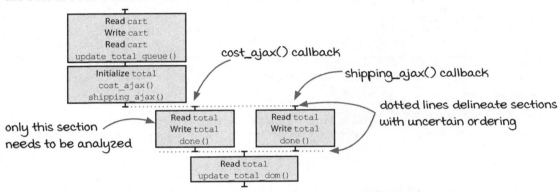

Let's first look at the more important thing: whether it gives us the correct behavior in all possible orderings.

We've chopped up our timeline pretty well with dotted lines, which will help tremendously in analysis. We can analyze it in sections.

Above our top dotted line, we've only got one timeline, so we have one possible ordering. Below the second timeline, the bottom section, we also have only one timeline. The one possible ordering is fine.

That leaves one section, the middle one between the two dotted lines. It has two timelines with one step each. Let's look at the orderings and check them:

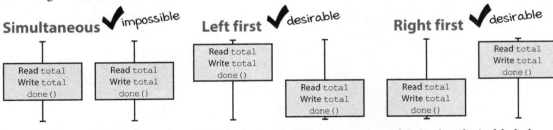

The JavaScript threading model makes simultaneous execution impossible, so we can rule it out. However, other threading models may have to consider this possibility.

This is desirable behavior. This shows adding the total cost before adding the shipping, and then calling `done()` the second time.

This is also desirable behavior. This shows adding the shipping, then adding the total cost, and then calling `done()` the second time.

Parallel execution analysis

We just analyzed the timeline for correct ordering. Now let's see if it really is faster:

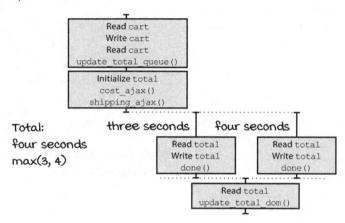

Again we can look at a hypothetical situation where the cost_ajax() response takes three seconds and the shipping_ajax() response takes four seconds. If we play that out on the diagram, we see that the total time is the greater of the two times, or four seconds.

So we win! We've got the speed of parallel execution and the correctness of serial execution.

We started with a timing bug that happened even when we clicked once. We cut the timeline so that two parallel timelines waited for each other before moving on. And now it works.

Well, it works for one click. Does it work for two or more? Let's find out on the next page.

Multiple-click analysis

We have seen that our code works correctly (and quickly) for a single click. What happens when we have two or more clicks? Does our queue work well with our cut? Let's see!

First, let's slightly redraw the timeline so that everything that happens in the queue is in a single line:

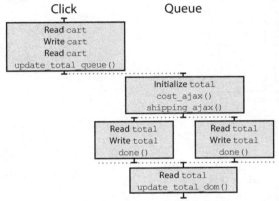

Now we can use this to see what happens when we have multiple clicks.

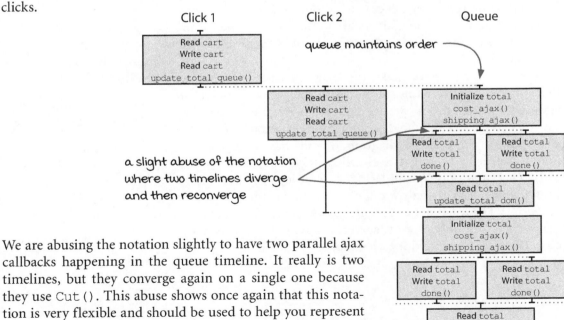

We are abusing the notation slightly to have two parallel ajax callbacks happening in the queue timeline. It really is two timelines, but they converge again on a single one because they use Cut(). This abuse shows once again that this notation is very flexible and should be used to help you represent the complexity of the situation in just the amount of detail you need in order to analyze it.

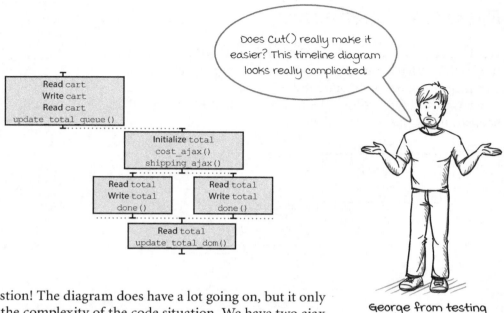

Tough question! The diagram does have a lot going on, but it only represents the complexity of the code situation. We have two ajax requests going in parallel. We need both responses to calculate the shopping cart's total, so we need to wait for both before updating the DOM with the answer, hence Cut(). But we also need to work correctly if they click the add to cart button quickly, hence the queue. That's quite a lot for one button to have to handle and quite a lot to analyze.

However, Cut() does make the diagram easier to analyze. Remember, shorter timelines are easier to analyze. We call it a *cut* because the dotted line means we can cut the timeline in two. We can analyze the section above the dotted line separately from the part below. In this timeline diagram, we only have one area running in parallel, with only two timelines (*t=2*) and one step each (*a=1*). There are only two orderings to consider (we considered simultaneous even though we don't need to—it's impossible in JavaScript). The rest is done in sequence, which the diagram makes clear. Cut() not only gives us correct behavior, but it makes the job of checking the behavior easier, too.

George from testing

Formula for number of possible orderings

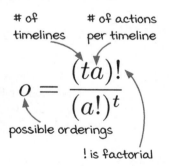

# of timelines

# of actions per timeline

$$o = \frac{(ta)!}{(a!)^t}$$

possible orderings

! is factorial

Is all this complexity really necessary? We just want to build a simple GUI in the browser.

Jenna from dev team

Excellent question. To answer this question, it's useful to think about where this complexity comes from. In our case, we're dealing with the complexity of three things:

1. Asynchronous web requests

2. Two API responses that need to be combined to form an answer

3. The uncertainty of the user's interactions

Numbers 1 and 3 are due to architectural choices. If we want to run in the browser as a JavaScript application, we have to deal with asynchronous web requests. And we want our shopping cart to be interactive, so we have to deal with the user. These follow necessarily from our architectural choices. Are complexities 1 and 3 necessary? No.

We could get rid of number 3 by making the app less interactive. We could present a form to the user. They type in all of the products they want to buy and submit the form. Of course, that would be a bad user experience. We probably want the app to be even more interactive than it is, not less.

We could get rid of number 1 by not using ajax requests. We could do a standard, non-ajax web app that uses links and form posts and reloads the page for each small change. But we don't want that.

Number 2, however, is different. We could imagine changing the API to make it a single request. We wouldn't have to worry about making requests in parallel and combining the answer. That wouldn't get rid of the complexity; it would just move the complexity to the server.

The server may be more or less able to deal with the complexity than the browser. It depends on the backend architecture. Does the backend have threads? Are the two calculations (total cost and shipping) doable from one database? Does the backend need to contact multiple APIs anyway? There are thousands of questions that uncover the choices that lead to this complexity.

So is the complexity necessary? No. But it follows from choices we probably don't want to change. Given those choices, there's a good chance that this complexity is unavoidable. We need good programming practices to help us manage it.

It's your turn

Here is code that shows multiple timelines that read and write to the sum global variable in order to count money from different cash registers. Draw the timeline diagram.

```
var sum = 0;

function countRegister(registerid) {
  var temp = sum;
  registerTotalAjax(registerid, function(money) {
    sum = temp + money;
  });
}

countRegister(1);
countRegister(2);
```

draw your diagram here

Answer

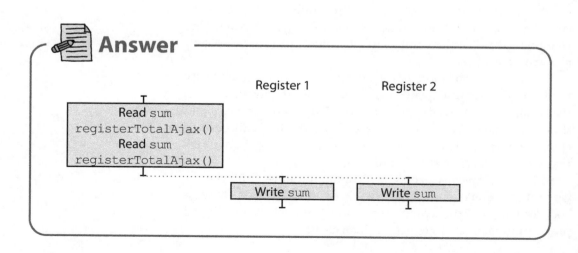

 **It's your turn**

Here is the timeline diagram from the previous exercise. It uses the sum global variable. Circle the actions that need to be analyzed and do the three-order analysis.

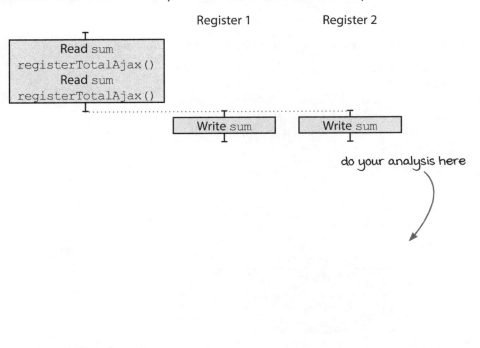

Register 1   Register 2

do your analysis here

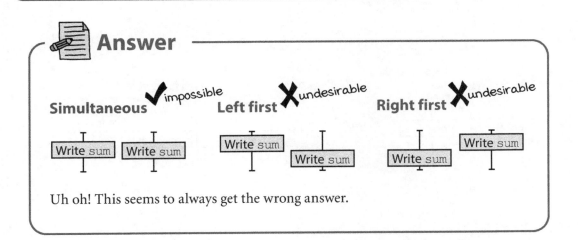 **Answer**

Uh oh! This seems to always get the wrong answer.

It's your turn

Here is the code from the last couple of exercises. There are no orderings that give the right answer. Can you find the bug? Fix the code, draw the diagram, and analyze the timelines.

Hint: What if you move the read to the sum closer to where you write to it?

```
var sum = 0;

function countRegister(registerid) {
  var temp = sum;
  registerTotalAjax(registerid, function(money) {
    sum = temp + money;
  });
}

countRegister(1);
countRegister(2);
```

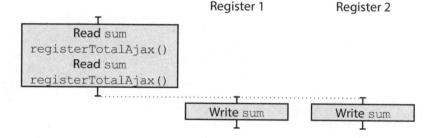

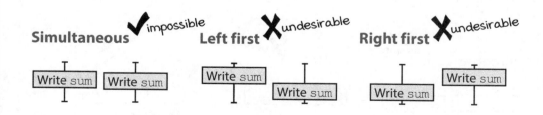

Answer

```
var sum = 0;

function countRegister(registerid) {
  registerTotalAjax(registerid, function(money) {
    sum += money;
  });
}

countRegister(1);
countRegister(2);
```

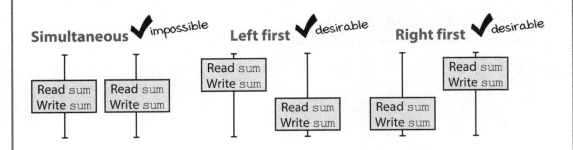

A primitive to call something just once

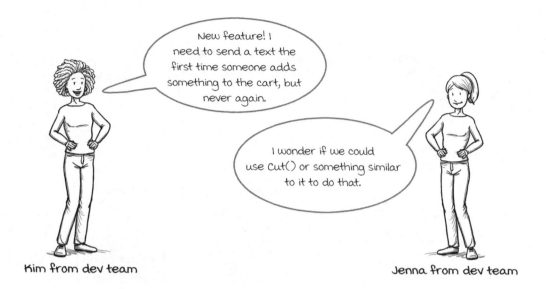

New feature! I need to send a text the first time someone adds something to the cart, but never again.

I wonder if we could use Cut() or something similar to it to do that.

Kim from dev team

Jenna from dev team

Kim: Really? Doesn't Cut() work by having all of the timelines finish before calling the callback?

Jenna: Yes. But look at it this way: Cut () calls the callback when the *last* timeline calls done(). That's how it coordinates them. What if we made a primitive that called the callback when the *first* timeline called it?

Kim: Oh! That way, the callback is only called once!

Jenna: That's right! We can call it JustOnce()! Let's see if we can do it on the next page.

Kim needs a way to perform an action just once, no matter how many times the code may call that action. That sounds like a job for a concurrency primitive. It will be a higher-order function that gives the callback a superpower—only running once.

Let's see what that might look like. Kim has a function that will text someone, welcoming them to use the site:

send a text every
time it's called

```
function sendAddToCartText(number) {
  sendTextAjax(number, "Thanks for adding something to your cart. " +
                       "Reply if you have any questions!");
}
```

Here is the code for a concurrency primitive that will wrap this function in a new function:

pass in an action

remember if we've
called it already

we're about to call
it, so remember

exit early if we've
called it before

call the action, passing
through the arguments

```
function JustOnce(action) {
  var alreadyCalled = false;
  return function(a, b, c) {
    if(alreadyCalled) return;
    alreadyCalled = true;
    return action(a, b, c);
  };
}
```

 Reminder

JavaScript has one thread. A timeline runs to completion before other timelines begin. JustOnce() takes advantage of this fact to safely share a mutable variable. Other languages would need to use locks or other coordination mechanisms so timelines can coordinate.

Just like we do in `Cut()`, `JustOnce()` shares a variable between
timelines, which is safe in JavaScript because this code is not
asynchronous. In languages with multiple threads, we would have
to use some kind of atomic update so that the threads could
coordinate. We can easily use this to wrap the function
`sendAddToCart()` so that it only runs once:

```
var sendAddToCartTextOnce = JustOnce(sendAddToCartText);

sendAddToCartTextOnce("555-555-5555-55");
sendAddToCartTextOnce("555-555-5555-55");
sendAddToCartTextOnce("555-555-5555-55");
sendAddToCartTextOnce("555-555-5555-55");
```

give sendAddToCartText()
a superpower

only the first one
sends a text

We have just created another concurrency primitive. It lets us share
an action among multiple timelines and dictates how they will col-
laborate to share it. Like most primitives, it is very reusable.

We've seen three concurrency primitives so far. We will see more
later in the book as we need them. The important point to stress is
that the primitives don't have to be hard to write. They are even
easier when you improve them incrementally and separate them
into the reusable, general part and the application-specific part.

Vocab time

An action that only
has an effect the first
time you call it is
called *idempotent*.
`JustOnce()` makes
any action
idempotent.

Implicit versus explicit model of time

Every language has an implicit model of time. That model describes two aspects of execution, ordering and repetition.

In JavaScript, the time model is quite simple:

1. Sequential statements execute in sequential order.
2. Steps in two different timelines can occur in left-first or right-first order.
3. Asynchronous events are called in new timelines.
4. An action is executed as many times as you call it.

ordering

repetition

This model is a great default because it's clear. We've used this model to draw our timeline diagrams:

1. Sequential statements execute in sequential order

2. Steps in two timelines can occur in two orders

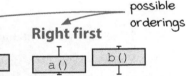

3. Asynchronous events are called in new timelines

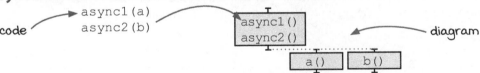

4. An action is executed as many times as you call it

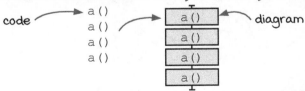

The implicit model is a good start. But it is only one possible way things can execute. In fact, it rarely matches *exactly* what we need. Functional programmers build a new model of time that is closer to what they need. For instance, we create a queue, which does not create new timelines for asynchronous callbacks. And we create a primitive called JustOnce() that only executes an action once, even if it is called many times.

 **Brain break**

There's more to go, but let's take a break for questions

Q: **The three concurrency primitives we've written have been higher-order functions. Are all concurrency primitives written that way?**

A: Good question. It's true that we've written three concurrency primitives that are higher-order functions. But they aren't always higher-order functions. You'll find that in JavaScript, because it is asynchronous, higher-order functions are used a lot since you need to pass callbacks. In the next chapter, we're going to see a concurrency primitive, called *cells*. Cells are used for sharing state. They make use of higher-order functions, but technically they aren't higher-order functions themselves.

There is one characteristic of concurrency primitives in functional languages that is almost universal: the use of first-class values. Making a thing first-class lets you use the whole of the language to manipulate it. You'll notice that we're using first-class actions in our code so that we can call them in a different context, for instance as part of the queue worker. As another example, we're taking the first-class action that sends a text and wrapping it in a new function that only calls it once. This is possible because we're making the action first-class.

Q: **Principle 5 says we're "manipulating time." Is that a little overblown?**

A: Ha! Maybe. What we're doing is building a new, explicit model of ordering and repetition—which are the important aspects of time when programming. We can then use that explicit model instead of relying on the implicit model of the language we're using. So, sure, we're not manipulating time. We're manipulating the model of time.

It's your turn

Here are the concurrency primitives we built in this book. How does each one build a new model of time? Describe them briefly and draw timeline diagrams. Remember, the elements of time are ordering and repetition.

- Queue()

- Cut()

- JustOnce()

- DroppingQueue()

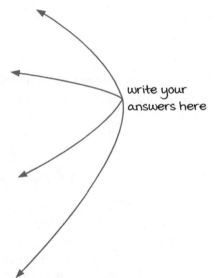

write your
answers here

 **Answer**

Queue()

Items added to the queue are processed in a separate, single timeline. Each item is handled in order to completion before the next is started:

```
var q = Queue(function() {
  a();
  b();
});

q();
q();
```

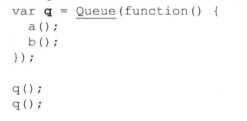
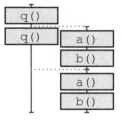

Cut()

Call a callback in a new timeline only after all timelines have completed:

```
var done = Cut(2, function() {
  a();
  b();
});

function go() { done(); }

setTimeout(go, 1000);
setTimeout(go, 1000);
```

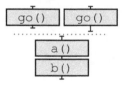

JustOnce()

An action wrapped in JustOnce() will only be executed once, even if the wrapped function is called multiple times:

```
var j = JustOnce(a);

j();
j();
j();
```

DroppingQueue()

This is like a Queue(), but will skip tasks if they build up quickly:

```
var q = DroppingQueue(1, function() {
  a();
  b();
});

q();
q();
q();
```

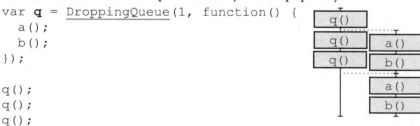

Summary: Manipulating timelines

Let's go over all of the ways we've improved our use of multiple timelines. They are listed in order of preference, most preferred first.

Reduce number of timelines

Simplify your system to create fewer threads, async calls, or server requests so as to use fewer timelines.

Reduce length of timelines

Use fewer actions in each timeline. Convert actions to calculations (which do not occur in the timeline). Eliminate implicit inputs and outputs.

Eliminate shared resources

Reduce the number of shared resources. Two timelines that don't share resources are free from ordering issues. Access shared resources from a single thread when possible.

Share resources with concurrency primitives

Replace shared access to an unsafe resource with shared access to safe resources, such as queues, locks, and so on, to share resources safely.

Coordinate with concurrency primitives

Use promises, cuts, and so on to coordinate timelines to constrain the ordering and repetition of their actions.

Conclusion

In this chapter, we diagnosed a race condition around the timing of web requests. If the requests came back in the same order as they were called, everything was good. But we couldn't guarantee that, so sometimes it gave us the wrong result. We created a primitive that let the two timelines work together so that they always get the same result. It was an example of coordination between timelines.

Summary

- Functional programmers build a new model of time on top of the implicit model provided by the language. The new model has properties that help them solve the problem they are working on.

- The explicit model of time is often built with first-class values. Being first-class means you have the whole language available to manipulate time.

- We can build concurrency primitives that coordinate two timelines. Those primitives constrain the possible orderings, helping us ensure the correct result is achieved every time.

- Cutting timelines is one way to coordinate between timelines. Cutting allows multiple timelines to wait for all timelines to finish before one continues.

Up next . . .

We've seen quite a lot of first-class functions and higher-order functions in this part. We've seen how to compose them into chains and build a new model of time. Now we're going to capstone part 2 with a discussion of design with a focus on the onion architecture.

In this chapter

- Learn how to build pipelines from actions using reactive architecture.

- Create a common mutable state primitive.

- Construct the onion architecture to interface your domain with the world.

- See how the onion architecture applies at many levels.

- Learn how the onion architecture compares to the traditional layered architecture.

We've learned quite a lot of applications of first-class functions and higher-order functions throughout part 2. Now it's time to take a step back and cap off those chapters with some talk about design and architecture. In this chapter, we look at two separate, common patterns. *Reactive architecture* flips the way actions are sequenced. And the *onion architecture* is a high-level perspective on the structure of functional programs that have to operate in the world. Let's get to it!

Two separate architectural patterns

In this chapter, we're going to learn two different patterns, *reactive* and *onion*. Each architecture works at a different level. Reactive architecture is used at the level of individual sequences of actions. Onion architecture operates at the level of an entire service. The two patterns complement each other, but neither requires the other.

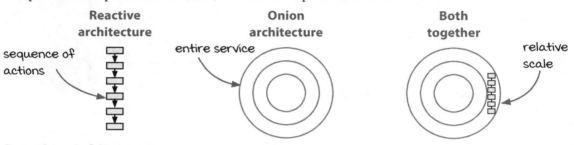

Reactive architecture

The reactive architecture flips the way we express the order of actions in our code. As we'll see, it helps decouple cause from effect, which can untangle some confusing parts of our code.

we'll see this architecture first

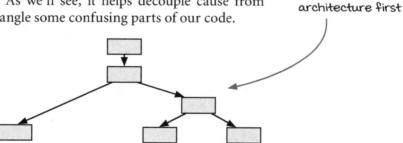

Onion architecture

The onion architecture gives a structure to services that must interact with the outside world, be they web services or thermostats. The architecture naturally arises when applying functional thinking.

we'll see this architecture second

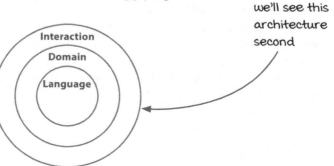

Coupling of causes and effects of changes

Jenna from dev team   Kim from dev team

Jenna: Every time I want to add some user interface (UI) element that shows something about the cart, I have to make changes in 10 places. A couple of months ago it was only three places.

Kim: Yeah, I see the problem. It's a classic $n \times m$ problem.

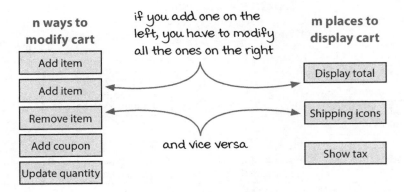

Kim: To add something to one column, you have to modify or duplicate all the things in the other column.

Jenna: Yep! That's the problem I'm feeling. Any idea how to solve it?

Kim: I think we can use reactive architecture. It decouples actions in the left column from actions in the right. Let's look at it on the next page.

What is reactive architecture?

Reactive architecture is another useful way of structuring our applications. Its main organizing principle is that you specify what happens in response to events. It is very useful in web services and UIs. In a web service, you specify what happens in response to web requests. In a UI, you specify what happens in response to UI events such as button clicks. These are usually known as event handlers.

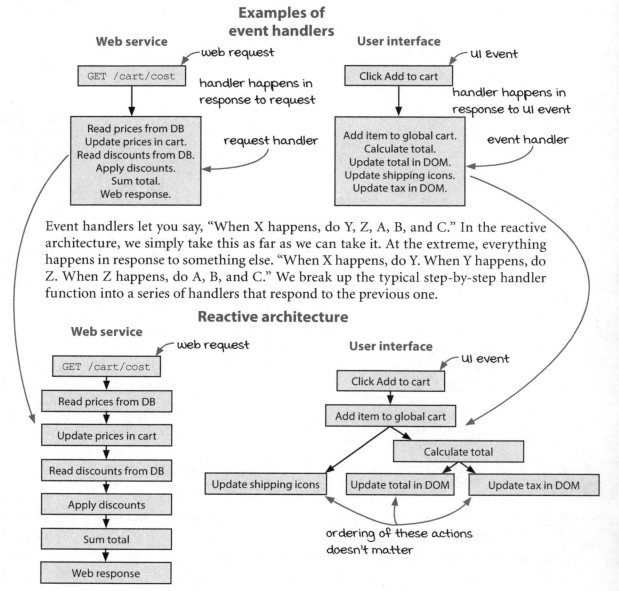

Event handlers let you say, "When X happens, do Y, Z, A, B, and C." In the reactive architecture, we simply take this as far as we can take it. At the extreme, everything happens in response to something else. "When X happens, do Y. When Y happens, do Z. When Z happens, do A, B, and C." We break up the typical step-by-step handler function into a series of handlers that respond to the previous one.

Tradeoffs of the reactive architecture

The reactive architecture flips the typical way we express ordering in our code. Instead of "Do X then do Y," a reactive style says, "Do Y whenever X happens." Sometimes this makes our code easier to write, read, and maintain. But sometimes it doesn't! It is not a silver bullet. You have to use your judgment to determine *when* to use it and *how* to use it. A deep understanding of what the reactive architecture lets you do will help you. You can then compare the two architectures (typical and reactive) to see if it achieves your goals.

Decouples effects from their causes

Separating the causes from their effects can sometimes make code less readable. However, it can also be very freeing and let you express things much more precisely. We're going to see examples of both situations.

Treats a series of steps as pipelines

We've already seen the power of composing pipelines of data transformation steps. We made good use of them by chaining functional tools together. That was a great way to compose calculations into more sophisticated operations. Reactive architecture lets you do a similar composition with actions and calculations together.

Creates flexibility in your timeline

When you reverse the expression of ordering, you gain flexibility in your timeline. Of course, as we've seen, that flexibility could be bad if it leads to unwanted possible orderings. But if used with skill, the same flexibility could shorten timelines.

To examine this, we're going to develop a very powerful first-class model of state that is common in many web applications and functional programs. State is an important part of applications, functional applications included. Let's dive into that model on the next page. We'll use what we develop to explain each of the headings.

Chapter 18 | Reactive and onion architectures

Cells are first-class state

The shopping cart is the only piece of global mutable state in our example. We've eliminated the rest. What we want to be able to say is, "do Y when *the cart changes*."

As it is right now, we don't know when the cart changes. It is just a normal global variable, and we use the assignment method operator to modify it. One option is to make our state first-class. That is, we can turn the variable into an object to control its operations. Here's a first pass at making a first-class mutable variable.

> I think I'm starting to get it. We say, "Do Y when X happens." How can we apply that to the cart?

Jenna from dev team

```
function ValueCell(initialValue) {
  var currentValue = initialValue;
  return {
    val: function() {
      return currentValue;
    },
    update: function(f) {
      var oldValue = currentValue;
      var newValue = f(oldValue);
      currentValue = newValue;
    }
  };
}
```

hold one immutable value (can be a collection)

get current value

modify value by applying a function to current value (swapping pattern)

The name ValueCell is inspired by spreadsheets, which also implement a reactive architecture. When you update one spreadsheet cell, formulas are recalculated in response.

ValueCells simply wrap a variable with two simple operations. One reads the current value (val()). The other updates the current value (update()). These two operations implement the pattern we have used when implementing the cart. Here's how we would use this:

Before

read, modify, write (swapping) pattern

```
var shopping_cart = {};

function add_item_to_cart(name, price) {
  var item = make_cart_item(name, price);
  shopping_cart = add_item(shopping_cart, item);

  var total = calc_total(shopping_cart);
  set_cart_total_dom(total);
  update_shipping_icons(shopping_cart);
  update_tax_dom(total);
}
```

After

replace manual swap with method call

```
var shopping_cart = ValueCell({});

function add_item_to_cart(name, price) {
  var item = make_cart_item(name, price);
  shopping_cart.update(function(cart) {
    return add_item(cart, item);
  });
  var total = calc_total(shopping_cart.val());
  set_cart_total_dom(total);
  update_shipping_icons(shopping_cart.val());
  update_tax_dom(total);
}
```

This change makes reading and writing to shopping_cart explicit method calls. Let's take it a step further on the next page.

We can make `ValueCells` reactive

On the last page, we defined a new primitive for representing mutable state. We still need to be able to say, "When the state changes, do X." Let's add that now. We'll modify the definition of `ValueCell` to add a concept of *watchers*. Watchers are handler functions that get called every time the state changes.

Original

```
function ValueCell(initialValue) {
  var currentValue = initialValue;

  return {
    val: function() {
      return currentValue;
    },
    update: function(f) {
      var oldValue = currentValue;
      var newValue = f(oldValue);

      currentValue = newValue;



    }

  };
}
```

keep a list of watchers

call watchers when value changes

add a new watcher

With watchers

```
function ValueCell(initialValue) {
  var currentValue = initialValue;
  var watchers = [];
  return {
    val: function() {
      return currentValue;
    },
    update: function(f) {
      var oldValue = currentValue;
      var newValue = f(oldValue);
      if(oldValue !== newValue) {
        currentValue = newValue;
        forEach(watchers, function(watcher) {
          watcher(newValue);
        });
      }
    },
    addWatcher: function(f) {
      watchers.push(f);
    }
  };
}
```

Watchers let us say what happens when the cart changes. Now we can say, "When the cart changes, update the shipping icons."

Vocab time

There's more than one name for the *watcher* concept. No name is more correct than the others. You may have heard these other names:

- *Watchers*
- *Listeners*
- *Callbacks*
- *Observers*
- *Event handlers*

They're all correct and represent similar ideas.

Now that we've got a way to watch a cell, let's see what it looks like in our add-to-cart handler on the next page.

We can update shipping icons when the cell changes

On the last page, we added a method to `ValueCell` for adding watchers. We also made watchers run whenever the current value changed. We can now add `update_shipping_icons()` as a watcher to the `shopping_cart ValueCell`. That will update the icons whenever the cart changes, for whatever reason.

*make the event handler
simpler by removing
downstream actions*

Before

```
var shopping_cart = ValueCell({});

function add_item_to_cart(name, price) {
  var item = make_cart_item(name, price);
  shopping_cart.update(function(cart) {
    return add_item(cart, item);
  });
  var total = calc_total(shopping_cart.val());
  set_cart_total_dom(total);
  update_shipping_icons(shopping_cart.val());
  update_tax_dom(total);
}
```

*we only have to write this
code once and it runs after
all cart updates*

After

```
var shopping_cart = ValueCell({});

function add_item_to_cart(name, price) {
  var item = make_cart_item(name, price);
  shopping_cart.update(function(cart) {
    return add_item(cart, item);
  });
  var total = calc_total(shopping_cart.val());
  set_cart_total_dom(total);

  update_tax_dom(total);
}
```

```
shopping_cart.addWatcher(update_shipping_icons);
```

There are two important things to notice here. First, our handler function got smaller. It does less. It no longer has to manually update the icons. That responsibility has moved into the watcher infrastructure. Second, we can remove the call to `update_shipping_icons()` from all handlers. It will run for any change to the cart, be it adding an item, removing an item, updating a quantity, or what have you. This is exactly what we want: The icons are always up-to-date with the state of the cart.

We've removed one DOM update from the handler. The other two only depend indirectly on the cart. More directly, they depend on the *total*, which is a value derived from the cart. On the next page, we implement another primitive that can maintain a derived value. Let's check it out.

FormulaCells calculate derived values

On the last page, we made ValueCells reactive by adding
watchers. Sometimes you want to derive a value from an existing
cell and keep it up-to-date as that cell changes. That's what
FormulaCells do. They watch another cell and recalculate their
value when the upstream cell changes.

```
function FormulaCell(upstreamCell, f) {
  var myCell = ValueCell(f(upstreamCell.val()));        ◄──── reuse the machinery
  upstreamCell.addWatcher(function(newUpstreamValue) {  ◄──── of ValueCell
    myCell.update(function(currentValue) {
      return f(newUpstreamValue);                       add a watcher to recompute
    });                                                 the current value of this cell
  });
  return {
    val: myCell.val,                                    val() and addWatcher()
    addWatcher: myCell.addWatcher                       delegate to myCell
  };                                                    FormulaCell has no way to
}                                                       change value directly
```

Notice that there is no method to directly update the value of a
FormulaCell. The only way to change it is to change the upstream
cell that it watches. FormulaCells say "When the upstream cell
changes, recalculate my value based on the upstream cell's new
value." FormulaCells can be watched as well.

Because they can be watched, we can add some actions that
happen in response to changes to the total:

*cart_total will change
whenever shopping_cart
changes*

Before

```
var shopping_cart = ValueCell({});




function add_item_to_cart(name, price) {
  var item = make_cart_item(name, price);
  shopping_cart.update(function(cart) {
    return add_item(cart, item);
  });
  var total = calc_total(shopping_cart.val());
  set_cart_total_dom(total);
  update_tax_dom(total);
}

shopping_cart.addWatcher(update_shipping_icons);
```

After

```
var shopping_cart = ValueCell({});
var cart_total = FormulaCell(shopping_cart,
                             calc_total);

function add_item_to_cart(name, price) {
  var item = make_cart_item(name, price);
  shopping_cart.update(function(cart) {
    return add_item(cart, item);
  });
}                       click handler is
                        now very simple


shopping_cart.addWatcher(update_shipping_icons);
cart_total.addWatcher(set_cart_total_dom);
cart_total.addWatcher(update_tax_dom);
```

*DOM will update in response
to cart_total changing*

Now we have three parts of the DOM updating whenever the cart
changes. What's more, our handler more directly states what it does.

Mutable state in functional programming

You may have heard functional programmers say they don't use mutable state and to avoid it at all costs. This is quite likely an overstatement since most software overuses mutable state.

Maintaining mutable state is an important part of all software, including software written using functional programming. All software must take in information from a changing world and remember part of it. Whether it's in an external database or in memory, something has to learn about new users and the users' actions in the software, to say the least. What's important is the relative safety of the state we use. Even though they are mutable, cells are very safe compared to regular global variables if you use them to store immutable values.

The update() method for ValueCells makes it easy to keep the current value valid. Why? You call update() with a calculation. That calculation takes the current value and returns the new value. If your current value is valid for your domain *and* the calculation always returns valid values if given a valid value, the new value will always be valid. ValueCells can't guarantee the order of updates or reads from different timelines, but they can guarantee that any value stored in them is valid. In a lot of situations, that is more than good enough.

> Wait a sec! I thought functional programmers don't use mutable state!

George from testing

always pass a calculation to update ⟶
`ValueCell.update(`*f*`)`

ValueCell consistency guidelines

- Initialize with a valid value.
- Pass a calculation to update() (never an action).
- That calculation should return a valid value if passed a valid value.

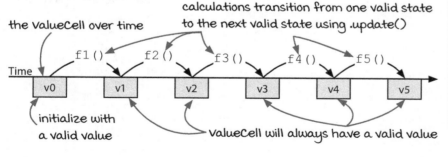

the ValueCell over time

calculations transition from one valid state to the next valid state using .update()

initialize with a valid value

ValueCell will always have a valid value

 **Vocab time**

The equivalent to `ValueCells` are found in many functional languages and frameworks:

- In Clojure: *Atoms*
- In React: *Redux store* and *Recoil atoms*
- In Elixir: *Agents*
- In Haskell: *TVars*

How reactive architecture reconfigures systems

We have just reconfigured our code into an extreme version of the reactive architecture. We made everything a handler to something else changing:

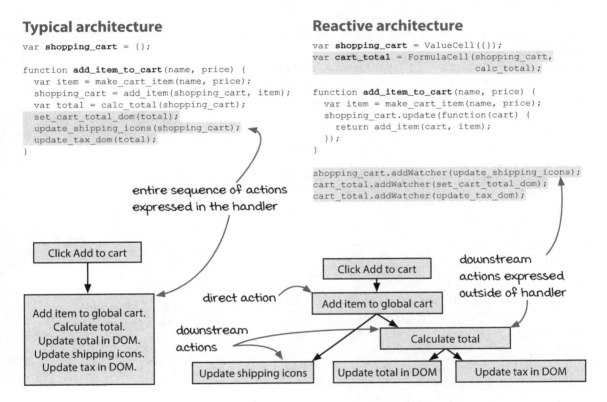

Typical architecture

```
var shopping_cart = {};

function add_item_to_cart(name, price) {
  var item = make_cart_item(name, price);
  shopping_cart = add_item(shopping_cart, item);
  var total = calc_total(shopping_cart);
  set_cart_total_dom(total);
  update_shipping_icons(shopping_cart);
  update_tax_dom(total);
}
```

Reactive architecture

```
var shopping_cart = ValueCell({});
var cart_total = FormulaCell(shopping_cart,
                             calc_total);

function add_item_to_cart(name, price) {
  var item = make_cart_item(name, price);
  shopping_cart.update(function(cart) {
    return add_item(cart, item);
  });
}

shopping_cart.addWatcher(update_shipping_icons);
cart_total.addWatcher(set_cart_total_dom);
cart_total.addWatcher(update_tax_dom);
```

entire sequence of actions expressed in the handler

direct action

downstream actions

downstream actions expressed outside of handler

Click Add to cart → **Add item to global cart. Calculate total. Update total in DOM. Update shipping icons. Update tax in DOM.**

Click Add to cart → **Add item to global cart** → **Calculate total**, **Update shipping icons**, **Update total in DOM**, **Update tax in DOM**

We should explore the consequences of this fundamental reorganization of the architecture. As we've seen before, reactive architecture has three major effects on our code:

1. Decouples effects from their causes
2. Treats series of steps as pipelines
3. Creates flexibility in your timeline

Let's address these in turn on the next few pages.

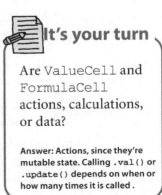

It's your turn

Are ValueCell and FormulaCell actions, calculations, or data?

Answer: Actions, since they're mutable state. Calling .val() or .update() depends on when or how many times it is called.

Decouples effects from their causes

you are here

> *Reactive architecture*
> 1. **Decouples cause and effect.**
> 2. Treats steps as pipelines.
> 3. Creates timeline flexibility.

Sometimes you have a rule you want to implement in your code. For instance, a rule that we've implemented in this book has been "The free shipping icons should show whether adding an item to the current cart would qualify for free shipping." That's a complex thing that we've implemented. However, it has that concept of *current cart*. It implies that whenever the cart changes, the icons may need to be updated.

The cart can change for different reasons. We've been focusing on clicking the add to cart button. But what about clicking the remove from cart button? What about clicking the empty cart button? Any operation we do to the cart will need us to run essentially the same code.

Typical architecture

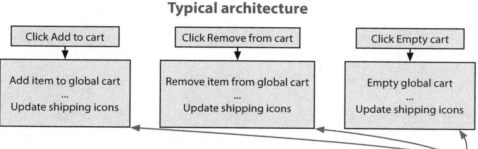

state the same effect three times

In a typical architecture, we would need to write the same code in every UI event handler. When the user clicks the add to cart button, update the icons. When they click the remove from cart button, update the icons. When they click the empty cart button, update the icons. We have coupled the cause (the button click) with the effect (updating the icons). A reactive architecture lets us decouple the cause and the effect. Instead, we say, "Any time the cart changes, regardless of the cause, update the icons."

Reactive architecture

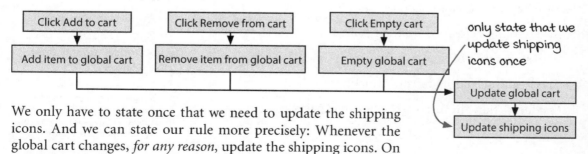

only state that we update shipping icons once

We only have to state once that we need to update the shipping icons. And we can state our rule more precisely: Whenever the global cart changes, *for any reason*, update the shipping icons. On the next page, let's look at what problem this architecture solves.

Decoupling manages a center of cause and effect

We just saw how the reactive architecture lets us decouple a cause from its effects. This technique is a powerful way to solve a really thorny problem. In our case, the problem manifested as many ways to change the cart and many things to do when the cart changes.

Ways to change the cart

1. Add item.
2. Remove item.
3. Clear cart.
4. Update quantity.
5. Apply discount code.

Actions to do when cart changes

1. Update shipping icons.
2. Show tax.
3. Show total.
4. Update number of items in cart.

the global shopping cart variable is a center of cause and effect

There are many more ways to change the cart and many more actions to do. And these change over time. Imagine that we have to add one more thing to do when the cart changes. How many places will we have to add it? Five, one for each of the ways to change the cart. Likewise, if we add one way to change the cart, we will need to add all of the actions into its handler. As we add more things on either side, the problem gets worse.

Really, we can say that there are 20 things that need to be maintained. That's five ways to change (causes) times four actions (effects). As we add more causes or effects, the multiplication gets bigger. We could say that the global shopping cart is a center of cause and effect. We want to manage this center so that the number of things to maintain doesn't grow as quickly.

This high growth is the problem that decoupling solves. It converts the growth operation from a multiplication to an addition. We need to write five causes and separately write four effects. That's $5 + 4$ places instead of 5×4. If we add an effect, we don't need to change the causes. And if we add a cause, we don't need to change the effects. That's what we mean when we say the causes are decoupled from the effects.

When that's the problem you have, this solution is very powerful. It lets you think in terms of changes to the cart when you're programming event handlers. And it lets you think in terms of DOM updates when you are showing things in the DOM.

When that's not the problem you have, the decoupling won't help and might make things worse. Sometimes the clearest way to express a sequence of actions is by writing them in sequence, line by line. If there's no center, there's no reason to decouple.

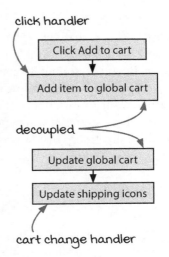

click handler

decoupled

cart change handler

Treat series of steps as pipelines

In chapter 13, we saw how we can compose multiple calculations using a chain of functional tools, which let us write very simple functions (easier to write) that could be used to make complex behaviors. In turn, we can get a lot of reuse from those simple functions.

Reactive architecture lets us build complex actions out of simpler actions and calculations. The composed actions take the form of pipelines. Data enters in the top and flows from one step to the next. The pipeline can be considered an action composed of smaller actions and calculations.

If you've got a series of steps that need to happen, where the data generated by one step is used as the input to the next step, a pipeline might be exactly what you need. An appropriate primitive can help you implement that in your language.

Pipelines are most often implemented using a reactive framework. In JavaScript, promises provide a way to construct pipelines of actions and calculations. A promise works for a single value as it passes through the steps of the pipeline.

If you need a stream of events instead of just one event, the ReactiveX (https://reactivex.io) suite of libraries gives you the tools you need. Streams let you map and filter events. They have implementations for many different languages, including RxJS for JavaScript.

There are also external streaming services, such as Kafka (https://kafka.apache.org) or RabbitMQ (https://www.rabbitmq.com). Those let you implement a reactive architecture at a larger scale in your system between separate services.

If your steps don't follow the pattern of passing data along, you either want to restructure them so that they do, or consider not using this pattern. If you're not really passing data through, it's not really a pipeline. The reactive architecture might not be right.

web request

Web service

GET /cart/cost

Read prices from DB

Update prices in cart

Read discounts from DB

Apply discounts

Sum total

Web response

you are here

Reactive architecture

1. Decouples cause and effect.
2. **Treats steps as pipelines.**
3. Creates timeline flexibility.

🛥 Deep dive

The reactive architecture has been gaining popularity as a way to architect microservices. See *The Reactive Manifesto* for a great explanation of the benefits (https://www.reactivemanifesto.org).

Flexibility in your timeline

Reactive architecture can also give you flexibility in your timeline, if that flexibility is desired. Because it flips the way we typically define ordering, it will naturally split the timelines into smaller parts:

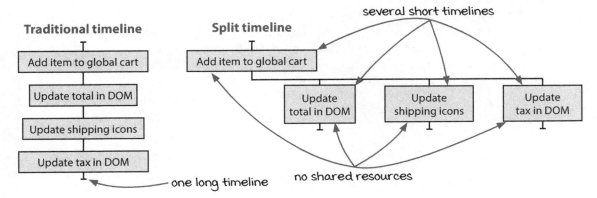

As we've seen starting in chapter 15, shorter timelines are easier to work with. However, more numerous timelines, in general, are harder to work with. The trick, as we've seen, is to split them in such a way as to eliminate shared resources.

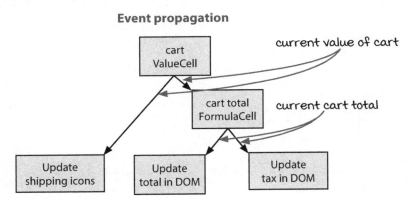

you are here

Reactive architecture

1. Decouples cause and effect.
2. Treats steps as pipelines.
3. **Creates timeline flexibility.**

The shopping cart `ValueCell` calls its watcher functions with the current value of the cart. The watcher functions do not need to read the cart `ValueCell` themselves, so they don't use the cart global as a resource. Likewise, the total `FormulaCell` calls its watcher functions with the current total. The DOM updates don't use the total `FormulaCell`, either. Each DOM update modifies a separate part of the DOM. We can safely consider them different resources; hence, none of these timelines have any resources in common.

 **It's your turn**

We need to design a user notification system to notify users of changes to their account, when the terms of service change, and when there are special offers. We might have other reasons to notify in the future.

At the same time, we need to notify the user in different ways. We send them an email, put a banner on the website, and put a message in their messages section of our site. And again, we may create more ways to notify them in the future.

A developer on the team suggested the reactive architecture. Would this be a good use of the reactive architecture? Why or why not?

write your answer here

Answer

Yes, it sounds like a very good application of the reactive architecture. We have multiple causes (reasons to notify the user) and multiple effects (ways to notify the user). The reactive architecture will let us decouple the causes from the effects so that they can vary independently.

It's your turn

Our newest document processing system has a very straightforward sequence of steps that needs to be executed to perform a routine task. The document is validated, cryptographically signed, saved to an archive, and recorded in a log. Would this be a good use of the reactive architecture? Why or why not?

write your answer here

Answer

Probably not. The sequence does not seem to have the center of cause and effect that reactive architecture really helps with. Instead, the steps are always sequential, and none seems to be the cause of the other. A more straightforward sequence of actions might be better.

Two separate architectural patterns

We've just seen the reactive architecture. Now we're going to focus on an entirely different architecture called the *onion architecture*. The onion architecture occurs at a larger scale than the reactive architecture. The onion architecture is used to construct an entire service so that it can interact with the outside world. When used together, you often see the reactive architecture nested inside an onion architecture, though neither requires the other.

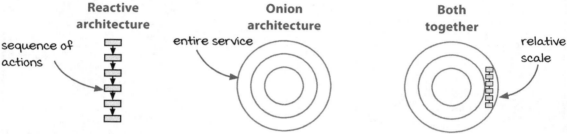

Reactive architecture

The reactive architecture flips the way that we express the order of actions in our code. As we'll see, it helps decouple cause from effect, which can untangle some confusing parts of our code.

we just saw this architecture

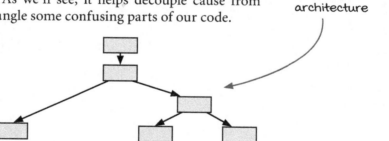

Onion architecture

The onion architecture gives a structure to services that must interact with the outside world, be they web services or thermostats. The architecture naturally arises when applying functional thinking.

we'll see this architecture next

What is the onion architecture?

The onion architecture is a way to structure services and other software that have to interact with the world. As the name suggests, the architecture is drawn as a set of concentric layers, like an onion:

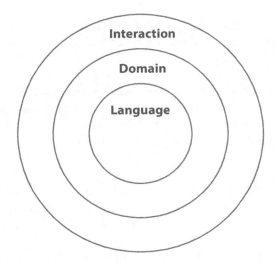

Interaction layer
- Actions that are affected by or affect the outside world

Domain layer
- Calculations that define the rules of your business

Language layer
- Language and utility libraries

The onion architecture is not specific about what layers you have, but they generally follow these three large groupings. Even this simple example shows the main rules that make it work well in functional systems. Here are those rules:

1. Interaction with the world is done exclusively in the interaction layer.

2. Layers call in toward the center.

3. Layers don't know about layers outside of themselves.

The onion architecture aligns very well with the action/calculation division and stratified design we learned in part 1. We will review those, and then see how we can apply the onion architecture to real-world scenarios.

Review: Actions, calculations, and data

In part 1, we learned about the differences between actions, calculations, and data. We'll review those here because they will inform a lot of our choices for building the architecture.

Data

We start with data because it is the simplest. Data is facts about events. It's numbers, strings, collections of those, and so on, anything that is inert and transparent.

Calculations

Calculations are computations from input to output. They always give the same output given the same input. That means calculations don't depend on when or how many times they are run. Because of that, they don't appear in timelines since the order they run in doesn't matter. Much of what we did in part 1 was to move code out of actions and into calculations.

Actions

Actions are executable code that has effects or is affected by the outside world. That means they depend on when or how many times they run. We spent a good portion of part 2 managing the complexity of actions. Since interacting with the database, APIs, and web requests are actions, we'll be dealing with those a lot in this chapter.

   If we follow the recommendations of chapter 4, which guided us to extract calculations from actions, we will naturally arrive at something very much like the onion architecture without meaning to. For this reason, many functional programmers may consider the onion architecture too obvious to even warrant a name. However, the name is used (so it's important to know it), and it is useful for getting a high-level view of how services might be structured when using functional programming.

Review: Stratified design

Stratified design is the perspective of arranging functions into layers based on what functions they call and what functions call them. It helps clarify what functions are more reusable, changeable, and worth testing.

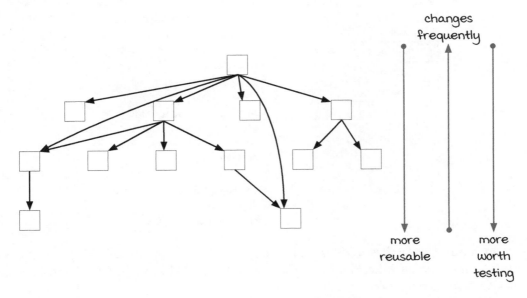

It also shows us a neat view of the spreading rule: If one of the boxes is an action, every box on the path to the top is also an action:

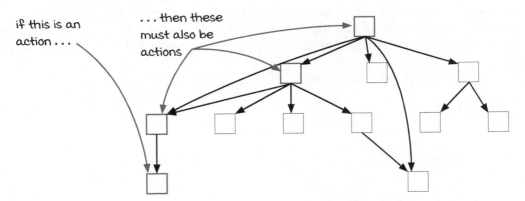

If you have any actions in the graph, the top of the graph will be an action. We spent much of part 1 separating the actions from calculations. Let's see what that looks like when we draw the graph with actions separated from calculations on the next page.

Traditional layered architecture

A traditional web API is often called layered, just like our layered design. However, the layers are different. Here is a typical layout for a layered web server:

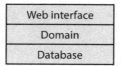

Web Interface layer
- Translate web requests into domain concepts, and domain concepts into web responses

Domain layer
- Application's custom logic, often translates domain concepts into DB queries and commands

Database layer
- Store information that changes over time

In this architecture, the database (DB) is the foundation at the bottom of everything. The domain layer is built out of, among other things, operations on the DB. The web interface translates web requests into domain operations.

This architecture is quite common. We see it in frameworks like Ruby on Rails, which builds the domain model (the M in MVC) using active record objects, which fetch and save to the database. Of course, we can't argue with the success of this architecture, but it is not functional.

The reason it is not functional is that putting the database at the bottom means everything in the path to the top above it is an action. In this case, it's the whole stack! Any use of calculations is incidental. A functional architecture should have a prominent role for both calculations and actions.

Let's compare this to a functional architecture on the next page.

A functional architecture

Let's compare the traditional (nonfunctional) architecture to a functional architecture. The main difference is that the database is at the bottom of the traditional layer scheme, while the database is pulled out to the side in a functional architecture. It is mutable, so access to it is an action. We can then draw the line dividing actions from calculations, and another one dividing our code from the language and libraries we use:

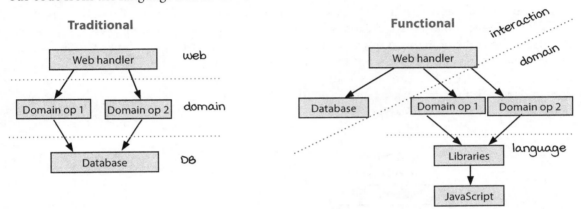

The database is mutable. That's the point of it. But that makes any access to it an action. Everything on the path to the top of the graph will necessarily be an action, including all of the domain operations. As we learned in part 1, functional programmers would rather extract calculations from the actions. They want a clean separation, to the point of building the entire business and domain logic in terms of calculations. The database is separate (though important). The action at the top ties the domain rules to the state in the database.

If we wrap those dotted lines of the functional architecture around to make circles, we get the original diagram of the onion architecture:

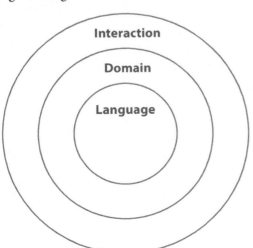

Rules of onion architecture

1. Interaction with the world is done exclusively in the interaction layer.

2. Layers call in toward the center.

3. Layers don't know about layers outside of themselves.

Facilitating change and reuse

In one sense, software architecture is about facilitating changes. What changes do you want to make easy? If you can answer that question, you're halfway to choosing an architecture.

We are examining the onion architecture, so we can ask, "What changes does the onion architecture make easy?"

The onion architecture lets you change the interaction layer easily. The interaction layer is at the top, which we've seen is easiest to change. Since the domain layer knows nothing about databases or web requests, we can easily change the database or use a different service protocol. We can also use the calculations in the domain layer with no database or service at all. This is the change that the architecture makes easy:

> The onion architecture makes it *easy to change* the interaction layer. It makes it *easy to reuse* the domain layer.

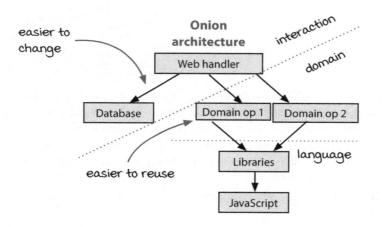

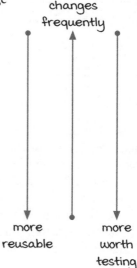

This is an important point, so we should restate it: External services, such as databases and API calls, are easiest to change in this architecture. They are only referred to by the top-most layer. Everything in the domain layer is easily tested because it makes no reference to external services. The onion architecture emphasizes the value of good domain models over the choice of other infrastructure.

Sarah from
dev team

In the typical architecture, domain rules do call out to the database. But in an onion architecture, that's not possible. In the onion architecture, the same work happens, just with a different call graph arrangement. Let's look at an example: a web service to calculate the total cost of a shopping cart. A web request is made to `/cart/cost/123`, where `123` is the cart's ID number. The ID number can be used to fetch the cart from the database.

Let's compare the two architectures:

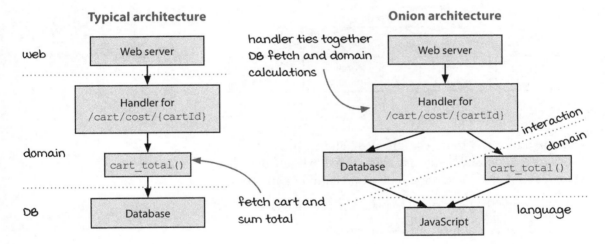

In the typical architecture, the layers are clearly stacked. A web request is routed to a handler. The handler accesses the database. Then it returns the response to the top-most layer, which sends it back to the client.

In this architecture, the domain rule for calculating the total for a cart fetches from the database and sums the total. It is not a calculation, since it fetches from the database.

In the onion architecture, we have to turn our heads to see the layers since the dividing line is skewed. The web server, handler, and database all belong in the interaction layer. `cart_total()` is a calculation that describes how to sum the prices of the cart into a total. It does not know where the cart comes from (from the database or somewhere else). The web handler's job is to provide the cart by fetching it from the database. Thus, the same work is done, but in different layers. The fetching is done in the interaction layer and the summing in the domain layer.

That's a great question. The short answer is that you *can* always make your domain out of calculations. We spent a lot of time in part 1 showing how to do this. Extract calculations from actions. The calculations and the actions become simpler, to the point where the lower-level actions have very little logic. Then, as we've shown in this chapter, the higher-level action ties together the actions and the domain calculations.

I get the pattern, but aren't there some situations where the domain rules need to be actions?

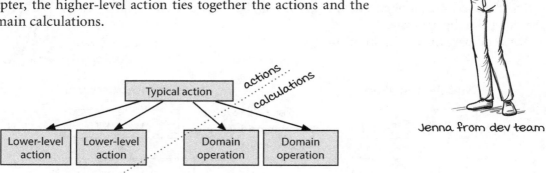

Jenna from dev team

The long answer is more complicated. The truth is, it depends. There are two factors you need to think about to figure out whether a particular domain rule should be a calculation or an action:

1. Examine the terms used to place the rule in a layer.

2. Analyze readability and awkwardness.

Let's look at these two factors on the following pages.

Examine the terms used to place the rule in a layer

We often think of all of the important logic of our program as a *domain rule* (sometimes it's also called a *business rule*). However, not all of the logic is about your domain. Usually, the terms your code uses help you decide if it's a domain rule. For example, you might have code that chooses which database to use. If the new database has an image for the product, use it. Otherwise, try the old database. Note that this code involves two actions (reads from databases):

```
var image = newImageDB.getImage('123');
if(image === undefined)
  image = oldImageDB.getImage('123');
```

Even though it's vitally important to your business, this isn't really a domain rule. It's not phrased in domain terms. The terms of the domain are *product, image, price, discount,* and so on. *Database* doesn't really describe the domain; *new* and *old* database even less so.

Domain rules are phrased in domain terms. Look to the terms in the code to know if it's a domain rule or if it belongs in the interaction layer.

This code is a technical detail to deal with the reality that some of your product images haven't been migrated to the new database. We need to be careful that we don't confuse this logic for a domain rule. This code squarely belongs in the interaction layer. It clearly deals with interacting with a changing world.

Another example of this is the logic for retrying failed web requests. Let's say you have some code that retries multiple times if a web request fails:

```
function getWithRetries(url, retriesLeft, success, error) {
  if(retriesLeft <= 0)
    error('No more retries');
  else ajaxGet(url, success, function(e) {
    getWithRetries(url, retriesLeft - 1, success, error);
  });
}
```

This also is not a business rule—even though retrying is important to the business. It is not phrased in domain terms. The e-commerce domain is not about *AJAX requests*. This is just some logic for dealing with the difficulties of unreliable network connections. As such, it belongs in the interaction layer.

Analyze readability and awkwardness

Okay, we're getting real here. Let's be really clear: Sometimes the benefits of a particular paradigm are not worth the cost. This includes choosing to implement parts of your domain as calculations. Even though it's totally possible to implement your domain entirely as calculations, we have to consider that sometimes, in a particular context, an action is more readable than the equivalent calculation.

Readability depends on quite a few factors. Here are some major ones:

- The language you are writing in
- The libraries you are using
- Your existing legacy code and code style
- What your programmers are accustomed to

The image of the onion architecture we've seen here is an *idealized* view of a real system. People can easily tie themselves in knots trying to reach that ideal of 100% purity of the onion architecture vision. However, nothing is perfect. Part of your role as architect is to trade off between conformance to the architecture diagram and real-world concerns.

Code readability

While functional code is usually very readable, occasionally the programming language makes a nonfunctional implementation many times clearer. Be on the lookout for those times. For short-term clarity, it may be best to adopt the nonfunctional way. However, be on the lookout for a clear and readable way to cleanly separate the domain layer calculations from the interaction layer actions, usually by extracting calculations.

Development speed

Sometimes we need features to get out the door faster than we would like for business reasons. Rush jobs are never ideal, and many compromises are made when rushed. Be ready to clean up the code later to conform to the architecture. You can use the standard skills we've learned throughout the book: extracting calculations, converting to chains of functional tools, and manipulating timelines.

System performance

We often make compromises for system performance. For instance, mutable data is undoubtedly faster than immutable data. Be sure to isolate these compromises. Better still, consider the optimization to be part of the interaction layer and see how the calculations in the domain layer can be reused in a speedier way. We saw an example of this on page 52 where we optimized email generation by fetching fewer from the database at a time. The domain calculations didn't change at all.

Applying a new architecture is always difficult. As your team's skills improve, it will become easier to apply the architecture the first time in a readable way.

How do you get optional data in the domain layer?

This is a good question. It's a scenario you might run into. Let's say you need to make a report of all the products that sold last year. You write a function that takes the products and generates the report:

```
function generateReport(products) {
  return reduce(products, "", function(report, product) {
    return report + product.name + " " + product.price + "\n";
  });
}


var productsLastYear = db.fetchProducts('last year');
var reportLastYear = generateReport(productsLastYear);
```

George from testing

All is good and functional. But then a new requirement comes in and the report needs to change. You now need to include discounts in the report. Unfortunately, the product record only includes an *optional* discount identifier, not the whole discount record. That discount record needs to also be fetched from the database:

product with discountID

```
{
  name: "shoes",
  price: 3.99,
  discountID: '23111'
}
```

product without discountID

```
{
  name: "watch",
  price: 223.43,
  discountID: null
}
```

The easiest thing to do is to fetch the discount given the ID in the callback to reduce. But that would make generateReport() an action. You need to do the actions at the top level—the same level as the code to fetch the products from the DB.

```
function generateReport(products) {
  return reduce(products, "", function(report, product) {
    return report + product.name + " " + product.price + "\n";
  });
}

var productsLastYear = db.fetchProducts('last year');
var productsWithDiscounts = map(productsLastYear, function(product) {
  if(!product.discountID)
    return product;
  return objectSet(product, 'discount', db.fetchDiscount(product.discountID));
});
var reportLastYear = generateReport(productsWithDiscounts);
```

augment the product at the top level

Remember, it is always possible to build your domain out of calculations and cleanly separate the interaction layer from the domain layer.

It's your turn

We are doing some work on public library software that tracks who has checked out what book. Write an I, D, or L next to the following pieces of functionality to indicate whether they go in the interaction layer, domain layer, or language layer.

1. A string processing library you've imported

2. Routines for querying a user record from the database

3. Accessing the Library of Congress API

4. Routines to determine which shelf a book is on given its topic

5. Routines to calculate the library fines due given a list of checked out books

6. Routine for storing a new address for a patron

7. The Lodash JavaScript library

8. Routines for displaying the checkout screen to a library patron

Key	
I	Interaction layer
D	Domain layer
L	Language layer

Answer

1. L, 2. I, 3. I, 4. D, 5. D, 6. I, 7. L, 8. I.

Conclusion

In this chapter, we got a high-level perspective on two architectural patterns: reactive architecture and onion architecture. Reactive architecture is a way to fundamentally reorient the way actions are sequenced so that you specify what actions happen in response to another action. Onion architecture is a pattern that occurs naturally when you apply functional programming practices. It's a very useful perspective because it shows up at every level of our code.

Summary

- Reactive architecture flips the way we sequence actions. It goes from "Do X, do Y" to "When X, then do Y."

- Reactive architecture, taken to its extreme, organizes actions and calculations into pipelines. The pipelines are compositions of simple actions that happen in sequence.

- We can create first-class mutable state that lets us control the read and write operations. One example is the `ValueCell`, which takes inspiration from spreadsheets and lets us implement a reactive pipeline.

- The onion architecture, in broad strokes, divides software into three layers: interaction, domain, and language.

- The outer interaction layer holds the actions of the software. It orchestrates the actions with calls to the domain layer.

- The domain layer contains the domain logic and operations of your software, including business rules. This layer is exclusively comprised of calculations.

- The language layer is the language plus utility libraries that your software is built with.

- The onion architecture is fractal. It can be found at every level of abstraction in your actions.

Up next . . .

We've just finished part 2. In the next chapter, we will conclude the journey with a look at what we've learned and where you can go in the future to learn more.

In this chapter

- Learn how to practice and apply your new skills without upsetting your boss.

- Pick up a new language or two to immerse yourself in functional features.

- Dive deep into the more mathematical aspects of functional programming.

- Open another functional programming book to learn more.

You've done it! You've reached the end of the book. Along the way, you've learned many useful, fundamental skills of functional programming. These skills are immediately useful to whatever kind of project you're working on. And they form a solid foundation on which to learn more. In this chapter, we'll get some practical advice for applying our new skills and learn a few ways to continue your learning after you put this book down.

A plan for the chapter

This chapter outlines a celebration of sorts, a kind of rite of passage. It will help you transition from theoretical knowledge to real skill. Here is a plan for this transition.

Review the skills you have learned

We will look back at the skills you've learned to appreciate how far you have come.

Form a model of the journey toward mastery

You've learned the skills. You are likely excited to start using them. As we learn skills, we go through a common trajectory. This section will give you a meta-perspective on that trajectory so you can navigate toward mastery. You will learn the two-track model.

Establish track 1: Sandbox

We want to establish safe places to play and experiment with new skills. We'll go over two kinds of sandboxes in detail:

- Side projects
- Practice exercises

Establish track 2: Production

As your skills mature, you will want the pressures of production to help hone them. You're welcome to apply them as you like, but these are some good places to start:

- Eliminate a bug today.
- Incrementally improve the design.

Continue your functional programming journey

You've come a long way and have built a strong foundation. When you hear the call to learn more, these paths will be waiting:

- Learn a functional language.
- Get mathy.
- Read more books.

We have learned the skills of professionals

Since we're at the end of the book, let's look back at how far we've come and do a high-level listing of the skills we've learned. These are the skills of professional functional programmers. They have been chosen for their power and depth.

Part 1: Actions, Calculations, and Data

- Identifying the most problematic parts of your code by distinguishing actions, calculations, and data

- Making your code more reusable and testable by extracting calculations from actions

- Improving the design of actions by replacing implicit inputs and outputs with explicit ones

- Implementing immutability to make reading data into a calculation

- Organizing and improving code with stratified design

Part 2: First-class abstractions

- Making syntactic operations first-class so that they can be abstracted in code

- Reasoning at a higher level using functional iteration and other functional tools

- Chaining functional tools into data transformation pipelines

- Understanding distributed and concurrent systems with timeline diagrams

- Manipulating timelines to eliminate bugs

- Mutating state safely with higher-order functions

- Using reactive architecture to reduce coupling between cause and effect

- Applying the onion architecture to design services that interact with the world

you are here

Chapter plan
- **List of skills**
- Two-track journey to mastery
- Track 1: Sandbox
- Track 2: Production
- Journey ahead

Big takeaways

In 10 years, you may only remember three things from this book. If you forget everything else, here are the three most important things you should remember:

There are often calculations hidden in your actions

It takes work to identify and extract calculations, but it is worth it. Calculations are easier to test, reuse, and understand than actions. They don't contribute to the length of your timelines. This distinction between actions, calculations, and data is fundamental to the skills of functional programming.

You can organize your actions, calculations, and data according to rate of change into distinct layers. At the global scale, it informs the architecture, leading to the onion architecture.

Higher-order functions can reach new heights of abstraction

Higher-order functions (functions that take functions as arguments and/or return functions) can liberate you from writing the same low-level code over and over. If you look at the future of your career, how many for loops will you write? How many try/catch statements? Higher-order functions let you write those once and for all, freeing you to write code about your domain. Higher-order functions are incredibly common in functional programming.

You can control the temporal semantics of your code

Many bugs are due to code executing in an undesirable order because it runs in multiple timelines. These days, most software runs in multiple timelines, so understanding how our code executes is very important.

Timeline diagrams help us visualize the execution of our code over time. They capture the sequential and parallel execution of actions. Remember, actions in particular depend on when they are called (ordering) and how many times they are called (repetition). Functional programmers recognize the need to control the ordering and the repetition. We can alter the semantics of execution by constructing primitives, which provide different ordering and repetition semantics.

The ups and downs of skill acquisition

Whenever we learn a new skill, we go through a similar process to make the skill our own. At first, we burn with the pleasure of new-found power. We seek to apply it everywhere, to play with our new toy. We are proud of our towers. But soon we build too high and they topple. Again and again, we learn the limits of the new skill. Gradually, we understand when to apply the skill. We learn how it interacts with the other things we know. And we learn when not to apply it.

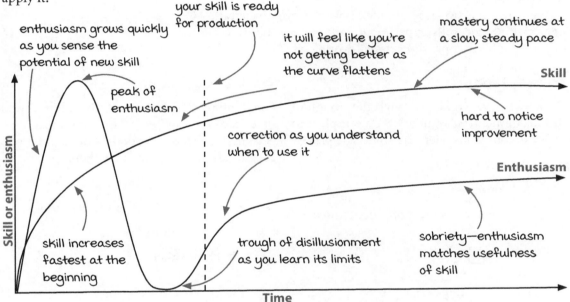

This process is the natural path that we all take as we learn functional programming. You should identify where you are on this path. Relish each moment of it. And when you have reached the end, the skill will be truly yours. You can look back and see all of the teachings, the experiments (successful and failed), the wrong turns and the right ones, that led you to mastery.

The real trouble in this curve is the overzealous application of new skills that are not quite mastered yet. Your excitement grows much quicker than your skill at first. There is a danger that you will over-apply them in production code, worsening readability and maintenance. But at a certain point, you have learned its limits, and you are ready to apply your skill to production. Let's look at a strategy for further mastering your skills and applying them to your existing work.

you are here

> *Chapter plan*
> - List of skills
> - **Two-track journey to mastery**
> - Track 1: Sandbox
> - Track 2: Production
> - Journey ahead

Parallel tracks to mastery

you are here

On the last page, we saw a model of how our skill evolves alongside our enthusiasm for that skill. The trouble is that our enthusiasm grows faster than our mastery. We wish to apply it everywhere, even when it should not be applied. We don't want to risk the undeveloped skills in production where they can worsen readability and maintainability. So how can we practice the skill to move past that peak of enthusiasm? And how can we know when we can trust our mastery?

We can use a two-track model, both running in parallel. On one track, we gleefully experiment and practice the skill. On the other, we soberly apply skills to real-world code.

> *Chapter plan*
> - List of skills
> - **Two-track journey to mastery**
> - Track 1: Sandbox
> - Track 2: Production
> - Journey ahead

Track 1: Sandbox

Before we have worked through the trough of disillusionment, we want to have a safe place to play with our skills. Here are some safe places:

- Practice exercises
- Side projects
- A throwaway branch of production code

Track 2: Production

Once you reach sobriety and the skill feels well practiced, you can begin to use it on real projects that depend on good coding practices. Here are some places to apply them:

- Refactoring existing code
- New features in an existing product
- A new, greenfield product
- Teaching others

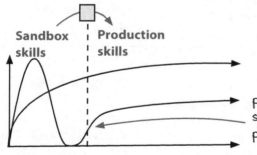

practice skills in the sandbox until you pass the trough

 Noodle on it

On page 543, there is a list of skills we've learned in this book. Evaluate where you are on the curve for each skill. Which ones are ready for production? Which ones need a sandbox?

Sandboxes are safe places to practice. And production is where the consequences become real. Please note that both these phases are important for mastering skills and that you will be at a different point of mastery for each skill. Your improvement will feel the fastest at the beginning. Then you reach a point where it is all about refinement and judgment. The beginning is all about experimentation and testing the limits. Then the pressures of production will guide you to refine the skills.

Sandbox: Start a side project

Side projects are fun ways to practice new skills. They give you the perfect opportunity to learn without big consequences of failure. However, how should you choose a side project? Here are four criteria that can help keep the project manageable and fun:

Keep the side project small at first

The last thing you want is to start a project that is so big that you never feel accomplished. Keep the scope of your side project small. You can always grow it as your skills improve.

Ask yourself these questions:

- What is the equivalent of Hello, World for web apps?
- What is the equivalent of Hello, World for a Twitter bot?

Make the side project whimsical

If a project is too serious, it risks failing for not meeting the arbitrary goals you set for it. But a whimsical project allows for free exploration and pivoting if you find fun stuff to work on. Playfulness and fun are a great attitude for learning.

Ask yourself these questions:

- What's something silly that won't feel like work?
- What would be fun even if it fails?

you are here

Chapter plan
- List of skills
- Two-track journey to mastery
- **Track 1: Sandbox**
- Track 2: Production
- Journey ahead

Use familiar skills plus one new skill

When you're learning to master timelines, it's probably not the time to also figure out a new web framework. Build something you are already confident with and apply one new skill.

Ask yourself these questions:

- What do I know how to make right now?
- How can I practice one skill on top of that?

Expand the project as you will

The best side project will be ready and waiting for when you are ready to practice a skill. It will have code that needs design work. It will have very basic features that you can expand with new skills. For instance, you could have a very basic blog. A weekend project might be to add user authentication to it.

Ask yourself these questions:

- What can be a stable foundation on which to explore?
- What basic features can I expand on later?

Sandbox: Practice exercises

Skills take practice. And sometimes the best kind of practice is an isolated exercise. The exercise is outside of a context and has clear requirements. It's basically a target to aim your skills at so that you can get some practice in with no consequences. Here are some great sources of exercises:

Edabit (`https://edabit.com/challenges`)

Edabit has lots and lots of coding exercises. They're small. They're clearly explained. They are graded Very Easy to Expert. Use these challenges as a way to practice your functional programming skills. See if you can solve the same problem in different ways by applying different skills.

Project Euler (`https://projecteuler.net`)

Project Euler has amassed many programming challenges. They are often very mathematical, but everything is clearly explained. The great thing about these challenges is that they will force you to face real limits. For instance, figuring out the first 10 prime numbers is easy. Figuring out the 1,000,000th prime number before the sun dies out is a real challenge! You'll face memory limitations, performance limitations, stack size limitations, and more. All of these limits will force you to make your skills practical and not just theoretical.

CodeWars (`https://codewars.com`)

CodeWars has a large collection of exercises that are challenging enough to test your skills but small enough to solve in a few minutes. These are great for practicing different skills on the same problem.

Code Katas (`https://github.com/gamontal/awesome-katas`)

Code Katas are a kind of practice where you solve the same problem multiple times. We perform a kata more for practicing the process of programming than for solving some challenge. These are also good because they let you integrate your new functional programming skills with your other development skills, such as testing.

you are here

Chapter plan
- List of skills
- Two-track journey to mastery
- **Track 1: Sandbox**
- Track 2: Production
- Journey ahead

Production: Eliminate a bug today

Every skill in this book was chosen so that it could be immediately applicable. But when you're staring at 100k lines of code, you may wonder where to start. Don't worry; that's really common. The key is simply to start small and start somewhere. You can improve your code a little at a time.

Some of the skills you've learned can be applied today to directly eliminate major sources of bugs. These places are your best bet for big wins in your codebase and high-fives from your team.

Reduce the number of global mutable variables by one

In chapters 3–5, we learned to identify the implicit inputs and outputs to a function. Some of those are global mutable variables. They allow parts of the code to share data. However, sharing mutable data is a huge source of bugs. Getting rid of just one global mutable can be a big win. Make an inventory of global variables, pick one, and refactor the functions that use it until the global variable is not needed anymore. Then move on to the next one! Your teammates will thank you.

Reduce the number of crazy timelines by one

In chapters 15–17, we learned how to use timeline diagrams to understand the behavior of our code. They helped us identify race conditions and other ordering problems. And the skills of isolating, sharing, and coordinating helped us eliminate undesirable orderings. When we program in a codebase long enough, we get a sense of where bugs pop up. Are any of those due to race conditions? Pick one of them, draw out the diagram, and use your skills to eliminate the wrong orderings.

Chapter plan
- List of skills
- Two-track journey to mastery
- Track 1: Sandbox
- **Track 2: Production**
- Journey ahead

you are here

Production: Incrementally improve the design

Some of the skills you've learned in this book can be used right now to incrementally improve the design of your code. Incremental is the name of the game. Design is really important, but you might not feel the gains right away. However, over time, as the improvements add up, the benefits of a better design will start to shine through.

Extract one calculation from an action

It's really hard to eliminate an action from your code. Most actions have a real purpose. The ones that are superfluous are rare. However, one thing you can do is make the action smaller. Look for an action that has a lot of logic in it. Extract the logic into a calculation. A simple, straightforward action is a happy action.

Convert one implicit input or output to explicit

Again, it's very difficult to eliminate a given action outright. It's more fruitful to eliminate one implicit input or output. If there are four implicit inputs to an action, getting it down to three is a great improvement. While it will still be an action, it will be a slightly better action. The action will be less coupled to the state of the system.

Chapter plan
- List of skills
- Two-track journey to mastery
- Track 1: Sandbox
- **Track 2: Production**
- Journey ahead

you are here

Replace one for loop

In chapters 12–14, we learned some really useful functions that replace for loops. While eliminating a single for loop might not feel like much, for loops make up a lot of the logic of our algorithms. Begin to replace for loops with functions like `forEach()`, `map()`, `filter()`, and `reduce()`. For loops are the stepping stones of a path to a more functional style. Along the way, you might start finding new functional tools unique to your code.

Popular functional languages

Here is a list of functional languages that are practical to learn. Although there are many more that are not listed here, these are popular and have libraries for doing just about anything. Any of these would be a great choice for a general-purpose programming language. On the next few pages, we will organize them according to different purposes—to get a job, to run on particular platforms, or to learn different aspects of FP.

Clojure (`https://clojure.org`)
Clojure runs on the Java Virtual Machine and JavaScript (in the form of ClojureScript).

Elixir (`https://elixir-lang.org`)
Elixir runs on the Erlang Virtual Machine. It uses actors to manage concurrency.

Swift (`https://swift.org`)
Swift is Apple's open source, flagship language.

Kotlin (`https://kotlinlang.org`)
Kotlin combines object-oriented and functional programming into one JVM language.

Haskell (`https://haskell.org`)
Haskell is a statically typed language used in academia, startups, and enterprises alike.

Erlang (`https://erlang.org`)
Erlang was built for fault tolerance. It uses actors for concurrency.

Elm (`https://elm-lang.org`)
Elm is statically typed and used for frontend web applications that compile to JavaScript.

Scala (`https://scala-lang.org`)
Scala combines object-oriented and functional programming into one language. It runs on the Java Virtual Machine and JavaScript.

F# (`https://fsharp.org`)
F# is statically typed and runs on the Microsoft Common Language Runtime.

Rust (`https://rust-lang.org`)
Rust is a system language with a powerful type system designed to prevent memory leaks and concurrency errors.

PureScript (`https://www.purescript.org`)
PureScript is a Haskell-like language that compiles to JavaScript to run in the browser.

Racket (`https://racket-lang.org`)
Racket has a rich history and a large and vibrant community.

Reason (`https://reasonml.github.io`)
Reason is statically typed and compiles to JavaScript and native assembly.

> *Chapter plan*
> - List of skills
> - Two-track journey to mastery
> - Track 1: Sandbox
> - Track 2: Production
> - **Journey ahead**

you are here

Functional languages with the most jobs

You may be thinking of learning a new language to get a job doing functional programming. Functional programming jobs are considered rare in the industry, but they do exist. To maximize your chances of learning a language you can get a job in, you should pick one of these languages. Although all of the languages listed previously are production-ready, these five languages have a lot of jobs listed:

Elixir - Kotlin - Swift - Scala - Rust   ordered roughly from easiest to hardest to get started with

These three languages don't have as many jobs as the previous list, but there are still many opportunities out there:

Clojure - Erlang - Haskell   ordered roughly from easiest to hardest to get started with

Unfortunately, the other languages can't be recommended purely for getting a job.

Functional languages by platform

Another way to organize functional languages is by what's available on the platform you are targeting.

Browser (JavaScript engine)

These languages compile to JavaScript. In addition to the browser, they can also run on Node:

Elm - ClojureScript - Reason - Scala.js - PureScript   ordered roughly from easiest to hardest to get started with

Web backend

These languages are commonly used to implement the server for a web application:

Elixir - Kotlin - Swift - Racket - Scala - Clojure - F# - Rust - Haskell

ordered roughly from easiest to hardest to get started with

Mobile (iOS and Android)

Native: **Swift**
Via JVM: **Scala - Kotlin**
Via Xamarin: **F#**
Via React Native: **ClojureScript - Scala.js**

Embedded devices

Rust

Functional languages by learning opportunity

Immersing yourself in a language can help you learn. You can choose a language based on what it can teach you. Here, you'll find the languages organized by prominent features. They can create a wonderful, immersive learning environment.

Static typing

The most advanced type systems found today are in functional languages. These type systems are based on mathematical logic and are proven to be consistent. Types do more than prevent errors. They can also guide you to design better software. Having a good type system is like having a logician on your shoulder, coaching you into good software. If you'd like to learn more, these languages will immerse you:

ordered roughly from easiest to hardest to get started with

Elm - Scala - F# - Reason - PureScript - Rust - Haskell

Swift, Kotlin, and **Racket** have type systems, too, though they are less powerful.

Functional tools and data transformation

Most functional languages have good functional tools for doing data transformation. But these languages excel at it. Instead of encouraging you to define new types, these languages operate on a small number of data types and a large number of operations on them:

ordered roughly from easiest to hardest to get started with

Kotlin - Elixir - Clojure - Racket - Erlang

Concurrency and distributed systems

Most functional languages are good at dealing with multiple threads, mostly because of immutable data structures. However, some excel at it by focusing primarily on that task. These languages have great facilities for correctly managing multiple timelines in a straightfoward way. They are organized by different classes of facilities:

With concurrency primitives: **Clojure - F# - Haskell - Kotlin**
Using the actor model: **Elixir - Erlang - Scala**
Through the type system: **Rust**

> *Chapter plan*
> - List of skills
> - Two-track journey to mastery
> - Track 1: Sandbox
> - Track 2: Production
> - **Journey ahead**

you are here

Get mathy

Functional programming borrows a lot of ideas from mathematics. Many people like that about functional programming. If you're into the far-out mathematical stuff, here's a list of areas of functional programming you might find to be up your alley.

Lambda Calculus

Lambda calculus is a powerful and simple mathematical system that includes function definitions and function calls. Because it uses a lot of functions, FP can use lambda calculus ideas freely.

Combinators

One interesting corner of lambda calculus is the idea of *combinators*. Combinators are functions that modify and combine other functions.

Type theory

Type theory is another aspect of lambda calculus that has made its way into functional programming. Type theory is basically logic applied to your code. It asks the question, "What can be derived and proven without introducing logical inconsistencies?" Type theory forms the basis of static type systems in functional languages.

Category theory

At the risk of oversimplifying, category theory is a branch of abstract mathematics that explores the structural similarities between different types. When applied to programming, it has opened a treasure box of ideas about how to design and implement software.

Effect systems

Effect systems borrow mathematical objects from category theory like *monad* and *applicative functor*. People have run with the concepts and used them to model all sorts of actions, like mutable state, thrown exceptions, and other side effects. The actions are modeled using immutable data, pushing the boundaries of what's possible using only calculations and data.

Chapter plan
- List of skills
- Two-track journey to mastery
- Track 1: Sandbox
- Track 2: Production
- **Journey ahead**

you are here

Further reading

I'd love to recommend a bunch of functional programming books. Out of all the ones I've read, these are the ones I'd recommend for your next steps.

Functional-Light JavaScript by Kyle Simpson

This is a mix of JavaScript style guide and introduction to many of the functional programming terms you'll come across. It explains lots of concepts I didn't think could be explained without a deeper entry into the academic side of FP. And it does it in a wonderful, helpful way. It is highly recommended.

Domain Modeling Made Functional by Scott Wlaschin

This book shows how to go from conversations with a customer to a full-fledged functional implementation of a workflow. It shows how to use types to model a domain. It's also the best explanation of Domain Driven Design I've found.

Structure and Interpretation of Computer Programs by Harold Abelson and Gerald Jay Sussman with Julie Sussman

This book is a classic. It was used as an introductory textbook for Massachussets Institute of Technology Computer Science students. That makes it a little more difficult for the rest of us. However hard it may be to get through, it's still the most accessible way to learn many important ideas. And if you do get stuck, don't worry. This is the kind of book you work through over years, as your functional skills grow.

Grokking Functional Programming by Michał Płachta

This book is a great introduction to functional programming from a different perspective. If you liked this book, *Grokking Functional Programming* will deepen your understanding of pure functions, functional tools, and immutable data. It goes deeper into data modeling than we were able to in this book.

Besides these general programming books, I'd recommend picking up popular books for programming languages that you are using or are interested in. There are books about functional programming in most languages. And functional languages have books about them, too.

> **Chapter plan**
> - List of skills
> - Two-track journey to mastery
> - Track 1: Sandbox
> - Track 2: Production
> - **Journey ahead**

you are here

Conclusion

In this chapter, we celebrated the skills you've learned throughout the book. You've got the power to apply functional programming to your code. We also saw a perspective that will allow you to continue practicing and refining your skill. Finally, when the time is right, you've got several ways to learn more.

Summary

- We've learned a lot of important skills. It is worth planning how to master them.

- We are deceptively enthusiastic about skills before we are ready to use them with discernment. Find a safe place to play and experiment.

- Functional programming can improve your production code. The pressures of production code can help you refine your skills.

- There are many functional languages that are practical for side projects and commercial products. There has never been a better time to build a career on functional programming.

- Functional programming is used as a playground for mathematical ideas. If that's your thing, dig in! There's plenty to learn.

- There are some nice books that can help you learn more about functional programming. Check them out.

Up next . . .

Nothing! Take care!

index